WITHDRAWN

LEGACIES

The publisher gratefully acknowledges the generous
contribution to this book provided by the General Endowment Fund
of the Associates of the University of California Press.

Legacies

The Story of the
Immigrant Second Generation

ALEJANDRO PORTES

RUBÉN G. RUMBAUT

UNIVERSITY OF CALIFORNIA PRESS

Berkeley   Los Angeles   London

RUSSELL SAGE FOUNDATION

New York

University of California Press
Berkeley and Los Angeles, California

University of California Press, Ltd.
London, England

Russell Sage Foundation
New York, New York

© 2001 by
The Regents of the University of California

Portes, Alejandro, 1944–
  Legacies : the story of the immigrant second
generation / Alejandro Portes, Rubén G. Rumbaut.
    p. cm.
  Includes bibliographical references and index.
  ISBN 0-520-22847-2 (cloth : alk. paper) — ISBN
0-520-22848-0 (pbk. : alk. paper)
    1. Immigrants—United States—Economic
conditions. 2. Immigrants—United States—Social
conditions. 3. United States—Emigration and
immigration. I. Rumbaut, Rubén G. II. Title.

JV6471 .P67 2001
305.990691—dc21   00-061993

Printed in the United States of America
08   07   06   05   04   03   02   01
10   9   8   7   6   5   4   3   2   1

The paper used in this publication meets the minimum requirements of ANSI/NISO Z39.48-1992
(R 1997) (*Permanence of Paper*).

To Lisa, Charles, and Andrea;
and Rob, Audra, and Rubén Darío

CONTENTS

List of Tables and Illustrations   xi

Preface   xvii

Acknowledgments   xxi

1. Twelve Stories   1

Miami Stories   2

María de los Angeles and Yvette Santana: August 1993   2
Melanie Fernández-Rey: September 1993   3
Aristide Maillol: August 1993   4
Armando and Luis Hernández: July 1995   4
Mary Patterson: February 1995   6
Efrén Montejo: May 1994   7

San Diego Stories   8

Jorge, Olga, Miguel Angel, and Estela Cardozo:
January 1994   8
Quy Nguyen: December 1987   9
Bennie and Jennifer Montoya: October 1995   11
Sophy Keng: November 1987–June 1988   12
Yolanda and Carlos Muñoz: March 1994   14
Boua Cha: 1988–1990   15

2. The New Americans: An Overview   17

Immigration Yesterday and Today   17

The Size and Concentration of the Second Generation   19

Studying the New Second Generation:
The Children of Immigrants Longitudinal Study   22

The New Second Generation at a Glance   33
Census Results   33
CILS Results   37

3. Not Everyone Is Chosen: Segmented Assimilation and Its Determinants   44

How Immigrants Are Received: Modes of Incorporation and Their Consequences   46

Acculturation and Role Reversal   49

Where They Grow Up: Challenges to Second-Generation Adaptation   55
   Race   55
   Labor Markets   56
   Countercultures   59

Confronting the Challenge: Immigrant Social Capital   62
   Parental Status, Family Structure, and Gender   62
   The Immigrant Community   64

Conclusion   69

4. Making It in America   70

Early Adaptation and Achievement   72
   General Trends   72
   Nationality and Achievement   73
   Determinants of Parental Economic Achievement: Additive Effects   76
   Determinants of Parental Economic Achievement: Interaction Effects   82

Nationality and Family Composition   85

Conclusion   90

5. In Their Own Eyes: Immigrant Outlooks on America   91

Aura Lila Marín, Cuban, 53, Single Mother (1994)   91

Pao Yang, Laotian Hmong, 57, Father (1995)   93

Optimism   94

Permissiveness   97

Ambition   103

Community and Pride   107

Conclusion   111

6. Lost in Translation: Language and the New Second Generation   113

Bilingualism: Yesterday and Today   115

Shadow Boxing: Myth and Reality of Language
Acculturation   118
   General Trends   118
   National Differences   122

Forced-March Acculturation   128

What Makes a Bilingual?   134

A Game of Mirrors: Language Instruction and Types
of Acculturation   143

**7. Defining the Situation: The Ethnic Identities
   of Children of Immigrants**   147

Sites of Belonging: The Complex Allegiances of Children
of Immigrants   149
   Developing a Self   149
   Past Research   152

Who Am I? Patterns of Ethnic Self-Identification   154
   Ethnic Identity Shifts   154
   Stability and Salience   157
   Ethnic Self-Identities by National Origin   160

Where Do I Come From? Nation, Family, and Identity   161

Correlates of Self-Identities   166
   Family Status, Composition, and Language   166
   The Influence of Parental Self-Identities   171
   Region, Schools, and Discrimination   171

The Race Question   176

Determinants of Ethnic and Racial Identities   181

Conclusion: From Translation Artists to Living Paradoxes   189

**8. The Crucible Within: Family, Schools,
   and the Psychology of the Second Generation**   192

San Diego Families   194

Family Cohesion, Conflict, and Change   197

School Environments and Peer Groups   203

Psychological Well-Being: Self-Esteem and Depressive Affect   207

School Engagement and Effort   211

Educational Expectations   215

Determinants of Psychosocial Outcomes   220
   Self-Esteem and Depression   220

Ambition   225
Conclusion   230

9. School Achievement and Failure   233

Early Educational Achievement   234
  Preliminary Results   234
  Determinants of Early Achievement   238
Educational Achievement in Late Adolescence   244
  Grades in Senior High School   245
  Change over Time   250
  Dropping Out of School   251
Two Achievement Paradoxes   258
  Southeast Asians   258
  Cuban Americans   261
Conclusion   267

10. Conclusion: Mainstream Ideologies and the Long-Term Prospects of Immigrant Communities   269

Two Mainstream Ideologies   270
A Third Way: Selective Acculturation and Bilingualism   274
The Mexican Case   276
Theoretical Reprise   280
  Time and Acculturation   281
  Reactive Ethnicity and Its Aftermath   284

Appendix A. Children of Immigrants Longitudinal Study: Follow-up Questionnaire   287

Appendix B. Children of Immigrants Longitudinal Study: Parental Questionnaire   307

Appendix C. Variables Used in Multivariate Analyses: Chapters 6 to 9   339

Notes   349
References   369
Index   389

TABLES AND ILLUSTRATIONS

Tables

2.1 The Immigrant-Stock Population of the United States: The First and Second Generations in the Top Metropolitan Areas, 1997   20

2.2 Characteristics of Children of Immigrants Interviewed in Southern Florida and Southern California, 1992   26

2.3 Original and Follow-up Surveys in Southern Florida and Southern California   28

2.4 Correlations between First Survey Predictors and Respondent Presence in the Follow-up, 1995–1996   30

2.5 Basic Demographic Characteristics of Immigrant Parents Interviewed in 1995–1996   32

2.6 Characteristics of Children, 18 Years or Younger, Living in Immigrant-Headed Households, 1990   35

2.7 Social and Economic Characteristics of Immigrant Parents Interviewed in Southern Florida and Southern California, 1995–1996   36

2.8 Characteristics of Children of Immigrants in Southern California and Southern Florida, 1992   40

3.1 Immigrant Nationalities and Their Modes of Incorporation, 1990   50

3.2 Types of Acculturation across Generations   53

4.1 Nationality, Education, and Socioeconomic Attainment   74

4.2   Breakdowns of Family Earnings and Personal
Incomes, by Selected Predictors, 1996   77

4.3   Determinants of Parental Economic Outcomes   79

4.4   Effects of Human Capital Variables on Monthly
Earnings for Selected Nationalities ($)   83

4.5   Determinants of Family Composition:
Children Living with Both Parents (CILS Student
Sample, 1992)   87

4.6   Determinants of Family Composition: Children
Living with Both Parents (CILS Parental Sample,
1995–1996)   89

5.1   Parental Outlooks on Schools, Neighborhoods,
and Opportunities   96

5.2   Parental Outlooks on School Influences and
Socialization   100

5.3   Parental Educational Expectations and Rules   104

5.4   Parental Perceptions of Co-ethnic Community   109

6.1   Foreign Languages Knowledge and Use, Full Sample   121

6.2   Correlations between Bilingualism and
Its Components   121

6.3   Language Use and Preferences of Second-Generation
Youth, by Major Nationality Groups, 1995–1996   123

6.4   Second-Generation Children's and Parents' Scores
in Language Composite Indices, by Detailed National-
Origin Groups, 1995–1996   128

6.5   Predictors of Fluent Bilingualism and English
Monolingualism   136

6.6   Determinants of Bilingual Fluency in Late
Adolescence, Children of Immigrants, 1995–1996   139

6.7   Determinants of Change in Bilingual Fluency during
High School, Children of Immigrants, 1995–1996   142

7.1   Continuity and Change in the Ethnic Self-Identities
of Children of Immigrants, 1992 and 1995–1996   158

7.2   Ethnic Self-Identities of Children of Immigrants, by
      National Origin Groups, 1995–1996   162

7.3   Nativity Patterns of Children of Immigrants and
      of Their Parents   164

7.4   Correlates of Ethnic Self-Identities in 1992 and
      1995–1996: Parental Status, Family Composition,
      and Acculturation   168

7.5   Correlations of Ethnic Self-Identifications of Parents
      and Children, 1992 and 1995–1996   172

7.6   Correlates of Ethnic Self-Identities in 1992 and
      1995–1996: Region, Schools, and Discrimination   174

7.7   Self-Reported Race of Children of Immigrants and
      Their Parents, by National Origin Groups, 1995–1996   178

7.8   Determinants of Ethnic Self-Identification, 1995–1996 182

7.9   Determinants of Racial Self-Identification, 1995–1996 184

8.1   Stressful Family Events and Perceptions of Family
      Relationships, by National Origin, Parental
      Socioeconomic Status, and Language Adaptation,
      1995–1996   198

8.2   School Safety and Perceptions of Teaching Quality
      in High School, by National Origin, Parental
      Socioeconomic Status, and Peers' School Plans,
      1995–1996   204

8.3   Psychological Well-Being: Self-Esteem and
      Depressive Symptoms, by Selected Variables,
      1995–1996   208

8.4   School Engagement and School Work Discipline,
      by Selected Variables, 1992–1996   212

8.5   Educational Aspirations and Educational Expectations,
      by Selected Variables, 1995–1996   217

8.6   Determinants of Self-Esteem and Psychological
      Depression, 1995–1996   222

8.7   Determinants of Educational Aspirations and
      Expectations, 1995–1996   228

9.1   Educational Achievement, by Nationality and Length
       of U.S. Residence, 1992   236

9.2   Models of Early (Middle School) Educational
       Attainment, 1992   240

9.3   Correlations between Indicators of Educational
       Achievement   247

9.4   Determinants of Grade Point Average in Late
       High School   248

9.5   Determinants of School Attrition   256

9.6   Time of Arrival and Academic Performance
       of Cuban Americans in Miami   264

9.7   Student Outside Employment, by Nationality, 1995   265

Figures

3.1   The Process of Segmented Assimilation: A Model   63

3.2   Types of Relationships in Dense versus Dispersed
       Immigrant Communities   66

3.3   Determinants of Immigrant Adaptation
       across Generations   68

4.1   Immigrant Education and Socioeconomic Attainment   75

4.2   Annual Incomes by Nationality and Different
       Human Capital and Gender Profiles   81

4.3   Monthly Earnings by Nationality and Different
       Human Capital and Gender Profiles   82

4.4   Family Composition by Nationality   86

5.1   Obstacles to Parental Aspirations for Children   106

5.2   Immigrant Parents' Perception of Their Own
       Ethnic Communities   110

6.1   English Knowledge and Preferences   119

6.2   Foreign Language Knowledge and Use   120

6.3   English Language Preference by
      Mexican-American Students   125

6.4   Types of Language Adaptation and Their
      Social Psychological Correlates   132

6.5   Types of Language Adaptation and Their
      Family Correlates   133

6.6   Generational Language Knowledge and Types
      of Acculturation   145

7.1   Ethnic Self-Identity Shifts among Children
      of Immigrants, 1992 to 1995–1996   155

7.2   Percent of Children of Immigrants Selecting
      Various Types of Panethnic Identities, 1992
      and 1995–1996   156

7.3   Stability and Salience of Ethnic Self-Identities,
      1995–1996   159

7.4   Ethnic Self-Identities by Native Origin of Self
      and Parents, 1995–1996   165

7.5   Correlates of Racial Self-Identification   180

8.1   Family Orientations by Length of U.S. Residence   202

8.2   School Indices and Dropout Status of Close Friends,
      1995–1996   206

8.3   Level of Self-Esteem by Family and School Indices,
      1995–1996   211

8.4   School Engagement and School Work Effort,
      by Year of Arrival in the United States   214

8.5   Educational Expectations and Its Correlates,
      1995–1996   220

9.1   Gross and Net Effects of Nationality on
      Grade Point Average, 1992   245

9.2   Gross and Net Effects of Nationality on
      Reading Scores, 1992   246

9.3   Indicators of School Attrition by Nationality, 1995   254

9.4   School Dropout Rates of Student Population
       and Children of Immigrants, 1992–96   259

9.5   Effects of Outside Employment and Parental
       Year of Arrival: Cuban Americans in
       Southern Florida, 1995   266

10.1   Paths of Mobility across Generations   283

Plates

Following page 112

PREFACE

Major events have a way of bursting upon society unawares, their unfolding phases receiving little attention until they are upon us. The major problems that preoccupy society today—the implosion of the inner city, the demise of the traditional family, the drug epidemic—all entered public consciousness after the forces that gave rise to them had become too entrenched to be easily dislodged. A mass of scientific studies and well-meaning policies followed after the fact, usually to no avail.

This book concerns a phenomenon that has not yet moved to center stage but whose transformative potential, for better or worse, is immense. This is the growth of the new second generation spawned by accelerated immigration during the last third of a century. By 1998, fully one-tenth of the U.S. population was foreign born, and in 1999 the number of their U.S.-born children surpassed the prior record set up by children of earlier European immigrants. Already the first and second generations of immigrants and their children total 55 million persons—one out of every five Americans. As in the past, immigration begets ethnicity, and hence the emerging ethnic groups of the twenty-first century will be the offspring of today's immigrants. Whether this new ethnic mosaic reinvigorates the nation or catalyzes a quantum leap in its social problems depends on the forms of social and economic adaptation experienced by this still young population. Unlike their immigrant parents who remain, in one form or another, tied to the land of their birth, these children are Americans and can be expected to become an integral part of this society. Their numbers and diversity ensure that the process will have a profound impact.

A sizable portion of today's second generation is still young, their parents having come mostly from Asia and Latin America. The series of stories in the first chapter provides a firsthand look at this emerging population, its situation, and its dilemmas. While some of these dilemmas may appear inconsequential at first glance—everyday events in the lives of adolescents and their families—in the aggregate they have profound effects. Some of the ethnic groups being created by the new immigration are in a clearly upward path, moving into society's mainstream in record time and enriching it in the process with their culture and energies. Others, on the contrary, seem poised for a path of blocked aspirations and downward mobility, reproducing the plight of today's impoverished domestic minorities. The size of the problems of American cities may increase concomitantly, the only difference being that the participants may come from new ethnic quarters. Were this outcome to become dominant among the second generation, a new rainbow underclass would be the prospect facing urban America by the middle of the next century.

While much public and scholarly attention continues to focus on the problems of the day, a new society is arising in our midst. Combining American culture with the sights and sounds of a host of foreign lands, seeking to balance the pressures of immigrant families and native peers, and striving to fulfill the goals of material success and personal freedom that drove their parents here, the new second generation holds the key to what will happen to their respective ethnic groups and, to a large extent, to the cities where they cluster. This book seeks to anticipate these developments by providing a close look at this rising population.

The opening chapter presents 12 real-life stories of immigrant families—from Mexico, Cuba, Nicaragua, the Dominican Republic, Haiti, Trinidad, the Philippines, Laos, Cambodia, and Vietnam—now living in southern Florida and southern California, two of the areas most heavily affected by the new immigration. Their stories exemplify not only the extraordinary variety of today's newcomers but also the often surprising ways in which parental histories, the surrounding context, and the children's own development combine to mold particular modes of "growing up American." Chapter 2, "The New Americans," sketches a detailed portrait of the immigrant-stock population of the United States, relying on information from two main sources: the decennial census and Current Population Surveys of the U.S. Census Bureau and the Children of Immigrants Longitudinal Study (CILS), the largest survey to date of the new second generation, upon which much of the rest of the book is based. Chapter 3, "Not Everyone Is Chosen," describes the theoretical perspectives that have both emerged from and guided our study, focusing on the central concept of segmented assimilation and the factors that condition diverse aspects of the adaptation process of second-generation youth. We draw on this theoretical framework to organize the presentation of results in the chapters that follow.

Chapter 4, "Making It in America," examines the socioeconomic adaptation of immigrant parents, their differences in economic attainment and family composition by national origin, and the determinants of immigrant economic achievement and family structure. The relative success or failure of these first-generation immigrants in integrating themselves to American society then sets the stage for the diverse courses of adaptation of their children. Chapter 5, "In Their Own Eyes," further explores the characteristics, situations, and perceptions of immigrant parents, with an emphasis on their experiences in raising their children on American soil—a challenge fraught with opportunity and threat at virtually every turn. In their eyes, America emerges as a gigantic puzzle: the place to come for the fulfillment of dreams and also the place to avoid if family ties and traditional cultures are to have a chance.

Chapter 6, "Lost in Translation," shifts attention to the children, focusing on the fundamental issue of language: the degree to which, over time, they come to use, prefer, and become proficient in English relative to the parental tongue and the determinants and consequences of linguistic acculturation. Chapter 7, "Defining the Situation," analyzes another central aspect of the adaptation process of children of immigrants, namely, the evolution of different types of ethnic self-identities and how these are shaped by a variety of factors, including personal experiences with and expectations of discrimination. Chapter 8, "The Crucible Within," explores further the subjective world of second-generation youth, looking at patterns of parent-child conflict and cohesion within immigrant families, differences in self-esteem, and aspirations for the future. Self-esteem and ambition are important adaptation outcomes in their own right, reflecting as they do the cumulative experiences of growing up in different corners of American society. But they also can be expected to bear on the future as they narrow or expand the range of goals that foreign-stock children believe possible.

Chapter 9, "School Achievement and Failure," addresses perhaps the most important question considered in this study: the factors that affect the children's academic performance and their chances of educational success. While it is still too early to tell how second-generation youths will fare in adult life, their adaptation and achievement in school can be expected to prefigure their future labor market opportunities and modes of insertion in society. Academic success or failure emerges from this analysis as a well-patterned outcome reflecting the cumulative bearing of earlier factors, from different forms of acculturation to the context that had originally received their immigrant parents.

The concluding chapter, "Mainstream Ideologies and the Long-Term Prospects of Immigrant Communities" reviews the study's findings in the light of the principal ideological positions informing public debate on contemporary immigration. The gap between the intent of policies derived from such positions and their actual effects raises serious concerns about the long-term adaptive prospects of many immigrant groups and, hence, of the communities where they have settled. It also points to the urgent need of educating the American mainstream as to where its true interests lie and how poorly they have been served by nativist and assimilationist policies in the past.

ACKNOWLEDGMENTS

This book was born in a conversation in an Atlanta café back in 1988. Having just completed the manuscript of our first book, *Immigrant America: A Portrait,* we agreed on the pressing need to address the study of the children of today's immigrants. It seemed to us then, as now, that the impact of the growing foreign population in America and the future of the cities and regions where it concentrates pivoted on what happened to this new second generation. In the 12 years that it has taken to complete the study, we have counted on the support of a large number of people without whose collaboration this book would not have materialized.

The study is based on a series of surveys with immigrant children and their parents conducted between 1992 and 1996 in Miami/Ft. Lauderdale and San Diego. Our colleague Lisandro Pérez of Florida International University ably led the fieldwork for the original and follow-up surveys in southern Florida. He and his team of field interviewers and coders deserve much of the credit for the success of the project in this area. In particular, Liza Carbajo, now Lisandro's wife, deserves mention for her tenacity and ingenuity in tracing and reinterviewing respondents during the follow-up survey. Completion of the parental survey in Miami was due to the ability and efforts of Victoria Ryan, Nidia Paz, and Vicente Espinosa. We owe a special debt of gratitude to Patricia Fernández-Kelly, who personally conducted the original intensive interviews with immigrant families in the summer of 1993 and then located and interviewed many parents, previously given up for lost, in 1996.

In San Diego, we benefited from the extraordinary commitment and competence of our research staff, in particular, Linda Borgen, Norm Borgen, Kevin Keogan, Laura Lagunas, and James Ainsworth. We appreciate as well the first-rate work of a team of over two dozen interviewers fluent in Spanish, Tagalog, Vietnamese, Cambodian, Lao, Hmong, and other Asian languages representative of the immigrant families that have settled in the San Diego area. Many of the immigrant stories reported in the following pages are drawn from the fieldwork of Patricia Fernández-Kelly in Miami and of this interview team, led by Kevin Keogan and Linda Borgen, in San Diego.

Much of the data on which the following analysis is based did not come from interviews but from school records. Indeed, the entire project could not have been conducted without the active cooperation and support of the Dade (Miami), Broward (Ft. Lauderdale), and San Diego school systems. We thank the administrators and research staff of each system, and especially the principals and teachers of the dozens of schools that participated in the project, for their indispensable collaboration. In Miami, we owe a special debt of gratitude to Gisella Fields of the Office of Educational Accountability, who gave generously of her time to ensure that we gained access to the latest school data and who has followed attentively the findings and publications from the study. At San Diego City Schools, we owe special thanks to Peter Bell and Gary W. Knowles of the Planning, Assessment, and Accountability Division for their consistent assistance with our data requests.

Our graduate assistants, Richard Schauffler, Tomás Rodriguez, Dag MacLeod, and Patricia Landolt, competently organized the coding and storage of survey data and collaborated in the successive stages of data analysis. The project was originally based at Johns Hopkins University and at San Diego State University. At Johns Hopkins University we acknowledge the devoted and efficient work of Angela Decker, Portes's secretary at the time, and the competent administrative assistance of Virginia Bailey. At San Diego State University, we are grateful for the help of the staff of its sociology department, where the project was housed throughout. At Michigan State University, we acknowledge the staff of its sociology department and the research assistance of Bryan Fry, who collaborated with Rumbaut on the administration of the project during and after the follow-up survey.

The study has been supported in its successive stages by grants from the National Science Foundation (SBR 9022555), the Andrew W. Mellon Foundation, the Spencer Foundation, and the Russell Sage Foundation. The Mellon Foundation supported both phases of the project in San Diego as well as exploratory interviews with immigrant parents in the period between surveys; we especially thank Stephanie Bell-Rose, its former program officer. The Spencer Foundation deserves our particular gratitude for its core support of all phases of the project and the sustained encouragement of its staff, in particular its past president, Patricia Albjerg Graham. We owe a similar debt to the Russell Sage Foundation, whose board adopted the new second generation as one of its research priorities and whose president, Eric Wanner, gave us unfailing support throughout the years. Two Russell Sage fellowships to the authors in different years gave decisive momentum to the process of data analysis—from its initial conceptualization to its final stages. Russell Sage staffers Kerry Woodward and Rebecca Hanson collaborated effectively in the last stages of project organization and data analysis. Reynolds Farley, Russell Sage's former vice president, gave generously of his time in providing technical assistance for the analysis of census data. We benefited greatly from his expertise.

Results from the baseline survey were originally published as a special issue of the *International Migration Review* (Winter 1994). We thank IMR's editor, Lydio Tomasi, and his board for their support. This collection of articles was subsequently re-edited and published by the Russell Sage Foundation as *The New Second Generation* (1996), the immediate predecessor of the present book. We thank Russell Sage's director of publication at the time, David Haproff, and Suzanne Nichols, for their careful and competent supervision of this edition. Suzanne, now Russell Sage Foundation's director of publications, has continued working diligently with us in carrying this book to completion.

We recognize in a very special way our long-term editor at the University of California Press, Naomi Schneider, who believed in this project before the first field interview was ever conducted and who followed and supported our efforts during all the ensuing years. A dear friend, Naomi deserves credit and gratitude for seeing the study through to its final stage. And we are once again indebted to Steven J. Gold, whose original photos of immigrant youths in communities throughout the country illustrate the great diversity of the new second generation.

In 1997, the project's headquarters moved to Princeton University. Its Office of Population Research (OPR) currently houses the data archives, and its Web site offers a fully documented data file from the study's first survey. We thank OPR's director, Marta Tienda, for her enthusiastic assistance and consistent support. Preparing the many versions of the following chapters and coordinating the thousand details of taking the manuscript to publication was the responsibility of Barbara McCabe. Barbara is our closest collaborator, whose grace, patience, and technical skills were key elements in the effort of conceiving, drafting, and revising each chapter. We can only hope that the final version of the book is up to the quality of her work.

Our wives, María Patricia and Irene, have been an integral part of the study, both as direct collaborators and as sources of indispensable support along a lengthy and often difficult road. They have our deepest affection for their loyalty and patience.

The final and most crucial recognition goes to the over 5,000 children and their immigrant families who are the subjects of this story. We learned what we know of the second generation from endless hours of talking to them and listening to their histories, worries, and dreams. The book will be justified if it succeeds in capturing, at least in part, the rich complexity of these families' lives and the gamut of experiences that they shared with us over the years.

Alejandro Portes and Rubén G. Rumbaut
Princeton and East Lansing
March 2000

Chapter 1

TWELVE STORIES

The following stories are real. The names are fictitious, but the places where they took place and the nationality of the participants are true. They provide a glimpse of the life of immigrant families in the United States today as it takes place in two of its main gateway cities. Both cities where the stories occurred—Miami and San Diego—have been thoroughly transformed by contemporary immigration but in ways more complex than meet the eye. That complexity is due, at least in part, to the very diverse flows of foreigners coming to each place and the distinct ways in which they have adapted to their new environment. These stories serve to illustrate that extraordinary diversity, and they will be used in later chapters to help frame and interpret general statistical results.

In part for this reason, we attempt no a priori organization of the narratives other than by the place where they took place. If the reader does not get past this first chapter, we at least want to leave with him or her a durable impression of who the newcomers to U.S. shores are, how varied are their attempts to make sense of their new reality, and what are the principal challenges facing their American-raised children.

Miami Stories

María de los Angeles and Yvette Santana: August 1993

When María de los Angeles, Yvette's Cuban mother, arrived in New York's Kennedy Airport in the 1970s, she experienced no trouble at all.[1] Cubans were welcome at the time, and the immigration authorities gave her and her family their residency permit—the green card—on the spot. The troubles started after the family moved to Chicago. At first they lived among immigrants, but when María de los Angeles's father saved the money to buy a home in the suburbs, their new neighbors and her classmates did not take kindly to their presence. Blond and fair skinned, María de los Angeles meshed well in her new surroundings until she opened her mouth and heavily accented English poured forth. "'Spic,' the kids called me. They used to yell, 'Spic, get out of here, go back to where you belong.' Once, a boy asked how come I was Cuban when I wasn't black. Another wanted to know whether I had always been white or had turned white after coming to the United States. . . . They were so ignorant."

María de los Angeles married a young Cuban printer, Fermín, in Chicago, and Yvette was born there. The family could not "go home" as her neighbors had urged, but it did the next best thing, which was to leave Chicago for Miami. There, Fermín pooled their savings to set up a printing shop, and María de los Angeles went to work for a local bank. Neither had a college education, but the family was on a clear upward path. By 1993, their combined earnings exceeded $50,000, and the house they had bought was neat, comfortable, and in a good part of town.

All of this had its effects on Yvette. In school, she has never been called names, never been taunted with ethnic slurs. Unlike her mother in Chicago, she speaks English fluently; more important, however, many of her teachers and most of her peers are also Cuban American. In this secure environment, Yvette has had time to drift. She wears smart clothes but wants jewelry and, at 16, a car. She does not see the need for college since jobs are plentiful for a bilingual girl like her in stores and offices close to home. María de los Angeles says: "We are not really poor, but there are things I can't give her because they are too expensive. . . . Besides, that's not the way we were raised."

The lack of motivation in her assimilated daughter is a cause of sorrow since she recalls all too well her own difficult path to get where she is. "Yvette may be able to get an office job through our Cuban friends, a receptionist or secretary maybe. She is lazy in her studies. She does not have the drive to become a professional."

Melanie Fernández-Rey: September 1993

Milagros is Melanie's mother by a previous marriage. She is currently living with Roberto, who has four children of his own. Roberto and Milagros are Nicaraguans who came to the United States in 1986, escaping the Sandinista revolution. They are not married but have been living together for eight years and share their rented two-bedroom apartment with four of their children. Two boys sleep in the living room. Melanie and her half-sister Marcela share one of the bedrooms. Despite the cramped quarters, the apartment is tidy and features new furniture.

Like many Nicaraguans, Milagros and Roberto have experienced rapid downward mobility in the United States. In Nicaragua, Milagros worked as a manager in an insurance company, and Roberto ran his own farm after getting a degree in agronomy. In Miami, Milagros has only advanced as far as a waitress job at Denny's. She is now a cocktail waitress working for $6.00 an hour plus tips. He has been a busboy and now works delivering pizzas for $4.50 an hour without benefits.

The problem they face is their uncertain legal status. For years they have had a work permit but no guarantee of permanent residence. This made it impossible for the couple to obtain jobs commensurate with their education or to seek assistance in learning English. They simply worked at whatever jobs they could find, hoping for an end to their uncertain status. Milagros finally received approval of her request for permanent residency but is still awaiting her card to arrive and make it official. Roberto's status is still up in the air.

In the meantime, Melanie has gone from grade to grade, growing fluent in English, gradually forgetting her home Spanish, and dreaming of a brilliant American life. Her modest circumstances seem to spur her ambition. She gets excellent grades and is determined to go to college. This is Milagros's greatest cause of anguish because neither she nor Roberto has the means to pay for a college education. In the legal limbo where they live, there are no means to obtain outside assistance, and even with the new green card, prospects are dim. As Milagros puts it, "When children don't want to continue studying, that's one thing; you don't worry too much. But to be unable to support your own child when she clearly has the ambition, it breaks your heart."

Alone in her room, Melanie plugs away at her homework and dreams her dreams. She has recently become a member of her school's cheerleading team. Her life becomes ever more American, oblivious of the tenuous hold of her family in their new country.

Aristide Maillol: August 1993

Being admitted into the home of Aristide Maillol in the Haitian section of Miami transports the visitor into a new reality.[2] The location is American, but the essence is rural Haiti. Aristide's mother speaks no English. Her eyes drift to the floor when explaining in Creole that her husband is hospitalized and that she had to leave her job as a maid at a local motel to attend to his needs. Both came as boat people and were granted temporary work permits under the federal Cuban-Haitian Entrant Program. Both have little education, and their earnings are minimal. There is consternation in the woman's demeanor as she contemplates her situation.

In the tiny sitting area adjoining the front door, a large bookcase displays the symbols of family identity in an arrangement suitable for a shrine. Framed by paper flowers at the top is the painted portrait of Mrs. Maillol and her husband. Below, on three separate shelves, several photographs show Aristide's brother and three sisters. The boy smiles confidently in the cap and gown of a high school graduate. The girls are displayed individually and in clusters, their eyes beaming, their attire fit for a celebration. Mixed with the photographs are the familiar trinkets that adorn most Haitian homes. Striking, however, is the inclusion of several trophies earned by the Maillol children in academic competitions.

At 17, Aristide's brother has already been recruited by Yale University with a scholarship. Young Aristide, who is 15 and plans to be a lawyer, explains his brother's and his own achievements as follows: "We are immigrants, and immigrants must work hard to overcome hardship. You can't let anything stop you. I know there is discrimination, racism, but you can't let that bother you. Everyone has problems . . . but God has brought us here, and God will lead us farther." Sitting to his side, in her humble dress, the mother nods agreement. While the immediate situation looks bleak, her son gives her a firm promise for the future.

Armando and Luis Hernández: July 1995

For Armando Hernández Bueno, life in America has never been a bed of roses. An illegal immigrant at first, he managed to legalize his situation by marrying a woman from his native Dominican Republic who had acquired U.S. citizenship. Armando toiled at a series of menial jobs in New York before coming down to Miami in hopes of a better life. Things did not improve much, and discrimination became worse. Armando, a light mulatto, had thought himself white in his native country; in America, however, he became black.

The lowest point of his new life came when his son called 911. Luis was 13 at the time and, after five years in the United States, thoroughly acculturated. Early adolescence brought out the common rebelliousness of the age, compounded by Luis's perceptions of his parents' ways as old fashioned and authoritarian. The child became progressively distant as his parents complained of his poor school performance, pointed to their own hard life, and exhorted him to do better. One day leaving the supermarket, Armando ordered his son to carry the bags to their old car and wait for him there as he ran another errand. "I'm not your slave," the child replied. "Carry them yourself."

Armando responded as his own father would have done in his native Cibao—by whacking Luis twice across the ears and shaking him by the shoulders. "Until you grow up, you will do as you're told. Who do you think you are?" he told his son. Luis complied with the order, but upon arriving at home, he called the police and denounced his father. Armando was taken to the police station and booked for child abuse. He had to appear before a magistrate and make bail. Only a sympathetic Spanish-speaking judge and the fact that this was his first brush with the law saved him from doing time. Armando did not seek revenge on his teenage son. Wisely, he understood that Luis had simply absorbed the ways of his new environment. As a father, however, he was quite alarmed at the permissiveness and loss of family values that he saw around him.

So Armando bid his time until the following summer when school let out. During vacation, it was customary for the family to travel back to Cibao for recreation and to see the grandparents. So Luis saw nothing unusual in the travel preparations, not suspecting that it would put an end to his American education. Alerted by Armando, his parents prepared to receive their grandchild in a tight embrace of love and discipline, Dominican style. No higher authority could be called there to overthrow parental rule. A tutor was engaged to freshen up Luis's Spanish and prepare him for enrollment in a private school come September. Neither tutor nor grandparents had to spare the rod if things got out of hand with the child.

It is now two years since that one-way trip to the Dominican Republic. Luis's parents report that after much initial crying and protest, he adapted to the new situation and is doing well. He is finishing his last year of secondary school and is preparing to enter the national university in Santo Domingo. Armando says that he will eventually bring his son back to the United States when he has matured sufficiently. This means at least two years of college in the Dominican Republic. "This is the strangest country in the world: the richest and most powerful but all twisted in knots as far as children are concerned," Armando says. "We had to send him back. It was either that or lose him to the gangs."

Mary Patterson: February 1995

Mary Patterson had a dilemma. Being black, she was treated in most places as part of the American black population. Clerks followed her in stores to prevent her from shoplifting. Whites from whom she asked a service or bought something added that extra measure of curtness to the transaction—all of this despite her family's home in Coral Gables (an affluent section of Miami) and the achievements of her parents, both successful professionals from Trinidad. When white people knew she was West Indian, their demeanor changed. "Ah, you are Jamaican, hard-working people. Good English, too," they would say. Never mind that Trinidad and Jamaica are different countries.

Mary consciously sought to project her image as second-generation Trinidadian—or, at least, West Indian—by carrying a key chain with the name and map of her parents' country and by caring for her attire and body language. In a busy world, few people paid attention to such details, and she continued enduring the same aggravations. Mary noticed, however, that when Patricia, her mother, spoke, the situation changed instantly. Patricia uses firm, well-modulated, heavily British-accented English—the English that she learned as a child in Trinidad. Having grown up in American schools, Mary speaks American English to which she has added local black inflections. She did this deliberately, searching for acceptance among her black school peers in junior high.

But now, approaching high school graduation and seeking a job to help pay for college, the situation is different. That West Indian identity must be conveyed to employers. It must be there, up front, as her best defense against standard white racism. Mary's solution was eminently practical: She has been taking lessons from her mother, seeking to regain an island accent. "My mother is so self-assured. She stands tall everywhere . . . at work, when shopping in the stores. I need some of that," Mary says. While she considers herself American, the question of language is just too important to be left to itself. "Blacks in this country carry a lot of baggage, like the way they dress and speak. I respect them, but I don't have to carry that load. I'm an immigrant." Despite discrimination, Mary is determined to succeed. She plans to surpass her mother, who is head nurse at a local hospital, by attending medical school.

Efrén Montejo: May 1994

Efrén Montejo is a senior at Belén Prep, an old Jesuit school in Havana transplanted to Miami in the 1960s. Efrén's parents arrived during those years and were quickly granted political asylum. His father studied civil engineering in Cuba and continued his career without pause in the United States. He is now a naturalized U.S. citizen and works as an engineer for a large Cuban construction company in Miami. His mother graduated from college and now works as a nurse in the office of a plastic surgeon. The couple's combined income exceeds $100,000. The family has never lived anywhere in the United States but Miami.

Both parents speak English fluently, but they try to speak Spanish at home so that Efrén and his younger brother Luis do not lose the language. In the public school that Efrén previously attended, he was rapidly forgetting Spanish. When his parents' economic situation allowed them to pay the steep Belén tuition, he was transferred. Instruction in Belén is bilingual, and children are taught Cuban history and geography. Though Efrén's Spanish is now much better, he still prefers English when talking to his friends.

The Montejos see themselves as Cuban Americans, and both parents and children have high aspirations for the future. Efrén plans to become a physician like his grandfather in Cuba. Since his grades are good and Belén has an excellent track record for placing its graduates in good universities, his parents are confident that he will reach his goal. They intend to assist him financially both in college and in medical school. "It will be a big sacrifice for us, but we can do it and will do it for him," his mother says.

Mr. Montejo would have preferred to raise his children in Cuba since he sees the United States as too permissive and too full of dangers for children. Nevertheless, he is grateful to the new country for the opportunities to succeed in his career and is satisfied with the progress made by his children in school. Surrounded by other Cuban Americans in

Belén and with strong support from his family, Efrén is growing up fully bicultural and with solid confidence in his future. He feels secure and reports that he has never felt discriminated against. His counselors have already started to help him select a college. For Efrén, the world is his oyster.

San Diego Stories

Jorge, Olga, Miguel Angel, and Estela Cardozo: January 1994

Jorge and Olga Cardozo and their two teenage children, Miguel Angel and Estela, live in a small house they recently bought in south central San Diego. The neighborhood, populated by Mexican immigrants like themselves and African Americans, is poor and run down, with several vacant lots filled with tumbleweeds; a boarded-up crack house is across the alley from the Cardozo home. Drug dealers hang out on corners down the block from the Mexicans, close to a seedy commercial district. The Cardozos used to give bread to the crack addicts on the street as part of their evangelical outreach to the poor, but now they, too, have boarded up the windows that face the crack house to avoid seeing anything going on there.

Mr. Cardozo and his family entered the country illegally 14 years ago in the trunk of a car. He had failed in his first attempt to cross on foot and was hospitalized afterwards. Their original goal was to make enough money to buy a house in their hometown of Michoacán; smiling, the Cardozos say they accomplished the first part of their goal—they bought the house—but are still here. They became legal permanent residents under the 1986 federal amnesty for illegal immigrants. Jorge works as a busboy in a tourist restaurant, a job he got through a Mexican friend and has held for 10 years. Olga works at a small Chinese-owned laundry, ironing clothes. They are poor but extremely proud of their son, Miguel Angel, expecting him to become a civil engineer. Miguel Angel gets good grades in school, was recently elected to the honor society, and is recognized by his teachers as a serious student.

Living in a combat zone of a neighborhood, the family has withdrawn from it. The parents speak very little English. The mother's friends are a mix of Latin Americans, almost all drawn from her church—Olga became a devout Pentecostal after coming to the United States—but the father has only Mexican friends, as does their son.

Miguel Angel stays home, playing video games and attending to his school work, rather than risk going outside and getting harassed by gangs. He told a painful story of riding the new bike his parents had given him and being surrounded by gang members who tried to steal it from him. They ripped off a gold chain instead, but ever since he keeps his bike locked up inside the house and does not use it.

Miguel Angel is angrier about experiences of anti-Mexican prejudice he has had in school and elsewhere. The family used to live in an apartment building where Jorge was a resident manager yet was frequently abused by the tenants. One day Miguel Angel's mother came home and found him speechless with rage. He said he could not stand seeing his father insulted so and that he would get a gun and shoot the neighbors. This event led Olga to insist that they move.

His father wants Miguel Angel "to be better than [him]" and not work all day and come home exhausted. "No one wants to wash dishes, that's the truth," he says, but he is proud that his family has never been on public assistance. Olga worries that her son does not want to go to church and sometimes talks back loudly; she also worries about Miguel Angel's younger sister, Estela, who is more rebellious and dresses gang style. Miguel Angel, for his part, continues to plan on becoming an engineer, but his biggest worry is economic. Sometimes, he says, it seems that his parents work just to pay the bills and never help him get ahead.

Quy Nguyen: December 1987

Quy Nguyen is a 19-year-old Vietnamese student in her first year at a local university.[3] Her family, including her father's parents, left Vietnam in 1975, when Quy was 7 years old. In their recent move from Texas to San Diego, the grandparents and other kin stayed behind. Quy's brothers are enrolled in colleges in Texas, where they pursue computer science and premed courses of study. Eventually the grandparents will resettle in California as part of the father's plan of family reunification. Quy's parents are Catholic, and both are college educated. The father has attended community college in the United States and now works in the computer field. The mother—who had seven children born in Vietnam and two more in the United States—is a seamstress and does alterations for a department store.

Quy talked about her oldest brother's educational history and its significance for the rest of them: "We were not really into academic things until my brother graduated third in his high school class. He ended up being third without really trying or anything. And so my parents felt that now that he's gone though it, he knows the system. That sort of opened our eyes. There was not that much pressure to do very well until then; once my brother did so well, that started us off . . . and everybody followed. We kind of knew the system. But the key thing is . . . how the older ones start off, because if the older children start on the wrong foot, it's very hard to get the younger ones in the right track. I have seen that happen, even to my relatives." With responsibility for tutoring shifted down the sibling line, the entire family becomes a mini–school system.

Quy's second-oldest brother graduated from his Houston high school as class valedictorian. Her third-oldest brother graduated fourth in his class. And Quy herself was covaledictorian: "It was a very close race with a Korean girl. We had been friends since the sixth grade, and we studied together, and she was also pressured a lot by her parents." Quy remained in Houston during her senior year, after her parents moved to San Diego, so that she could stay in the race to become valedictorian—competing not only against her Korean friend but also against the record of her brothers.

Quy believes that the reason for her studiousness is to be found in "the nature of the family" and involves a combination of competition and cooperation: "To us there's always the competition. There's always challenge . . . each of us urging each other to do better. . . . It creates a really neat atmosphere. And then there's a certain feeling that you get when you're trying to help younger brothers and sisters." During all her years in junior and senior high school, her parents never met her teachers. They assume that schools have their authority and that when their children are at school, teachers are in charge. Parents support the idea of education but only at home.

Quy is now a freshman at the local branch of the University of California (UC), majoring in biochemistry and aspiring to go to medical school. At UC she was surprised at the number of Vietnamese students, and she hasn't done as well as she had hoped. "There are a lot more Vietnamese than I expected. They make it harder, because there's a lot more competition, really. The majority of Vietnamese are either enrolled in engineering or in science or in something premed, like biology or biochemistry, to get into medical school. And the Vietnamese study all the time, every time you see them, they're always . . . studying, or talking to the TAs and stuff."

The single-mindedness with which Vietnamese students pursue technical fields also reflects their English-language handicap. The Vietnamese want to compete and to win, but they can't succeed against American students in English-based courses. Quy remembers that because of the language handicap, she and her brothers and sisters were held back a grade by the nuns at the Catholic school they first attended in Houston, and she still feels cheated out of that year.

She recalls that "the one thing that gave me satisfaction was math, because in Vietnam you were taught at a much faster pace. I remember the things that I learned in second grade were not taught to the students here until the fourth or fifth grade." So "math is the language that the Vietnamese do know, where they feel they're not handicapped." She calculated her way to the covaledictorian honor, she explained, by focusing on accelerated math and science classes that yielded extra grade points for her grade point average, unlike classes such as history that did not.

Bennie and Jennifer Montoya: October 1995

The Montoyas live in a predominantly Filipino, middle-class neighborhood in San Diego with their four U.S.-born children and Mrs. Montoya's elderly mother. Their home is well furnished, with a huge television set in the living room. The two oldest children, Bennie and Jennifer, attend different high schools in the San Diego area—but not the one that is closest to their home. Mrs. Montoya says that the neighborhood school is "the worst place to send a child right now," due to the poor quality of the teaching and administrative staff. So the kids have to travel long distances to get to other schools.

The parents both hail from Manila. Mrs. Montoya is a registered nurse—she trained in the Philippines—and works at a local hospital. Mr. Montoya is employed as a manufacturing technician; unlike his wife, he did not finish college, but he says that education is very important. "The Filipino way is to have a good education for [the] kids. The kids can then help their parents. They show the world that they are good parents." Still, he seems ambivalent in his career expectations for the children. He wants them to get good grades in school but does not encourage Bennie (a senior) or Jennifer (a junior) to seek to attend a top university or to go to college outside the San Diego area.

Mrs. Montoya says that her daughter Jennifer has the usual problems of wanting to socialize more, and her grades suffer as a result. "There are gangs anywhere you go, there's drugs anywhere you go, you teach your kids to do what's right and hope that they find good friends, that's all you can really do." Jennifer minimizes those concerns: At her current high school, she said, the kids break down along social lines (socialites, brains, dropouts) rather than ethnic lines, but her junior high was majority Filipino, and social life was shaped by Filipino "gangs," organized by where they lived. "At the time everybody was like 'cliqueing' together; it was totally like a bunch of kids saying, 'We're together now and we'll be called so-and-so.'"

Mr. Montoya is dissatisfied with Bennie's academic performance, which has deteriorated lately despite their efforts to send him to a better school—"I would like that A, if possible." Bennie's GPA in ninth grade was 3.2, but in his junior year he managed only a C average. According to Mr. Montoya, an inability to communicate is one of the difficulties he has with his son. Another problem is "the materialism of the youth in this country. Sometimes Bennie has an attitude, the way he dresses, the expensive things he wants."

Bennie and Jennifer have lost much of their ability to speak the parents' (and grandmother's) native tongue, Tagalog. Ironically, Bennie is now taking Spanish at school even though a Tagalog class was also offered. But Bennie is not motivated and recently received a D in that class. When asked why Bennie cannot speak Tagalog well, his father replies: "They're embarrassed to speak it because they think we're making fun of them." Bennie shrugged and said simply, matter-of-factly, "I do all the customs."

Sophy Keng: November 1987–June 1988

Sophy Keng, an 18-year-old Cambodian girl, had just turned 6 when Phnom Penh fell in 1975 and her life was turned upside down.[4] The apartment complex where she now lives is rundown, but numerous Cambodian children are happily running about. Although the complex is shabby, the inside of Sophy's apartment is neat. Despite the obvious poverty of the place, a corner of the living room boasts a stereo system, a color TV set, and pictures of Sophy's roommate and her children.

Sophy's father was of mixed Vietnamese, Chinese, and Khmer ancestry, and her mother was of Thai and Khmer background. In 1974 her father, a soldier, disappeared and was not heard from again. Her mother had been a clerk in Cambodia with about a seventh-grade education. After the Khmer Rouge came, her mother and two siblings were sent along with Sophy to a small village in Cambodia where they stayed until 1979. However, during this time Sophy was separated from her family and forced to work on a farm from 5 A.M. to 6 P.M. every day. She was fed only gruel, which consisted of a little rice and water: "Everybody got skinny." One day she was lonely for her mother and left the farm without permission to go see her. When she returned, she was beaten with a branch so severely that she still bears the scars on her back. She witnessed killings and feared for her own life. She recalls the horror of being called out of bed one night and taken to a field with sharp stakes sticking out of holes in the ground. There she saw babies thrown up in the air and impaled to death as they fell onto those stakes.

In 1979, her family fled to Thailand, where they lived in several refugee camps until the early 1980s, when they were resettled in San Diego and sponsored by an American family. When Sophy lived with her mother in San Diego, as she did until recently, her mother received supplemental security income (SSI) cash assistance from the welfare department. But her mother was distraught and had difficulty taking care of her family. Sophy and her younger brother had received cash assistance through the Aid to Families with Dependent Children (AFDC) program. Her older sister stayed in school for a year but dropped out. Her brother was supposed to be in the eighth grade, but at the time we met with Sophy, he was missing after having run away from home.

While in high school, Sophy was married unofficially in the Cambodian fashion, got pregnant, and bore a son. Her "husband" has since disappeared. After her baby was born, Sophy moved in with her girlfriend. She doesn't want to move back to her mother's apartment. "At home it's lonely; nobody visits me there." Her mother sends her $100 per month, and her friend helps her out when she can. She is thinking of applying for AFDC herself, but she doesn't know how that is done. She does recall seeing the social worker when she was pregnant but hasn't seen one since then.

She likes school and would like to finish high school. But it's very difficult now with the baby. Her mother is not a reliable resource, so she is often unable to find a baby-sitter during school days, causing Sophy to stay home and thus resulting in school absences. She claims she got good grades before the baby (A's and B's), but this semester it's been all F's. When asked about her career goals, she selected "clerk" because her mother was one and so was her grandfather. But other than this, she has no idea about future occupations.

About her adoptive country, she says: "How could I be American? I black skin, black eyes, black hair." She expresses this very emphatically and insisted on defining *American* in racial terms. When asked about how she has been treated by Americans, she eluded the question but later repeated that "my English not good enough and my skin color black." She speaks Khmer most of the time, though her girlfriend does speak English, and she is seen by the black assistant manager of the apartment complex as the tenant who can speak English best. Sophy is distraught and confused about both her past and her future. Life is something that has happened to Sophy, and she experiences it as largely outside her control.

Yolanda and Carlos Muñoz: March 1994

Carlos Muñoz was born in San Diego, the only child of Rafael and Yolanda Muñoz. Both of Carlos' parents were born in Mexico, but they met and were married in the United States. They divorced several years ago, and Carlos alternates living with his mother and father. His father is an attorney and lives with his new wife in a middle-class suburban home. His mother has long worked as a teacher's aide in the local school district; she lives in a tidy house in a working-class, mostly Mexican area near downtown San Diego. She periodically takes Carlos on trips to Mexico.

Mrs. Muñoz graduated from a high school in the same district where she is now employed, and she is knowledgeable about the educational system here. She is happy with Carlos' high school—which is not over-crowded and understaffed as his junior high school had been—but is worried about his school performance, saying that he lacks *ganas* (desire) and is not spending enough time or effort on his studies. "He tries to do everything fast. . . . He's getting an F in biology and C's in most other classes." Of her career hopes for Carlos, she says that "it would be perfect for him to be a lawyer, but he needs to work harder. I don't think that he can do it." His father has now taken a more active role in Carlos' education, hoping to get him on the right track again.

At school, Carlos is involved with the Movimiento Estudiantil Chicano de Aztlán (MEChA) organization. He calls himself Chicano and identifies with *La Raza*. His father, according to Mrs. Muñoz, also identifies as Chicano. But she thinks of herself as Mexican, saying that "even though I'm a U.S. citizen, I am Mexican because I was born there." She does not consider herself political, like her son and ex-husband. She would rather that Carlos identified as Mexican, too, to show he is proud of his Mexican heritage. This has caused some discord between Carlos and his mother, though she understands why he feels as he does. "Now that he started with MEChA," she comments, "he feels that he has to fight for stuff."

Carlos has been upset by the anti-immigrant climate in California, especially against illegals. He has witnessed Border Patrol sweeps through their neighborhood. And not long ago he was questioned on the bus en route to his father's house, because he had been seated next to a Mexican woman detained by the Immigration and Naturalization Service (INS) during one of its routine checks of buses heading north from San Diego. Carlos also has more Mexican friends (*recién llegados,* or recent immigrants) at his high school now than he did when he was in junior high. Although Mrs. Muñoz has a much less sympathetic appraisal of recent immigrants than her son, she welcomes the change in his peer group. It is good, she says, because now Carlos (who cannot read or write in Spanish) is learning more of the language than ever before.

Boua Cha: 1988–1990

Boua Cha was an 18-year-old Hmong student completing her senior year at a San Diego High School.[5] She arrived in the U.S. in 1980 at the age of 10 and now speaks English effortlessly and without an accent. She is the second child of her father's first family, which consisted of eight children at the time they fled Laos in 1975. A ninth died at childbirth, along with Boua's mother, in a refugee camp in Thailand when Boua was 8 years old. The father remarried and has six additional children with his second wife.

Because their family was so large, they split it in half and lived in separate two-bedroom apartments a block away from each other. Her father works for low wages as a laborer, her grandparents are on general assistance, and the bulk of the household income comes from AFDC. Boua lost her AFDC eligibility when she turned 18, forcing her to work part time to help make up for the loss of household income. But as the oldest female, Boua also had the responsibility of running her household, including shopping, cooking, cleaning, and other duties that her mother would have managed—in addition to being a full-time high school student. This required her to get up at 5 A.M. each weekday to prepare breakfast for the family, as her classes started at 7:30 A.M.; after school she cooked and served the evening meal, and she attended to her homework only after all household chores were done.

Of her siblings, one sister had a 4.0 GPA in school; her older brother had a 3.5 GPA, and she herself had a 3.3 average in senior high. She became a member of a local Mormon church (which she joined on her own) and cultivated close ties with some of her teachers. Despite her heavy family burdens, Boua seemed posed to succeed. Indeed, she graduated with honors, was admitted to the local state university, received some financial aid, and was supported by teachers and members of her church. Yet soon after her graduation she met a Hmong man from Fresno and three weeks later married him and eloped north. He hadn't finished high school and worked as a laborer.

Church sponsors who had placed great hopes in her college education even thought of filing a suit to prevent the marriage but were persuaded by clan leaders that Boua was old enough to make her own choices. Besides, these elders pointed out that supporting a female through college is a poor economic investment because daughters have no obligation to support members of their blood family and instead become contributors to her husband's family. In traditional Hmong society, girls are seen as "lost" upon marriage and are devalued accordingly. According to one young Hmong activist, cases like Boua's are all too common and amount to a "tragic waste of talent."

Two years later we caught up with Boua at her modest home in Fresno. She said she felt happier and freer but was ashamed that she had let down those who had helped her in San Diego; she had one baby and was expecting another. She still vaguely hoped to enroll in community college classes and to become a writer some day, but not under her present circumstances, without the financial wherewithal or the support of her family and community.

Chapter 2

THE NEW AMERICANS
An Overview

Immigration Yesterday and Today

Like the early 1900s, the final decades of the twentieth century witnessed a growing wave of immigration that is once again remaking the fabric of American society. Because of its recentness, attention has focused on the adult newcomers—their places of origin, qualifications, and legal status. As is now well known, the bulk of the new immigration comes from Latin America and Asia; it includes a sizable number of professionals and entrepreneurs along with many poorly educated manual workers and comprises both legal residents and a large, underground migrant population.[1]

Less attention has been paid so far to another key aspect of the new immigration, namely, its transformation over time into a variety of new ethnic groups as the first generation gets settled and the second generation comes of age. The experiences of adult immigrants are important for the future of these ethnicities, but even more decisive is the fate of their children. Immigrants always have a point of reference in the countries they left behind, and if they are unsuccessful, they can go back. Many actually return home on their own after accumulating sufficient resources. In contrast, the U.S.-born second generation grows up American, and the vast majority of them are here to stay. Their common point of reference is life in this country, and their relative educational and economic achievements will set the course of their respective ethnic groups for the long term.[2] Indeed, the children of today's immigrants represent the most consequential and lasting legacy of the new mass immigration to the United States.

Growing up American with foreign parents is not an unusual experience. It is the stuff of which innumerable films, novels, and personal retrospectives have been made. The experiences of descendants of Jewish, Italian, Polish, and German immigrants occupy a central place in twentieth-century American literature. On the other hand, the experiences and situation of children of the more recent arrivals are less well known. Because not only their countries of origin but also the society receiving them has changed, extrapolating the well-known saga of the old second generation to the new is questionable. For reasons to be examined in later chapters, the United States today is a very different place from the society that greeted southern and eastern Europeans in the early twentieth century. These differences interact with the racial, educational, and cultural characteristics of first-generation parents to produce very different adaptation outcomes.

The 12 real-life stories in the preceding chapter illustrate this diversity. They show some of the multiple ways in which parental histories, the surrounding U.S. context, and the children's own development come together, as well as the paths that grow out of this confluence. As we move to examine quantitative evidence on the condition and attitudes of the new second generation in the following chapters, it will be helpful to keep these stories in mind. They were selected because they exemplify certain key trends found in the survey data and provide a human context for those numerical results.

Some of the stories illustrate the peculiar paradox that greater family economic achievement and security sometimes lead to lower aspirations among secure and acculturated children, while legal insecurity and a precarious economic situation spur their ambition, often to the chagrin of penniless parents. Here the stories of María de los Angeles, Yvette Santana, and Carlos Muñoz, on the one hand, contrast with those of Miguel Angel Cardozo and Melanie Fernández-Rey on the other. The same is the case with the ambitious Aristide Maillol, who is set in comparison with Efrén Montejo. Both boys are bound for professional careers, but in Efrén's case, this is the natural course of events for the child of stable, white, and affluent parents, while in Aristide's, it is the outcome of family support and a heroic determination to overcome discrimination and poverty.

The story of Quy Nguyen is representative of the remarkable way in which some Vietnamese families have organized around the relentless pursuit of academic success, while those of Sophy Keng and Boua Cha offer poignant reminders of the ways in which even the most resilient young people can be overcome by the oppressive weight of their circumstances. Finally, the stories of Bennie and Jennifer Montoya, of Armando Hernández and his son Luis, and of Mary Patterson and her mother illustrate the pitfalls of rapid assimilation and the various ways in which parents and children seek to overcome it. All these stories show that the process of "growing up American" ranges from smooth acceptance to traumatic confrontation depending on the characteristics that immigrants and their children bring along and the social context that receives them.

The Size and Concentration of the Second Generation

In 1990 demographers estimated that 24.3 million Americans—9.8 percent of the U.S. population—were the children of foreign-born parents.[3] The absolute figure had remained about the same since the 1920s, when the children of earlier European and other immigrants numbered 22.8 million, or 21.6 percent of the national population. Because the size of this population is driven by the influx of immigrants, it has grown rapidly in the 1990s and will expand further at the beginning of the twenty-first century. National censuses show that between 1960 and 1990 the size of the foreign-born population doubled, from 9.7 million to 19.8 million, or 7.9 percent of the population.[4] By 1997, the foreign-born population had grown to about 26.8 million, or 10 percent of the total U.S. population, and the foreign-stock population (the first and second generations) had grown to about 54.7 million, or 20.5 percent of the national total.[5] The children of this new immigration represent our focus of interest.

Immigrant children and U.S.-born children of immigrants are the fastest-growing segment of the country's total population of children under 18 years of age. By 1997, they accounted for one out of every five American children. In that year, as Table 2.1 shows, there were an estimated 3 million foreign-born children under the age of 18 and another 10.8 million U.S.-born children under 18 living with one or two foreign-born parents. These immigrant families, moreover, are heavily concentrated in a few areas of settlement, making their presence and impact

	Total Population	Foreign-Born First Generation	U.S.-Born Second Generation	Immigrant Stock
Total U.S. population	266,726,726 100.0%	26,845,381 10.1%	27,797,013 10.4%	54,642,394 20.5%
U.S. children under 18	71,206,051 100.0%	2,962,381 10.1%	10,799,755 15.2%	13,761,844 19.3%
Los Angeles	9,547,461 100.0%	3,526,395 36.9%	2,389,024 25.0%	5,915,419 62.0%
New York	8,806,186 100.0%	2,900,972 32.9%	1,880,989 21.4%	4,781,961 54.3%
Chicago	7,793,189 100.0%	1,081,571 13.9%	1,193,271 15.3%	2,274,842 29.2%
Miami	2,279,644 100.0%	1,108,618 48.6%	521,419 22.9%	1,630,037 71.5%
Orange County	2,775,937 100.0%	926,657 33.4%	564,787 20.3%	1,491,444 53.7%
San Diego	2,678,255 100.0%	650,503 24.3%	501,653 18.7%	1,152,156 43.0%
Houston	3,992,738 100.0%	662,654 16.6%	484,286 12.1%	1,146,940 28.7%
Washington, D.C.	4,423,737 100.0%	625,456 14.1%	374,856 8.5%	1,000,312 22.6%

NOTE: Total U.S. and Primary Metropolitan Statistical Areas (PMSA) population estimates from the 1997 Current Population Survey (CPS); immigrant-stock population estimates from the 1996–1997 merged CPS. *Immigrant stock* is defined as the sum of the first (foreign-born) and second (native-born of foreign-born parents) generations of the U.S. population. In 1997, of the 27.8 million persons making up the second generation, about 55 percent had two foreign-born parents, while 45 percent had one foreign-born parent and one U.S.-born parent. The immigrant-stock total of 54.6 million does *not* include another 2.8 million citizens residing in the U.S. mainland who were born in Puerto Rico or other U.S. territories.

SOURCE: U.S. Census Bureau, 1997 and 1996 Annual Demographic Data Files, (March) Current Population Survey.

felt most keenly in local school districts. Table 2.1 ranks the eight primary metropolitan areas of the country with immigrant populations greater than 1 million. In Los Angeles County, a remarkable 62 percent of the area's 9.5 million residents were of immigrant stock (first or second generation), as were 54 percent of New York's and Orange County's, 43 percent of San Diego's, and 72 percent of Miami's.

The rapid rise and concentration of this population reflects the accelerated rate of recent immigration to the United States. Of the 26.8 million foreign-born persons in 1997, fully 60 percent had come since 1980, and 90 percent—over 24 million persons—had immigrated since 1960. Of those post-1960 immigrants, the majority (52 percent) had come from Latin America and the Caribbean, with Mexico alone accounting for 28 percent of the total. Another 29 percent had come from Asia, with Filipinos, Chinese, and Indochinese alone accounting for 15 percent.

The youthfulness of today's immigrant population is another salient feature. Some 40 percent of the post-1960 immigrants arrived in the United States as children under 18, and another 40 percent arrived as young adults between the ages of 18 and 34. Only 1 in 10 immigrated after the age of 40. To be sure, about a third of the nearly 28 million persons who made up the second generation in 1997 were born before World War II to parents who had immigrated to the United States, mostly from Europe, in the early part of the twentieth century; they are the remnants of the "old" second generation. But the number of second-generation persons born between 1960 and 1997 was 16 million, or 58 percent of the total. And that number is growing significantly through natural increase: already by 1995, foreign-born mothers accounted for nearly a fifth of all U.S. births (18 percent).[6]

Other demographic research has confirmed the relative youth of this population. Using data from the 1990 census, Hirschman concludes that the new second generation is still, by and large, in its infancy or early adolescence.[7] For example, the median age of native-born offspring of Cuban parents was only 15.9; of Dominicans, 18.9; of Chinese, 14.7; of Koreans, 9; of Vietnamese, 6.7; and of Cambodians and Laotians, 5. In 1990, according to this estimate, there were fewer than 90,000 second-generation Chinese between the ages of 15 and 24; the census indicates that there were fewer than 80,000 second-generation Cubans and fewer than 40,000 second-generation Dominicans and Koreans as well. The only major exceptions are Mexicans, whose sustained migration over the past century has produced sizable third and fourth generations, and Japanese, whose peak immigration waves took place earlier in the twentieth century and whose native-born members are mostly third generation or higher. In these cases, foreign ancestry cannot be equated with second-generation status among the native born. For other Asian, Latin American, and Caribbean nationalities, the native born are usually second generation, and they are mostly young.[8]

Thus, the process of adaptation among today's second generation is a matter of coping with the challenges of growing up in an environment foreign to themselves or to their parents. The principal outcomes of this process are determined by school performance, language knowledge and use, ethnic identities, the level of parent-child generational conflict, and the extent to which peer relations reach beyond the ethnic circle. The fact that these are children's outcomes does not make them any less important. On the contrary, they will largely determine the chances for social stability and economic ascent of this population as adults. And neither does the census provide much information on these key outcomes. The information available from this source will be summarized in the following section, but it clearly does not suffice for a precise portrayal of the challenges faced by these children.

Studying the New Second Generation: The Children of Immigrants Longitudinal Study

The study from which most of the stories summarized in the first chapter were taken represents our attempt to fill this vacuum. The Children of Immigrants Longitudinal Study (CILS) focused on a baseline population of mean age fourteen, corresponding to the census estimate of the average age for children of Asian and Latin American immigrants in 1990. In addition to this correspondence, there was another powerful reason to focus on this age group: At this early age, most children are still in middle school or junior high school, which makes it possible to generate representative samples by tapping the school population. As they get older, an unknown number drops out of school, biasing samples restricted to a purely student cohort.

The study's design called for taking large samples of students of foreign parentage in the eighth and ninth grades, ranging in age from 13 to 17, and following them for three to four years until their last year of high school. At this point, a second survey took place of all those students who had remained in school and were about to graduate as well as those who had abandoned their schooling. Through this strategy, it was possible to examine adaptation outcomes at the crucial school-to-work or school-to-college transition and, more important, to unambiguously establish the causal forces determining these outcomes; the study did not measure potential causes and consequences at the same time but over a span of three to four years. Hence, for example, a positive relationship between school grades and high parental aspirations may be due to the greater motivation for achievement spurred in the child by ambitious parents or, alternatively, to the adjustment of parental expectations to the child's actual performance. With data collected at one point in time, it is not possible to tell the difference. With surveys at two different points in time, we can establish the order of causation more confidently as well as examine how particular outcomes (in this case, grades) change over time.

In total, 5,262 students took part in the first survey. Their parents came from 77 different countries. To be eligible for an interview, the student had to be U.S. born or to have lived in the United States for at least five years and to have at least one foreign-born parent. Thus, even the oldest foreign-born youths in these grades, at age 17, would have had to have arrived in the United States by age 12 to be included. This corresponds to a broad operational definition of *second generation* as native-born children of foreign parents or foreign-born children who were brought to the United States before adolescence.

The samples were drawn in 49 schools in the metropolitan areas of Miami/Ft. Lauderdale, Florida, and San Diego, California. These cities were selected because they represent two of the areas most heavily affected by the new immigration, as shown by figures in Table 2.1, and because they serve as entry points for significantly different groups. Miami receives immigrants mainly from the Caribbean—especially Cubans, Haitians, Dominicans, Jamaicans, and other English-speaking West Indians; from Central America, mostly Nicaraguans; and from South America, primarily Colombians, Venezuelans, and Brazilians. San Diego is one of the main entry points and places of settlement for the large migrant inflow from Mexico; it also receives large numbers of Salvadorans and Guatemalans and is one of the cities preferred by immigrants from Asia—such as Filipinos, Vietnamese, Cambodians, and Laotians and, to a lesser extent, Chinese, Japanese, and Koreans.

In both cities, the sample design called for inclusion of schools in areas of heavy immigrant concentration as well as those where the native born predominated. This strategy allows analysis of how various adaptation outcomes are affected by different school contexts. The San Diego school district is sufficiently diverse to contain both types of schools. Miami has been so heavily affected by immigration that most of its schools include large proportions of first- and second-generation students. For this reason, the sample encompassed the schools of Ft. Lauderdale (in Broward County), where native-parentage students predominate. In addition, we encountered a well-developed bilingual private school system in Miami, serving primarily the children of former Cuban exiles. Two such schools were included in the sample.

In the absence of prior knowledge of the second generation's distribution, the sample could not be drawn with exact probabilities of inclusion. Instead, the survey team in each city combined its own knowledge of the area with the cooperation of the respective school districts to target schools serving the principal immigrant nationalities, those containing students from smaller immigrant groups, and a control sample of schools where students of native parentage were dominant. In terms of national origin, the sampling goal was to include roughly proportional numbers of students from the principal immigrant groups in each area while reserving approximately one-fourth of the interviews to represent smaller nationalities. This goal was met. As shown in Table 2.2, the major groups in both areas—Cubans, Nicaraguans, Colombians, and Haitians in southern Florida and Filipinos, Mexicans, and Vietnamese in southern California—jointly compose 75 percent of the sample. The remainder is represented by children of immigrants from 70 other countries.

The average age of the sample was 14 at the time of the survey, and it was evenly divided by sex and by grade in school (see Table 2.2). Similarly, about half of the respondents were native born of foreign parentage (corresponding to a strict definition of *second generation*), and the remainder were members of the 1.5 generation (born abroad but brought at an early age to the United States.) This first survey was conducted in 1992. Shortly after completion of this survey, detailed interviews were conducted with a sample of 120 parents, 60 in each metropolitan area. The purpose of these interviews was to learn more about the family context of students who represented distinct types of adaptation experiences.[9]

In 1995, three years after the original survey, the follow-up was launched. As described previously, its purpose was to measure adaptation outcomes at a key juncture in the life of these youths when they left school for work or college. Whenever possible, interviews were conducted in school, first with the original ninth graders as they reached their senior year and then with the original eighth graders as they, in turn, became seniors. For students who had dropped out or moved to other areas, questionnaires were completed in two other forms—either a member of the survey team visited the last known address and asked the student to fill out the schedule, or it was mailed to the student with an addressed, stamped envelope and instructions. In a few cases, students who had returned to their country of origin were located and interviewed by telephone.

The follow-up schedule repeated many questions of the original one to examine how the situation and outlooks of these children had changed over time. In addition, a number of items drawn from national surveys of comparable native-born students were included to allow analysis of similarities and differences between the two populations. The follow-up interview questionnaire is presented in Appendix A. A problem of potential bias exists because the follow-up survey did not retrieve all original respondents; the total follow-up sample is 4,288, or 81.5 percent of the original. The question is whether lost cases are random or whether they overrepresent a particular class of respondents. In the latter case, a sampling bias exists. To test this possibility, we compared retrieved and lost respondents on their characteristics measured in the first survey and correlated presence in the follow-up with potential determinants, also ascertained in 1992.

Tables 2.3 and 2.4 present this exercise's results, which by and large show that the follow-up sample faithfully reproduces the different categories of respondents in the original survey. For example, the second survey retrieved almost identical proportions of boys and girls, of native-born and foreign-born youth, and of U.S. citizens and noncitizens. Similarly, the proportions represented by different nationalities in both surveys are very similar. There is a slight tendency for children from intact families (both parents present) to be overrepresented in the follow-up survey. With this exception, all other differences are statistically insignificant.

Along the same lines, Table 2.4 shows that correlations with presence or absence from the follow-up are small for most predictors. With samples this large, almost any correlation is statistically significant.[10] For this reason, we use an absolute criterion of 1.15 as the indicator of sizable bias in the data. As shown in Table 2.3, almost all the relevant correlations fall below this figure. The only exception valid for both regional samples is intact family; other partial exceptions are family

Variable	Number of Cases	Percent
Location		
Miami/Ft. Lauderdale	2,842	54.0
San Diego	2,420	46.0
Grade in School		
Eighth	2,833	53.8
Ninth	2,429	46.2
Sex		
Male	2,575	49.0
Female	2,687	51.0
Length of U.S. Residence		
U.S. born	2,507	47.6
10 years or more	1,426	27.1
9 years or less	1,329	25.3
U.S. Citizen		
Yes	3,335	63.4
No or does not know	1,927	36.6
Father's Education		
Less than high school	2,172	41.3
High school graduate	1,889	35.9
College grad or more	1,201	22.8
Mother's Education		
Less than high school	2,163	41.1
High school graduate	2,034	38.7
College graduate or more	1,065	20.2

TABLE 2.2 (*continued*)

Variable	Number of Cases	Percent

National Origin

Cuban	1,226	23.3
Filipino	819	15.6
Mexican	755	14.4
Vietnamese	370	7.0
Nicaraguan	344	6.5
Colombian	227	4.3
Haitian	178	3.4
Jamaican	156	3.0
Laotian	155	2.9
Other West Indian	116	2.2
Dominican Republic	104	2.0
Cambodian	95	1.8
Chinese	72	1.4
Hmong	53	1.0
Other Latin American	365	6.4
Other Asian	91	1.7
Other (Middle East, Europe, Canada, etc.)	136	2.6

Language Spoken at Home

English	371	7.0
Spanish	2,931	55.7
Tagalog/other Philippine	756	14.4
Vietnamese	326	6.2
Lao	158	3.0
Haitian Creole	150	2.8
Chinese	98	1.8
Cambodian	82	1.6
Hmong	51	1.0
Other languages	100	1.9
No information	41	0.8

Household Type

Father and mother present	3,338	63.4
Parent and stepparent	692	13.2
Single parent	1,061	20.2
Other	171	3.2

Family Home Ownership

Owns	2,856	54.3
Rents/other	2,406	45.7

SOURCE: Children of Immigrants Longitudinal Study, First Survey.

TABLE 2.3 ORIGINAL AND FOLLOW-UP SURVEYS IN
SOUTHERN FLORIDA AND SOUTHERN CALIFORNIA

Variables	Values	Miami/Ft. Lauderdale				San Diego			
		First Survey (1992)		Follow-up Survey (1995–1996)		First Survey (1992)		Follow-up Survey (1995–1996)	
		n	%	n	%	n	%	n	%
Sex	Male	1,366	48.1	1,046	47.0	1,209	50.0	1,023	49.6
	Female	1,467	51.9	1,179	53.0	1,211	50.0	1,040	50.4
Age (1992)	13 or less	549	19.3	468	21.0	479	19.8	419	20.3
	14	1,284	45.2	1,024	46.0	1,046	43.2	908	44.0
	15	804	28.3	594	26.7	736	30.5	617	29.9
	16 or more	205	7.2	139	6.3	158	6.5	119	5.8
Length of U.S. residence	9 years or less	596	21.0	467	21.0	733	30.3	605	29.3
	10 years or more	739	26.0	582	26.2	687	28.4	583	28.3
	U.S. born	1,507	53.0	1,176	52.9	1,000	41.3	875	42.4
U.S. citizen	Yes	1,886	66.4	1,461	65.7	1,449	59.9	1,260	61.1
	No/don't know	956	33.6	764	34.3	971	40.1	803	38.9
Household composition	Father and mother present	1,649	58.0	1,385	62.2	1,689	69.8	1,517	73.5
	Parent and stepparent	450	15.8	306	13.9	242	10.0	182	8.8
	Single parent	658	23.2	478	21.5	403	16.7	310	15.0
	Other	85	3.0	56	2.5	86	3.5	54	2.7
Father's education	Less than high school	1,066	37.5	809	36.4	1,106	45.7	924	44.8
	High school graduate	1,010	35.5	793	35.6	879	36.3	754	36.5
	College graduate or more	766	27.0	623	28.0	435	18.0	385	18.7

Mother's education								
Less than high school	891	31.4	676	30.4	1,272	52.6	1,050	50.9
High school graduate	1,319	46.4	1,037	46.6	715	29.5	616	29.9
College graduate or more	632	22.2	512	23.0	433	17.9	397	19.2
National origin								
Cuban (public school)	1,042	36.8	820	36.9	2	0.1	2	0.1
Cuban (private school)	183	6.5	146	6.6	0	0.0	0	0.0
Nicaraguan	340	12.0	277	12.4	4	0.2	4	0.2
Colombian	223	8.0	181	8.1	4	0.2	4	0.2
Haitian	177	6.2	134	6.0	1	0.0	1	0.0
West Indian	253	9.0	189	8.5	19	0.8	12	0.6
Mexican	28	1.0	21	0.9	727	30.0	578	28.0
Filipino	11	0.5	8	0.4	808	33.4	716	34.7
Vietnamese	8	0.3	7	0.3	362	15.0	303	14.7
Laotian	1	0.0	1	0.0	154	6.4	143	6.9
Cambodian	1	0.0	1	0.0	94	3.8	88	4.3
Hmong	0	0.0	0	0.0	53	2.2	50	2.4
Other Latin American	411	14.6	317	14.3	58	2.4	41	1.9
Other Asian	22	0.8	40	1.8	118	4.9	107	5.3
Other	120	4.3	83	3.8	16	0.5	14	0.7
Totals	2,842	100.0	2,225	100.0	2,420	100.0	2,063	100.0

NOTE: All variables measured in the original survey.
SOURCE: Children of Immigrants Longitudinal Study.

TABLE 2.4   CORRELATIONS BETWEEN FIRST
SURVEY PREDICTORS AND RESPONDENT
PRESENCE IN THE FOLLOW-UP, 1995–1996

First Wave (1992)	Respondent Present in Second Survey	
Variable	Miami/Ft. Lauderdale	San Diego
Age	–.118	–.074
Sex (male)	–.040	–.018
Grade in school	–.061	.026
Knowledge of English	.026	.100
Father U.S. citizen	–.014	–.064
Mother U.S. citizen	–.067	–.063
Intact family	.163[1]	.196[1]
Number of siblings	–.057	–.013
Father's occupation[2]	.038	.000
Mother's occupation[2]	.061	.018
Home ownership[3]	.076	.161[1]
Family socioeconomic status[4]	.081	.085
Occupational aspirations[5]	.069	.073
Math test scores[6]	.175[1]	.117
Reading test scores[6]	.098	.106
Percent white students in school	–.016	.052
Percent black students in school	–.067	–.066
Percent Hispanic students in school	.061	–.081

[1]Coefficient exceeds absolute criterion of strength of association.
[2]Socioeconomic index (SEI) occupational status scores.
[3]Family-owned homes coded 1; all others coded 0.
[4]Composite index of father's and mother's education, father's and mother's occupational status scores, and family home ownership standardized to mean 0, standard deviation 1.
[5]Occupation that student wants to have as an adult in SEI occupational status scores.
[6]Percentile scores in Stanford standardized achievement test administered in 1991–1992.
SOURCE: Children of Immigrants Longitudinal Study.

home ownership in California and scores in math achievement in Florida. The sign of these coefficients indicates that there is some over-representation in the follow-up sample of children from better-off and more stable families. This stands to reason as children from broken and lower-status families, particularly those who do not own their homes, are more likely to move frequently and hence are more difficult to locate. The relatively small size of these correlations, however, indicates that this bias is not large.[11]

An important limitation of the original student survey is that information on the families was obtained indirectly from relatively young teenagers and thus was often quite limited. It is obvious that the social context provided by immigrant parents plays a decisive role in the adaptation outcomes of their children. For this reason, we deemed it vital to extend the interviews conducted with a small group of parents following the first survey to a sizable subsample. This much larger parental survey took place simultaneously with the follow-up of students in their senior year. Questions in the parental questionnaire are designed to gauge the contexts that received these immigrants, the characteristics of their present neighborhood, their relationships with and aspirations for their children, and their socioeconomic condition and cultural adaptation.

Many immigrant parents do not speak English fluently, and for this reason the questionnaire had to be translated and the interview conducted face-to-face. In total, this instrument was translated into eight languages, including Spanish, Haitian Creole, Tagalog, Cambodian, Lao, Hmong, and Vietnamese. Appendix B presents only the English version. Because of the complexity of locating and interviewing so many non-English-speaking parents, the survey was conducted with a probability sample representing 50 percent of the student follow-up. The parental sample was drawn randomly but with differential probabilities by national groups to ensure sufficient representation of smaller nationalities, especially those comprised of immigrants of more modest socioeconomic background.

The goal of this strategy was to produce sufficient parental interviews with immigrants of all nationalities. As shown in Table 2.5, this goal was met, because the survey yielded sizable numbers of Haitian, West Indian, Nicaraguan, and other Latin American parents in Miami/Ft. Lauderdale and of Vietnamese, Laotian, Cambodian, and Hmong parents in San Diego. The larger nationalities—Cubans, Mexicans, and Filipinos—are proportionally underrepresented, although they still make up the greater absolute numbers in the parental as well as in the student surveys. Table 2.5 also shows that the majority of interviewed parents had been in the country for a considerable length of time, averaging 21.6 years, and that most had become U.S. citizens.

Close to 90 percent of our 2,442 respondents are the biological parents of students in the sample, and of these the majority are mothers. Three-fourths are married, and the vast majority have remained married to the child's other biological parent. Thus, we are dealing with a rather stable and settled adult population. Results from this survey provide context to findings on the adaptation outcomes of second-generation youths and indicate their possible long-term determinants. These uses will become evident in the following chapters.

TABLE 2.5 BASIC DEMOGRAPHIC CHARACTERISTICS OF IMMIGRANT PARENTS INTERVIEWED IN 1995–1996

	Miami/Ft. Lauderdale		San Diego		Totals	
	n	%	n	%	n	%
Parent's Country of Birth						
Cambodia	—	—	85	6.4	85	3.5
Colombia	83	7.4	3	0.2	86	3.5
Cuba	384	34.2	2	0.2	386	15.8
Haiti	75	6.7	—	—	75	3.1
Jamaica/West Indies	99	8.8	4	0.3	103	4.2
Laos (Hmong)	—	—	46	3.5	46	1.9
Laos (Lao)	—	—	140	10.6	140	5.7
Mexico	8	0.7	321	24.4	329	13.5
Nicaragua	203	18.0	3	0.2	206	8.4
Philippines	1	0.1	359	27.2	360	14.7
Vietnam	1	0.1	248	18.8	249	10.2
Other Latin American	207	18.5	17	1.3	224	9.2
Other Asian	11	1.0	64	4.9	75	3.1
Other country	51	4.5	26	2.0	77	3.2
Relationship to Child						
Parent	1,081	96.3	1,289	97.8	2,370	97.1
Stepparent	17	1.5	3	0.2	20	0.8
Guardian	25	2.2	26	2.0	51	2.1
Gender						
Male	338	30.1	583	44.2	920	37.7
Female	785	69.9	735	55.8	1,520	62.3
Marital Status						
Married	847	75.5	1,106	83.9	1,953	80.0
Divorced/separated	209	18.6	126	9.6	335	13.7
Widowed	39	3.5	64	4.9	103	4.2
Other	28	2.4	23	1.6	51	2.1
If Married, Partner's Relationship to Child						
Biological father/mother	713	84.2	1,001	90.5	1,714	87.8
Stepparent	119	14.1	88	8.0	207	10.5
Other	15	1.7	17	1.5	32	1.7

TABLE 2.5   (*continued*)

	Miami/Ft. Lauderdale		San Diego		Totals	
	n	%	*n*	%	*n*	%
Present Citizenship						
Foreign	514	45.8	675	51.3	1,189	48.7
U.S.	609	54.2	643	48.7	1,252	51.3
Year of Arrival in U.S.						
Before 1960	43	3.8	37	2.8	78	3.2
1960–1969	292	26.0	121	9.2	412	16.9
1970–1979	330	29.4	551	41.8	882	36.1
1980–1984	303	27.0	368	27.9	671	27.5
1985 and after	155	13.8	241	18.3	398	16.3
Totals	1,123	100.0	1,319	100.0	2,442	100.0

SOURCE: Children of Immigrants Longitudinal Study, Parental Survey.

The New Second Generation at a Glance

Census Results

From the preceding discussion, it is clear that there are at present two major sources of information on the present second generation of immigrants to the United States. One is the decennial U.S. Census, which covers the nation but is shallow in its coverage.[12] The second is the CILS, which is limited to two metropolitan areas but, as seen earlier, provides a wealth of information on these children and their parents. A key difficulty in census data is the impossibility of identifying members of the second generation directly because no question about parental nativity appeared in the 1980, 1990, and 2000 censuses. In the absence of this question, demographers have resorted to different, indirect approaches.

One approach consists of cross-tabulating declared national ancestry with place of birth to arrive at estimates of the size of the second generation and certain characteristics of its members, as done by Hirschman.[13] A second strategy takes advantage of the fact that most of the new second generation is still young enough to live with their parents. By comparing children living in households headed by a foreign-born person with those living in households of native parents, it is possible to obtain a partial glimpse at the population of interest. The approach is partial because it excludes second-generation members old enough to be living on their own as well as those living with a single native-born parent when the other biological parent is foreign born. Nevertheless, the strategy provides important information on the general characteristics of this population. This approach has been used by Oropesa and Landale to estimate its size.[14]

Table 2.6 reports a second exercise based on this strategy conducted by Jensen and Chitose. From the 1990 household sample, these authors selected all households with children under the age of 18 whose heads or spouses of heads were foreign born. The data allow a distinction between native- and foreign-born children of immigrants. For comparison, a sample of native-born children of native parentage was also drawn. As shown in the table, children of immigrants are much more likely to live in urban areas and in five specific states than native-parentage youth. Not surprisingly, these states—California, New York, Florida, Texas, and Illinois—are those receiving the bulk of today's immigration. Predictably, as well, the second generation is more likely to speak languages other than English at home, with Spanish being by far the most common.[15]

Table 2.6 shows that immigrant households are much less likely to be non-Hispanic white and much more likely to be Asian or Hispanic than those of natives. Relative to the latter, the education of immigrant parents is clearly bimodal: There are slightly more college graduates among immigrant than native household heads, but at the other extreme, the foreign born are far more likely to have eight years or less of education. That figure is still higher among more recently arrived immigrants, whose children are themselves foreign born.

These census data pertain to the homes and the parents of the second generation. Results can be fruitfully compared and extended by those stemming from our own survey of immigrant parents in California and Florida. Although the latter is not representative of the national population, it contains detailed information on a much larger number of variables. These surveys confirm the absolute dominance of Spanish among languages spoken in the homes of children of immigrants and the bimodal character of their parents' education. Table 2.7 shows the close correspondence of these results with those from the census. In both instances, Spanish is by far the dominant home language. Parents with eight years of education or less and those with a college degree jointly represent about 60 percent in both data sets. There is, however, a sharp

TABLE 2.6   CHARACTERISTICS OF CHILDREN,
18 YEARS OR YOUNGER, LIVING IN
IMMIGRANT-HEADED HOUSEHOLDS, 1990

	Second Generation (Foreign-Born Parents)			Third Generation and Higher (Native-Born Parents)
	Foreign-Born Children (%)	Native-Born Children (%)	Total (%)	(%)
Lives in Metropolitan Area				
California	39.7	32.3	33.9	8.3
New York	12.5	11.4	11.7	5.7
Texas	9.5	11.6	11.1	7.0
Florida	7.1	6.3	6.5	4.1
Illinois	4.1	5.3	5.1	4.6
Language Spoken at Home				
English only	7.7	19.1	16.5	88.6
Spanish	47.3	45.8	46.2	7.2
Other European language	15.3	16.2	16.0	3.4
Other Asian language	26.3	15.5	17.9	0.3
Other	3.4	3.4	3.4	0.5
Socioeconomic Characteristics of Household				
Below poverty line	32.3	18.7	21.8	16.5
Owns home	32.5	58.7	52.8	66.8
Average household income ($1,000s)	33.4	42.8	40.7	40.9
Race/Ethnicity				
Non-Hispanic White	30.1	59.6	53.2	83.8
Black	13.1	11.4	11.7	14.5
Asian	55.9	28.2	34.2	0.5
Hispanic[1]	47.4	44.2	44.9	5.5
Household Heads				
Male	80.3	83.8	83.0	76.1
Married	83.4	87.9	86.9	78.1
Household Head Education				
College graduate or more	25.4	34.6	33.7	31.7
Eight years or less	35.1	22.9	25.7	3.4

[1]Hispanics can be of any race.

SOURCE: Leif Jensen and Yoshimi Chitose, "Today's Second Generation" in *The New Second Generation* (New York: Russell Sage Foundatiuon, 1996), 82–107.

		Miami/ Ft. Lauderdale (%)	San Diego (%)	Total (%)
Language Most	English	40.5	15.8	27.2
Spoken at Home	Spanish	52.8	21.6	36.0
	Haitian Creole	5.4	—	2.5
	Tagalog/other Philippine	—	16.2	11.1
	Vietnamese	—	20.6	8.8
	Cambodian	—	6.0	3.2
	Laotian	—	10.8	5.8
	Hmong	—	3.6	1.9
	Other	1.3	5.4	3.5
		100.0	100.0	100.0
Education	8 years or less	4.2	35.7	21.2
	9 to 12 years	31.1	24.0	27.3
	Some college	41.2	22.6	31.2
	College graduate	23.5	17.6	20.3
		100.0	100.0	100.0
Mean Knowledge of English[1]		3.06	2.62	2.83
Labor Market	Works full time	69.9	47.3	57.7
Participation	Works part time	8.9	11.1	10.1
	Unemployed	6.0	10.5	8.4
	Retired, disabled, homeworker, student	15.2	31.1	23.8
		100.0	100.0	100.0
Occupational	Manual services	10.7	26.5	18.1
Status of Those	Blue collar	24.7	32.4	28.3
in Labor Force	White collar	45.0	27.5	36.7
	Professional and managerial	19.6	13.6	16.9
		100.0	100.0	100.0
Self-employed		16.8	8.3	12.2
Family has Health Insurance		70.2	61.9	65.7
Mean Number of Children		2.8	4.0	3.5
Mean Number of Persons Living in Household		4.7	5.3	5.0
Family's Average Yearly Income ($1,000s)		26.0	24.7	25.3
	Percent below $15,000	20.0	26.5	23.5
	Percent above $50,000	22.1	19.1	20.5

[1]Four-point index ranging from 1 (low) to 4 (high).
SOURCE: Children of Immigrants Longitudinal Study, Parental Survey.

break between immigrant parents in southern Florida, who tend to approximate the educational profile of immigrant household heads nationwide, and the southern California sample, where immigrants of very low education represent the absolute majority. This difference is due to the heavy presence of Mexican immigrants and southeast Asian refugees in our California sample. Unlike the nationalities most heavily represented in Florida, these groups include large numbers of low-skilled manual workers and very poor refugees.

The contrast across these two regions also highlights a point commonly obscured by national figures, namely, the enormous diversity in socioeconomic origins and modes of incorporation of adult immigrants. Again looking at cross-regional differences, we observe them reproduced in the occupational status and entrepreneurial rates of interviewed parents. The proportion of immigrants occupied in professional and managerial occupations in southern Florida is comparable with the national averages, while the figure for San Diego drops to just 14 percent. The unemployment rate at the time of the original interview in Florida was 6 percent, while in California it reached 10 percent, or almost double the national average. Immigrants who owned their own businesses represent a remarkable 17 percent of the Miami/Ft. Lauderdale sample, a figure that is more than twice the national self-employment rate among working adults; the rate of entrepreneurship in the California sample, while still high by national standards, drops to half of the Florida figure.

These differences are accounted for by the distinct composition and immigration histories of the major groups flowing to each area. Notice that despite the educational and occupational disadvantages of California parents, the family income levels in both areas are quite similar. This is partially a consequence of government assistance programs benefiting southeast Asian refugees, a topic to which we will return in later chapters. For the time being, these data show clearly that this is a population of mixed educational backgrounds, with generally modest but different trajectories in the U.S. labor market, high levels of entrepreneurial initiative, mostly low family incomes, and diverse family structures. These heterogeneous circumstances provide the contexts in which today's second-generation children grow.

CILS Results

To supplement the preceding census data with firsthand information on second-generation youths, we make use of the first survey of our longitudinal study, conducted when the children were in the eighth or ninth grades. The results, broken down by nationality, are presented in Table 2.8. It shows that the vast majority of the new second generation has at least some knowledge of a foreign language, since only a tiny minority reports speaking English only. The exception are children of Canadian, Jamaican, and other West Indian immigrants, most of whom are native English speakers. This near universal familiarity with other languages (mostly the parents' mother tongue) does not imply that they hold sway over English. As shown in the next row, majorities of every nationality, with the important exception of Mexicans, already preferred English at this early age. Yet all students, Mexicans included, have a superior command of English relative to their parents' language. The mean English proficiency score for the total sample is 3.7 (out of 4), indicating near universal fluency; it reaches only 2.8 for foreign languages spoken at home, indicating knowledge but not fluency in most of them.

In the sample as a whole, educational expectations are very high, with the average student saying that he or she realistically expected to at least graduate from college. However, a majority of children of Mexican, Laotian, and Cambodian immigrants often do not aim for a college degree, while on average, the rest of the sample plans to earn a graduate degree. An extensive research literature shows that educational expectations play an important role in guiding future academic achievement.[16] As will be seen in subsequent chapters, this is confirmed by the survey's results.

An important set of findings has to do with children's relationships with their parents. The student data support results from the parental survey by showing that about two-thirds of second-generation youth live in intact families. The exception are Haitians and other West Indian-origin students, less than half of whom live with both biological parents. This finding is in line with the known instability of family relations in Caribbean island societies.[17] Despite intergenerational pressures of acculturation, most children appear to get along fairly well with their parents. Only 17 percent of the total sample report feeling embarrassed by their parents' cultural ways, although the figure ranges from a low of 8 percent among Mexican Americans to a high of over 30 percent among offspring of Cambodian and Hmong refugees.

However, relations with outside society have already begun to show significant tensions. A majority of second-generation youths report feeling discriminated against in school and other settings. The major source of discrimination is white student peers, teachers, and neighbors. But again there is considerable variability among nationalities. Only a minority of Cuban Americans growing up in the protected Cuban enclave of Miami report feeling discriminated against. The figure drops to less than one-third among those attending bilingual private schools in this area. The opposite is the case among offspring of nonwhite immigrants or refugees. Two-thirds of children of Mexican, Haitian, Filipino, and Vietnamese origin report discrimination against themselves. The number rises to over 70 percent among Laotians and Jamaicans.

More meaningful still are responses to the question of whether respondents would still be discriminated against if they managed to attain a high level of education. Over two-thirds of the total sample are optimistic, indicating that they would not be. A significant exception, however, are children of black immigrants—Haitians, Jamaicans, and West Indians—among whom one-half or more expect future discrimination despite high academic achievement. These negative expectations are also reflected in the distinctly less enthusiastic stance of black second-generation youths about their adopted country. While solid majorities of Vietnamese, Filipino, and Cuban children proclaim the United States to be the best country in the world, only a minority of Jamaican and Haitian children think so.

This overview of the new second generation reveals a great deal about its situation, internal composition, and attitudes. The combination of census and survey data gives us a far richer and more nuanced profile of this population than was available previously. Yet the information presented in this chapter is only preliminary. First, it is not clear whether trends in family composition, educational plans, language preferences, and other factors observed in early adolescence persist over time. Some of these figures may represent stable patterns, while others may evolve over time or simply be passing fads due to the early age of respondents. Second, it is not clear what leads to what. Do high school grades stimulate loftier educational goals for the future or vice versa? Does preservation of the parental language lead to better parent-child relationships, or does a good family environment stimulate foreign language retention? Do experiences of race discrimination lead to a more contentious attitude toward the white mainstream, or does an a priori negative attitude stimulate greater sensitivity to racial affronts? Such questions cannot be elucidated with data from a single survey.

Third, major differences in a range of variables across national groups cannot be taken as proof of distinct social or cultural effects. Differences in language loyalties, ambition, intrafamilial relations, and

TABLE 2.8 CHARACTERISTICS OF CHILDREN OF IMMIGRANTS IN
SOUTHERN CALIFORNIA AND SOUTH FLORIDA, 1992

	Mexico	Cuba	Nicaragua	Colombia	Other Latin America	Haiti	Jamaica	Other West Indies
Speaks English only (%)	2.4	0.7	0.6	1.3	4.2	4.5	47.1	56.6
Average knowledge of English (1–4)[1]	3.5	3.9	3.7	3.8	3.8	3.8	3.9	3.9
Average knowledge of foreign language (1–4)[2]	3.2	3.1	3.2	3.1	3.0	2.3	2.1	1.7
Prefers English (%)	45.2	82.3	74.4	70.5	73.6	80.9	71.0	85.9
Educational expectations (1–5)[3]	3.9	4.4	4.4	4.4	4.4	4.4	4.5	4.4
Attends inner-city school (%)	61.0	20.0	23.8	8.4	23.0	36.0	8.4	24.5
Intact family (%)[4]	59.3	58.7	62.8	58.6	57.3	44.9	39.4	46.2
Embarrassed by parents (%)	8.1	16.5	16.9	16.3	12.1	25.3	6.5	13.2
Discrimination against self (%)	64.9	38.1	51.2	45.3	48.7	62.7	74.2	61.9
Expects discrimination in the future (%)[5]	34.7	19.1	25.7	19.8	25.0	48.6	60.3	47.8
Believes U.S. is the best country in the world (%)	54.0	70.2	51.4	45.4	57.3	32.6	32.2	37.8
n	755	1,226	344	227	469	178	156	116

	Philippines	Vietnam	Laos (Lao)	Laos (Hmong)	Cambodia	Chinese, Other Asian	All Others	Total
Speaks English only (%)	18.0	1.6	0.0	0.0	0.0	19.1	35.6	8.0
Average knowledge of English (1–4)[1]	3.8	3.3	3.3	3.1	3.4	3.7	3.9	3.7
Average knowledge of foreign language (1–4)[2]	2.1	2.6	2.4	2.7	2.4	2.2	2.1	2.7
Prefers English (%)	88.3	51.5	52.3	64.2	65.6	75.3	88.2	71.7
Educational expectations (1–5)[3]	4.4	4.2	3.7	3.5	3.9	4.5	4.5	4.1
Attends inner-city school (%)	5.5	48.5	66.5	83.0	91.7	18.5	27.9	29.5
Intact family (%)[4]	79.5	73.1	71.6	77.4	68.8	77.8	66.2	63.3
Embarrassed by parents (%)	17.2	25.9	20.7	35.9	31.3	33.3	13.2	16.7
Discrimination against self (%)	63.5	67.2	72.1	55.8	59.6	59.4	61.5	55.1
Expects discrimination in the future (%)[5]	38.1	35.4	43.9	39.6	38.7	31.0	27.4	31.2
Believes U.S. is the best country in the world (%)	62.4	66.4	67.1	66.0	64.6	67.9	60.3	59.3
n	819	370	155	53	95	163	136	5,262

[1]Unit-weighted sum of ability to speak, understand, read, and write English. Index ranges from 1 (no knowledge) to 4 (complete fluency.) Internal consistency reliability (Cronbach's alpha) is .92.

[2]Unit-weighted sum of ability to speak, understand, read, and write a foreign language. In almost all cases, this is the parental language. Index ranges from 1 (no knowledge) to 4 (complete fluency.) Internal consistency reliability (Cronbach's alpha) is .93.

[3]Student's report of highest level of education that she or he realistically expects to attain. Answers range from 1 (high school or less) to 5 (postgraduate degree). College graduation scores 4.

[4]Student's report of living with both biological parents.

[5]Student's reported expectation that he or she would be discriminated against regardless of his/her educational achievements.

SOURCE: Children of Immigrants Longitudinal Study, First Survey; Rubén G. Rumbaut, "The Crucible Within: Ethnic Identity, Self-Esteem, and Segmented Assimilation among Children of Immigrants," in The New Second Generation, ed. Alejandro Portes (New York: Russell Sage Foundation, 1996), 119–170. Some frequency distributions have been recomputed for clarity.

perceptions of the outside world may be due to the timing of migration of various immigrant groups, their socioeconomic composition, and their contexts of reception in the United States. Once such factors are taken into account, initial differences between Cubans and Mexicans or between Filipinos and Cambodians may evaporate. Alternatively, however, nationality effects may linger after controlling for other variables, indicating that there is something unique, socially or culturally, in the makeup of immigrant communities affecting their children's adaptation.

Fourth, we do not know how the causal process leading to important adolescent outcomes compares between children of immigrants and those of native parentage. The availability of extensive information on the latter population makes it possible to establish whether the same factors play a determining role in achievement, self-esteem, and aspirations for the future or whether there are again unique effects specific to the second generation. The following chapters elucidate these points using results from the first and follow-up student surveys as well as the parental survey. We begin with a review of theories that have sought to account for immigrant and second-generation adaptation in a general way and continue with more detailed analyses of specific aspects of the process.

As we have progressed in the analysis of these survey results, we have been surprised by the unique twists and turns that the efforts to cope with life in the United States has taken for immigrant parents and their children. The case of Mario González, a Salvadoran parent interviewed in California, offers a suitable example. A farmer with a third-grade education, Mr. González crossed the U.S. border to escape the violent civil war in his country. He later managed to bring his family, although at present they are still illegal residents. González cuts grass, plants trees, and paints houses for a living, but he also acts as president of the La Esperanza Improvement Association, a civic group set up by immigrants from his hometown to support their kin and friends left behind. Asked about discrimination in the United States, he describes vividly the many times that he has suffered it. His earthy mestizo features do not help; he is commonly followed around in stores and has been stopped several times by police.

Yet at a different moment in the interview, González declares himself satisfied with his life in the United States and states his firm intention of remaining here. "But wait, sir," the interviewer remarks, "you have told us that you have been severely discriminated against here, that almost every American feels superior to you and treats you accordingly. How come that you want to stay?" González smiles for a while, contemplating his reply. "I really live in El Salvador. I work and earn money in Los Angeles, but my thoughts are always there. When I visit La Esperanza as president of the committee, I am as important as the mayor. We have paid for many works there . . . and it's only three hours away." And what about his sons? "They will become Americans, but I took the elder in my last trip so that he would learn about his roots and take pride in them. This, I think, will help him along."[18]

Chapter 3

NOT EVERYONE IS CHOSEN
Segmented Assimilation and Its Determinants

> Since most immigrants' children are now in school and not yet in the labour force, it is essential that the school careers and future job possibilities of these children be understood.
> —**Herbert J. Gans, "Second Generation Decline," p. 183**

> When you see someone go downtown and get a good job, if they be Puerto Rican, you see them fix up their hair and put some contact lens in their eyes. Then they fit in. And they do it! . . . Look at all the people in that building, they all turn-overs. They people who want to be white. Man, if you call them in Spanish it wind up a problem.
> —**Phillipe I. Bourgois, *In Search of Respect*, p. 170**

This chapter presents the theoretical perspectives that have developed in the course of our study and that guide the analysis of data in the following chapters. The story of how a foreign minority comes to terms with its new social surroundings and is eventually absorbed into the mainstream of the host society is the cloth from which numerous sociological and economic theories have been fashioned.[1] For the most part, this story has been told in optimistic tones and with an emphasis on the eventual integration of the newcomers. In other words, increasing contact over time is expected to end in the gradual merging of foreigners and natives, and the speed of the process depends on how close descendants of immigrants come to resemble the mainstream population.

For this reason, the notion of assimilation became the master concept in both social theory and public discourse to designate the expected path to be followed by foreign groups in America. The concept conveys a factual prediction about the final outcome of the encounters between foreign minorities and the native majority and, simultaneously, an assertion of a socially desirable goal.[2] More than half a century ago, sociologists Lloyd Warner and Leo Srole introduced their study of an American city as "part of the magnificent story of the adjustment of ethnic groups to American life" and went on to predict that "oncoming generations of new ethnics will . . . climb to the same heights."[3] In reality, the process is neither as simple nor as inevitable. To begin with, both the immigrant population and the host society are heterogeneous. Immigrants, even those of the same nationality, are frequently divided by social class, the timing of their arrival, and their generation. American society is not homogeneous either. Depending on the timing of their arrival and context of reception, immigrants can find themselves confronting diametrically different situations, and hence the course of their assimilation can lead to a number of different outcomes.

There are groups among today's second generation that are slated for a smooth transition into the mainstream and for whom ethnicity will soon be a matter of personal choice. They, like descendants of earlier Europeans, will identify with their ancestry on occasion and when convenient. There are others for whom their ethnicity will be a source of strength and who will muscle their way up, socially and economically, on the basis of their own communities' networks and resources. There are still others whose ethnicity will be neither a matter of choice nor a source of progress but a mark of subordination. These children are at risk of joining the masses of the dispossessed, compounding the spectacle of inequality and despair in America's inner cities. The prospect that members of today's second generation will join those at the bottom of society—a new rainbow underclass—has more than a purely academic interest, for it can affect the life chances of millions of Americans and the quality of life in the cities and communities where they concentrate.

Hence, while assimilation may still represent the master concept in the study of today's immigrants, the process is subject to too many contingencies and affected by too many variables to render the image of a relatively uniform and straightforward path credible. Instead, the present second generation is better defined as undergoing a process of *segmented assimilation* where outcomes vary across immigrant minorities and where rapid integration and acceptance into the American mainstream represent just one possible alternative. Why this is so is a complex story depending on a number of factors, among which four can be considered decisive: 1) the history of the immigrant first generation; 2) the pace of acculturation among parents and children and its bearing on normative integration; 3) the barriers, cultural and economic, confronted by second-generation youth in their quest for successful adaptation; and 4) the family and community resources for confronting these barriers. This chapter provides a theoretical description of each of these factors and their expected consequences as a way of fleshing out the concept of segmented assimilation and paving the way for the analysis of its diverse aspects in later chapters.

How Immigrants Are Received: Modes of Incorporation and Their Consequences

It stands to reason that the adaptation of second-generation youths is conditioned by what happens to their parents and that the latter's economic performance and social status are likely to vary. In contrast to journalistic and political characterizations of immigrants as a uniform population, every scholarly analysis of the subject begins by emphasizing their great diversity.[4] Today's immigrants differ along three fundamental dimensions: 1) their individual features, including their age, education, occupational skills, wealth, and knowledge of English; 2) the social environment that receives them, including the policies of the host government, the attitudes of the native population, and the presence and size of a co-ethnic community; and 3) their family structure.

The skills that immigrants bring along in the form of education, job experience, and language knowledge are referred to as their *human capital* and play a decisive role in their economic adaptation. The economic attainment of immigrants does not entirely depend on human capital, however, because its utilization is contingent on the context in which they are incorporated. Yet, by and large, educated immigrants are in a much better competitive position and are more likely to succeed occupationally and economically in their new environment. The same is true of those with extensive occupational experience.[5]

On arrival, however, immigrant workers and entrepreneurs do not confront American society as a level playing field where only their education and work experience count. Instead, a number of contextual factors shape the way in which they can put their skills to use. The policies of the receiving government represent the first such factor confronting newcomers. Although a continuum of possible governmental responses exists, the basic options are exclusion, passive acceptance, or active encouragement. When enforced, exclusion precludes immigration or forces immigrants into a wholly underground and disadvantaged existence. The second alternative is defined by the act of granting immigrants legal access to the country without any additional effort on the part of authorities to facilitate their adaptation. This neutral stance places newcomers under the protection of the law but does not grant them any special concessions to compensate for their unfamiliarity with their new environment. Most economically motivated immigration to the United States in recent years has taken place under this alternative. A third governmental option occurs when authorities take active steps to encourage a particular inflow or facilitate its resettlement. At various times during the last century, the U.S. government was directly involved in the recruitment of different categories of foreign workers and professionals deemed to be in short supply. During the last 30 years or so, active governmental support and assistance has been granted only to selected refugee flows, arriving mostly in the aftermath of communist takeovers during the cold war.[6] Government support is important because it gives newcomers access to an array of resources that do not exist for other immigrants. This edge provides refugees who have high levels of human capital with a chance for rapid upward mobility. It also improves the economic condition of those from modest backgrounds by providing job apprenticeships and direct economic assistance.

The second contextual factor is the host society and its reception of newcomers. A well-established sociological principle holds that the more similar new minorities are in terms of physical appearance, class background, language, and religion to society's mainstream, the more favorable their reception and the more rapid their integration. For this reason, educated immigrants from northwestern Europe face little difficulty in gaining access to U.S. middle- and upper-class circles and are readily able to deploy their educational and work skills to their advantage.[7] Though race is in appearance a personal trait, in reality it inheres in the values and prejudices of the culture so that individuals with the same physical appearance can be treated very differently depending on the social context in which they find themselves.

In America, race is a paramount criterion of social acceptance that can overwhelm the influence of class background, religion, or language. Regardless of their class origin or knowledge of English, nonwhite immigrants face greater obstacles in gaining access to the white middle-class mainstream and may receive lower returns for their education and work experience. A racial gradient continues to exist in U.S. culture so that the darker a person's skin is, the greater is the social distance from dominant groups and the more difficult it is to make his or her personal qualifications count.[8] This social context and its differential evaluation of newcomers account, for example, for the generally favorable reception accorded to Irish immigrants in northeastern U.S. cities and the much greater barriers faced by Haitian immigrants in the same areas, despite the fact that many Haitians are legal immigrants and many Irish are actually undocumented.[9]

The immigrant community's own compatriots represent the third and most immediate context of reception. In some cases, no such community exists, and newcomers must confront the challenges of adaptation by themselves. More common, however, is the arrival of immigrants into places where a community of their conationals already exists. Such communities can cushion the impact of a foreign culture and provide assistance for finding jobs. Help with immediate living needs, such as housing, places to shop, and schools for the children, also flow through these co-ethnic networks.[10]

This regularity in the process of adaptation conceals, however, significant differences among the ethnic communities that immigrants join. While all such communities help their own, they do so within the limits of their own information and resources. For purposes of future socioeconomic mobility, the central difference is whether the co-ethnic group is mainly composed of working-class persons or contains a significant professional and entrepreneurial element. For newcomers in working-class communities, the natural thing to do is to follow the path of earlier arrivals into the host labor market. The help that ethnic communities can offer for securing employment in these situations is constrained by the kind of jobs held by their more established members. In this fashion, immigrants with considerable human capital can be channeled to below-average occupations as a function of the co-ethnic context that they encounter and the "help" that its members can provide.[11]

On the contrary, immigrants fortunate enough to join more advantaged ethnic communities can translate their education and occupational skills into economic returns, even when still unfamiliar with the new language and culture. The main feature of this situation—where a substantial number of conationals holds professional occupations or are independent entrepreneurs—is that the support of ethnic networks does not come at the cost of accepting a working-class lifestyle or outlook. Instead, these networks open a whole range of possibilities—from employment in the outside labor market to jobs within the ethnic community—that make full use of the immigrants' potential.[12]

Jointly, these three levels of reception—governmental, societal, and communal—comprise the mode of incorporation of a particular immigrant group. These modes condition the extent to which immigrant human capital can be brought into play to promote successful economic and social adaptation. No matter how motivated and ambitious immigrants are, their future prospects will be dim if government officials persecute them, natives consistently discriminate against them, and their own community has only minimum resources to offer.

A third dimension of importance for second-generation adaptation is the composition of the immigrant family, in particular the extent to which it includes both biological parents. Immigrant family composition varies significantly across nationalities, reflecting both different cultures and social structures in sending countries and patterns of arrival in the United States. Different modes of incorporation, in particular the outlook of authorities and strength of co-ethnic communities, can affect family composition by facilitating family reunification and reinforcing cultural norms. In turn, family contexts can be expected to affect various second-generation outcomes, even after taking parental human capital and modes of incorporation into account.

Summarizing this discussion, Table 3.1 presents a profile of the human capital, modes of incorporation, and family contexts of several of the largest immigrant groups arriving in the United States during the last two decades. These are also the groups best represented in our study, so these profiles provide a set of preliminary expectations concerning parental adaptation and subsequent second-generation outcomes. Specifically, we expect parental human capital, in the form of education and occupational skills, to positively affect their own socioeconomic attainment. In turn, achieved parental status and family composition will affect the pace and character of second-generation acculturation and subsequent adaptation outcomes. Modes of incorporation are expected to significantly affect the socioeconomic attainment of first-generation parents and to influence their family structure. The importance of these contextual variables may even extend beyond the first generation to directly affect second-generation outcomes. This is one of the main questions to be examined in the following chapters.

Acculturation and Role Reversal

In the family of José María Argüelles, a 40-year old Nicaraguan immigrant in Miami, power has drifted steadily away from him and his wife and toward their two teenage sons. José María does not speak English and has only a high school education. His and his wife's lack of per-

TABLE 3.1   IMMIGRANT NATIONALITIES AND
THEIR MODES OF INCORPORATION, 1990

Nationality	Size	Status Characteristics[1]			
		Median Age	College Graduates (%)[3]	Poverty Rate (%)[4]	Median Family Income ($)[4]
Mexican	4,298,014	29.9	3.5	29.7	21,585
Filipino	912,674	38.8	43.0	5.9	47,794
Cuban	736,971	49.0	15.6	14.7	32,007
Chinese					
People's Republic	529,837	40.5	30.9	15.7	34,225
Taiwan	244,102	33.2	62.2	16.7	45,325
Hong Kong	147,131	30.3	46.8	12.7	49,618
Korean	568,397	34.9	34.4	15.6	33,406
Vietnamese	543,262	30.3	16.0	25.5	30,496
Dominican	347,858	33.6	7.5	30.0	19,694
Jamaican	334,140	35.7	14.9	12.1	34,338
Colombian	286,124	35.3	15.5	15.3	30,342
Haitian	225,393	34.6	11.8	21.7	25,556
Laotian	171,577	27.0	5.1	40.3	19,671
Nicaraguan	168,659	30.0	14.6	24.4	24,416
Cambodian	118,833	29.0	5.5	38.4	19,043

[1]U. S. Bureau of the Census, *The Foreign-Born Population of the United States* (Washington, D.C.: U.S. Department of Commerce, 1993).
[2]Typology based on past studies of individual nationalities.
[3]Persons 25 years of age or over.
[4]Annual figures (1989).
[5]Children under 18 residing with both biological parents.
[6]Percent of households headed by women with no husband present.

manent immigration papers means that they have been dependent on a string of odd menial jobs, like dishwashing and house cleaning, for survival. However, they have remained in the United States long enough for their children to grow up and learn the language. At 19, Pepe Argüelles already holds a waiter's job at a good restaurant and drives a better car than his parents. His younger brother, Luis, has been drifting toward a local gang dealing drugs, but the money that he brings home helps pay

Family Structure		Mode of Incorporation[2]		
Both Parents Present (%)[5]	Female Head (%)[6]	Governmental[7]	Societal[8]	Co-ethnic Community[9]
73	14	Hostile	Prejudiced	Working class, concentrated
78	15	Neutral	Neutral to prejudiced	Professional, dispersed
72	16	Favorable to hostile	Neutral to prejudiced	Entrepreneurial, concentrated
87	8			
81	10	Neutral	Prejudiced	Professional/entrepreneurial, concentrated
84	10			
87	11	Neutral	Prejudiced	Entrepreneurial, concentrated
73	15	Favorable	Prejudiced	Entrepreneurial/working class, concentrated
47	41	Neutral	Prejudiced	Working class, concentrated
53	35	Neutral	Prejudiced	Professional/working class, dispersed
65	21	Hostile to neutral	Prejudiced	Professional/working class, dispersed
56	28	Hostile	Prejudiced	Working class, concentrated
81	12	Favorable	Prejudiced	Poor, concentrated
66	21	Hostile	Prejudiced	Professional/working class, concentrated
71	24	Favorable	Prejudiced	Poor, concentrated

[7]Favorable reception accorded to groups composed of legal refugees and asylees; neutral reception to groups of legal immigrants; hostile reception to groups suspected to harbor large numbers of unauthorized immigrants or being involved in the drug trade, becoming targets of deportation by U. S. immigrant authorities.

[8]Prejudiced reception accorded to nonwhite immigrants and to those with perceived involvement in the drug trade; neutral to groups defined as mostly white.

[9]Concentrated ethnic communities are those that have large and highly visible concentration in at least one metropolitan area.

the rent and meet other urgent needs when his father is out of a job. José María feels powerless to discipline Luis or guide the future of their sons. "It's too late to send them back to Nicaragua," he says. "Here, they know English and know their way around far better than us . . . all that their mother and I can do is pray."[13]

One of the most poignant aspects of immigrants' adaptation to a new society is that children can become, in a very real sense, their parents'

TABLE 3.2   TYPES OF ACCULTURATION ACROSS GENERATIONS

Children's Learning of English and American Customs	Parents' Learning of English and American Customs	Children's Insertion into Ethnic Community	Parents' Insertion into Ethnic Community	Type	Expected Outcomes
+	+	–	–	Consonant acculturation	Joint search for integration into American mainstream; rapid shift to English monolingualism among children
–	–	+	+	Consonant resistance to acculturation	Isolation within the ethnic community; likely to return to home country
+	–	–	+	Dissonant acculturation (I)	Rupture of family ties and children's abandonment of ethnic community; limited bilingualism or English monolingualism among children
+	–	–	–	Dissonant acculturation (II)	Loss of parental authority and of parental languages; role reversal and intergenerational conflict
+	+	+	+	Selective acculturation	Preservation of parental authority; little or no intergenerational conflict; fluent bilingualism among children

SOURCE: Adapted from Alejandro Portes and Rubén G. Rumbaut, *Immigrant America, a Portrait*, 2d ed. (Berkeley: University of California Press, 1996), p. 242.

parents. This role reversal occurs when children's acculturation has moved so far ahead of their parents' that key family decisions become dependent on the children's knowledge. Because they speak the language and know the culture better, second-generation youths are often able to define the situation for themselves, prematurely freeing themselves from parental control.

Role reversal was a familiar event among offspring of working-class European immigrants at the beginning of the twentieth century, and it was often seen as part of the normal process of assimilation to America. Children of Italian, Russian, and Polish laborers raced past their parents to take jobs in the expanding industrial economy of the time, set themselves up in business, or claw their way into the corporate world.[14] Today, second-generation Latins and Asians are repeating the story but with an important twist. For reasons that we will see in detail later on, the social and economic context that allowed their European predecessors to move up and out of their families exists no more. In its place, a number of novel barriers to successful adaptation have emerged, making role reversal a warning sign of possible downward assimilation. Freed from parental control at a premature age, the options available to second-generation youths can be different and sometimes more dangerous than those available to children of Europeans earlier in the century.

Role reversal, like modes of incorporation, is not a uniform process. Instead, systematic differences exist among immigrant families and communities. It is possible to think of these differences as a continuum ranging from situations where parental authority is preserved to those where it is thoroughly undermined by generational gaps in acculturation. The process of acculturation is the first step toward assimilation, as both immigrant parents and children learn the new language and normative lifestyles. Yet the rates at which they do so and the extent to which this learning combines with retention of the home culture varies, with significant consequences for second-generation adaptation.[15] Table 3.2 presents a typology of possible situations depending on the acculturative gaps across generations and the children's insertion in the ethnic community.

Three of the outcomes portrayed in this figure are especially important. *Dissonant acculturation* takes place when children's learning of the English language and American ways and simultaneous loss of the immigrant culture outstrip their parents'. This is the situation leading to role reversal, especially when parents lack other means to maneuver in the host society without help from their children. *Consonant acculturation* is the opposite situation, where the learning process and gradual abandonment of the home language and culture occur at roughly the same pace across generations. This situation is most common when immigrant parents possess enough human capital to accompany the cultural evolution of their children and monitor it. Finally, *selective acculturation* takes place when the learning process of both generations is embedded in a co-ethnic community of sufficient size and institutional diversity to slow down the cultural shift and promote partial retention of the parents' home language and norms. This third option is associated with a relative lack of intergenerational conflict, the presence of many co-ethnics among children's friends, and the achievement of full bilingualism in the second generation.[16]

Dissonant acculturation does not necessarily lead to downward assimilation, but it undercuts parental authority and places children at risk. Consonant acculturation does not guarantee success because parents' and children's striving for acceptance into the American mainstream may be blocked by discrimination. Still, consonant acculturation lays the basis for parental guidance and mutual intergenerational support in confronting external challenges. Lastly, selective acculturation offers the most solid basis for preservation of parental authority along with the strongest bulwark against effects of external discrimination. This happens because individuals and families do not face the strains of acculturation alone but rather within the framework of their own communities. This situation slows down the process while placing the acquisition of new cultural knowledge and language within a supportive context.

Types of acculturation do not occur in a vacuum but are conditioned by the variables discussed previously, namely parental socioeconomic achievement, family composition, and modes of incorporation. When parents have greater resources—in the form of higher education, economic status, intact families, or the support of strong co-ethnic communities—intergenerational acculturation tends to shift toward the consonant or selective modes. Parent-child conflict is reduced, and children are less prone to feel embarrassed by their parents' ways. On the other hand, parents whose educational and economic resources are modest, and especially those who are socially isolated, are more likely to experience dissonant acculturation and role reversal.

Where They Grow Up:
Challenges to Second-Generation Adaptation

To a greater extent than at the beginning of the twentieth century, second-generation youths confront today a pluralistic, fragmented environment that simultaneously offers a wealth of opportunities and major dangers to successful adaptation.[17] In this situation, the central question is not whether the second generation will assimilate to U.S. society but *to what segment* of that society it will assimilate. In the present historical context, there are three major challenges to educational attainment and future career success by children of immigrants. The first is the persistence of racial discrimination, the second is the bifurcation of the U.S. labor market and its growing inequality, and the third is the consolidation of a marginalized population in the inner city.[18]

Race

One of the key features that children inherit from their parents is their race. Just as the mode of incorporation of adult immigrants is defined by how the native majority typify them racially, so is the second generation affected by inheriting the same physical features as their parents. Defined by contemporary standards, the majority of today's second generation are nonwhite, comprising children of Asian immigrants; of blacks from the West Indies and Africa; and of blacks, mulattos, and mestizos from Latin America. The minority of white immigrants also come from Latin America and, in declining numbers, from Europe and Canada.[19] Although it is true that Irish, Italian, Polish, and other early immigrants were originally defined as separate races and subjected to extensive discrimination, their phenotypical similarity with members of the mainstream American population eventually asserted itself. Once second-generation youths learned unaccented English, adopted American patterns of behavior and dress, and climbed a few rungs in the social ladder, they became by and large indistinguishable from the rest of the population. From that point on, the question was not whether they could melt into the mainstream population but whether they were willing to abandon their ethnic niches or would persist in remaining attached to them.

To the contrary, children of Asian, black, mulatto, and mestizo immigrants cannot so easily reduce their ethnicity to the level of a voluntary decision. Their enduring physical differences from whites and the equally persistent practice of discrimination based on those differences, especially against black persons, throws a barrier in the path of occupational mobility and social acceptance. Immigrant children's perceptions of discrimination in American society, their ethnic identities and self-esteem, their aspirations, and their patterns of school behavior are affected accordingly.[20]

Labor Markets

A second major barrier is the deindustrialization and progressive inequality in the U.S. labor market. As the prime industrial power of its time, the United States generated a vast demand for industrial labor during the first three decades of the twentieth century. Indeed, this was the reason why European immigrants first and southern black migrants second were recruited and came in such vast numbers to northern U.S. cities.[21] The availability of industrial jobs and the existence of a ladder of occupations within industrial employment created the possibility of gradual upward mobility for the European second generation without the need for an advanced education. This continuing labor demand was behind the rise of stable working-class communities in northeastern and Midwestern cities where supervisory and other preferred industrial jobs afforded a reasonable living standard for European ethnics.[22]

The depression and its aftermath reduced industrial demand and led to high levels of unemployment. The crisis was short lived, however, as a combination of governmental pump-priming under the New Deal and renewed demand for manufactured goods during World War II reopened the industrial labor market, creating new opportunities for second- and third-generation workers. Their gradual mobility into the higher tiers of blue-collar employment and then into the white-collar middle class furnished the core empirical basis for theories of assimilation, which was conceived as a gradual and straightforward process.[23]

Beginning in the 1960s and accelerating thereafter, the structure of the U.S. labor market started to change under the twin influences of technological innovation and foreign competition in industrial goods. The advent of Japan as a major industrial competitor took American companies by surprise, accustomed as they were to lacking any real foreign rivals in the post–World War II era. As two prominent students of American deindustrialization have concluded: "What caused the profit squeeze was mainly the sudden emergence of heightened international competition—a competition to which U.S. business leaders were initially blind. In the manufacturing sector a trickle of imports turned into a torrent. The value of manufactured imports relative to domestic production skyrocketed—from less than 14 percent in 1969 to nearly triple that, 38 percent only ten years later."[24]

Caught in this bind, many companies resorted to the "spatial fix" of moving productive facilities abroad to reduce labor costs.[25] Technological innovations made the process easier by lowering transportation barriers and making possible instant communication between corporate headquarters and production plants located overseas. The garment industry represents a prime example of this process of restructuring. While fashion design and marketing strategies remained centralized in the companies' American headquarters, actual production migrated, for the most part, to industrial zones in less developed nations.[26]

Industrial restructuring and corporate downsizing brought about the gradual disappearance of the jobs that had provided the basis for the economic ascent of the European second generation. Between 1950 and 1996, American manufacturing employment plummeted from over one-third of the labor force to less than 15 percent. The slack was taken by service employment, which skyrocketed from 12 percent to close to one-third of all workers. Service employment is, however, bifurcated between menial and casual low-wage jobs commonly associated with personal services and the rapid growth of occupations requiring advanced technical and professional skills. These highly paid service jobs are generated by knowledge-based industries linked to new information technologies as well as complex tasks associated with the command and control functions of a restructured capitalist economy.[27]

The growth of employment in these two polarized service sectors is one of the factors that has stalled the gradual trend toward economic equality in the United States and then reversed it during the last decades of the twentieth century. Between 1960 and 1990, the income of the top decile of American families increased in constant (1986) dollars from $40,789 to $68,996. In contrast, the income of the bottom decile barely budged, from $6,309 to $8,637. The income of the bottom half of families, which in 1960 represented about 50 percent of what those in the top decile earned, declined by almost 10 percent relative to this wealthiest group in the following 30 years.[28]

These and related figures contradict the euphoric impression prompted by the economic expansion of the late 1990s that "everybody is getting rich."[29] Indeed, the economic expansion has benefited large sectors of the American population, but these are the sectors linked, directly or indirectly, to the new information technologies and having the requisite educational credentials, skills, and capital to take part in them. At the other extreme, many Americans have been left behind. The median household net worth climbed 10 percent during the 1990s to about $80,000. However, almost half of households (44 percent) did not reach $25,000, and exactly a third had annual incomes below this figure. More than half of American families (57 percent) did not own any equities at all, causing them to fall further behind in terms of economic power.[30]

From the point of view of new entrants into the labor force, including children of immigrants, these structural changes mean the end of the old industrial ladder of unskilled, semiskilled, skilled, and supervisory occupations and the advent of growing labor market bifurcation. In this changed market, high demand exists at the low end for unskilled and menial service workers and at the high end for professionals and technicians, with diminishing opportunities for well-paid employment in between. Adult immigrants, especially those with low levels of education, confront this new "hourglass" labor market by crowding into low-wage service jobs.[31] On the other hand, their children, imbued with American-style status consciousness and consumption aspirations, are generally not satisfied with the same roles. As Gans notes: "If these young people are offered immigrant jobs, there are some good reasons why they might turn them down. They come to the world of work with American standards, and may not even be familiar with the old country conditions. . . . Nor do they have the long-range goals that persuaded their parents to work long hours at low wages. . . . From their perspective, immigrant jobs are demeaning."[32]

Increasing labor market inequality implies that to succeed socially and economically, children of immigrants today must cross, in the span of a few years, the educational gap that took descendants of Europeans several generations to bridge. They cannot simply improve on their parents' typically modest skills but must sharply increase them by gaining access to an advanced education. This, plus the cultivation of the requisite networks, is required to reach into the upper half of the hourglass—that is, to obtain professional-level occupations yielding high incomes and making possible a middle-class lifestyle. For this reason, the educational goals and academic achievement of today's second generation acquire a singular importance.

For children of professional immigrants and successful entrepreneurs, the journey toward the heights of the American labor market may not be so difficult because their parents have already gained access to the needed resources to finance an advanced education or because their co-ethnics control economic niches where profitable business opportunities are still open. These children can afford to adopt a more relaxed stance toward their future. For offspring of working-class immigrants—by far the majority among many nationalities—the task of bridging the gap from their parents' modest starting position to their own aspirations is daunting. This barrier, superimposed on the second generation's general reticence to accept "immigrant" jobs, prompts concern about the future of these children and their chances for successful adaptation.[33] Key questions for our empirical analysis are the extent to which modest parental resources and unfavorable contexts of incorporation translate into lower educational aspirations and poorer achievement and the factors that can reverse these trends among the least privileged.

Countercultures

The third external challenge confronting children of immigrants is that the social context they encounter in American schools and neighborhoods may promote a set of undesirable outcomes such as dropping out of school, joining youth gangs, or participating in the drug subculture. This alternative path has been labeled *downward assimilation* because the learning of new cultural patterns and entry into American social circles does not lead in these cases to upward mobility but to exactly the opposite. The emergence of an adversarial outlook and deviant lifestyles in American inner cities is partially linked to the transformation of the labor market that did away with the ladder of blue-collar jobs facilitating the upward mobility of earlier children of immigrants. The first victims of this transformation were not members of today's second generation but the children and grandchildren of their predecessors—southern blacks, Mexicans, and Puerto Ricans—brought to fill the labor needs of the American industrial economy during and after World War I.[34]

As descendants of these earlier waves reached working age, they confronted a situation of diminished industrial opportunities and blocked economic mobility. The disappearance of jobs in industry, coupled with racial discrimination, kept second- and third-generation offspring of "colored" minorities bottled up in the inner city while simultaneously preventing them from taking advantage of emerging opportunities in the new postindustrial economy. The result was the rise of what Wacquant and Wilson have called the "hyperghetto"—veritable human warehouses where the disappearance of work and the everyday reality of marginalization led directly to a web of social pathologies.[35] Proliferation of female teenage pregnancy, high involvement of youngsters in crime, and the disappearance of work habits and discipline are common traits in these areas.

Contemplating the dismal landscape of Liberty City, the main ghetto area of Miami, a prominent black leader of the local Urban League remarked:

> Incorporating blacks into mainstream institutions or programs can't do anything today about what's going on in Liberty City. . . . We have allowed people to develop a prescription for survival which creates a kind of character that is in the long run suicidal. So to say to the guy who has never seen anyone go to work, who's never had a steady job, who has never seen an adult male bring a paycheck home; to say to him "you're unemployed, therefore we are going to give you a training program" does not even begin to understand what has happened to him, to his everyday experience, to his life.[36]

A crucial consequence of social and economic marginalization is the emergence of a measure of solidarity in opposition to external discrimination, based on the central notion that the plight of the minority is due to the hostility of mainstream institutions. Among the young, this form of minority solidarity translates into a denigration of schools and their staffs as instruments of racial oppression and of education itself as incapable of bettering their situation.[37] In her study of Mexican-origin students in a California high school, Matute-Bianchi highlights the oppositional stance toward school authorities of second- and third-generation Chicanos and *cholos* and their low levels of academic achievement. According to Matute-Bianchi, these children are caught in a forced-choice dilemma in which doing well in school is perceived as "acting white" and hence being disloyal to one's group.[38]

Suárez-Orozco, an anthropologist who has studied the same ethnic group, refers to this process as "learning not to learn."[39] Since group solidarity is based precisely on the view that mainstream institutions are discriminatory and block minorities' progress, instances of individual success through the same institutions undermine the common bond. The quote at the start of this chapter, drawn from Bourgois's study of Puerto Rican youths in the Bronx, exemplifies this orientation. Though correct historically, this oppositional ideology ends up reinforcing the very blockage of opportunities that it denounces. In the language of the ghetto, those wanting to escape by doing well in school are "wannabes" and are derided accordingly.[40]

Recently arrived immigrants confront these features of life in American cities as a fait accompli conditioning their own and their children's chances for success. Because of their poverty, many immigrants settle in close proximity to urban ghetto areas. In this environment, they and their families are often exposed to norms of behavior inimical to upward mobility as well as to an adversarial stance that justifies these behaviors. For second-generation youths, the clash of expectations is particularly poignant when the messages that education does not pay and that discrimination prevents people of color from ever succeeding are conveyed by native peers of the same race or ethnic origin.

In Miami, Stepick and Fernández-Kelly and Schauffler portray the plight of Haitian American students caught between their parents' dream of a professional career and the realities of the schools that they must attend. In Miami inner-city schools, Haitian youths are often ridiculed because of their obedience to school staff, and some have been physically attacked. To survive in this environment, they must adopt the same tough aggressive stance of the ghetto and, along with it, a common rejection of their parents' expectations. Although some Haitian students (exemplified by Aristide Maillol in Chapter 1) manage to survive and advance under these harsh conditions, others assimilate. In this case, assimilation is not to the middle-class mainstream but downward to the attitudes and norms of the inner city.[41]

Children of black West Indian immigrants in New York face a similar plight. Mary Waters remarks on the gap across generations that follows from this cultural encounter:

> The first generation tends to believe that, while racism exists in the United States, it can be overcome or circumvented through hard work. . . . The second generation experiences racism and discrimination constantly and develops perceptions of the overwhelming influence of race on their lives. . . . The boys adopt black American culture, wearing flattops, baggy pants, and certain types of jewelry. While parents tell their children to strive for upward mobility, and to work harder . . . the American-identified teens think the rewards for doing so will be very slim.[42]

Some parents become so distraught at what they see as the permissiveness of American culture and the specific threat posed by the ghetto that they send their children back home to be educated in the care of grandparents or other kin. The experience of Luis Hernández Bueno in Chapter 1 is thus not an isolated incident. Private schools have actually sprung up in the Dominican Republic, Belize, and other countries of emigration to reeducate these "refugees" from American streets.[43] As we will see when we review parental outlooks in Chapter 5, the rise of these schools attests to the resolve of many adult immigrants who become willing to part with their children to protect them from what they see as the looming threat of gangs, drugs, and other forms of downward assimilation.

Segmented assimilation emerges from the different ways in which second-generation youths approach these challenges and the resources that they bring to the encounter. Figure 3.1 presents a theoretical model of the process by relating parental factors, including modes of incorporation, family contexts, and intergenerational acculturation, to the ways in which children of immigrants confront these barriers. The expectation is that typical assimilation outcomes for children in these varying situations will flow naturally from the interaction between external challenges, family and community resources, and patterns of acculturation. We use this model as a broad framework to guide our analysis in later chapters and as a point of reference for key empirical results.

Confronting the Challenge: Immigrant Social Capital

Parental Status, Family Structure, and Gender

Most parents want the best for their children, have high aspirations for their future, and invest extraordinary resources in them. This is especially true of immigrants, who commonly see fulfillment of their ambitions not in their own achievement but in those of their offspring. Yet not all families possess the means to promote educational success and ward off the threats posed by discrimination, narrowing labor market options, and street culture.

Resources necessary to do so are of two kinds: those that provide access to economic goods and job opportunities and those that reinforce parental normative controls. Parents with higher levels of human capital are in a better position to support their children's adaptation for two reasons: First, they have greater information about opportunities and pitfalls in the surrounding environment; second, they can earn higher incomes giving them access to strategic goods. A home in the suburbs, a private school education, or a trip to the home country to reinforce family ties are all expensive propositions not within the reach of the average family. Those able to afford them can confront the challenges of second-generation adaptation with a measure of equanimity.

Figure 3.1 The Process of Segmented Assimilation: A Model

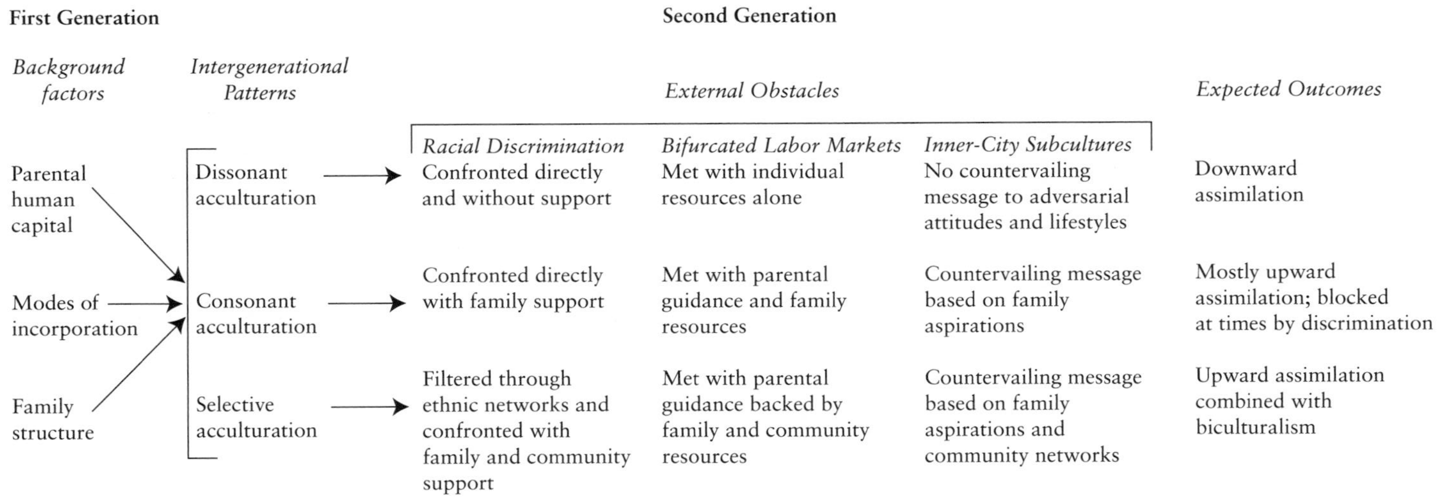

First Generation

Second Generation

Background factors	Intergenerational Patterns	External Obstacles			Expected Outcomes
		Racial Discrimination	Bifurcated Labor Markets	Inner-City Subcultures	
Parental human capital	Dissonant acculturation →	Confronted directly and without support	Met with individual resources alone	No countervailing message to adversarial attitudes and lifestyles	Downward assimilation
Modes of incorporation	Consonant acculturation →	Confronted directly with family support	Met with parental guidance and family resources	Countervailing message based on family aspirations	Mostly upward assimilation; blocked at times by discrimination
Family structure	Selective acculturation →	Filtered through ethnic networks and confronted with family and community support	Met with parental guidance backed by family and community resources	Countervailing message based on family aspirations and community networks	Upward assimilation combined with biculturalism

In addition to human capital, the character of the family itself plays a significant role. Children growing up in families with both biological parents have access to both greater economic resources and greater adult attention and guidance. Hence, immigrant groups that combine high levels of human capital with high proportions of nondisrupted families make available to their children an extraordinary set of resources, where family assets support parental guidance. This is backed, in turn, by the more extended networks that two adults make possible.[44]

Gender enters the picture in an important way because of the different roles that boys and girls occupy during adolescence and the different ways in which they are socialized. As a general rule, females tend to be more under the influence of their parents because of the less autonomous and more protective character of their upbringing. In traditional immigrant families, boys are encouraged to excel in various outside pursuits, while girls are reared to be mothers and homemakers.[45] Even in less traditional homes, teenage girls are more likely to conform to parental expectations and to experience the challenges of the external environment differently than their male siblings.[46] We expect these gender differences to affect important adaptation outcomes such as language acculturation, aspirations, and academic achievement. Because of the different roles that adolescent boys and girls are expected to play in American society, we can also anticipate significant gender effects on various dimensions of psychosocial adaptation, including self-esteem.

The Immigrant Community

Yet immigrant parents' human capital, family composition, and gender socialization do not exhaust the range of forces molding types of acculturation and subsequent outcomes. The outside environment—in particular, the co-ethnic community—supplies the other main determinant. This is shown in Figure 3.1, where selective acculturation is portrayed as contingent on the existence of supportive networks. The varying character of co-ethnic communities determines the level of social capital available to immigrant families.[47] Social capital, grounded on ethnic networks, provides a key resource in confronting obstacles to successful adaptation. First, it increases economic opportunities for immigrant parents, giving them a better chance to put to use whatever skills they brought from their home country and sometimes providing additional entrepreneurial training.[48] Second, strong ethnic communities commonly enforce norms against divorce and marital disruption, thus helping preserve intact families. Third, the same networks directly reinforce parental authority.

Social capital depends less on the relative economic or occupational success of immigrants than on the *density* of ties among them. It makes little difference whether fellow nationals are highly educated and wealthy if they feel no obligation toward one another. It does not matter either that many doctors and business owners come from the same country when they are geographically dispersed or otherwise unreachable. On the other hand, modest but tightly knit communities can be a valuable resource, as their ties support parental control and parents' aspirations for their young. Among immigrants of limited means, this function of social capital is vital.

Consider the two situations portrayed in Figure 3.1. In a foreign land, parental normative control can wane quickly when confronted with the sustained challenges of new lifestyles, media-driven consumption aspirations, and native peer influences. For isolated families, the situation can easily devolve into a pattern of dissonant acculturation and role reversal. Panel A in Figure 3.2 depicts this situation where a lack of ties or "structural holes"[49] deprive parents of this crucial resource. On the contrary, when parental expectations are reinforced by others in the community, the probability of selective acculturation is enhanced. In this situation, parents can support each other's efforts in guiding their youths, creating a far more formidable barrier against premature consumerism and the lure of the streets. This is the situation portrayed in panel B of Figure 3.2. In well-integrated communities where children have internalized the goals of success through educational achievement, the threat of downward assimilation effectively disappears.[50]

Modes of incorporation of different immigrant groups clearly play a role in the types of ethnic communities that they create. In particular, the governmental reception accorded to different nationalities conditions the chances for the rise of cohesive ethnic networks. Groups that have benefited from a favorable reception and resettlement assistance appear more likely to develop such ties than those subject to systematic persecution. The following contrasting histories of former Nicaraguan professionals in Miami and former Vietnamese farmers and fishermen in New Orleans provide a preliminary illustration of these differences.

In their study of the Nicaraguan refugee community in southern Florida, Fernández-Kelly and Schauffler report the presence of a number of professionals who came to escape political persecution at home but

Figure 3.2   Types of Relationships in Dense versus Dispersed Immigrant Communities

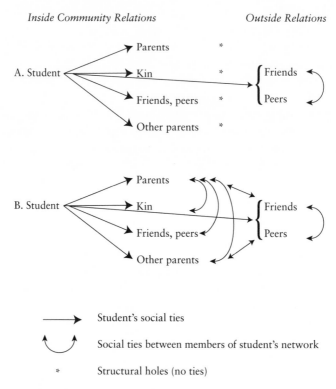

SOURCE: Adapted from Alejandro Portes, "Children of Immigrants: Segmented Assimilation and Its Determinants," in *The Economic Sociology of Immigration* (New York: Russell Sage Foundation, 1995), 261.

were denied asylum by U.S. immigration authorities. Lacking legal permanent residence, they were shunted to the margins of the labor market, forced to work either in manual jobs or as informal service providers for a fraction of the income of legal professionals.[51] A trained chemist back in Nicaragua summarized his situation as follows: "We came with high hopes, escaping the Sandinistas, thinking this was the land of opportunity . . . but we were stopped in our tracks. We haven't been able to legalize our situation. Every so often, we get these notices saying we'll be thrown out of the country. As a result, we haven't been able to move ahead. . . . I work for an hourly wage without benefits, although I perform the duties of a professional for a pharmaceutical company. They know they can abuse my condition because I can't go anywhere; no one will hire me!"[52]

His and his wife's high levels of human capital did not count for much because of an unfavorable context of reception. Left to fend for themselves in Miami, they had to move to an impoverished area of the city and send their two children to schools attended mostly by inner-city minority youths. Conflict was rampant, and academic standards were low. Even more distressing, the older son had forgotten most of his Spanish and could not speak English fluently. At 17, he had no aspirations beyond high school and no job prospects beyond menial service work.

In their study of the Vietnamese community of New Orleans, Zhou and Bankston note that most of its members are former farmers and fishermen with very little education. Lacking any economic means, the Vietnamese have been forced to cluster in the poorest area of a poor city, where their neighbors are mostly impoverished native minorities. Based on the human capital profile of these refugees and the external challenges that they confront, prospects for successful adaptation look dim. The situation is counterbalanced, however, by the high levels of social capital within the community. As refugees from communism, the Vietnamese were beneficiaries of generous government resettlement assistance that helped them reconstitute families and build close community ties.[53]

Only 7 percent of Vietnamese families in this area are headed by a single parent, as compared with 18 percent of local white families and 55 percent of African American families. The majority of Vietnamese families are not only headed by two parents but are also extended, including married children, unmarried grown children, and grandparents. Youngsters are taught that the family always comes first. These norms are supported externally because close ties link Vietnamese families around places of residence, work, and church. The local Catholic church serves as the focal point of community events and provides a powerful symbolic means of reasserting common values: "The Vietnamese have come to believe that education is the chief means to achieve this goal and they have adjusted their cultural patterns to orient the younger generation toward educational and occupational attainment. . . . Because the norms of individual families stem from the ethnic community and are supported by it, the behavior expected by parents and by others around the children are essentially the same."[54]

Figure 3.3 Determinants of Immigrant Adaptation across Generations

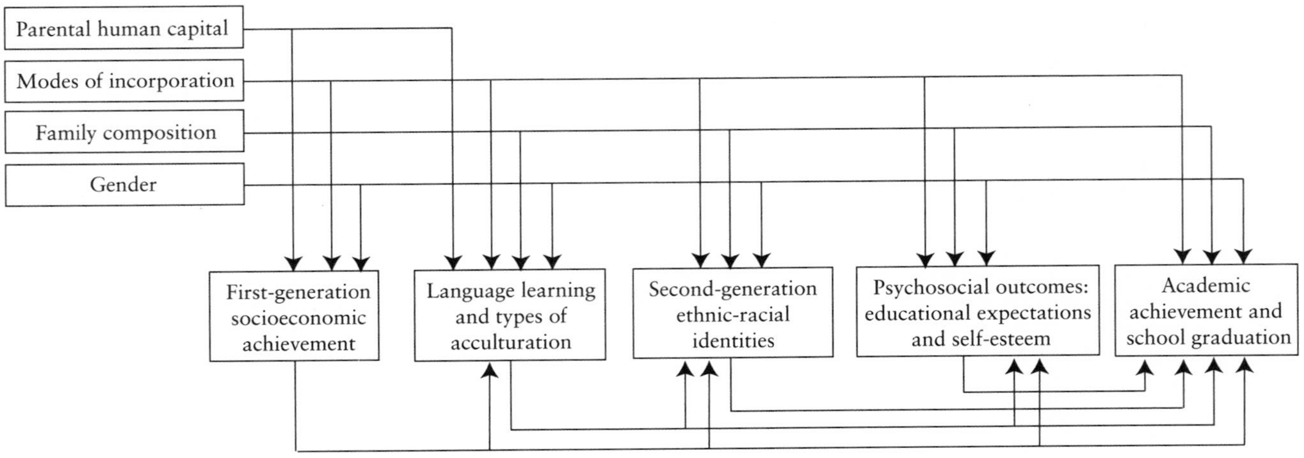

These contrasting histories modify the picture concerning the role of human capital and parental socioeconomic achievement in the prospects of the second generation. High human capital in the first generation can be expected to play a powerful role, but even immigrants of modest endowments can successfully overcome challenges to their children's mobility when they can count on strong families and communities supporting their efforts. Groups that have not had to cope with official persecution and have, on the contrary, benefited from a favorable reception are usually in a better position to restructure themselves along solidary lines and to provide each other with the requisite support. Contextual as well as individual factors can hence be expected to guide the adaptation of the first generation and its transmission of privilege or disadvantage to the second.

Conclusion

In the following chapters, we apply these ideas to the analysis of results from our student and parental samples. The analytic framework presented in Table 3.2 and Figures 3.1 and 3.2 systematizes the illustrative materials presented in Chapter 1 and our theoretical interpretation of existing research in this area. We do not intend these models to function as an exhaustive set of hypotheses to be tested against the data but as ideal types guiding the empirical analysis and being, in turn, susceptible to refinement. The overall logic of this theoretical approach is of a cumulative process where immigrant backgrounds and contexts of reception influence early adaptation outcomes that, in turn, condition subsequent ones. This approach is graphically portrayed in Figure 3.3. The figure also summarizes the analytic program for the following chapters: It begins with parental socioeconomic achievement, attitudes, and aspirations and culminates with the most important outcome for second-generation youths—their educational attainments.

While an analysis of survey data is necessarily oriented toward individual variables, we try not to lose sight of contextual effects arising from the communities in which these children grow up and the schools that they attend. Similarly, while statistical analysis must perforce emphasize averages, we make use of the extensive qualitative material gathered by the CILS to illustrate these trends as well as their exceptions. Exceptional cases and individual variations are important to remind us of the tentative character of theoretical models and the presence in real life of multiple alternative paths.

Chapter 4

MAKING IT IN AMERICA

"We took our two children out of Colombia to escape the poverty, the politics, and the drugs," says Rodolfo Restrepo.[1] "Then we arrive in Miami and find that people believe all Colombians are drug dealers, and Colombians themselves seem to believe it because they avoid each other. Outside of the family, no one trusts anybody and to top it all, jobs are hard to find. The Cubans arrived earlier, and they have taken all the good jobs."

A lawyer by training, Mr. Restrepo left his native Cali with his wife and children five years ago. A legal immigrant, he had counted on his English skills and his education to land a job in a bank or corporation doing business with Latin America. Things did not turn out this way. His friends and kin already living in Miami did not have the requisite connections, and in any case, Colombians are often suspicious of fellow nationals because of the pervasive presence of the drug trade. After being forced into several blue-collar positions, Mr. Restrepo finally found a job as an accounting clerk in a Latin-oriented supermarket chain. The job rescued him from his previous occupation as a truck driver, but it pays modestly and offers few opportunities for promotion. Mr. Restrepo and his wife rent a three-bedroom apartment in North Miami. His teenage sons attend a public school in the central city with a lively drug trade.

Nghi Van Nguyen managed to escape the inner city to attend a good school in the suburbs of San Diego.[2] He was able to do this because his family pooled resources together to buy a tract house outside the city. "The Vietnamese family is like a corporation. We all bring our money together—the grandparents, the parents, the children. Everyone works. Since Vietnamese food is cheap, we could save for the down payment." As an employee of the U.S. embassy in Saigon, Nghi's father was lucky to leave in the first wave, taking his parents, wife, a sister, and eight children along. They landed in Arkansas, where the father worked as a translator in a refugee resettlement camp for several months. With help from the voluntary agencies in the camp, he moved to Kansas City first and then to San Diego, taking his family with him.

To support his eight children, Mr. Nguyen worked two and even three janitorial jobs. Their mother found an operator's job in a local electronics firm, and even the grandfather became employed as a grocery vendor. After the teenage children enrolled in school, they, too, got part-time jobs, and following Vietnamese custom, they turned over a third of their earnings to their mother. Hence, though individual earnings were low, the pooled total allowed the family to save by living frugally. Those savings bought the house and also helped Nghi's father to take the first steps to open a restaurant specializing in Vietnamese cuisine. At the time, the Vietnamese population of San Diego was fairly small but growing fast, and it clung together tightly for mutual support in a strange land. Knowledge of English and his past clerical experience—together with co-ethnic connections made through mutual aid associations—gave Mr. Nguyen a foothold for setting himself up in business. His wife and children provided the requisite labor, at least at the start. "Americans think that big families are a problem, but that's not the Vietnamese way," says Nghi. "Your family is your social security. We know that we need each other to pull ahead." He is currently a medical student at the University of California. His family still owns the restaurant.

Whether prompted by the need to escape political persecution at home or by the urge to seek a better life for oneself and one's family, the motivations of immigrants converge in a remarkable way as they reach U.S. shores: to survive in any manner possible and then to move ahead, seeking all the possible support mechanisms, the open and hidden avenues for mobility that a complex, advanced society makes available. The streets of America may be paved with gold, but for newcomers that promise quickly becomes an aspiration rather than a reality. The country seldom makes its wealth easily accessible. Instead, it demands hard toil and much ingenuity from newcomers, and it can throw obstacles, sometimes unsurpassable, in the path of some of them. In the eyes of immigrants, America can be a harsh place, shattering the dreams of many and leading others to lower their sights and adjust in any way they can to its realities.

The possession of credentials helps to move ahead but does not guarantee success. This is because the transfer of credentials does not occur in a vacuum but in the context set by the way immigrants and their families are received. His law degree did not help Mr. Restrepo escape downward occupational mobility and a difficult economic situation in Miami. With less education but much more assistance at arrival, Mr. Nguyen promptly left these conditions behind, allowing his children to escape inner-city schools. In this and the following chapter, we explore the first steps of the adaptation process involving the parents. We present first general trends in the CILS parental sample and then focus on economic attainment and its determinants. This analysis concentrates on the effects of parental human capital and the extent to which it accounts for the differential economic performance of major nationalities.

Next, we examine family structure and its determinants. In agreement with the theoretical argument put forth in Chapter 3, parental socioeconomic achievement and family composition are expected to flow from differences in human capital and other individual traits as well as from the contexts of incorporation confronted by different groups. Parental achievement and family structure lead in turn to different acculturation patterns and later second-generation outcomes. Accordingly, the following chapter complements the analysis of objective family situations with the subjective outlooks of parents as they confront a foreign environment and seek to guide their children. The attitudes and ambition of parents then set the stage for examining how language acquisition, a key aspect of acculturation, and other adaptation outcomes have evolved among the children.

Early Adaptation and Achievement

General Trends

Our sample of 2,442 parents is formed primarily of immigrants of modest origins who arrived in the United States between 1970 and 1985 and who, for the most part, are here to stay. As seen in Chapter 2, just 20 percent have a college education, and two-thirds have a high school diploma or less. As a result, neither their occupational attainment nor their earnings are exceptional. Only 19 percent held a professional or managerial position at the time of the interview (1995–1996), and just 20 percent earned $50,000 or more. Average family income was slightly over $25,000.

Whatever these families have managed to accomplish has been mostly on their own. During their first year in the United States, less than half had any contact with government agencies of any kind, and only 28 percent received economic assistance from these agencies or any other source. Legally recognized political refugees, such as Cubans and southeast Asians, are in a category apart since many did receive government assistance. For regular immigrants, though, this sort of help was minimal. Today, most immigrants live in nuclear families—parents and children alone. The absence of extended family arrangements is signaled by the dearth of other adult kin living at home. Just 13 percent of these families, for example, have a grandparent living with them, and no nationality departs significantly from that figure.

Only 27 percent of immigrant parents speak English at home, and this figure includes those who, like Jamaicans, Filipinos, and most East and West Indians, spoke fluent English prior to coming to the United States. In agreement with the national origins of immigration to south Florida and southern California, Spanish is dominant among foreign languages, being spoken in 35 percent of the homes. This figure is five times larger than the next most commonly used foreign language. Eighty-four percent of our immigrant parents arrived before 1985, and by the mid-1990s, they were already firmly settled in the United States. By then, slightly over half (51 percent) had become citizens, and an overwhelming majority intended to stay. Only 14 percent planned to return home, mostly among recent arrivals.

Nationality and Achievement

Table 4.1 presents the distribution of individual monthly earnings, occupational status, education, and related variables among major nationalities in our sample. The data show evident differences both in economic success and in the factors associated with it. Hence, individual monthly earnings range from a low of $1,178 among Haitian parents to a high of $5,232 among Canadian, European, and Middle

TABLE 4.1   NATIONALITY, EDUCATION,
AND SOCIOECONOMIC ATTAINMENT

National Origin	Monthly Earnings ($)	College Graduates (%)	Professionals and Managers (%)	Self- Employed (%)	U.S. Citizen (%)	Speaks English Well (%)
Chinese/other Asian	3,983	41.9	20.3	20.3	62.2	37.5
Colombian/other Latin American	2,022	18.8	13.7	18.1	55.6	27.1
Cuban	2,410	20.9	19.1	20.4	69.0	44.2
European/other[1]	5,232	31.3	53.1	15.6	84.4	96.9
Filipino	2,623	45.5	16.8	6.4	85.0	67.9
Haitian	1,178	9.3	9.3	3.5	47.7	24.4
Jamaican/West Indian	2,037	20.0	22.3	9.7	64.8	98.4
Laotian/Cambodian	1,989	2.6	1.8	0.7	14.6	3.3
Mexican	1,263	2.6	2.9	10.9	27.0	16.8
Nicaraguan	1,827	32.5	17.0	15.5	15.5	17.5
Vietnamese	1,990	7.6	5.6	13.9	57.4	5.2

[1]All other smaller nationalities represented in the sample, mostly from Canada, the Middle East, and Africa.

Eastern parents grouped in the Other category. Similarly, the proportion of college graduates ranges from a minute 2.6 percent among Mexicans, Laotians, and Cambodians to 45.5 percent among Filipinos, far above the national average of approximately 22 percent for the native adult working population.[3]

It is worth noting at this point that Filipinos, although the best-educated group, are not the best paid on average; similarly, West Indians, another well-schooled group, have relatively low earnings for their education. On the other hand, Cubans have relatively high earnings, despite middling educational credentials, and southeast Asian refugees report monthly earnings close to the sample average despite the near absence of college graduates among them. The last column of Table 4.1 presents average figures in a second important dimension of human capital—knowledge of English. Fluency in English is nearly universal among West Indians and Europeans and almost nonexistent among southeast Asian refugees. Both Asian and Latin parents tend to have low average levels of English competence, with the exception of Filipinos. Yet a perusal of the figures shows that nationalities that speak English best are not necessarily those that earn the highest incomes or have the highest number of managers and professionals.

Figure 4.1   Immigrant Education and Socioeconomic Attainment

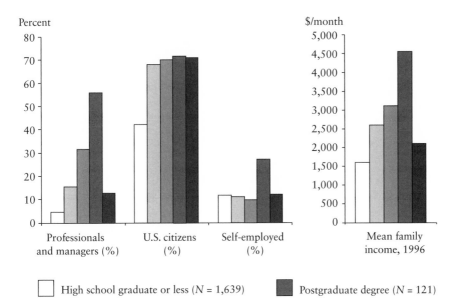

This imperfect association between *average* group credentials and economic mobility opens up the question of what is the influence of human capital on *individual* socioeconomic mobility. Figure 4.1 provides an initial answer by showing the relationship between personal educational attainment and key outcomes including earnings, occupational status, citizenship, and self-employment. As shown in the figure, the proportion employed in professional and managerial occupations ranges from less than 5 percent for parents with a high school education or less to 56 percent among those holding a post-graduate degree. Similarly, monthly incomes range from $1,605 among parents in the lowest educational category to $4,556 for those in the highest. Citizenship status follows a similar trajectory, with the more educated immigrants being significantly more likely to have naturalized first. Finally, only among the most educated is the number of the self-employed significantly higher than the average. The proportion of immigrants who are entrepreneurs hovers around 10 percent, but the figure is more than 20 percent for those with an advanced education. This corresponds to past findings on determinants of self-employment.[4]

These results strongly highlight the importance of human capital in the socioeconomic mobility of first-generation immigrants and corroborate the theoretical argument advanced in the previous chapter. No matter how imperfect the association between average group skills and status characteristics is, it is evident that individuals derive significant rewards from their own educational credentials. The same conclusion is evident from the results shown in Table 4.2 which presents breakdowns of monthly earnings and family incomes by other individual characteristics, including knowledge of English. As one would expect from previous examples, both measures of economic attainment increase with English fluency, length of residence in the United States, and occupational status. In agreement with consistent results based on national samples, immigrant men earn significantly more than women on the average.

These preliminary findings lend support to the predicted causal linkage between human capital and socioeconomic achievement in the first generation but leave open the question of the extent to which human capital endowments account for all group differences across nationalities. The imperfect association between average group skills and status characteristics suggests that, powerful as it may be, human capital is not the only differentiating factor among national groups. In line with the argument advanced in Chapter 3, they are also influenced by different modes of incorporation that can exercise an independent collective effect on economic achievement. However, the evidence presented so far is not conclusive in itself. To test this theoretical argument, we must consider two alternative effects of group differences in contexts of reception: their direct causal impact on socioeconomic achievement and the extent to which they modify the influence of individual human capital and other variables. In statistical parlance, the first are *additive effects* and the second are *interactive effects*. We consider each of them in turn.

Determinants of Parental Economic Achievement: Additive Effects

The choice of income and earnings as the focus for the following analysis is based on its direct impact on the life chances of the second generation. Income largely determines the extent to which immigrant families can guide the education of their children and open career opportunities for them. It is not enough for parents to have high educational credentials if these do not translate into the wherewithal to

TABLE 4.2   BREAKDOWNS OF FAMILY EARNINGS AND PERSONAL INCOMES, BY SELECTED PREDICTORS, 1996

Predictor	Monthly Earnings ($)	Annual Income ($)
Sex		
Male	2,349	23,450
Female	1,729	21,150
E^1	.338**	.09*
Length of U.S. Residence		
Less than 10 years	1,499	17,245
Less than 20 years	1,755	19,780
Less than 30 years	2,167	23,415
30 years or more	2,556	30,820
E	.205**	.264**
Knowledge of English		
Little or none	1,437	15,895
Some	1,898	22,050
Fluent	2,602	30,900
E	.320**	.419**
Occupation		
Professional/executive	2,903	36,035
Other	1,769	20,235
E	.293**	.326**
Self-Employment		
Yes	2,143	26,110
No	1,955	21,575
E	.041*	.104**
Totals	1,979	22,035
N^2	2,011	2,436

[1]E = Eta coefficient of strength of association.
[2]Actual frequencies vary depending on missing data in predictor variables.
*Probability of differences being due to chance less than 5 in 100.
**Probability of differences being due to chance less than 1 in 1,000

move to areas where schools are good, to pay for private schooling, or to help their children's early career steps in other ways. The initial model for this analysis follows the conventional specification in sociological and economic studies of income attainment by including education, work experience, and knowledge of English as indicators of human capital plus gender, occupational status, and self-employment. Education is measured as a set of dummy variables with separate indicators for postgraduate training, college graduation, and incomplete college or post–high school vocational training. A high school education or less is the reference category.

Knowledge of English is a composite of self-reported ability to understand, speak, read, and write the language, ranging from no knowledge to full fluency. This index is a highly reliable and statistically well-behaved measure. Work experience, in turn, is measured by two straightforward indicators: first, the age of the respondent and second, his or her length of residence in the United States. The latter serves as a measure of country-specific experiences expected to bear on U.S. earnings. Lastly, we introduce dichotomous variables representing major individual nationalities in the parental sample. They provide direct indicators of modes of incorporation, since the history of early reception and settlement of each of these groups is known. Hence, for example, we expect southeast Asian refugees, such as Vietnamese and Laotians, to enjoy a certain advantage by virtue of a positive governmental reception that included considerable resettlement assistance. On the contrary, Haitian and Mexican immigrants combine modest average human capital with a governmental stance that defined them as potential illegal aliens and treated them accordingly.

Table 4.3 presents these results. For each indicator of achievement—family monthly earnings and individual yearly income—we introduce first the human capital indicators plus occupational status and gender and then add the effects of the nationality variables. Note that individual nationality effects are computed relative to a reference category composed of the remainder of the parental sample. This reference category, comprised of numerous small nationalities, has higher mean earnings than the sample as a whole, thus providing a strict standard of comparison. There are two sets of results that deserve attention. The actual *strength* of effects controlling for other variables is represented by the number of asterisks following each coefficient. The *size* of the effect is given by the coefficient itself. By using actual monthly earnings and yearly incomes as dependent variables, this coefficient represents

TABLE 4.3   DETERMINANTS OF PARENTAL
ECONOMIC OUTCOMES[1]

Predictor	Family Monthly Earnings[2]		Individual Yearly Income[2]	
	I	II	I[3]	II[3]
Sex (male)	$ 562***	$ 429***	$ 2,365***	$ 1,795*
Age	6 ns	−1 ns	−30 ns	−60 ns
Years of U.S. residence	10*	16**	135**	165**
Post–high school education	327**	407**	5,425***	5,120***
College graduate	851***	866***	8,680***	7,265***
Postgraduate education	1,565***	1,679***	8,305***	8,450***
Knowledge of English	233***	275***	2,485***	2,330***
Occupational status	511***	540***	3,605**	3,930***
Self-employment	−49 ns	56 ns	580 ns	1,015 ns
Nationality				
Colombian		−454*		−865 ns
Cuban		−192 ns		1,500 ns
Filipino		91 ns		4,305**
Haitian		−697*		−5,930**
Laotian/Cambodian		901***		4,960**
Mexican		−401*		−1,910*
Nicaraguan		−583**		−475 ns
Vietnamese		324*		1,220 ns
West Indian		−441*		−1,015 ns
R^2		.248	.313	.311	.354
N	2,010		2,010	

[1]Ordinary least squares regressions with untransformed dependent variables.
[2]Unstandardized regression coefficients; amounts in U.S. dollars.
[3]Decimals (cents) suppressed. Coefficients evaluated at the mean interval of the income distribution.
*Moderate effect (coefficient exceeds 2.5 times its standard error).
**Strong effect (coefficient exceeds 4 times its standard error).
***Very strong effect (coefficient exceeds 6 times its standard error).
ns: Nonsignificant effect.

the net dollar gain associated with each predictor while controlling for all others.[5]

The first columns of each panel of Table 4.3 show the powerful effects of education on earnings and incomes. A post–high school education, for instance, yields an average monthly benefit of $327, which increases to $851 for college graduates and to $1,565 for those with postgraduate training. Knowledge of English also has a strong effect with each unit of our four-point index, increasing monthly earnings by $233 and annual incomes by approximately $2,480. As expected on the basis of prior research, sex continues to influence both economic indicators significantly, with male immigrants receiving much higher returns after other variables are controlled.[6]

Age does not affect economic achievement, but years of U.S. experience do. This effect is statistically reliable, indicating that what counts in terms of first-generation economic mobility is not overall work experience but rather work experience specifically acquired in the United States. Lastly, a professional or executive occupation yields net monthly earnings $511 above others and has a similarly strong effect on annual incomes. Controlling for occupation, the original positive influence of self-employment disappears in both equations. As a whole, these linear human capital models correspond to theoretical expectations and do a good job of accounting for economic outcomes, explaining between one-fourth and one-third of the variance in each dependent variable. Yet as the second columns of each panel of the table show, human capital variables do not entirely eliminate nationality effects, a result corresponding to the earlier imperfect association of average group credentials with earnings. Resilient nationality coefficients support the expected effect of different contexts of reception, especially as they run in a direction congruent with the history of each group.

Thus, Haitian, Mexican, and Nicaraguan immigrants experience a significant loss in monthly earnings even after controlling for their education, knowledge of English, and occupation. The same is true for yearly incomes, although in this case the Nicaraguan effect becomes insignificant. Hence, no matter how educated a Mexican or Haitian parent is, his or her chances of moving ahead economically are significantly constrained by the social environment in which his or her group has become incorporated. On the other hand, statistically insignificant nationality effects in these models indicate that the original observed group differences are entirely accountable by the average characteristics that immigrants brought along and by their achieved occupational status and work experience. Thus, for Cubans, a refugee group with a presence of many years in the United States, the advantages of an earlier favorable reception had largely dissipated by the mid-1990s, giving way to individual factors as the significant determinants of their economic situation.

By contrast, southeast Asian refugees enjoy an advantage in relation to their human capital endowments that corresponds to their more recent and favorable contexts of reception. This is especially the case for Laotians (Lao and Hmong) and Cambodians, refugees of very low average education who nevertheless retain a significant economic edge after controlling for other factors. The positive nationality effect in this case is entirely attributable to generous resettlement assistance since the

Figure 4.2   Annual Incomes by Nationality and Different Human
Capital and Gender Profiles

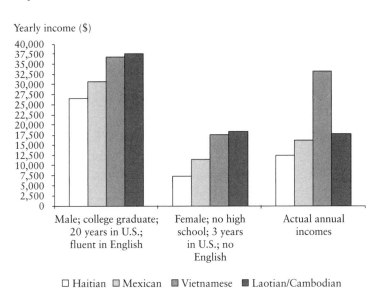

Yearly income ($)

□ Haitian   ◫ Mexican   ▨ Vietnamese   ■ Laotian/Cambodian

human capital profile of these groups would otherwise lead to much
lower incomes. The lingering influence of different modes of incorporation is nowhere more visible than in the gap between southeast Asian
refugees and Haitian immigrants, signaled by the opposite sign of their
respective coefficients and the marked disadvantage of the latter group.

Figures 4.2 and 4.3 graphically illustrate these results by presenting
income and earnings figures for immigrants of different nationalities
possessing two hypothetical human capital profiles. The first is for a college-educated male who is fluent in English and has extensive experience in the United States; the second is for a recently arrived female
with no English skills and less than a high school education. The difference in projected earnings, based on our models, is stark. Yet in each
polar situation, major differences persist among selected nationalities.
Hence, monthly earnings of our hypothetical educated male would
range from $2,950 if he were a Haitian to about $4,000 if he were a
southeast Asian refugee. At the opposite end, an uneducated Haitian
woman could expect to earn no more than $560 per month, but a Lao-
tian in the same situation could receive over $2,100.

Actual average earnings for each nationality, presented in the third
panel of each figure, show that they come closer to the low–human capi-

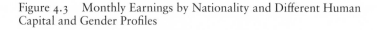

Figure 4.3   Monthly Earnings by Nationality and Different Human Capital and Gender Profiles

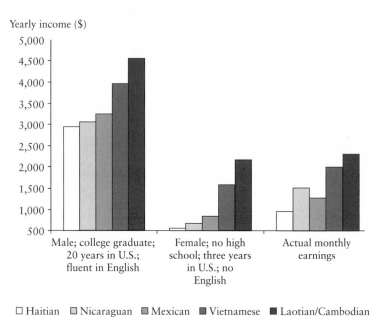

Yearly income ($)

Male; college graduate; 20 years in U.S.; fluent in English

Female; no high school; three years in U.S.; no English

Actual monthly earnings

□ Haitian   ◫ Nicaraguan   ▨ Mexican   ▰ Vietnamese   ■ Laotian/Cambodian

tal profile. Yet in all instances but one, they exceed this figure by a considerable margin, indicating higher levels of human capital than our hypothetical low-end case. The exception is the Laotian/Cambodian group, for which actual earnings come close to those projected on the basis of minimum human capital. This result reflects, once again, the low education and skill endowment of these groups and their almost exclusive reliance on a favorable context of reception.

Determinants of Parental Economic Achievement: Interaction Effects

The second possible influence that modes of incorporation can have is on the actual effects of human capital variables on earnings. In this case, the experiences of a national group do not affect its economic performance directly so much as facilitate or constrain the influence of individual-level predictors. In the language of statistics, this is an *interaction effect*. We focus the analysis on four nationalities for which data are available for a sizable number of cases and which have had very different experiences of incorporation in the United States. As seen previously, Mexican and

TABLE 4.4   EFFECTS OF HUMAN CAPITAL VARIABLES
ON MONTHLY EARNINGS FOR SELECTED
NATIONALITIES ($)

Predictor	Mexican	Nicaraguan	Cuban	Vietnamese
Sex (male)	460**	492*	1,223***	247
Length of U.S. residence	8 (ns)	178 (ns)	14*	90**
Some college/vocational school	336*	79 (ns)	429*	672*
College graduate	−139 (ns)	58 (ns)	1,015**	1,208*
Postgraduate degree	2,427**	615*	2,858***	519 (ns)
Knowledge of English	170*	329*	281*	770**
Professional/executive	79 (ns)	368*	180 (ns)	925**
Intercept	1,332	1,014	2,330	1,806
R^2	.274	.344	.547	.458
N	269	154	294	245

NOTE: Predictors lacking any significant effects are omitted from the model.
***Very strong effect (coefficient exceeds 5 times its standard error).
**Strong effect (coefficient exceeds 3.5 times its standard error).
*Moderate effect (coefficient exceeds 2 times its standard error).
ns: Nonsignificant effect.

Nicaraguan immigrants were confronted with a rather negative reception, marked by official hostility, public discrimination, and the lack of strong co-ethnic communities. In contrast, Cuban and Vietnamese refugees arrived under more favorable circumstances, defined primarily by generous governmental resettlement assistance and a measure of initial public sympathy as refugees from communism.

Cuban and Vietnamese refugees also regrouped in certain areas, creating economic enclaves in their places of concentration. These ethnic economies, in turn, created occupational and business opportunities for later arrivals.[7] In this analysis we examine how these diverse experiences may impinge on the process of economic achievement. Results are presented in Table 4.4. Variables found to be significant predictors of earnings in the full parental sample are included in this model, with equations computed separately for each national group. The findings of interest are the direction of the coefficients and their relative size. We limit the following discussion to monthly earnings since results based on our second economic indicator, personal income, yield similar results. Because the dependent variable is measured in dollars, coefficients are interpretable as the net gain associated with each individual variable.

The first result of note is that length of U.S. residence has essentially no effect on earnings for Mexicans and Nicaraguans. In other words, no matter how long these immigrants have lived and worked in the United States, their net earnings remain flat. This is not the case for Cubans and Vietnamese, for whom each additional year of experience in the country yields a small but significant gain. Similarly, a college education has a minimal effect on the earnings of Mexican and Nicaraguan immigrants. In particular, a college degree yields no improvement in earnings, a surprising result in light of the strong effect of this variable in the full sample. Only among the few members of these groups who have attained a postgraduate degree do we detect a reliable effect of education on earnings. That effect is quite sizable, particularly for Mexicans.

These results indicate that it takes a very advanced education for immigrants to overcome the handicap of a negative context of reception. For immigrants in this situation, including those who have completed a college degree, education indeed does not pay, or its returns are meager. Notice that this is not the case for Cubans and Vietnamese, among whom even an incomplete college education has higher returns and a college degree pays off handsomely. For the Vietnamese, this is the key economic outcome since practically none had achieved a postgraduate degree. The latter variable's lack of effect is compensated, in their case, by the strong coefficient associated with a professional occupation that absorbs the remaining influence of education on earnings.

A final difference worthy of attention is that human capital predictors are more effective in accounting for economic achievement among the two groups of former refugees than among Mexicans and Nicaraguans. This is indicated by the R^2 coefficients at the bottom of the table that show that human capital plus gender account for about half of earnings variance in the Cuban and Vietnamese samples but for only a third or less among the other two groups. These differences are again indicative of the relative weakness of individual skills in leading to better economic outcomes among disadvantaged groups. Cuban and Vietnamese refugees have been able to make their U.S. work experience, education, and occupation pay, leading in the process to a more predictable process of economic achievement. The weakness of the same effects for Mexicans and Nicaraguans produces, in turn, a more random process, with the exception of the few who have attained a very advanced education.

Together with the additive effects of nationality discussed previously, these interactions between national origin and human capital provide evidence about the impact of membership in specific national groups on economic achievement. Since coefficients run consistently in the direction expected on the basis of knowledge of the experiences of incorporation of each group, these results add up to a strong case supporting the role of social context in the success or failure of the immigrant first generation. Family and group differences in socioeconomic achievement then set the stage for the socialization of the second generation and directly mold the experiences that it will confront during the process. We will retake this line of argument in subsequent chapters as we examine effects of parental socioeconomic status on different aspects of second-generation adaptation.

Nationality and Family Composition

After the interview with his mother, a single parent, came to an end, Roberto Santos, a young Mexican American, pulled the interviewer aside, speaking in English so that his mother would not understand:

> She doesn't know about those things, like those questions you asked her about the neighborhood. She answered them all wrong. I would have answered your questions differently because I get out and see things. I live what I would call a typical teenage life. Drugs, gangs, these are part of my daily life. She doesn't know. In every way, we are opposites. She doesn't get out except to go to work. I keep up with my friends and stay social. I look for work but can't find any. I had my rebellious stage when I didn't care, but she doesn't realize that I've changed now. I see how important education is. I've had to do it myself from first to twelfth grade, with no help, no tutor, no help with homework, nothing. I got burned out. But now I see it is very important, and I want to get ahead.[8]

Roberto confirmed his family's isolation and lack of resources—it was just he and his lone mother. Dissonant acculturation and the consequent lack of parental control were followed by drugs and an active period of gang membership. Roberto mercifully pulled out of that scene but not thanks to his family. As he tells us in earnest, he barely managed to reach senior year, having to do everything himself. What other children, such as Efrén Montejo in Chapter 1, pretty much take for granted have been quasi miracles for Roberto.

Aside from parental poverty or wealth, the difference is in the structure of the family. Two-parent families double, by their very character, the scope of resources to guide and influence the acculturation of children. Clearly, all families are different, and the presence of both biological parents does not guarantee successful results in every case. But on

Figure 4.4   Family Composition by Nationality

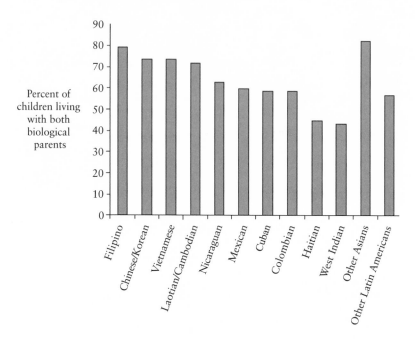

average, intact families can be expected to have a positive influence on second-generation outcomes, including the outlooks and aspirations of children, their self-esteem, and their school performance. Family stability provides children growing up in a new culture with a solid psychological and social anchor. Almost two-thirds of the children in the CILS sample had this resource, but there are significant variations around the sample mean.

As shown in Figure 4.4, the proportion of intact families ranges from 80 percent for Filipinos to slightly above 40 percent for West Indians. There is a clear rank order in this dimension among immigrant groups in our sample, with Asian immigrants being the most likely to hold families together and Caribbean immigrants the least. Reasons for these differences are multiple and have to do with characteristics of the culture of origin, the experiences of the group on arrival, and its age and educational composition. To further clarify the determinants of family structure, we conducted a series of multivariate analyses based on both student and parental data. The dependent variable in these analyses is

TABLE 4.5   DETERMINANTS OF FAMILY
COMPOSITION: CHILDREN LIVING WITH BOTH
PARENTS (CILS STUDENT SAMPLE, 1992)

Predictor	Coefficient[1]	Wald Statistic[2]	Probability[3]
Father's age	.04	30.9***	.01
Father's education	–.02	ns	—
Mother's age	.04	14.1**	.01
Mother's education	.12	6.4*	.03
Nationality			
Colombian	–.31	ns	—
Cuban	–.35	ns	—
Filipino	.3655	ns	—
Haitian	–.58	2.7*	–.14
Laotian/Cambodian	1.47	6.3*	.25
Mexican	.04	ns	—
Nicaraguan	.07	ns	—
Vietnamese	.63	3.1*	.13
West Indian	–.78	6.5*	–.19
Other—Asian	.54	ns	—
Other—Latin	–.28	ns	—
Constant	–2.65	31.48	—
Model chi square[4]	211.96	N = 3,053[5]	
(degrees of freedom)	(15)		

[1]Effect on the logarithm of the odds of living with both biological parents, controlling for other variables.

[2]Coefficient of strength of association omitted for nonsignificant effects.

[3]Net increase/decrease in the probability of living with both biological parents per unit change of each predictor evaluated at the sample mean. Omitted for nonsignificant effects.

[4]Model's goodness of fit. Probability that model improvement is due to chance is less than 1 in 1,000.

[5]Model limited to cases with valid data on all variables.

*Moderate effect (coefficient exceeds twice its standard error).

**Strong effect (coefficient exceeds thrice its standard error).

***Very strong effect (coefficient exceeds five times its standard error).

ns: Nonsignificant effect.

the presence/absence of both biological parents in the household, as reported by the child and by the parents themselves. Since this variable is dichotomous, we use logistic regression with intact families coded 1; others are coded 0. Logistic regression coefficients are not readily interpretable in their raw form. To clarify their meaning, we transformed them into net probabilities associated with each predictor.

Table 4.5 presents results of this analysis on the basis of data from the student sample. In addition to national origin, our predictors include the education of the father and the mother and their respective ages.[9] Again, results of interest include the strength of the effect, as indicated by the number of asterisks attached to each coefficient, and its magnitude, as indicated by the associated probabilities. Results indicate that the age of both parents contributes to family stability, with older parents being far more likely to stay together. The education of mothers, but not of fathers, also increases stability, with each upward shift in our five-level education variable increasing by 3 percent the probabilities of parents staying together. Based on these results, a child whose mother is a college graduate and whose parents are both 10 years older than the sample average is about 25 percent more likely to live in an intact family than his or her peers.

Taking parental age and education into account does not eliminate the earlier noted differences among nationalities. Children of southeast Asian origin (Vietnamese, Laotians, and Cambodians) are still far more likely to have been raised in intact two-parent families, while those of West Indian and Haitian parentage are much less likely to have done so. The relative family instability in the English-speaking Caribbean is well known and has been the subject of an extensive literature. This trait of the societies of origin is well reflected in the sizable negative West Indian effect.[10] On the other hand, other significant nationality effects may be directly influenced by different contexts of reception. Family reunification represented a priority of the resettlement program for southeast Asian refugees with various government agencies providing assistance to this end;[11] Haitians did not receive such help, and indeed their settlement process confronted numerous barriers created by official harassment.[12]

It is possible to replicate this analysis with data from the CILS parental survey. In addition to parents' age, the data allow us to consider the possible effect of length of U.S. residence. To examine in greater detail the effect of education, this variable is broken into bivariate measures with completion of high school, college, and postgraduate education as predictors. We also consider the separate influence of parental professional and executive occupations on the assumption that achievement of high status positions in the United States can also affect family stability. Results, presented in Table 4.6, show a pattern of effects very similar to those based on the student sample. Parental age and education again have strong positive effects on the likelihood of intact families. College-educated parents are significantly more likely to have remained together. Controlling for these variables, neither years of U.S. residence nor occupational success after arrival affects family composition. The likelihood of immigrant families remaining together appears to reflect

TABLE 4.6   DETERMINANTS OF FAMILY
COMPOSITION: CHILDREN LIVING WITH BOTH
PARENTS (CILS PARENTAL SAMPLE, 1995–1996)

Predictor	Coefficient[1]	Wald Statistic[1]	Probability[1]
Age	.02	13.0**	.01
Year of arrival	.01	ns	—
High school graduate[2]	.02	ns	—
College graduate	.41	5.9*	.08
Postgraduate education	.53	4.4*	.10
Professional/executive	.13	ns	—
Nationality			
Colombian	.02	ns	—
Cuban	.02	ns	—
Filipino	.96	25.0**	.16
Haitian	−.69	7.1*	−.15
Laotian/Cambodian	.30	2.5*	.06
Mexican	.21	ns	—
Nicaraguan	.04	ns	—
Vietnamese	.78	14.5**	.13
West Indian	−1.03	19.8**	−.25
Constant	−.724		—
Model chi square			
(degrees of freedom)[1,3]	142.07 N = 2,436		

[1]See definitions in Table 4.5.
[2]Includes some college.
[3]Probability that model's improvement is due to chance is less than 1 in 1,000.
*Moderate effect. See definitions in Table 4.5.
**Strong effect. See definitions in Table 4.5.
***Very strong effect. See definitions in Table 4.5.
ns: Nonsignificant effect.

more the original demographic and human capital characteristics of parents than their subsequent U.S. career trajectories.

Yet again, national origin continues to affect family composition after taking individual factors into account. In this instance, Filipino parents join southeast Asians in being significantly more likely to remain together. With education controlled, this effect cannot be attributed to this group's high level of human capital. In the absence of any official family reunification assistance for Filipinos after arrival, this effect seems traceable to characteristics of their culture of origin. Overall, the hierarchy of family stability portrayed in Figure 4.4 remains fairly constant even after taking other predictors into account. Asian families are, by and large, the most stable, and that trait is not solely explainable by demographic or educational composition; Latin families are in the middle, with stability largely determined by individual characteristics; black Caribbean families are the most unstable, and this is also a resilient effect, jointly attributable to characteristics of the culture of origin and their modes of incorporation.

Conclusion

So far we have established that parental human capital and demographic characteristics directly affect the structure and achievement of immigrant families in the United States but that these family outcomes also vary significantly among nationalities. Key questions for the ensuing analysis are the effects of family variables on acculturation and other aspects of second-generation adaptation and the extent to which they mediate the original influence of contexts of reception. For this purpose, we will need to examine nationality differences in language learning, ethnic self-identities, ambition, academic achievement, and other outcomes and then establish the extent to which family variables account for the differences.

First, however, it is important to consider some aspects of the acculturation of the first generation itself, in particular its outlook on U.S. society and its aspirations for the future. Immigrant views of America are complex and at times surprising, as they are based on perceptual frameworks brought from abroad that are often quite different from those of the native population. This tour into the subjective world of adults complements the objective dimensions of family socioeconomic achievement and family composition and will help us understand how parents cope with the task of raising their children in a foreign land. All too often immigrants are painted with broad strokes, neglecting differences and imputing motives and values quite at variance with reality. The resulting portrait leads, in turn, to unjustifiable prejudices. To avoid this common error, we listen to the immigrants and let them tell of their struggles and fears.

Chapter 5

IN THEIR OWN EYES
Immigrant Outlooks on America

Aura Lila Marín, Cuban, 53, Single Mother (1994)

Mrs. Marín lives in a modest Miami home with luscious greenery on the front porch.[1] The style is vintage working-class Cuban. Trophies for academic achievement of the children, a miniature sculpture of José Martí,[2] and many family photographs decorate the living area. This is a female-headed household dependent on public assistance. Mrs. Marín is on disability because she has a back problem. She suffers from obesity and nervous distress caused largely by her divorce. She had been married for 20 years when her husband left her for another Cuban woman. The impact of exile and divorce was so serious that she has been under periodic psychiatric care.

Mrs. Marín was born in Camagüey, Cuba. She is a legal resident, not a citizen of the United States, because she always thought she would go back to her country. She has only six years of schooling. In Cuba, she worked as an assistant nurse but was mostly dedicated to raising her children. In the United States, she worked in informal jobs for 10 months. At the time of the interview, she was receiving approximately $310 in public assistance and another $305 in food stamps per month and was supplementing that income by working as a kitchen helper in a Cuban restaurant. Her eldest daughter, Ana María, pays the electricity and mortgage. Much of Mrs. Marín's time is spent filling out forms and navigating the arduous paths of the welfare system.

Despite her poverty, she keeps a tidy home. She thinks of herself as Cuban and does not like the term *Hispanic* because it is too broad: "We all have the same roots, but there are important differences." She expresses disapproval of recent immigrants from Central America: "Although Cubans left their country many years ago, they always had a sense of self-respect, cleanliness, duty towards children, a work ethic." Aura Lila's daughter, Maribel, is 18. She was 3 when she came from Cuba. She speaks English without an accent and has just finished high school. Because Maribel has shown ambition and ability, her mother expects her to go through college and earn a graduate degree. The girl is so determined that even when there were money problems and little to eat at home, she did her homework first.

It was not always this way. When Maribel first went to school in Miami, she experienced serious learning difficulties. She was then attending Southside Elementary. Her mother volunteered to assist in school although she spoke not a word of English. Aura Lila felt terrible that she could not help her daughter because she did not know the language. Maribel was not misbehaving in school but was simply unable to perform. On the advice of friends, she was transferred to a Cuban bilingual private school, where she made no progress. Mrs. Marín transferred her yet again to another private school, La Luz, where Maribel went through the fourth grade with only marginal improvement. The family faced grave financial problems and could barely afford the tuition. At the time, her estranged husband paid $50 a month for child support, but the tuition cost double that figure plus books and other fees.

In desperation, Mrs. Marín took her daughter to a mental health agency to be evaluated. The staff laughed at her since it was a clinic for adults and referred her to Miami Jackson Hospital. The psychiatrist who finally examined Maribel determined that there was nothing wrong with the girl and sent her to the public school system's main office to get counseling. She was re-enrolled in compensatory special education and in nine months moved forward about four years in academic performance. As a result, Aura Lila and her daughter are big supporters of the public school system.

Looking back, Maribel explains her early problems as a result of insecurity and low self-esteem. After her transfer back to public schools and despite being in special education, she was able to join the school's Trust Club. That changed her perspective. As a member of the club, she performed public service and became a peer counselor. The other key factor was support within her family circle, especially from her mother, who never abandoned hope. At present, Maribel is collecting information to gain admission to college. She plans to become a mental health therapist.

Pao Yang, Laotian Hmong, 57, Father (1995)

The San Diego home of Mr. Pao Yang and his family was in disarray at the time of the interview because they were packing to move to Fresno.[3] As refugees, both Mr. Pao and his wife Zer Vue receive federally supported assistance. Pao Yang complements this with some odd jobs, but his options are limited as he speaks little English. The interview was conducted in Hmong. Before starting, the interviewer asked for his 18-year-old son, Khae, who had not yet completed the project's follow-up schedule. Pao responded that his son had just stepped out of the house, but they could begin the interview. Ten minutes into it, the porch screen door slammed, and Khae stepped in. He wore no shirt and had shaved his head.

The father called, "Khae, come here; you have some questionnaire to fill up." The young man replied, "No, I don't care for it or anybody." He went to his bedroom, slamming the door after him. Fifteen minutes later he was out; he was now confronted by his mother who politely asked him to cooperate. Khae answered, "No, all of this is shit." He left the home, again slamming the front door. In Hmong, the mother reported, "It was not like this before. He was obedient, well-behaved, went to school every day. Two years ago, he joined the Mesa Kings [a local gang] and last year he quit school. He does what he likes, does what he pleases. If you try talking to him, he yells louder and leaves."

Pao added, "We cannot control him; once I hit him and he pulled a gun on me. He knows English better than us—thinks that he knows everything. If he continues this way, he'll never finish high school; he'll be killed first." By the end of the conversation, it became clear that Khae was the reason why the family was moving to Fresno. There is a larger, more concentrated Hmong population there, and the family had several relatives living in the city. The parents hoped to put him back to school and garner the help of the extended family and clan to keep him away from gangs. Zer, the wife, accompanied the interviewer to the door. "I want to apologize for the bad attitude of my son," she said. "It would not have been like this back home; it is this country that is so hard to understand."

Accounts about immigrants commonly focus only on their struggles in labor markets and their efforts to gain social acceptance. An equally important task is coping with growing children whose problems and crises can often derail the best–laid out family plans. General trends exist, of course, as we will shortly see, but equally important are the variations around these averages and the unexpected features found in individual family histories. Of the two preceding stories, that of Aura Lila and Maribel shows how a single mother with next to no human capital can still pull through on the strength of a favorable social environment. What Mrs. Marín did not emphasize, in part because she took it for granted, was that as a legal refugee, she was entitled to generous government assistance and that most of the officials whom she saw in her pilgrimage to save Maribel were fellow Cubans. The principals at the private schools, the psychiatrist who saw the girl at Jackson, and many of the remedial teachers at Dade County public schools were part of the same large exile community and thus lent a sympathetic ear. This explains, at least in part, how a woman with no English and little education could successfully mobilize complex bureaucracies to save her daughter.

Pao Yang and Zer Vue were not so lucky as they confronted the estrangement of their son in isolation. As political refugees, they also received governmental assistance, but there was no surrounding co-ethnic presence to provide support. As farmers and herdsmen from the Laotian highlands, most Hmong refugees arrived in the United States with virtually no formal education and skills ill suited for urban life. Co-ethnic professionals and officials in school bureaucracies are non-existent. Even so, the family was moving to Fresno in search of what San Diego could not provide—a larger, more densely knit community of their own. They were betting that only with this kind of support could they extricate their son from almost certain tragedy. These stories are among the thousands that could have been selected to illustrate the challenges faced by immigrant families as they seek to guide their youths and how external factors—in particular, the social context surrounding families—interact with individual traits to produce very different outcomes.

Optimism

The purpose of interviewing immigrant parents was less to study their own histories than to understand how their experiences and attitudes frame the immediate environment of their children. Out of this analysis, a number of significant themes emerged. Some are found, to a substantial extent, in all nationalities and at all status levels, while others vary widely. Among common themes, none is more salient than generalized optimism among adult parents. Despite problems, setbacks, and much suffering, most of these immigrants view their American lives in a positive light, an outlook they then translate into high expectations and a sustained effort to achieve them. It is likely that some of the optimism evident in these responses reflects a desire on the part of these immigrant adults to give the "right" answer. However, the numbers are so overwhelming and the pattern of results so consistent across nationalities that they clearly indicate a real trend beyond any desire to please.

Table 5.1 presents several illustrations of this pattern. It shows that parents are seldom dissatisfied with the education offered to their children in American schools or with their own situation in the country. Over 75 percent indicate that they have had fair opportunities to succeed in their occupations and believe that their children should face no great difficulty if they wish in the future to marry a white American, move into a white neighborhood, or join a white club.[4] This optimism about fairness of opportunities and lack of serious social barriers extends to their appraisal of their immediate environment. Contrary to what could be expected given the relatively modest neighborhoods where most immigrants live, strong majorities hold a positive evaluation of these areas.

For example, over 80 percent report that there is no serious interethnic conflict or lack of respect for laws in their neighborhoods. Most importantly, there is a generalized feeling that neighbors can be counted on to come to the assistance of children if they were getting into trouble. Over 75 percent of the sample state their belief in this form of community support. Along the same lines, a majority of the sample report an abundance of role models for their children among adults living in the area.

These findings place into perspective the difficult living situations and despair encountered in some immigrant households. These conditions exist but do not represent the dominant trend. Most parents hold on resolutely to a positive outlook on their lives, neighborhoods, and opportunities. By the same token, general optimism and the expectations that flow from it must be qualified by significant differences across nationalities in the real situation of immigrant households and the support that they derive from the outside environment. As we saw

TABLE 5.1   PARENTAL OUTLOOKS ON SCHOOLS,
NEIGHBORHOODS, AND OPPORTUNITIES

Variable	Categories	Percent
1. How satisfied are you with the education your child has received in the U.S.?	Not satisfied	8.1
	Satisfied	39.8
	Very satisfied	52.1
2. Compared to people of other races or nations, how many opportunities have you had to succeed in your occupation?	Less than others	24.0
	The same or more	76.0
3. Would your child experience opposition if in the future she/he would want to		
• join a club of white Americans?	No	82.1
• move into a white American neighborhood?	No	85.9
• marry a white American?	No	84.5
4. How much of a problem in your neighborhood are		
• different races or ethnic groups that do not get along?	Not a problem	86.4
• lack of respect for laws, rules, authority?	Not a problem	80.8
• assaults and muggings?	Not a problem	74.4
• delinquent and drug gangs?	Not a problem	76.6
5. Would people in your neighborhood intervene if		
• someone was being beaten?	Likely	78.1
• someone was trying to sell drugs to your child?	Likely	75.8
• your child was getting into trouble?	Likely	77.0
6. There are a lot of adults around here that my child can look up to.	Agree	60.5
7. In total, how satisfied are you with having come to live in the United States?	Satisfied	96.4
	N = 2,442	

SOURCE: Children of Immigrants Longitudinal Study, Parental Survey, 1995–1996.

in the preceding chapter, differences in socioeconomic status and family structure reflect the play of parental human capital and the contrasting reception met by immigrant groups. Differences are also apparent in three other themes consistently present in immigrant parents' outlooks: 1) their fear of excessive freedoms given to their children, 2) their simultaneous high ambition for the future, and 3) the importance they attribute to community support and national pride. Each is evident in detailed interviews and in the sample tabulations presented next.

Permissiveness

Why? Why? Why should this country, the richest in the world, have such low educational standards and disruptive behavior? It is sad to see this country's children smoking grass or wearing their hair in spikes. How are these youngsters paying back for the opportunities they receive? . . . Some say that teachers are responsible for this situation, but you have to remember that these teachers are not like teachers in our countries. Here, American society leads them to fulfill their obligations mechanically, like robots. They can't address discipline problems because that falls outside their mandate. You can wear anything to school, you can talk in class—no one can stop you.

—**Roger, 38, Nicaraguan father, arrived in Miami in 1987**

For example, take discipline; in this country you are not allowed to beat children. My boss says it's not right to give kids a whipping. Yet I raised my children with discipline and that meant beating them when needed. Now that they are older, I do not hit them anymore.

Parents in this country are just too tolerant and that harms children because they do not know any limits to their actions. When children are reprimanded in school, some American parents are so immoral as to complain to the teacher without realizing that they are the cause of their children's problems.

—**Carmela, Colombian mother, 40, arrived in Miami in 1982**

This is a bad area to live in because of the many homeboys using alcohol and drugs. Every night there is the sound of police sirens and helicopters. My family gets used to it. It's simple. I want to move but the rent is cheap here.

I am concerned about my younger children. I'm afraid they will join with the homeboys. The reason I'm concerned is because I feel I cannot control the peer pressure; when they step out of the house, it's all over them.

—**Botum, 51, Cambodian mother of six, arrived in San Diego in 1983**

We all live together, children, parents, and grandparents. The grandparents are in charge of discipline here and they are tough—from school to home and back. Kids are taught that our family comes first and that parents must always know where their children are . . . this is about the only way to survive here. American parents and grandparents do not control their children and that's why so many turn into bad people.

—**Huu Tran, 47, Vietnamese father, arrived in San Diego in 1979**[5]

The voices of immigrant parents speak in unison when it comes to the challenges of educating their children on American soil. They are less worried about racial discrimination and lack of opportunities than about their young doing themselves in because of excessive freedom and lack of institutional restraints. Schools come in for particular criticism as the centers of all that is wrong with America. Despite satisfaction with the quality of education that they provide (see Table 5.1), there are also widespread complaints about their atmosphere of permissiveness— teachers who can't discipline, unruly classes, and the ominous presence of gangs.

These complaints give expression to parents' own interpretation of the process of dissonant acculturation. Deprived of institutional supports, especially by the schools, some parents feel powerless to control their young and must passively witness how children's lives unfold. Working-class parents are in a particularly difficult predicament because they lack the means to move to better neighborhoods or gain access to better schools and are simultaneously prevented from disciplining their children when necessary. Many immigrants see parental administration of physical punishment as a natural, even necessary, tool for child-rearing. In the United States, however, children can counter with the threat of calling the police. Parents of modest education, who often lack the skills to devise other means of social control, thus fall at the mercy of peer pressure and the external environment.

Consistent evidence from our parental survey on this point is reinforced by other sources. In Chapter 1, we saw how Dominican immigrants resort to sending their children back home to escape what they perceive as the multiple threats of New York City schools. A recent report from the Dominican Republic found that as many as 20 percent of students in certain private schools were returned children of New York immigrants and that their total number may be as high as 10,000. As Betty Cruz, the immigrant mother of a 14-year-old attending private school in the city of Santiago, Dominican Republic, reports, "I don't want my kid growing up in a drug-infested area where I am always worrying that somebody is going to drive by and shoot him. . . . I wanted him away from all that, and that's the reason every parent sends their kids home."[6]

The permissiveness of U.S. culture has led to a common perception among immigrants that "becoming Americanized" is a negative, even dangerous, thing for their young. This represents an important shift from the attitudes of earlier immigrant waves. At the turn of the twentieth century, poor European parents commonly aspired to their young becoming Americanized (i.e., assimilated) as a way to escape the squalor of tenements and working-class life. They did so even if it entailed accepting the frustrations of role reversal.[7] Today, the opposite is the case as parents see premature acculturation as a barrier, preventing children from taking advantage of the multiple educational and occupational opportunities available to them. In some situations, rapid acculturation can become a ticket for downward mobility and permanent disadvantage.

For this reason, immigrants who do not have access to the enforced return option used by Dominicans have come to rely on the social capital from extended families or ethnic communities to countermand the anomic pressures of American culture. As the case of Huu Tran exemplifies, some Vietnamese families live in extended compounds where grandparents and other adults create an atmosphere supportive of parental authority. The same is the case in other closely knit communities where social networks ensure that children are supervised and, when necessary, disciplined by other adults.

Several immigrant groups have successfully overcome the challenge of premature Americanization in this manner, which may help explain their optimism about life chances in the United States. Yet many cases exist where parents find themselves isolated and where processes of dissonant acculturation are well underway. Even when events do not take this dramatic turn, preoccupation with the negative influences experienced by children in their schools and in the streets is widespread, as much indeed as the optimism shown earlier.

Table 5.2 provides evidence of this parallel trend through replies to four survey items. Asked how worried they are about negative influences on their children in school, only one-fifth (21.8 percent) of the sample said that they were not worried. The remaining four-fifths reported varying degrees of concern about such influences. This preoccupation is common among all nationalities, regardless of differences in socioeconomic status. While southeast Asian refugees (Vietnamese, Laotian, and Cambodian) are the most worried, majorities of all national groups express the same feeling. Table 5.2 also shows that this broad concern with negative school influences does not vary with education—close to 80 percent of parents at all educational levels endorse it.

The following columns in the table confirm the same perception on the basis of other survey items. Preoccupation about external influences drops appreciably when the source of these is the child's close friends.

TABLE 5.2 PARENTAL OUTLOOKS ON SCHOOL INFLUENCES AND SOCIALIZATION

	How worried are you about negative influences on your child in school?		How worried are you about negative influences on your child from his/her close friends?		How different are your ideas and views from those of your child's close friends?	
	Not at All Worried	Worried[1]	Not at All Worried	Worried[1]	Not at All Different	Different[2]
Nationality						
Chinese/other Asian	13.5	86.5	29.7	70.3	14.9	85.1
Colombian/other Latin American	28.2	71.8	50.9	49.1	10.5	89.5
Cuban	28.5	71.5	45.3	54.7	16.9	83.1
European/other	21.9	78.1	43.8	56.3	12.5	87.5
Filipino	20.9	79.1	37.4	62.6	16.6	83.4
Haitian	32.6	67.4	48.8	51.2	18.6	81.4
Jamaican/West Indian	35.4	64.6	54.6	45.4	19.2	80.8
Laotian/Cambodian	3.7	96.3	4.8	95.2	8.1	91.9
Mexican	23.8	76.2	28.7	71.3	15.0	85.0
Nicaraguan	37.4	62.6	50.5	49.5	22.8	77.2
Vietnamese	1.2	98.8	2.0	98.0	1.2	98.8
Education						
High school or less	21.4	78.6	30.5	69.5	12.8	87.2
Some college	23.0	77.0	37.9	62.1	16.5	83.5
College graduate	22.0	78.0	42.6	57.4	16.4	83.6
Postgraduate degree	23.1	76.9	46.3	53.7	12.4	87.6
Total	21.8	78.2	34.0	66.0	13.8	86.2
N[3]	531	1,910	831	1,610	337	2,104

How different are the messages that your child gets from you and from his/her close friends about becoming a successful person?

How do you want your child raised?

	Not at All Different	Different[2]	The American Way	My Country's Way	A Mix of the Two[4]
Nationality					
Chinese/other Asian	16.2	83.8	25.7	23.0	51.4
Colombian/other Latin American	9.0	91.0	39.4	41.9	18.8
Cuban	23.2	76.8	32.7	28.0	39.3
European/other	40.6	59.4	40.6	15.6	43.8
Filipino	25.4	74.6	13.1	19.8	67.1
Haitian	23.3	76.7	17.4	39.5	43.0
Jamaican/West Indian	30.8	69.2	26.9	24.6	48.5
Laotian/Cambodian	5.9	94.1	1.1	75.8	23.1
Mexican	18.5	81.5	42.2	34.9	22.9
Nicaraguan	23.8	76.2	41.7	28.2	30.1
Vietnamese	1.6	98.4	3.2	74.9	21.9
Education					
High school or less	15.1	84.9	25.5	44.6	29.9
Some college	23.3	76.7	25.6	31.7	42.7
College graduate	22.5	77.5	19.6	27.9	52.5
Postgraduate degree	21.5	78.5	34.7	23.1	42.1
Total	17.6	82.4	25.0	39.4	35.6
N[3]	429	2,012	611	961	869

[1]Includes "a little worried" to "very worried."
[2]Includes "a little different" to "very different" plus those who do not know their child's friends or their views. "Don't know" responses represent approximately 7 percent of the total sample.
[3]Total number of parents endorsing each response alternative.
[4]Includes negligible percentages of "don't know" answers.

Still, two-thirds of parents (and sizable majorities within most nationalities) report varying degrees of concern. In this instance, educational status does make a difference, as preoccupation with friends' negative influences drops among the best educated. Yet the disparity between parental outlooks and those to which children are exposed, even among close friends, is evident in answers to the final items. Less than 20 percent of parents believe that their own views and aspirations are reinforced by their children's friends. This perceived dissonance is again general, being reported by majorities of parents of all nationalities and all educational levels.

Preoccupation with dissonant acculturation may explain why most immigrants do *not* want their children to be educated the American way. The majority would prefer an education based on their own country's customs or a mix of the two. A drive toward exclusive socialization in the home country's customs is strong among the Vietnamese and other southeast Asian refugees. For Filipinos, West Indians, and most immigrants with an advanced education, the modal response is a mix of American and home-country ways, signaling a clear preference for selective acculturation.

Overall, parents from all national backgrounds and all socioeconomic levels see the principal danger to their children's well-being and the fulfillment of their own aspirations in an external environment full of premature consumerism, permissiveness, and the alternative role models provided by street culture. Their dominant view of America is that of a dreamland of wealth and opportunity surrounded by many treacherous undercurrents. Only firm parental guidance and strong family and community ties can lead to the hoped-for destination.

Some authors have argued that immigrants have always been at odds with their children and that concerns voiced today by Mexican or Chinese parents are the same as those expressed by their Polish or Italian predecessors.[8] There is some truth to this, but the distinct character of the present situation is given credence by the different meanings attributed to Americanization yesterday and today and by repeated stories of young lives destroyed in the currents of today's society. The story of Khae Yang at the beginning of this chapter is symptomatic of the course of second-generation youths undergoing downward assimilation. These are the ones who are not making it to the promised shore, and their experience stands as an object lesson to all.

Ambition

The will to reach those shores, despite all obstacles, is very strong and represents a third common theme in our parental interviews. High expectations for children's educational achievement is common not only among the more successful and the better educated but also among those of more modest condition. Ambition is high among Filipino professionals and Chinese entrepreneurs as well as among southeast Asians on government assistance and unemployed Haitian mothers. Aristide Maillol, the child of one such mother, expressed this resilient optimism in eloquent terms in one of our opening stories (Chapter 1.) The same faith is evident in Aura Lila Marín, the Cuban welfare mother, and her daughter at the start of this chapter. Survey results confirm the trend. As shown in Table 5.3, 73.9 percent of parents expect their children to graduate from college, and of these, close to 50 percent expect them to earn a postgraduate degree. Majorities of all immigrant nationalities voice these goals. Predictably, college and postgraduate expectations rise with parental education, but even among those with a high school education or less, lofty goals are the norm.

Within this picture, there are still some noteworthy differences. College expectations exceeding 80 percent of the respective national samples are found among immigrants with a high average education, such as Filipinos and West Indians, and refugee groups that combine some educational credentials with a favorable official reception, such as the Vietnamese. Cubans, another group in the same category, have college expectations no higher than the sample mean, but a high proportion of these parents plan for their children's postgraduate education. Below-average educational goals are found among Mexicans and Laotian/Cambodians. The Mexican pattern reflects again the low educational endowment of the first generation and its difficult experiences of entry and incorporation. The Laotian/Cambodian result is more complex.

Further breakdowns reveal that this result is due exclusively to the low educational goals of Cambodian (Khmer) refugees, only 27 percent of whom expect their children to graduate from college. Lao and Hmong parents, on the other hand, voice high expectations for their children despite their own very low educational attainment. The Cambodian pattern appears influenced by the unique and traumatic experiences of persecution and flight confronted by these refugees. Many kin

TABLE 5.3   PARENTAL EDUCATIONAL EXPECTATIONS AND RULES

	Expects child to graduate from college (%)	Expects child to earn a post-graduate degree (among parents who have college expectations) (%)	Has rules for child about maintaining a minimum GPA (%)	Has rules for child's doing homework (%)	Talks to child regularly about future education (%)
		Nationality			
Chinese/other Asian	87.8	69.2	81.1	85.1	47.9
Colombian/other Latin American	67.5	74.9	98.5	98.9	91.3
Cuban	74.3	61.0	93.2	94.9	91.2
European/other	93.8	60.0	71.9	75.0	84.4
Filipino	92.2	33.0	75.7	91.2	67.4
Haitian	76.7	65.2	100.0	100.0	87.1
Jamaican/West Indian	80.8	55.2	96.9	99.2	89.2
Laotian/Cambodian	57.1	38.5	69.5	87.9	59.6
Mexican	54.5	39.2	86.4	90.5	74.1
Nicaraguan	73.3	55.0	91.7	97.1	88.3
Vietnamese	86.9	18.8	67.3	88.0	44.2
		Education			
High school or less	66.2	44.1	83.9	92.3	71.9
Some college	86.7	45.9	87.1	96.1	83.8
College graduate	89.8	49.3	82.8	91.4	79.1
Postgraduate degree	95.9	75.9	90.8	93.3	80.2
Total	73.9	47.4	84.5	92.7	74.9
N[1]	1,804	855	2,050	2,245	1,823

NOTE: Table data reflect total number of parents endorsing each indicated response alternative.

and friends were lost in the infamous Khmer Rouge killing fields, and these experiences have left an indelible mark.[9] A review of interviews with Khmer parents conducted in the course of the study reveals widespread concern with children's education, but this concern focuses on getting them through high school, with little thought of any advanced degree. The Khmer worry instead about their past, their physical and mental health, and their overall estrangement from U.S. society. As one parent put it: "All I hope is that Loeung does not fall into a gang. We have suffered much and now I don't know for what. . . . We live here without really knowing where we are or how we are going to survive."[10]

Despite these variations in educational ambition, there is remarkable consistency in the reported efforts to guide children through school and encourage them to succeed. As shown in the next two columns of Table 5.3, parents of all nationalities have sought to set standards about grade point averages and completing school homework. In total, about 90 percent of the entire parental sample have set such rules, a remarkable figure in view of the precarious circumstances of many families and their lack of familiarity with the outside environment.

Similarly, immigrants seek to engage their children in regular interaction about their education and future. As shown in the last column of Table 5.3, three-fourths of parents report talking to their children regularly about these matters. Heavy majorities are evident among parents of all nationalities except the Vietnamese, Chinese, and other Asians who report talking to their children occasionally. Choice of the word *occasional* seems to be a cultural preference in this instance rather than evidence of any less concern on the part of these parents. This is especially true in light of the high educational expectations and emphasis on family solidarity held by all of these Asian groups.

Parental expectations are important because they set the framework for the development of the children's own ambitions. The high goals expressed by most immigrants and their efforts to guide their children in the direction of educational success provide a powerful impulse forward. These influences help explain why many Haitian and Mexican youths, coming from poor and discriminated families, do well academically. Yet parental ambition and children's achievement do not always fall in line; for every Aristide Maillol and Roberto Santos there are also a number of Khae Yangs who stumble on the barriers of a difficult outside environment. Parental setting of rules is not the same as enforcing them since external factors can prevent effective guidance of children. From survey data and detailed parental interviews, three patterns

Figure 5.1   Obstacles to Parental Aspirations for Children

Normative Pattern

Parental ambition $\longrightarrow$ Children's aspirations $\longrightarrow$ Children's educational
                              and self-esteem   achievement

Obstacles   *Alternative Outcome*

Dissonant acculturation $\longrightarrow$ Low academic performance
                                            Downward assimilation

Family poverty $\longrightarrow$ Low educational attainment
                                            Frustrated aspirations

Family security $\longrightarrow$ Delayed career pursuits
and early job options   High dropout rates

emerge that block a smooth translation of parental ambition into their offspring's educational success.

The first is the trend toward dissonant acculturation, commonly found among isolated families. Premature Americanization—in the form of consumerism and socialization into school peer cultures—often stands in the way of parents who feel powerless to confront it because of lack of personal resources and social supports. The second pattern, exemplified by Melanie Fernández-Rey in Chapter 1, combines the absorption by children of high educational expectations with persistent poverty. The problem in these cases is how to find the means to pay for a college education within the constraints of low-wage jobs and an insecure legal status. Immigrant families who have experienced rapid downward mobility because of a negative official and public reception often find themselves in these straits. There is no conflict in these cases between parents and children, just the objective constraint of poverty and consequent lack of educational opportunities.[11]

The third pattern is actually the reverse of the second and consists of cases where the economic achievements of the first generation lead the young to be less concerned about the future or to avail themselves of job opportunities prior to school graduation. This relaxed attitude toward educational achievement among children of more economically successful groups is exemplified by the case of Yvette Santana in Chapter 1. Other Cuban American youths have also followed this contrary-to-expectations pattern, which will be given detailed attention in later chapters. Figure 5.1 summarizes these alternative obstacles to successful adaptation and their possible outcomes.

Despite these challenges, the dominant note in parents' outlook for the future is their high ambition, a view consonant with their basic optimism about their own lives. The impetus that parental expectations provide is considerable and can lead second-generation youths to overcome seemingly impassable barriers. The perils of dissonant acculturation and poverty are real and can derail many children from the normative achievement path. Yet the overall sense conveyed by our findings is that the majority of these children are poised to move ahead in school, riding on their family's support and ambition. Parental status, family structure, and the character of parent-child interaction all play a role in this process, with results to be examined in the coming chapters.

Community and Pride

San Diego, 1993. Mrs. Ly and her daughter Hoa Nguyen sit in their tiny apartment surrounded by several calendars and clocks, a small South Vietnamese flag, two Buddhist shrines, and four school achievement plaques. Two of Mrs. Ly's daughters have maintained perfect grades for two years in a row. Hoa, her mother explains, is behind: Her grade point average is only 3.8 rather than a perfect 4.0.

Since their arrival in the United States in 1989, neither Mrs. Ly nor her husband Tam Nguyen have held any jobs. They depend on government assistance, although Mrs. Ly is unclear about where exactly the money they receive comes from. Leaving their country was filled with trauma, and the family is still dazed. More than anything what keeps the Nguyens and other Vietnamese families apart is the language barrier: "We can't speak English," says Mrs. Ly, "so the girls don't go out much, they stay home. I raise my children here the same as I raised them in Vietnam: to school and back home, no point their being in the street."[12]

New Orleans, 1994. "More than 80 percent of Vietnamese in the Versailles area are Catholics, and the Mary Queen of Vietnam Church has served not only as a place of worship, but also as the focal point of secular community activities. As some members of the community have achieved a measure of material success, a system of formal civic organizations have been established, the most important of which are the Vietnamese-American Voter's Association, the Vietnamese Educational

Association, and the Vietnamese Parent-Teacher Association. Overall, this is a society in which individual members are integrated into a densely knit system of relations with the church as a physical and social center."[13]

These two snapshots of Vietnamese adaptation to the United States capture different times and family settings: one isolated and still uncertain of the surrounding environment and the other more firmly settled and well ensconced in ethnic community networks. In New Orleans, the mechanisms for social control and guidance of second-generation youths are well established. Ethnic pride is also present, however, in the little flag, shrines, and plaques in the Nguyens' home. Despite its poverty and disorientation, this family has also managed to guide their daughters toward academic achievement. Possibly, they have been helped in this effort by the presence of other refugee families in the vicinity: In San Diego, the Vietnamese are well known for their solidarity and mutual support.

In this last section, we return to a theme first broached in Chapter 3 and illustrated by several prior stories, namely, how co-ethnic communities play a central role in immigrants' modes of incorporation and in supporting parental efforts. This form of social capital is important for all immigrant groups but especially for those composed of relatively poor parents with modest educational credentials. In these instances, community networks are often the only factor compensating for the weakness of the parents' own economic position. Dissonant acculturation can be most effectively resisted when parental authority is reinforced by supportive kin and ethnic networks.

Immigrant groups are not uniform either in their achievement of economic success or in their internal solidarity and mutual support. Strong human capital endowments and a favorable context of reception have provided some groups with the means to forge ahead into the social and economic mainstream. Their collective success is subsequently transmitted to their young in the form of ethnic pride and validation of parental authority. Other groups have not fared as well, but in some cases, lack of economic success is experienced as a collective fate and compensated by internal solidarity, while in others, it is endured as an individual calamity with little external support.

These differences are illustrated in Table 5.4, which presents parental responses to items asking about the relative success of their own national group in America, the extent to which conationals support each other, and the level of mutual assistance rendered by conationals living in the same neighborhood. There are major differences in these subjective perceptions, which agree, in broad outlines, with the known situation of each major immigrant group. Fully 75 percent of Cambodian and Laotian

TABLE 5.4 PARENTAL PERCEPTIONS OF CO-ETHNIC COMMUNITY

Nationality	People from my country have not been economically successful in the United States.			People from my country are very supportive of one another.		People from my country who live in this neighborhood do not help each other.		
	True (%)	False (%)	Don't Know (%)	True (%)	False¹ (%)	True (%)	False (%)	Don't Know (%)
Chinese/other Asian	12.2	71.6	16.2	55.4	44.6	21.6	32.4	45.9
Colombian/other Latin American	12.6	71.1	16.2	35.7	64.3	5.4	55.6	39.0
Cuban	3.5	94.5	2.0	86.4	13.6	18.6	64.7	16.6
European/other	18.8	56.3	25.0	62.5	37.5	0.0	37.5	62.5
Filipino	6.1	82.6	11.2	78.9	21.1	14.7	64.4	20.9
Haitian	37.2	26.7	36.0	70.9	29.1	16.3	27.9	55.8
Jamaican/West Indian	6.9	76.9	16.2	70.0	30.0	13.8	49.2	36.9
Laotian/Cambodian	75.1	12.8	12.1	87.5	12.5	7.0	73.6	19.4
Mexican	39.0	44.9	16.1	54.0	46.0	37.0	41.6	21.4
Nicaraguan	30.6	61.2	8.3	39.8	60.2	32.0	35.0	33.0
Vietnamese	33.1	41.0	25.9	82.9	17.1	12.7	66.9	20.3
Totals	25.1	61.1	13.8	68.1	31.9	17.8	55.7	26.5
N	612	1,492	337	1,663	778	435	1,359	647

¹Includes a small proportion of "don't know" responses.

Figure 5.2   Immigrant Parents' Perception of Their own
Ethnic Communities

External Achievement

		Less Successful	More Successful
		A	**B**
Less Solidary		Mexicans, Nicaraguans	Europeans, Other Asians[1]
Internal Cohesion			
		C	**D**
More Solidary		Laotians, Cambodians, Vietnamese	Cubans, Filipinos

NOTE: Nationalities in each cell correspond to response averages in Table 5.4. They should be interpreted as approximations
that include significant variations within each national group.
[1]Both groups are formed by multiple small nationalities.

refugees report that their conationals have *not* been economically successful in the United States, and about 40 percent of Mexicans are of the
same opinion. On the other hand, an emphatic 82.6 percent of Filipinos
and 94.5 percent of Cubans believe that their own group has succeeded
in America. Smaller Latin and Asian nationalities, including the Chinese,
also have a high opinion of their group's economic performance.

A very different pattern emerges when we examine the next columns
of Table 5.4. It is possible to identify, on the basis of these data, four distinct parental outlooks on their respective ethnic communities. These are
summarized in Figure 5.2. Cells in this figure correspond to perceived
differences in external economic achievement and internal solidarity,
based on parental responses to our survey. Obviously, the best situation
is that of groups that see themselves as both economically successful and
solidary (cell D.) A different situation, portrayed by cell B, is characteristic of smaller nationalities that see themselves as moving ahead economically but are too dispersed and lacking sufficient numbers to forge
dense networks. The most significant contrast in these results, however,
is between nationalities that have not experienced economic success in
the United States but whose internal solidarity varies (cells A and C).

Southeast Asian refugees see themselves as part of supportive ethnic
networks even when, as in the case of Laotians and Cambodians, their
members are mostly poor. On the other hand, close to half of Mexican

immigrant parents and almost two-thirds of Nicaraguans report that they have received little support from their conationals. In agreement with the ethnographic evidence presented in Chapter 3, over 30 percent of Nicaraguan parents indicate having gotten little or no help from neighbors of the same nationality, together with Mexicans, who report the lowest level among all groups. In these cases, the dearth of socio-economic achievement among first-generation immigrants is not compensated by the support of community networks, thus giving rise to a set of cumulative disadvantages.

The pattern of dense networks, ethnic pride, and tight social control even in the absence of economic success is commonly found among Vietnamese families, as illustrated by the previous stories. The situation of poor and atomized immigrant households is exemplified by Mrs. Santos, a single Mexican woman and the mother of Roberto Santos, whose story was told in the last chapter:

> The interviewer asked Señora Santos if she thought people from Mexico helped each other here. The question elicited an emotional response in her. Tears came to her eyes as she expressed her disappointment that Mexicans as a group are not tight-knit like the other immigrants who work together and help each other. She cited jealousy and selfishness among people of her own group which alienated them from each other. "If they can't have it, they don't want anyone else to have it either. Not like the Vietnamese who cling together," Señora Santos said. "Listening to her," noted the interviewer, "I had the impression that this was a very lonely woman."[14]

Different socioeconomic origins and contexts of reception have promoted divergent patterns of immigrant adaptation, including the composition and solidarity of ethnic communities. Although most parents voice high aspirations for their children and there is a uniform note of optimism in their responses, some approach the future securely embedded in successful and tight-knit communities, others compensate for their humble origins and poverty with bonds of community support, while still others lack even this resource. Atomized households and the consequent lack of social capital mean that parents must confront the challenges of the outside environment and the threat of role reversal on their own. For those of modest condition, the challenge is all too often overwhelming.

Conclusion

With tears in his eyes, Luis Aparicio, a Filipino immigrant, tells about the death of his son, who was interviewed as part of our original sample in 1993:

It happened one day after school. Timothy and his friends were chased by their enemies on the way home. They came here and called some friends for help. These friends told them to go to their house. So Timothy and his two friends went to their friends' house but, unfortunately, their enemies followed and started shooting. Timothy was able to get to the friends' house and knock on the door. His friends thought that he was one of the enemies. When they opened the door, they fired and hit Timothy before they realized who he was.

Gangs are all over the school; kids have guns; teachers do nothing. What could we do?[15]

Many immigrants voice high ambitions for the future, which, as we will see in later chapters, will be reproduced in lofty aspirations and educational achievement among their children. But these averages should not let us forget those who do not make it. Reports of children being "chased by their enemies" who "followed them and started shooting" point to a harrowing reality that is each immigrant parent's worst nightmare. Some send their kids back to their home countries to escape it, others close ranks and surround their young with protective ethnic networks, and still others fail and must face the consequences of dissonant acculturation. Parental voices thus give us a rather complex picture, reflecting what they see as the Janus-faced nature of American society: unmatched educational and economic opportunities coupled with constant multiple threats to family cohesion and individual survival. The outcomes of this confrontation will be undoubtedly mixed. With different combinations of handicaps and resources, immigrant families soldier on, hoping that their children will be among those who make it to the promised shore.

PLATES

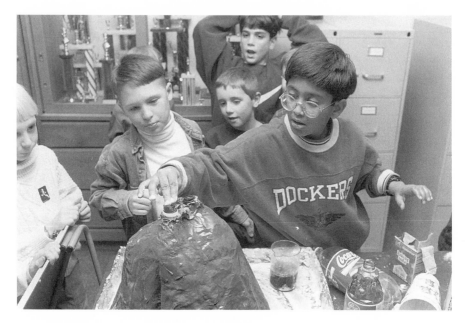

1. Indian-American child at science fair, Okemos, Michigan.

2. Chinese Cub Scouts, Monterey Park, Southern California.

3. Learning the ropes, Chinese-Vietnamese publisher and daughter.

4. Birthday party in a Mexican-American family, Los Angeles.

5. Children of Korean immigrants playing street hockey, East Lansing, Michigan.

6. Vietnamese Catholic youth, Feast of the Immaculate Conception,
Whittier, Southern California.

7. Yemeni boys, Dearborn, Michigan.

8. Arab Americans, Dearborn, Michigan.

9. Vietnamese child, Oakland, California.

10. Hmong family, Lansing, Michigan.

11. Vietnamese beauty shop, Little Saigon, Southern California.

12. Southeast Asian children, Tenderloin, San Francisco.

13. Girls at a martial arts demonstration, Tet festival (lunar New Year), Little Saigon.

14. Tet celebration, Orange County, California.

15. Chinese and Vietnamese students in a student association, Los Angeles.

16. Nicaraguan and Japanese students, Los Angeles.

17. Vietnamese students getting scholarships from a Japanese-American group, Los Angeles. Most plan to major in premed.

18. Chinese-Filipino and Chinese students' performance, Los Angeles.

19. Family-owned Dominican video store, Boston, Massachusetts.

20. Trinidadian-Panamanian students, Los Angeles.

21. Cambodian youth, Revere Beach, Massachusetts.

22. Southeast Asian boys, Tenderloin, San Francisco.

23. Chinese- and Anglo-American family, Los Angeles.

Chapter 6

LOST IN TRANSLATION
Language and the New Second Generation

We have room for but one language here, and that is the English language, for we intend to see that the crucible turns our people out as Americans, and not as dwellers of a polyglot boarding house; and we have room for but one sole loyalty, and that is loyalty to the American people.
— Theodore Roosevelt[1]

Language is much more than a means of communication. The relevant literatures have shown how its acquisition in childhood is closely linked to the development of the self as well as to mental ability. Language also defines the limits of communities and nations and leads to bounded national identities and ethnic solidarities. Through use of the same language, individuals learn to identify each other as members of the same bounded cultural community. Common inflections and a common accent in the same language tightens this sense of "we-ness" and links it firmly to a common historical past.[2]

Immigrants arriving in a foreign land face a significant dilemma, one whose resolution lies at the very core of the process of acculturation. On the one hand, the languages that they bring are closely linked to their sense of self-worth and national pride. On the other hand, these languages clash with the imperatives of a new environment that dictate abandonment of their cultural baggage and learning a new means of communication. Language assimilation is demanded of foreigners not only for instrumental reasons but for symbolic ones as well. It signals their willingness to seek admission into the circles of their new country, leaving past loyalties behind. Precisely because a common language lies at the core of national identity, host societies oppose the rise of refractory groups that persist in the use of foreign tongues.[3]

In the United States, in particular, the pressure toward linguistic assimilation is all the greater because the country has few other elements on which to ground a sense of national identity. Made up of people coming from many different lands, lacking the unifying symbols of crown or millennial history, the common use of American English has come to acquire a singular importance as a binding tie across such a vast territory. This explains the sense of urgency in the opening remark by Teddy Roosevelt and the regular emergence of organized movements seeking to defend English against foreign intrusions.[4] In this chapter, we turn to the analysis of language learning and use as a central element of acculturation. We consider how it varies from parents to children and how it relates to key empirical indicators of generational consonance/dissonance and psychological well-being. Given the observed association between bilingualism and these variables, we also examine the factors that lead to this outcome, as opposed to the more common transition to English monolingualism. This analysis continues the causal sequence outlined in Chapter 3, extending it now to the second generation.

The historical setting in which today's children of immigrants undergo this form of acculturation has been marked by the consistent success of assimilative forces. In no other country, among those studied by Lieberson and his associates, has the transition toward monolingualism been so swift and the disappearance of foreign languages so thorough.[5] In their view, assimilative pressures turned the United States into a veritable cemetery of other languages. This repeated triumph of nativism has come, however, at the cost of immigrants' efforts to balance acculturation with preservation of some aspects of their cultural heritage.

Adult immigrants in the United States typically combine instrumental learning of English with efforts to maintain their culture and language.[6] They also seek to pass this heritage to their children. Of all the distinct legacies transmitted across generations, language is arguably the most important, but it is also the most difficult to transmit because of strong opposing forces. Linguists Fishman and Veltman have outlined the pattern accounting for the remarkable language loss across generations: The instrumental acculturation of the first generation in the United States is followed by a second that speaks English in school and parental languages at home, often responding to remarks in those languages in English. Limited bilingualism leads, almost inevitably, to English becoming the home language in adulthood. By the third generation, any residual proficiency in the foreign language is lost since it is supported neither outside nor inside the home.[7]

Although this process is in agreement with nativists' desires, it is not necessarily in the interest of the children or of society at large. In the present global context, it is not clear that language acculturation and bilingualism are mutually exclusive or that preservation of foreign language skills represents a negative outcome. It may well be that the boundary-maintenance function of English is not incompatible with knowledge of other countries' languages. Reasons for this alternative outlook on language acculturation are based on the evolving scholarly understanding of bilingualism. We examine this literature as a prelude to our own findings on the new second generation.

Bilingualism: Yesterday and Today

Until recently, attacks on immigrant languages were buttressed by a powerful intellectual current that saw their preservation as inimical to the individual and the community. Up to the 1960s, the consensus in the linguistic and psychological literatures was that bilingualism and cognitive development were negatively associated. By the 1920s, the matter was considered settled, and the academic debate featured hereditarians and eugenics advocates who considered the continued use of foreign languages as an additional sign of the inherent intellectual limitations of immigrants versus supporters of the "nurture" school who attributed to bilingualism itself the cause of immigrant children's mental retardation.[8]

Illustrative of the first school was Carl Brigham's 1923 analysis of intelligence test scores among foreign-born draftees during World War I. Oblivious of the recent arrival of these soldiers, Brigham attributed their limited English vocabulary to the innate inferiority of southern and eastern Europeans, concluding that "the representatives of the Alpine and Mediterranean races in our immigration are intellectually inferior to the representatives of the Nordic race."[9] A prominent example of the second school was the work of Madorah Smith, whose research during the 1930s on the speech patterns of preschool Chinese, Filipino, Hawaiian, Japanese, Korean, and Portuguese children in Hawaii convinced her that the attempt to use two languages simultaneously was an important factor in the retardation of speech among children. Smith's results reinforced the generalized view that bilingual youths suffered from a "language handicap" and that "an important factor in the retardation of speech found in the preschool population is the attempt to make use of two languages."[10]

These conclusions reflected the zeitgeist of the time, which privileged unaccented English as a sign of full membership in the national community. Prominent political figures reinforced this view with forceful attacks of foreign languages and multiculturalism in general. Roosevelt's ringing denunciation, directed primarily at German Americans, was exemplary of the trend, but he was by no means alone. States such as Nebraska regularly administered language loyalty oaths to schoolchildren,[11] and attempts to explain the lower English fluency of immigrants on the basis of their recency in the country were dismissed as "special pleading for the alien."[12]

This atmosphere of hostility to foreign influences finds its contemporary equivalent in statements periodically issued by movements such as U.S. English: "Where linguistic unity has broken down, our energies and resources flow into tensions, hostilities, prejudices, and resentments—within a few years if the breakdown persists, there will be no retreat—society as we know it can fade into a noisy Babel and then chaos."[13]

The academic research that made such pronouncements respectable is by now thoroughly discredited. Recent evidence challenges both the alleged individual handicaps created by bilingualism and its supposed negative effects on national unity and progress. The studies that demonstrated the intellectual inferiority of bilingual children were flawed on two key counts. First, they failed to control for parental social class, so children of poor immigrant families were regularly compared with children from middle-class English-speaking backgrounds. Second, they failed to distinguish between fluent bilinguals, who spoke both languages correctly, and limited or quasi bilinguals, who spoke only one language fluently and had a poor or diminishing command of a second.

The turning point came with a landmark study of bilingualism among French Canadian children conducted by Peal and Lambert in 1962. These researchers compared a sample of fluent bilingual 10-year-olds with a sample of monolingual counterparts matched by sex, age, and family status. Contrary to most earlier reports, Peal and Lambert found that bilinguals outperformed monolingual students of the same socioeconomic status in almost all cognitive tests. A factor analysis showed that bilinguals had superior performance in concept formation and particularly in tasks that required symbolic flexibility. Although the design of the study had shortcomings that partially biased results in favor of the bilingual sample, subsequent research consistently upheld its major findings.[14]

Linguists have demonstrated that bilinguals in a number of different language combinations, such as English-French, English-Chinese, German-French, and others, possess greater cognitive flexibility. Leopold, for example, has concluded that this pattern is due to bilinguals' having more than one symbol for a concrete thing, thus liberating them from the tyranny of words.[15] For Cummins, bilinguals are able "to look *at* language rather than *through* it to the intended meaning."[16] Sociological studies based on larger samples have generally confirmed the better academic performance associated with bilingualism. Rumbaut has compared fluent bilingual students with limited bilinguals of the same national origins and with English monolinguals in the entire San Diego school system in the late 1980s. Without exception, fluent bilinguals outperformed the other two categories in standardized academic tests and GPAs within each ethnic and national group. On the average, fluent bilinguals also had higher GPAs and math achievement scores than their native-born monolingual peers.[17]

The positive associations between bilingualism, cognitive flexibility, and academic performance have held after controlling for socioeconomic background, but there are questions as to their causal order. Hence, though many linguists have vigorously argued that knowledge of two or more languages promotes cognitive development, it is also possible that the causal effect runs in the opposite direction. In this version, fluent bilingualism would be a *consequence* of greater cognitive ability rather than the other way around. A pioneer study by Hakuta and Diaz has addressed this issue by following samples of Spanish-speaking Puerto Rican students immersed in a bilingual education program in New Haven. Though the final usable sample was small, the study showed that bilingualism at a given time had the expected positive association with subsequent cognitive development. Furthermore, multivariate analyses indicated that bilingual ability was a significant predictor of subsequent academic performance, while the opposite causal sequence was weaker.[18]

Regardless of the exact causal order, the positive association of bilingualism with cognitive development has become commonly accepted in the contemporary literature. This positive relationship for individuals is coupled with an increasing demand for language skills in the labor market. As Sassen notes, the rise of "global cities" where control and command functions for the international economy concentrate has triggered a growing need for professionals and managers able to conduct business in more than one language. In the United States, New York is the prime example of a global city, and those with fluency in several languages can enter a major market there.[19] Other cities concentrate more specialized global functions. Miami, for example, has become the administrative and marketing center of the nation's Latin American trade and is often dubbed the financial capital of Latin America.[20] Business leaders in this city have recently complained about the dearth of fluent bilinguals among second-generation Latin children. Although many retain some speaking knowledge, their Spanish is not fluent enough to be able to conduct regular business transactions.[21]

The evolution of the world economy and America's position in it suggest the convenience of combining fluency in English with preserving or acquiring other languages. This additive approach to language learning has been advocated by a number of authors, based on the advantages of bilingualism for individual development and national competitiveness. Children of immigrants would thus do well to preserve what they have received as a cultural gift from their parents. On the other hand, nativists continue to argue for a subtractive approach based on the danger of cultural fragmentation. This danger, in their view, is especially serious in periods of high immigration where sizable linguistic enclaves emerge.[22]

It is well known that adult immigrants seldom abandon their original languages even while learning English. Hence, the central issue is what happens to the children. In the past, the shift of linguistic allegiances among children has been swift, but, in theory, two other outcomes are possible: First, second-generation youths may acculturate slowly, retaining their parental language as primary and acquiring only a limited command of English; second, they may become bilingual but maintain primary allegiance to foreign languages. It is those possibilities that worry the U.S. English movement and other nativists as they seek to stamp out the public use of other languages in America.

Shadow Boxing: Myth and Reality of Language Acculturation

General Trends

Evaluated against the alarm created by these messages, empirical findings are surprising indeed. In our large second-generation sample, knowledge of English is near universal, and the use and preference for English increases consistently over time. Figure 6.1 presents these

Figure 6.1   English Knowledge and Preferences

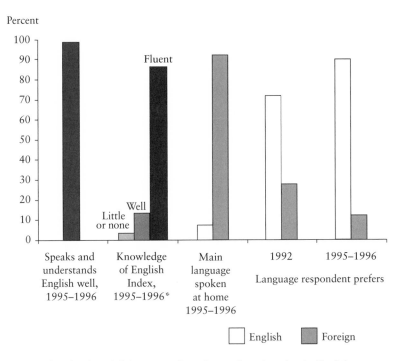

Percent

*Combined index of ability to speak, understand, read, and write English.

results, indicating that over 98 percent of respondents spoke and understood English well or very well by the time of the second survey. An
index of English fluency combining ability to speak, understand, read,
and write the language shows exactly the same pattern.[23] Not only is
knowledge of English near universal, but preference for the language is
overwhelming as well. Figure 6.1 also shows that while a foreign language is spoken in almost all immigrant homes, 72 percent of the children had opted for English as their preferred means of expression in
junior high school, with the figure increasing to 88 percent by the time
of high school graduation.

The story is quite different, however, when we turn to command and
use of foreign languages. While over 90 percent of the sample report
knowing a language other than English, their fluency in that language is
significantly poorer. This is shown in Figure 6.2, which presents the
proportion of respondents who report speaking or understanding a for-

Figure 6.2   Foreign Language Knowledge and Use

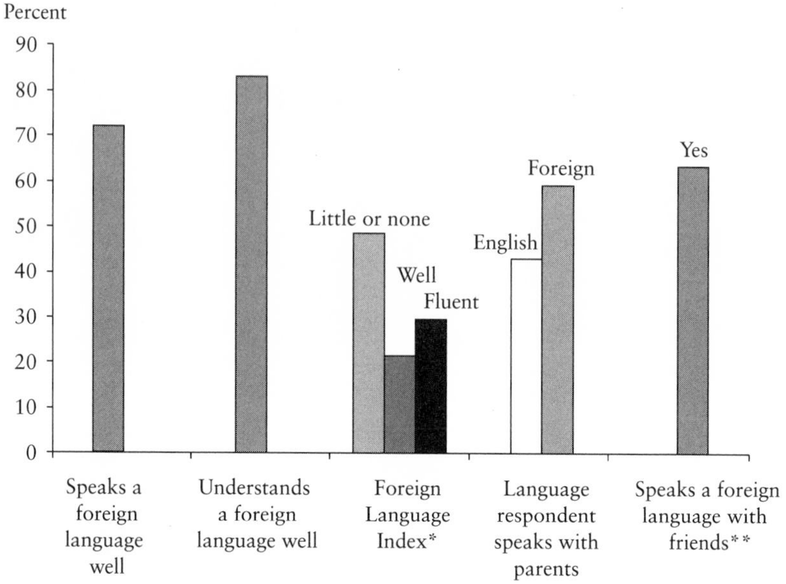

Percent

NOTE: All figures are from CILS follow-up survey, 1995–1996.
*Combined index of ability to speak, understand, read, and write a foreign language.
**At least occasionally.

eign language well or very well. These figures trail those corresponding to English by 15 to over 25 percent. The contrast is still more marked in the Foreign Language Index constructed in parallel fashion to the English Knowledge Index.[24] In this instance, only 30 percent of respondents report themselves fluent, that is, fully able to speak, understand, read, and write a foreign language, in contrast to 83 percent for English.

As shown in Table 6.1, Spanish has pride of place among foreign languages in this sample. It is by far the most common foreign language known by children, spoken at home, and used with peers. Tagalog and other Philippines languages come a distant second, followed by Vietnamese. The strength of Spanish reflects, in part, the design of the sample, drawn from two metropolitan areas of high Latin American concentration. As Table 6.1 indicates, Spanish comes next to English in order of preference by second-generation youths, although it trails the latter by a wide margin. In addition, preference for Spanish dropped markedly between our first and second surveys—from 14.8 to only 6.5 percent—indicating a rapid language shift.

TABLE 6.1   FOREIGN LANGUAGES
KNOWLEDGE AND USE, FULL SAMPLE

Language[1]	Known by Respondent (%)	Preferred by Respondent		Used with Parents[2] (%)	Used with Peers[2] (%)
		1992	1995–1996		
Cambodian	1.2	0.4	0.3	1.3	1.3
Chinese	2.3	0.6	0.6	1.7	0.6
French	0.9	0.2	0.0	0.0	0.3
Haitian Creole	2.7	0.5	0.2	1.3	2.1
Hmong	1.2	0.4	0.3	1.1	1.0
Lao	3.4	1.5	0.8	3.1	2.8
Tagalog	12.6	1.7	0.7	2.2	4.0
Spanish	56.3	14.8	6.5	34.6	43.8
Vietnamese	6.5	2.9	1.7	5.8	5.1
Others	3.8	3.9	2.2	4.3	1.9
N	4,288	5,262	4,288	4,288	4,288

NOTE: Unless otherwise indicated, figures are for the 1995–1996 survey; results did not change significantly from the initial (1992) survey.

[1]Relative frequency distributions computed with English as a valid category. Inclusion of exclusive English knowledge, preference, or use rounds percentages to 100.

[2]Occasionally or regularly.

TABLE 6.2   CORRELATIONS BETWEEN
BILINGUALISM AND ITS COMPONENTS

1992	1995–1996[1]		
	Knowledge of English	Knowledge of Foreign Language	Fluent Bilingualism[2]
Knowledge of English	.676	−.159	.188
Knowledge of Foreign Language	−.100	.709	.427
Fluent bilingualism[2]	.206	.375	.465

[1]Probability of all correlations being due to chance is less than 1 in 1,000.

[2]Speaks English very well (index score of 3.75 or higher) and a foreign language at least well (index score of 3.25 or higher).

Though related, foreign language retention and bilingualism are not the same thing. This is because bilingualism requires simultaneous fluency in English and a foreign language. As shown in Table 6.2, the correlations between English and foreign language fluency, on the one hand, and bilingualism, on the other, are all positive because both contribute to bilingualism. However, the correlation between knowledge of

English and knowledge of a foreign language is negative because of the propensity to lose one with the acquisition of the other. Bilingualism requires overcoming this tendency by retaining command of both. Not surprisingly, only one-fourth of our respondents in 1992 and in 1995–1996 could be classified as fluent bilinguals.[25] These average figures conceal, however, wide disparities among nationalities. These differences are important as they signal the distinct patterns of linguistic acculturation among immigrants from various cultural origins.

National Differences

> *Yo hablo español* especially if I get really ticked off and the words are simply not as strong, not as specific, not as subconsciously launched in English. To a lot of us bilingual South Floridians, Spanish is the language of love and war. It's just the way things are. *Punto.*[26]

In language, as in other things, there are different ways of remembering and forgetting. Some things are remembered faintly, even apologetically, while others are up there at the forefront, aggressively claiming their place. A lot depends on the social context. When surrounded by an overwhelming native-speaking majority, a foreign language becomes a private matter, a discreet subject, used by family and friends in quiet reunions and transmitted perhaps in low-profile weekend schools. When a language is spoken by many, however, it breaks out into the public realm to be used in several distinct settings. To the southern Floridian journalist quoted previously, those settings requiring strong emotional expression are the proper realm of Spanish. English remains the language of work and shopping.

Not surprisingly, nationality is one of the key dimensions along which remembering and forgetting vary. It could scarcely be otherwise, given the origins and different modes of incorporation experienced by immigrant groups in America. Here, as in other dimensions of second-generation adaptation, parental characteristics weigh heavily on the children. In applying the theoretical framework presented in Chapter 3 to language acculturation, the dimensions of parental national background, family socioeconomic status, and household values and norms play key roles. The resolve of parents in transmitting their language and the resources committed to this task are important, but so is the outside context in undermining or supporting these efforts.

As shown in Table 6.3, significant majorities of children of all nationalities retain at least some knowledge of parental languages by the time of high school graduation. Predictable exceptions are Jamaicans and

TABLE 6.3   LANGUAGE USE AND PREFERENCES OF SECOND-GENERATION YOUTH, BY MAJOR NATIONALITY GROUPS, 1995–1996

National Origin	Knows a Foreign Language (%)	Prefers to Speak English (%)	Communicates with Parents in Foreign Language (%)	Uses Foreign Language with School Friends (%)[1]	Bilingual (%)[2]	N
Latin Americans						
Colombian/Other South American[3]	96.3	90.1	69.6	67.6	43.2	543
Cuban (private school)[3]	100.0	95.2	43.8	80.8	61.6	146
Cuban (public school)[3]	98.5	94.6	59.4	65.2	44.0	822
Mexican	97.8	72.3	78.7	87.0	39.1	598
Nicaraguan	98.9	89.3	86.1	81.1	47.0	281
Asians						
Cambodian	98.9	86.5	89.9	73.0	3.4	89
Chinese/Other Asian	84.4	86.4	51.0	28.6	10.2	147
Filipino	81.9	96.1	13.4	27.5	9.8	724
Hmong	100.0	58.0	96.0	86.0	8.0	50
Lao	99.3	75.0	92.4	82.6	0.7	144
Vietnamese	98.7	74.5	88.7	71.6	6.1	310
West Indian						
Haitian	95.5	93.3	50.4	72.6	14.8	135
Jamaican/West Indian	44.3	95.0	7.5	25.4	10.9	201
European/Other[4]	60.4	94.8	17.7	22.9	12.2	98
Total	91.5	87.9	57.1	63.4	28.5	4,288

[1]Regularly or occasionally.
[2]Speaks English very well (four-point index score of 3.75 or higher) and a foreign language at least well (four-point index score of 3.25 or higher).
[3]School enrollment in 1992.
[4]Includes children of European, Canadian, and Middle Eastern origins.

other West Indians whose parents' tongue is predominantly English. Most children of immigrants prefer to communicate in English, but in this case, there are major differences. In the 1992 survey, second-generation Mexicans and southeast Asians departed from the common pattern by voicing strong preferences for their parents' language. In the case of southeast Asian refugees, this result was readily attributable to the recent arrival of these groups and the children's bond with parents, cemented by dramatic experiences of flight and resettlement.[27] By 1996, however, three-fourths of Mexicans and southeast Asians indicated a preference for English—an extraordinarily rapid shift—although most continued to communicate with parents in their own language.

Equally interesting is the contrast in language preferences between Cuban American and Mexican American respondents. It is reasonable to expect that Cuban students attending bilingual private schools in the heart of the Miami enclave would display a strong preference for Spanish. On the other hand, Mexican immigrants' greater contact with mainstream society because of the need to find jobs and the desire of children to climb the U.S. socioeconomic ladder may be expected to lead to a stronger preference for English. In reality, the opposite happens. In the case of Cuban Americans, preference for English reflects a longer period of settlement in the country, including a large proportion (70 percent) of respondents born in the United States. For these children, growing up under the protection of solid ethnic institutions may allow an easier and more confident shift into the cultural mainstream. Mexican Americans, on the other hand, are more likely to be foreign born (40 percent) and commonly live in working-class communities subject to much outside discrimination. Growing up under these conditions may trigger a reactive process, where parental language and culture become symbols of pride against external threats.

Data from CILS's second-generation Mexican sample provide support for this interpretation. As shown in Figure 6.3, a strong relationship exists between length of residence in the United States and preference for English, the latter increasing significantly among the native born. That preference is reinforced if one of the parents is American born. Preference for Spanish, on the other hand, is more common among children who are not embarrassed by their parents' ways, who do not prefer American customs, and who attend schools with a heavy concentration of co-ethnics. Jointly, these relationships suggest a convergent pattern of linguistic/cultural reaffirmation among Mexican American youths more closely identified with their family and ethnic group.

Figure 6.3   English Language Preference by Mexican-American Students

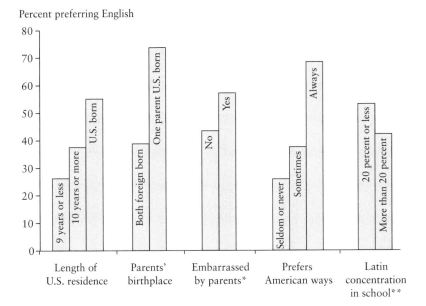

Percent preferring English

NOTE: CILS Follow-up Survey, 1995–1996.
*Percent who reported being embarrassed by their parents' language use and cultural ways.
**Proportion of Latin students in junior high school attended by respondent.

Despite a strong preference for English, majorities in most groups communicate with parents in their native tongues. Exceptions are second-generation West Indians, Filipinos, Canadians, and other nationalities among whom large proportions of parents speak English at home. On the other hand, at least two-thirds of Latin American parents and over 90 percent of southeast Asian refugees talk to their children in their native languages. Among the children, there is a noticeable gap between reported knowledge of these languages and their actual use at home. About 98 percent of second-generation Mexican, Vietnamese, and Latin American children say that they speak parental languages, but their actual use in communication with parents drops by between 10 and 50 percent.

In the case of older and more settled groups, it is likely that a significant proportion of immigrant parents have become fluent in English and shifted to that language at home. The situation then becomes similar to that observed in Filipino and West Indian homes. In other instances, however, where parents' knowledge of English is rudimentary or where they insist on speaking their home language, refusal by children to do so provides an initial indicator of dissonant acculturation. This situation was revealed in the course of qualitative interviews in immigrant homes where questions addressed to children in their parents' language were commonly responded to in English. Although the young understood perfectly what was being said to them, they refused to go along, indicating their growing distance from parents' culture.[28]

For Lourdes Alvarez, whose 11-year-old daughter Cristina spoke only Spanish before kindergarten, the effort to keep her bilingual turned into a losing battle. "She fights it," Mrs. Alvarez reported. For her part, Cristina, who says that she wants to be bilingual, protests that English just comes more easily to her. Despite her mother's attempt to force her to use Spanish, Cristina cannot write the language and barely reads it. A similar pattern is illustrated by the struggle of the Pérez-Apple family to raise their child as bilingual. A binational couple (he is American, she is Cuban), they even hired a Costa Rican nanny to speak to their son exclusively in Spanish but to no avail. "He knows he can speak English and people can understand him," Mrs. Pérez-Apple says. By an early age, he already insisted on responding in English to questions asked in Spanish, and there has been no way to budge him from this stance.[29]

Achieving fluent bilingualism is a demanding feat. It requires learning English while resisting assimilative pressures toward full monolingualism. As seen previously, only 28 percent of our sample could be considered full bilinguals by the time of high school graduation. Nationalities characterized by parents speaking English at home are naturally the least able to preserve or create bilingual fluency among children. Many Asian immigrants speak their native tongue exclusively at home but suffer from lack of external support for their languages. Asian children generally take longer to learn English, but when they do, they tend to shift to exclusive monolingualism. As shown in Table 6.3, less than 10 percent of second-generation Asians remain fluent bilinguals by their senior year of high school.

The advantage in this respect displayed by Latin American students results from a combination of factors. The fact that Spanish is a Western language with grammatical and phonetic affinities to English undoubtedly plays a major role. However, if this were the only reason for the observed differences, Haitian American students whose parents speak French or its island derivative, Creole, would also exhibit high rates of bilingualism, which is not the case. A second advantage of Spanish is its use by a large immigrant population, buttressed by institutions that include ethnic media such as newspapers, radio stations, and even major television networks.

This development affects the second generation because parents' efforts to transmit their language are not isolated but supported by a broader framework. Yet even with these outside external supports, the absorptive capacity of American culture is so powerful as to reduce fluent bilinguals to a minority among second-generation Latins. The sole exceptions are Cuban Americans attending private bilingual schools in Miami, a predictable outcome of the exceptional environment created by this ethnic enclave.

A closer look at the components of bilingualism shows that the prime reason for its relative absence is not lack of English fluency but the loss of parental languages. Table 6.4 presents scores in the English Knowledge Index and Foreign Language Knowledge Index for a detailed breakdown of immigrant nationalities represented in both our student and parental samples. In both variables, scores range between 1 and 4, with those above 3.0 reflecting good combined ability to speak, understand, read, and write the language and those above 3.5 representing close to full fluency. The table also presents the proportion of parents who report addressing their children in a language other than English at home. A first significant result is that children of every nationality score above 3.0 in English knowledge and all but four (the southeast Asian groups) score above 3.5. With few exceptions, English knowledge among the young is far superior to that of their parents. Major linguistic gaps thus separate Cambodian, Laotian, and Hmong parents from their children, and the same trend can be seen, to a lesser extent, among Vietnamese, Mexicans, and Nicaraguans.

In contrast, and despite the fact that over 70 percent of parents use a foreign language at home, not a single second-generation nationality scores above 3.5 in the Foreign Language Index, and only 11 (all Latin American) score above 3.0. Hence, *no* second-generation group on the average can be considered fluent in their parents' native tongue. This lack of knowledge of parental languages, coupled with the wide parent-child gap in English among many Asian and some Latin American nationalities, points to the likelihood of dissonant acculturation. That possibility is enhanced by the inability of some parents to learn English and the strong assimilative pressures on children. In the extreme, fluent communication across generations ceases, opening the way for affective separation and weakening of parental authority. The common com-

TABLE 6.4   SECOND-GENERATION CHILDREN'S AND
PARENTS' SCORES IN LANGUAGE COMPOSITE
INDICES, BY DETAILED NATIONAL-ORIGIN GROUPS,
1995–1996

National Origin	Children's Knowledge of English	Children's Knowledge of Foreign Language	N	Parent's Knowledge of English	Parent Speaks Foreign Language with Child (%)
		Latin America			
Argentinians	3.93	3.02	37	3.32	71
Chileans	3.86	2.97	26	2.89	79
Colombians	3.90	3.22	185	2.78	86
Costa Ricans	3.91	3.02	11	2.83	83
Cubans	3.90	3.13	968	3.10	83
Dominicans	3.80	3.09	78	2.84	88
Ecuadoreans	3.89	3.00	27	2.88	72
Guatemalans	3.89	2.85	25	2.89	67
Hondurans	3.76	3.08	42	2.87	81
Mexicans	3.62	3.33	599	2.45	85
Nicaraguans	3.78	3.23	281	2.59	95
Panamanians	3.92	2.82	15	3.75	17
Peruvians	3.88	3.13	28	3.25	80
Salvadorans	3.84	3.35	26	2.79	85
Venezuelans	3.87	3.08	13	3.33	67
Latin Americans (other)	3.90	2.84	30	3.19	70
		West Indies			
Haitians	3.87	2.44	135	2.66	77
Jamaicans	3.94	1.78	118	4.00	0
Trinidadians/other	3.95	1.58	83	3.94	2

plaint from immigrant parents that they cannot control their children because of the latter's English superiority points clearly in this direction.

Forced-March Acculturation

Would any of this have been different if my transition had been eased by a good bilingual program? I don't know but I do know I suffered in the sink-or-swim gamble I was thrown in. . . . When I sat in class those first few months, I was lost. I couldn't follow the teacher. It was complete nonsense to

TABLE 6.4   (*continued*)

National Origin	Children's Knowledge of English	Children's Knowledge of Foreign Language	N	Parent's Knowledge of English	Parent Speaks Foreign Language with Child (%)
		Asia			
Cambodians	3.38	2.40	89	1.52	99
Chinese (Hong Kong)	3.78	2.28	17	2.00	100
Chinese (People's Republic)	3.54	2.23	35	2.71	78
Chinese (Taiwan)	3.57	2.24	18	2.82	70
Filipinos	3.87	2.08	724	3.62	37
Hmong (Laos)	3.21	2.66	50	1.73	100
Indians	3.89	2.42	16	4.00	37
Japanese	3.93	2.07	24	3.05	54
Koreans	3.63	2.27	15	3.62	50
Lao (Laos)	3.37	2.42	144	1.90	99
Pakistanis	3.95	2.38	10	4.00	50
Vietnamese	3.42	2.54	310	2.32	94
Asians (other)	3.83	2.00	12	2.67	80
Middle East, Africa	3.97	1.88	42	3.50	12
Europe, Canada	3.98	2.06	55	3.96	26
Totals	3.77	2.75	4,288	2.83	73

NOTE: Range of English and foreign language knowledge are rated on a four-point index. Higher scores indicate better knowledge. See text for explanation.

me. I couldn't talk to my classmates either. Funny, huh? Actually, it was horrible. I was in a fog of depression for six months.[30]

I felt stupid and ignorant for years before learning that there was nothing abnormal with me. I learned (and then unlearned) that if I spoke Spanish I was less than the others. In the COBOL class in my first year in college, I could not understand the teacher very well. After asking him something, he answered, "You gotta be really stupid to ask that question." I dropped the course. Well, now that I am the computer expert in my office, I know that I am not stupid nor allergic to cybernetics. . . . But for a long time, I had my doubts, all because of lack of a little translation.[31]

Many immigrant children have not only learned English quickly but have also had to do it under harrowing conditions. While it could be argued that this is a natural part of the immigrant experience—the price of coming to and finding one's way in a foreign land—the fact is that these harsh experiences can produce enduring negative consequences— first, in lowered self-esteem and heightened alienation and second, in a strong tendency toward loss of fluency in the original language. As our informant put it, children are caught in a fog where confusion about self-identity and disorientation in school couple with a growing stigma about speaking a foreign language. The result is limited bilingualism, at least in the short run, as imperfect English acquisition accompanies the rapid loss of the language brought from home. Some actually remain in this situation, which for children represents a telling indicator of dissonant acculturation—being increasingly unable and unwilling to communicate with parents in their native language while still lacking full English fluency.

A strong movement has recently arisen against schooling imparted in foreign languages to immigrant students. This form of remedial schooling is erroneously called bilingual education, for it is not aimed at promoting fluent command of two languages but at mainstreaming students as soon as possible into English classes. This remedial training has been attacked by nativists as perpetuating linguistic divisions and creating a population of second-class students.[32] The proposed solution is English immersion, held to be the most effective means to promote linguistic unity. In 1998, for example, California voters approved Proposition 227, the so-called English for the Children initiative, which abolished remedial classes in favor of one-year English immersion for foreign children, followed by their transfer to regular classes.[33]

This proposition and similar proposed policies in other states reflect the vision of a uniformly monolingual country that has underlain nativist movements for over a century. These policies seek to promote English fluency at any cost, including the stigmatization and loss of other languages. The loss for children forced into such programs is double—first, in the sacrifice of valuable linguistic skills and second, in increasing distance from parents who are implicitly defined as carriers of an inferior culture. Intentionally or not, forced English immersion promotes dissonant acculturation with negative consequences that can far exceed the alleged benefits of such programs. Limited bilingualism in children is a common reflection and outcome of this situation.

An alternative to forced-march acculturation is found in programs designed to promote English fluency while supporting parental efforts toward bilingualism. Cooperation between schools and families in promoting this form of additive learning is likely to have precisely the opposite results of the subtractive approach now being implemented in California schools. More needs to be said on the question of educational policy, but first it is important to document differences among children who have achieved fluent bilingualism, limited bilinguals, and exclusive English monolinguals who are the products of the subtractive vision advocated by nativists.

Figures 6.4 and 6.5 present a profile of our sample categorized into four mutually exclusive categories. *Fluent bilinguals* are defined as respondents who know English very well and who know a foreign language at least well. *English-dominant* children have fluency in English but much weaker knowledge of a foreign language. *Foreign-dominant* children are in the opposite situation—they speak the parental language well but are less fluent in English. Finally, *limited bilinguals* have lost fluency in the home language but have not yet acquired full command of English. Figure 6.4 presents data on children's aspirations and psychosocial adjustment; Figure 6.5 describes their relationships with parents as indicators of different types of acculturation. Results are quite clear in showing a pattern of advantage for fluent bilinguals relative to other categories, especially those with limited command of both languages. In both junior and senior high school, fluent bilinguals have high educational aspirations, surpassing by a considerable margin the rest of the sample, including English monolinguals. The same result obtains for occupational aspirations although in this case the main gap is between fluent and limited bilinguals.

A third indicator of this trend is given by test scores in high school. Unlike middle schools, where taking standardized math and reading tests is compulsory, in later years students are not required to take them and do so on a voluntary basis. As a result, selectivity of these data renders them useless as indicators of school achievement. Yet the fact that some students *chose* to take the tests even when not required to do so reveals higher motivation. As results in Figure 6.4 show, fluent bilinguals surpass other language categories, including English monolinguals, in their willingness to put themselves through this trial.

Figure 6.4 presents relationships between types of language adaptation in the first survey and motivational variables in the second to establish a preliminary causal order. Yet exactly the same results emerge when we relate variables measured at the same time in time. The consistency of results within and across surveys provides an indicator of their reliability. Equally important is the association of language adaptation with two key dimensions of psychological well-being—self-esteem and depression.

Figure 6.4 Types of Language Adaptation and Their Social Psychological Correlates

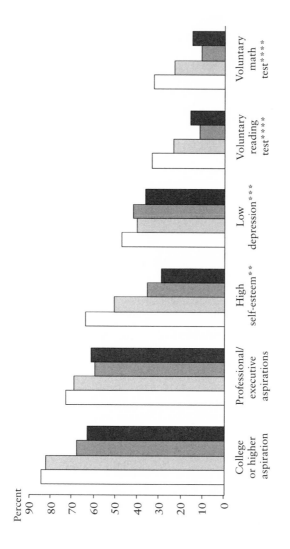

*See text for description of types of language adaptation.
**Mean scores of 3.5 or higher in Rosenberg's Self-Esteem Scale. Range is 1 (low) to 4.
***Mean scores of 1.5 or less in Center for Epidemiological Studies–Depression Subscale (CES-D). Range is 1 (low) to 4.
****Percent taking optional standardized achievement test in senior high school.

Figure 6.5   Types of Language Adaptation and Their Family
Correlates

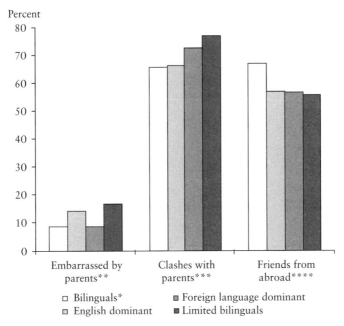

Percent

*See text for description of types of language adaptation.
**Percent of students who feel embarrassed by their parents' cultural
ways.
***Percent of students who get in trouble with parents sometimes or
frequently because of different ways of doing things.
****Percent of students whose close friends include other children of
immigrants.

These two variables were measured on the basis of standardized scales
of known reliability and validity—Rosenberg's Self-Esteem Scale and
the Center for Epidemiological Studies Short-Form Depression Scale
(CES-D). Once again, results indicate a close correspondence between
language adaptation and second-generation outcomes. Fluent bilinguals
are the best adjusted on the basis of these data. Their advantage is particularly noteworthy with regard to limited bilinguals, but it extends as
well to children who have completed the transition to monolingualism.

Despite relating language adaptation in middle school to psychosocial outcomes three years later, Figure 6.4 cannot be interpreted as a
final demonstration of causality. All that is shown by these results is that
contrary to earlier speculation, the achievement of fluent bilingualism is

not linked to negative psychosocial outcomes. On the contrary, possession of two languages is associated with higher goals for the future and better personality adjustment. One possible reason for this is that fluent bilingualism makes possible better intergenerational communication because children can talk to their parents *regardless* of the latter's English ability. Thus, even when parents' language learning lags behind, dissonant acculturation and its negative consequences can be prevented.

Figure 6.5 illustrates this possibility by relating types of language adaptation to two indicators of intergenerational dissonance in our data—whether students are embarrassed by their parents and whether they clash with their parents frequently. Figure 6.5 also presents the proportion of students who report that many or most of their friends are other children of immigrants, an indicator of selective acculturation. Results show that fluent bilinguals are the least embarrassed by their parents, have the least conflictive relationship with them, and are most prone to maintain friendships with co-ethnic children. These findings are consistent within and across the two surveys. The data thus show a clear pattern where fluency in two languages is associated with benign social and psychological outcomes. On the contrary, the rapid loss of parental languages unaccompanied by English fluency is associated with negative consequences, including poor self-esteem and a more common sense of shame at their parents' culture.

What Makes a Bilingual?

The old Jewish Market on North Collins Avenue, Miami Beach, had changed its name to Latin Market. The proprietor remained the same, but having witnessed the rapid change in the store's clientele, he decided to stock it with a new brand of ethnic products and a new name. The old Brooklyn Jewish tourist visiting the store was at a loss. A regular winter visitor to the area, he now had a hard time making himself understood. Finally, he addressed the store's owner in halting Spanish, seeking to make his wishes clear: "Yo querer un botella de vino Manischewitz y un caja de cigaros." Despite the store's name change, the owner's Spanish was even worse, so he took his customer for one of the new brand of ethnic clientele and essayed to respond in his language: "Que es lo que tu desear." Other clients were treated to the spectacle of two old New Yorkers seeking to communicate in a language that neither understood and that each presumed the other spoke.[34]

Limited bilingualism has its costs. And neither is there another kind of bilingualism for many Americans, even educated ones, for whom knowledge of a foreign language is limited to a few high school or college courses. By late high school, which is when most students are first exposed to a foreign tongue, their capacity to learn it is already limited. A noted educational analyst put the matter this way:

> During the first years of life, a child programs his brain with phonemes—or basic phonetic sounds—of the language he hears around him. If he is casually exposed to a second language, a child learns that too, programming its basic sounds into his developing brain as he does his native tongue. He will be able to speak both languages easily—and switch effortlessly from one to another. Most American school systems continue to teach foreign languages primarily in high school, years after the brain has lost its ability to learn a new language easily. It's hard going for most students. And much of what they do learn is soon forgotten once school is over.[35]

In agreement with the vision of a uniformly monolingual nation, most school systems today practice a form of subtractive bilingualism, giving native-born students only a late and rudimentary command of foreign languages while seeking to channel immigrant students who spoke them fluently in childhood into English-only classes. Adults who seek to make use of their lost or painfully acquired "second language" later in life may find themselves in a plight akin to that of our friends in the new "Latin" market. For the most part, American public schools are not the place at present to learn and preserve fluent bilingualism. The acquisition of that skill takes place in other contexts and with different institutional supports.

Table 6.5 presents a profile of some of the variables that can be plausibly associated with the onset of bilingualism. For purposes of contrast, we present their distribution both for students identified as fluent bilinguals and for those who have become English monolinguals. In line with previous results, Latin-origin students are far more likely to be bilingual than those from other nationalities. Less than 10 percent of the latter retain fluency in their parents' languages along with English; the number is more than four times greater among those whose home language is Spanish. Parental education increases English knowledge but does not affect bilingualism. On the other hand, parents' use of their own language at home does have a strong positive association with its preservation by children.

The significance of family composition is again evident in the difference between children whose parents are both foreign born and those

TABLE 6.5   PREDICTORS OF FLUENT
BILINGUALISM AND ENGLISH
MONOLINGUALISM

Predictors (1992)	Fluent Bilinguals (1995–1996)	p^1	English Dominant (1995–1996)	p^1
Sex (%)				
Male	20.8	<.01	38.5	ns
Female	25.4		40.3	
National Origin (%)				
Latin American	34.9	<.001	27.9	<.001
Other	7.4		55.0	
Father's Education (%)				
Less than high school	26.0	ns	28.2	<.001
High school graduate[2]	22.4		46.0	
College graduate	27.0		45.3	
Mother's Education (%)				
Less than high school	24.4	ns	29.3	<.001
High school graduate[2]	24.9		43.4	
College graduate	25.3		49.8	
Foreign Language Use at Home (%)				
Seldom	7.8		58.1	
From time to time	13.7	<.001	49.5	<.001
Often	22.2		46.5	
Always	29.7		28.2	
Close Friends from Abroad (%)				
None	14.3	<.001	43.7	<.01
Some	17.9		41.7	
Many or most	26.9		37.8	

with one American-born parent. The lesser prevalence of bilingualism
in the latter group is partially attributable to the lower likelihood of a
foreign language being spoken at home. Results also show a noticeable
disparity in the ways that school ethnic composition relates to language.
A heavier proportion of Latin-origin students significantly increases the

TABLE 6.5   (*continued*)

Predictors (1992)	Fluent Bilinguals (1995–1996)	p^1	English Dominant (1995–1996)	p^1
Length of U. S. Residence (%)				
U. S. born	24.5	ns	47.0	<.001
10 years or more	20.8		43.0	
9 years or less	23.2		23.5	
Parents' Birthplace				
Both foreign born	24.8	<.001	37.0	<.001
One parent U. S. born	13.0		54.8	
Mean proportion of Latin students in school[3]	62.0	<.001	38.1	<.01
Mean proportion of Asian students in school[4]	8.2	<.001	17.6	ns
Attends Private Bilingual School (%)				
No	22.2	<.001	40.2	<.001
Yes	47.8		20.8	
Totals (%)	23.2		39.4	
N	1,220		2,076	

NOTE: This table utilizes fluent bilingualism and English monolinualism as the types of language adaptation ascertained during the second survey in 1995–1996. See Figure 6.4 for full sample distribution. Types other than those listed in the columns are omitted from this analysis.

[1]Probability of differences being due to chance. Mean differences are calculated relative to the total sample. Percentage differences are calculated relative to the average within each language type. ns: not significant.

[2]Includes some college.

[3]Mean for the total sample is 45.2. Tests of significance are computed relative to this figure.

[4]Mean for the total sample is 15.3. Tests of significance are computed relative to this figure.

chances of fluent bilingualism and decreases those of monolingualism, but a higher proportion of Asians has the opposite result. This pattern again points to the importance of lack of a common language among Asian students. Private bilingual schools also increase bilingualism, although in our sample they are limited to Cuban and other Latin students in Miami. Actual effects of these schools must therefore be untangled from those attributable to their ethnic composition.

These preliminary results pave the way for a more detailed analysis of what makes a bilingual. For this purpose, we ran a series of logistic regressions with fluent bilingualism in the year of high school graduation as the dependent variable. Predictors were all measured in junior high school to establish clear time order between variables. We also limited this set of predictors to objective characteristics of the student, the family, and the school to avoid the problem of reverse causality with attitudinal and other subjective predictors. For purposes of clarity, significant logistic coefficients are translated into net probabilities. The number of asterisks following each Wald statistic indicates the relative strength of each effect, controlling for other variables.

Consistent with the theoretical framework guiding the study, we included a series of parental variables as predictors. Parental socioeconomic status is a composite standardized index of parental education, occupational status, and home ownership. This index is a reliable and statistically well-behaved measure yielding more consistent results than its individual components. Family composition is represented by two variables: first, nativity of parents (both parents foreign born versus one native born) and second, frequent use of a foreign language by intact families. We reason that the support provided by families for language maintenance ought to be most evident in homes with both biological parents present. Since nativity of parents is controlled, this effect is interpretable as reflecting the influence of linguistic practices in intact families where both parents are foreign born.[36] National origin also plays an important role in language acculturation, but as we have seen, the decisive cleavage in this case is between children whose parents speak Spanish and all others. This influence is represented by the dichotomous variable *Latin* in the following equations. Finally, in agreement with the reviewed literature on the relationship between academic achievement and language, we include GPA in 1992 as a possible influence on bilingualism three years later.

Table 6.6 presents nested regressions, with the first including effects of individual and family variables and the second adding the influence of school type and composition. Panel I of the table shows the powerful effect of national origin. Controlling for other variables, a Latin background remains the strongest predictor; Latin-origin students in our sample have a remarkable 51 percent greater probability than the rest of retaining their parental language. The next pair of effects are of opposite signs, but both reveal the importance of family composition. When one parent is U.S. born, the probability of fluent bilingualism drops

TABLE 6.6 DETERMINANTS OF BILINGUAL FLUENCY IN LATE ADOLESCENCE, CHILDREN OF IMMIGRANTS, 1995–1996

Predictors (1992)	I Logistic Coefficient	I Wald Statistic[1]	I Probability[2]	II Logistic Coefficient	II Wald Statistic[1]	II Probability[2]
Sex (female)	.301	15.3**	.06	.362	20.8**	.07
Age	-.002	.5	ns	.006	.0	ns
National origin (Latin)	2.240	518.5***	.51	2.023	274.0**	.46
Length of U.S. residence[3]	-.030	6.8*	-.01	-.031	7.5*	-.01
U.S.-born parent[4]	-.637	23.0**	-.09	-.545	16.4**	-.08
Foreign home language[5]	.309	15.7**	.06	.323	16.9**	.06
Number of friends from abroad	.229	11.1*	.04	.165	5.5*	.03
Grade point average	.132	8.1*	.02	.125	7.1*	.02
Parental socioeconomic status	.173	10.7*	.03	.122	4.9*	.02
Percent Latin students in school				.004	5.1*	.001
Percent Asian students in school				.000	.0	ns
Private bilingual school				.614	9.8*	.13
Constant	-3.545			-3.653		
Model chi square (degrees of freedom)	823.86 (9)			849.76 (12)		
Significance	.0001[6]			.0001[6]		

[1] Measure of strength of effects. Higher numbers indicate more reliable or stronger effects.
[2] Probability of increase/decrease in bilingual fluency associated with a unit change of each predictor, net of the others.
[3] Years.
[4] Children of one foreign-born and one U.S.-born parent.
[5] Use of foreign home language "always" or "often" in families with both biological parents present.
[6] Probability of model predictive improvement being due to chance is less than 1 in 10,000.
ns: Statistically nonsignificant effect.
* Moderate effect (coefficient exceeds twice its standard error).
** Strong effect (coefficient exceeds 4 times its standard error).
*** Very strong effect (coefficient exceeds 10 times its standard error).

markedly, even after controlling for home language use. On the other hand, when both parents always use a foreign language at home, chances for bilingualism increase. Jointly, these effects highlight the contrast between mixed (immigrant/native) marriages that tend to provide contradictory cultural messages and those in which both parents reinforce maintenance of key elements of their culture.

With other factors controlled, U.S. residence leads to a net decline in the probability of bilingualism of about 1 percent per additional year in the country. On the other hand, parental socioeconomic status contributes to language preservation. Since, as seen in Chapter 4, immigrant economic status increases with years of U.S. residence, the parental socioeconomic status effect is interpretable as partially countermanding the passage of time. In other words, if additional years of U.S. residence promote the loss of foreign languages, they also improve the resources of immigrant families to foster their preservation.

An important finding in this model is the effect of gender. On the average, girls are approximately 6 percent more likely to be bilingual than boys of similar class, family, and ethnic backgrounds. This effect, one of the strongest in the model, reflects differential patterns of socialization of both sexes, as discussed in Chapter 3. Girls are commonly more sheltered and tend to spend greater time at home.[37] Since a large majority of immigrant families speak a foreign language, females are naturally more subject to these influences and hence more likely to retain their parents' language. The finding fits the theoretical expectation of stronger bilingualism among youths less subject to dissonant acculturation.

Panel II in Table 6.6 adds school influences on bilingualism. In particular, it seeks to answer the question of whether the strong effect of national origin is due to compositional differences in the ethnic makeup of schools. It is possible that at least part of the influence of Latin origin is mediated by the supportive environment provided by co-ethnic peers and by bilingual instruction. Results in Table 6.6 shows that this is the case, as the strength of the national origin coefficient drops by half. The reduction is entirely due to the presence of other Latin students and enrollment in private bilingual schools. Each 10 percent increase in the proportion of other Latins increases bilingualism by 1 percent; enrollment in bilingual schools leads to a sharp 13 percent increase in the probability of retaining both languages.

Though reduced in half, the coefficient associated with Latin origin remains very strong, reflecting an influence that transcends that of family and school. In other words, children whose cultural background includes Spanish are more likely than other second-generation youths to preserve that language, regardless of what school they attend or what type of family they come from. Based on model coefficients,[38] a female Latin student is 53 percent more likely to be bilingual than a non-Latin male. This figure increases to 62 percent if her parents speak Spanish at home and if she has many co-ethnic friends and to 75 percent if she happens to be enrolled in a bilingual private school. By contrast, the number of Asian students in school has no effect on bilingualism. The absence of a common language among Asian-origin students dilutes whatever support a co-ethnic presence could provide for language preservation. Despite parental efforts in this direction, no Asian language compares at present with Spanish in its intergenerational resilience and external support.

Despite the time order between variables, the causal line between some predictors and fluent bilingualism can still be reasonably challenged because of the possibility that the relationship was already present in early adolescence. For example, children may have had foreign friends in junior high school because they were able to speak their language, but these friendships might not have fostered or strengthened bilingualism by themselves. Similarly, the correlation between language knowledge and grades could have existed earlier, and academic performance may not produce further increases in bilingualism.[39]

To examine this possibility, we introduce bilingual fluency in junior high school as an additional predictor. Introduction of this variable leads to a change in the interpretation of other coefficients. The latter cease to be net effects on language adaptation and become effects on the *change* in language ability in the years between both surveys. Results are presented in Table 6.7. They show the same pattern of effects noted earlier, although some of the coefficients become attenuated. Panel I of the table, including all individual and family predictors, indicates that national origin, gender, foreign language at home, co-ethnic friends, and parental status all contribute to improve bilingual fluency over time. On the other hand, the effect of academic performance is reduced. Although the sign of the coefficient is positive, the reduction suggests that a good part of the observed effect of grades on bilingualism could be due to their earlier association.

As in the previous analysis, length of U.S. residence and having a U.S.-born parent reduce the likelihood of bilingual fluency over time. Thus, a native-born 17-year-old with one U.S.-born parent is about 25

TABLE 6.7 DETERMINANTS OF CHANGE IN BILINGUAL FLUENCY DURING HIGH SCHOOL, CHILDREN OF IMMIGRANTS, 1995–1996

	I			II		
Predictors (1992)	Logistic Coefficient	Wald Statistic	Probability	Logistic Coefficient	Wald Statistic	Probability
Fluent bilingual (T1)	1.902	466.3***	.44	1.889	456.1***	7.43
Sex (female)	.241	8.2*	.05	.291	11.5*	.06
Age	.004	.0	ns	.011	.1	ns
National origin (Latin)	1.792	294.5***	.41	1.672	169.2***	.38
Length of U.S. residence	-.035	8.2*	-.01	-.036	8.8*	-.01
U.S.-born parent	-.545	14.4**	-.08	-.487	11.2*	-.08
Foreign home language	.319	14.2**	.06	.327	14.6**	.06
Number of friends from abroad	.145	3.8*	.03	.102	1.8	ns
Grade point average	.064	1.6	ns	.055	1.2	ns
Parental socioeconomic status	.127	4.9*	.02	.094	2.5	ns
Percent Latin students in school				.003	1.9	ns
Percent Asian students in school				.001	.1	ns
Private bilingual school				.524	5.9*	.11
Constant	-3.382			-3.512		
Model chi square (degrees of freedom)	1,320.10 (10)			1,333.69 (13)		
Significance	.0001			.0001		

NOTE: See Table 6.6 and text for explanation of the meaning of coefficients.

percent less likely to maintain such fluency by the time of high school graduation. On the other hand, a child of high-status parents who speaks a foreign language at home and who has many co-ethnic friends has an approximately 16 percent greater probability of improving his or her bilingual fluency.[40]

The introduction of school variables in Panel II of Table 6.7 reduces the influence of parental status and co-ethnic friendships. This result suggests that parental status increases bilingualism over time by helping place children in the appropriate school contexts, which also facilitate greater co-ethnic friendships. Having enrolled in a private bilingual institution in junior high school increases the probability of bilingualism by 11 percent. This type of schooling as well as nationality, gender, and family composition represent the most consistent predictors in the entire analysis. Together, they provide a fairly consistent answer to the question of what "makes" a bilingual: Children of two foreign-born parents who have remained together and speak their language at home are more likely to be fluent bilinguals; that likelihood increases among females and with enrollment in schools that explicitly promote selective acculturation through preservation of the parental culture.[41]

Despite these various positive influences, we must return to the fact that by age 18 or so, second-generation bilingualism is exceptional. Among the languages lost to the 85 percent of non-Latin students in our sample who have become English monolinguals or limited bilinguals are French, Chinese, Portuguese, Japanese, Vietnamese, Cambodian, Korean, and Tagalog, tongues spoken by millions of people. This loss affects individuals who did not have to learn these languages from scratch but inherited them from birth as a gift. Even among Latin-origin children, approximately half have lost fluency in Spanish, and only 40 percent preserve it along with English. The dissipation of these resources constitutes a cultural loss for individuals compelled to join a monolingual world and for an economy whose global interdependence demands increasing multilingual competence.

A Game of Mirrors: Language Instruction and Types of Acculturation

> There are 600,000 Hispanics in Miami, and we have a hard time hiring a person who can write a proper business letter in Spanish.[42]
> — Miami businesswoman

They have become Americans in their own eyes, but they do not have the advantages of white Americans. So, they lose the direction that their Vietnamese culture can give them. Since they do not know where they are going, they just drift.[43]

—Joseph Vuong, school counselor, New Orleans

Anyone who has traveled to Europe knows that young people all over Europe are fluent in two and often three languages. I see no reason why our children should not be their equals. Some children already come to school with the ability to speak two languages. We should build on this linguistic base and recognize that our nation will be better for it in the global environment.[44]

—Secretary of Education Richard W. Riley, on California Proposition 227

Losing a language is also losing part of one's self that is linked to one's identity and cultural heritage. When children move decisively in this direction while parents remain steeped in their own language and culture, the conditions for dissonant acculturation are set. Communication across generations becomes more difficult, and the resultant gap reduces parental authority and control. As a recent study of Khmer (Cambodian) immigrants and their children concludes, the difference between successful and downward assimilation in the second generation commonly lies in the ability of parents to keep up with and guide their children's acculturation. The study offers vivid examples of what happens when communication breaks down, as in this statement from a 32-year-old Cambodian woman: "I have a niece living in East Boston who knows only English. I cannot talk to her because I don't speak English. . . . Those children act and talk like Americans. They eat American food like pizza and McDonald's . . . and they say to their parents, "I don't want to live with you; I want to move in with a roommate!"[45]

As we saw earlier in the chapter, a foreign language is spoken in most immigrant homes, and children claim at least some knowledge of this language. Thus, parent-child communication does not commonly reach the complete breakdown suggested by this example. Most parents learn at least some words of English, and most children preserve some facility in the parental tongue, leading to constrained but not ruptured communication between them. Still, extreme cases are important because they represent the logical end point of acculturative dissonance. Figure 6.6 presents the theoretical relationship between language ability and types of acculturation across generations. Since most parents are not fluent in English and most children have ceased to be fluent in their

Figure 6.6   Generational Language Knowledge and Types of Acculturation

Parents' Knowledge of English	Children's Knowledge of Parental Language		
	None	*Limited*	*Fluent*
None	Dissonant acculturation and role reversal	Partial dissonant acculturation	Selective acculturation
Limited	Partial dissonant acculturation	Partial consonant acculturation	Selective acculturation
Fluent	Consonant acculturation	Consonant acculturation	Selective acculturation

NOTE: See Chapter 3 for explanation of types of acculturation.

parental tongue, most cases actually fall in the intermediate categories of partial dissonant and partial consonant acculturation.

The figure makes two other important points: First, when parents are fluent in English, the expected outcome is consonant acculturation regardless of children's language loss. Parents are able to accompany the acculturation of the children and to maintain open channels of communication in all circumstances. Second, when children are fully bilingual, selective acculturation is the expected outcome, regardless of parents' language learning. Children in this situation preserve significant elements of the parental culture as well as full communication with their parents. The point is exemplified by the case of Aura Lila Marín, the Cuban mother in the preceding chapter, who, despite her own lack of English, was still able to support her daughter and help her overcome learning difficulties because of the child's own command of Spanish.[46]

Extreme cases of acculturative dissonance are illustrated by the examples of the Hmong family of Pao Yang and the Mexican single-parent household of Mrs. Santos in Chapter 5. Khmer American families also provide frequent and poignant examples.[47] For the most part, however, second-generation youths retain some knowledge of their parents' tongue, enough for limited exchange at home but not sufficient for public communication. This limited fluency is what the Miami businesswoman quoted at the beginning of this section deplored in her complaint about the inability of young Hispanics to write a proper letter in Spanish.

Limited bilingualism and dissonant acculturation are partly traceable to the inability of public schools to support immigrants' efforts to preserve their language. In the game of mirrors that the debate on language has become, *bilingual education* has come to mean "temporary instruction in a foreign language for children unable to speak English." This is not bilingual education at all but remedial training geared toward mainstreaming immigrant students as soon as possible. Use of the term *bilingual education* in this context confuses two objectives: first, how to teach English to foreign children so that they can join regular classes and second, how to create or preserve fluency in a second language.

True bilingual education must start early, in elementary school if possible, and involve the teaching of selected subjects in a foreign language. This type of education can be made available not only to children of immigrants but to children of natives as well, as a means to acquire a valuable lifelong skill. Only in this fashion will the alternative vision outlined by Secretary of Education Riley at the start of this section be implemented: a society where universal English competence is accompanied by fluent knowledge of various foreign languages by sizable groups of citizens.

Despite the personal and societal advantages of multilingualism, the subtractive vision promoted by U.S. English and other nativist organizations continues to correspond to the reality on the ground. For the foreseeable future, public education and social pressures in American society will continue to extinguish foreign languages at a brisk pace. The corresponding profile for the new second generation will feature a minority of bilinguals who have managed to preserve foreign language fluency on the strength of family and community social ties; a majority of English monolinguals with residual and declining knowledge of their parents' languages; and a sizable group for whom school immersion programs have produced the loss of those languages without full acquisition of English. The psychosocial and educational consequences of these different types of language adaptation are examined in the coming chapters.

Chapter 7

DEFINING THE SITUATION
The Ethnic Identities of Children of Immigrants

"Being American means that you feel like you're the norm," one of my
friends tells me. . . . [But] in a splintered society, what does one assimilate
to? . . . I want to figure out, more urgently than before, where I belong in
this America that's made up of so many subAmericas. I want, somehow,
to give up the condition of being a foreigner. . . . I have to make a shift in
my innermost ways. I have to translate myself.
—Eva Hoffman, *Lost in Translation*, pp. 202, 210–11

Stephanie Bernal liked to call herself a "mixed chocolate swirl." Half
Latina and half Anglo by her reckoning, the well-acculturated southern
California native and high school senior had not had more than a fleet-
ing and apolitical connection with Mexico, her mother's homeland, until
Proposition 187 exacerbated ethnic tensions in California in the autumn
of 1994. The measure aimed to "Save Our State," as Proposition 187
was called, by denying social and nonemergency health care services—
and access to public schools—to undocumented immigrants and their
children. It also required school districts to verify the legal status of students' parents or guardians and to report to state officials any persons
suspected of being in the United States unlawfully so that they may be
detained and deported. Stephanie reacted by joining with friends who
were organizing her school's anti-187 movement and by affirming the
identity of her maternal ancestry: "When we get together to talk about it,
we speak Spanish and just feel good about being Mexican."[1]

The week before, more than 70,000 people had marched in protest
through downtown Los Angeles—the largest such march in memory,
which was heavily covered on television and by the news media—
spawning subsequent marches and student walkouts in local campuses.

To the marchers, who included many second-generation youths from area high schools, Proposition 187 was an affront to their parents, their friends, and their neighbors, according to local news accounts of the events at the time.[2] Parents, too, joined in some of the marches or encouraged their children's participation, making the initiative an issue through which the budding teenage activists could bridge the generational divide and express themselves in solidarity with their parents.

Referring to "that commercial," a frequently repeated ad on television that showed people running across the California-Mexico border, sophomore Jorge Higareda complained, "They show Mexicans, but they don't show Asians coming over in boats or anybody else. It's like we're the only ones coming here. And then they call us illegal." A student at another high school, Vicky Velasco, reported that "this is mostly a Latino school and everyone's proud of their heritage—they want to defend it." And in yet another school, a 16-year-old Armenian immigrant, Serob Zetilyn, was among 200 students who walked out of school in protest, explaining that "I've got a lot of friends who will have to quit school if Prop 187 passes because they're illegal. Plus classes will get smaller and some teachers will get fired."[3] In that protest, as in the huge march that preceded it, the teenagers carried banners saying "No on 187"—and waved Mexican flags.

Proposition 187 won in a landslide, getting 59 percent of the statewide vote; in populous San Diego and Orange counties, south of Los Angeles, the measure passed with 67 percent of the votes cast.[4] But Stephanie's Mexican ethnic self-identity was "thickened" in the process, a sense of belonging made more salient than ever as she came to define who she was and where she came from in opposition to who and what she was not.[5] The divisive campaign had the unintended consequences of accentuating group differences, heightening group consciousness of those differences, and promoting ethnic group solidarity and political mobilization.

This process of forging a reactive ethnicity in the face of perceived threats, persecution, and exclusion is not uncommon.[6] On the contrary, it is one mode of ethnic identity formation, highlighting the role of a hostile context of reception in accounting for the rise rather than the erosion of ethnicity. A few years earlier, second-generation Korean Americans saw over 2,300 Korean-owned stores in Los Angeles's Koreatown targeted by African Americans and burned during the rioting that followed a not-guilty verdict in the 1992 trial of four white police officers charged with the brutal beating of a black motorist. The event caused many young Koreans born or raised in the United States to become self-conscious about their common fate and distinctiveness as Koreans. They reacted by participating in multigenerational solidarity rallies and by moving to organize politically to protect the interests of their parents' generation and the image of the group in the larger society.[7]

To cite a third example, in 1980, the chaotic boatlift of 125,000 Cubans from the port of Mariel to southern Florida—and the deliberate placement aboard some of the boats of exconvicts and mental patients by the Castro government—tarnished the "success story" image of Cuban exiles in the United States.[8] *The Miami Herald* launched a campaign against the exodus, and as an outgrowth of these events, a grassroots movement of native whites in Miami was organized to put an anti-bilingual referendum on the November 1980 ballot, which was passed overwhelmingly. That referendum victory marked both the highpoint of the Anglo-centered effort to hang on to local hegemony and the onset of a process of reactive formation among Cuban Americans. As a Cuban-American Miami official put it at the time, "The antibilingual referendum . . . was a slap in our face. People began to feel 'more Cuban than anyone.'" The unintended consequence of the establishment's campaign was to transform the exile community, which until then had concerned itself largely with events in Cuba, into a self-conscious ethnic group that went on to organize effectively for local political competition.[9]

Sites of Belonging: The Complex Allegiances of Children of Immigrants

Developing a Self

In contrast, conventional accounts of identity shifts among the descendants of European immigrants, conceived as part of a larger, linear process of assimilation, pointed to the thinning of their ethnic identities in the United States. For children and grandchildren of European immigrants, one outcome of widespread acculturation, social mobility, and intermarriage with the native population is that ethnic identity became an optional leisure-time form of symbolic ethnicity.[10] As the boundaries of those identities become fuzzier and less salient, less relevant to everyday social life, the sense of belonging and connection to an ancestral past faded "into the twilight of ethnicity," in Richard Alba's vivid phrase.[11]

This mode of ethnic identity formation, however, was never solely a simple linear function of socioeconomic status and degree of acculturation—that is, of the development of linguistic and other cultural similarities with the dominant group—but hinged also on the context of reception and the degree of discrimination experienced by the subordinate group. Milton Gordon, in his seven-stage portrayal of assimilation in American life, saw "identificational assimilation"—a self-definition as an unhyphenated American—as the culmination of a complex sequence made possible only if and when it was accompanied by an absence of prejudice and discrimination in the core society.[12] Whether ethnicity will become similarly optional—a matter of individual choice—for the descendants of immigrants who are today variously classified as nonwhite or whether they will be collectively channeled into enduring racially marked subordinate statuses remain open empirical questions.

Drawing on the European experience and on the eve of the new immigration from Asia and Latin America, the prevailing view of the matter was framed succinctly by Nahirny and Fishman: "The erosion of ethnicity and ethnic identity experienced by most (but not all) American ethnic groups takes place in the course of three generations . . . ethnic heritage, including the ethnic mother tongue, usually ceases to play any viable role in the life of the third generation."[13] However, compared with language loyalty and language shift, generational shifts in ethnic self-identification are more conflictual and complex. To those authors, the "murky concept of ethnic identification" did not lend itself to intergenerational analysis along a unidimensional attitudinal continuum since "fathers, sons, and grandsons may differ among themselves not only in the *degree* but also in the *nature* of their identification with ethnicity."[14]

Indeed, as was the case with respect to language maintenance and language shift, revisited in the previous chapter, the decisive turning point for change in ethnic and national self-identities can be expected to take place in the second, not in the first, generation. For the children, the process of becoming American today has itself taken a new turn and may now include the adoption or rejection of such constructed pan-ethnic categories as Hispanic and Asian/Pacific Islander, which lump together scores of nationalities into one-size-fits-all minority-group labels.[15] Relative to the first generation, the process of ethnic self-identification of second-generation children is more complex and often entails the juggling of competing allegiances and attachments. Situated within two cultural worlds, they must define themselves in relation to multiple reference groups (sometimes in two countries and in two languages) and to the classifications into which they are placed by their native peers, schools, the ethnic community, and the larger society.

Pressure from peers and from parents can tighten the tug-of-war of ethnic and national loyalties, contributing unwittingly to a sense of marginality. Thus, a young Korean woman feels the sting of being called a "twinkie" ("yellow on the outside, white on the inside") by co-ethnics during her freshman year in college "just because I grew up in a white suburb and was a cheerleader," while her mother does not let her forget that she has to marry a Korean. More complicated is the identity juggling act of 17-year-old José Mendoza, a U.S.-born, Spanish-speaking Dominican who is not black enough for many African Americans, not light enough for most Hispanics, and is advised by his parents to "marry light." The way he figures it, "From the inside we're Dominicans; from the outside we're black." And while with his friends he talks mostly in "black Spanglish"—a mix of Spanish and hip-hop English— he feels that "I'm still part Dominican. That's my nationality. If you become African American you give your nationality away. That's like saying you're betraying your country."[16]

Youths see and compare themselves with those around them, based on their social similarity or dissimilarity with the reference groups that most directly affect their experiences—especially with regard to such socially visible and categorized markers as gender, phenotype, language, and nationality.[17] Their social identities, forged in terms of those contrasts with others, represent the way they self-consciously define the situation in which they find themselves and construct an ongoing account of who "we"—and "they"—are. Ethnic identification begins with the application of a label to oneself in a cognitive process of self-categorization, involving not only a claim to membership in a group or category but also a contrast of one's group or category with other groups or categories. Such self-definitions also carry affective meaning, implying a psychological bond with others that tends to serve psychologically protective functions.[18]

For majority-group youths in a socially supportive context, ethnic self-identity tends to be taken for granted and is not salient, but a dissimilar context heightens the salience of ethnicity and of ethnic boundaries.[19] People whose ethnic, racial, or other social markers place them in a minority status in their group or community are more likely to be self-conscious of those characteristics. Youths may cope with the psychological pressure produced by such differences by seeking to reduce conflict and to assimilate within the relevant social context—the modal response of the children of European immigrants in the American experience. An alternative reaction may lead to the rise and reaffirmation of ethnic solidarity and self-consciousness, as exemplified by Stephanie Bernal in the vignette sketched earlier. For Stephanie, the newfound sense of belonging she experienced in joining the movement against Proposition 187 helped dissolve the ambiguity and marginality of a "mixed chocolate swirl" identity.

Past Research

A variety of field studies have sought to portray the patterning of these paths to identity resolution in the second generation. Such adaptations have been observed for the same ethnic group, in the same ethnic neighborhood, in the same school, and even in the same family. In a social psychological study of second-generation Italian immigrants in New Haven in the late 1930s, Irvin Child described three main modes of reaction to the dilemma of remaining within the sphere of the immigrant family or breaking out of it altogether: the *rebel* (who assimilated into the American milieu), the *in-group* type (who retained an Italian ethnicity), and the *apathetic* or marginal reaction, each shaped by a set of centripetal and centrifugal social and psychological forces.[20] Writing during World War II, when the United States was at war with Italy, Child was prescient in his analysis of the likely effects of inclusionary versus exclusionary contexts of reception:

> If during the present period, the general American population encourages people of Italian origin to regard themselves as Americans and really offers them the full rewards of membership in American society, the rebel reaction should be by far the most frequent, and adoption of American culture traits should therefore proceed at a tremendous rate. It is also predicted that, if during this period of war, the non-Italian members of the population uniformly suspect Italian Americans of treasonable activity and do not offer them the full rewards of membership in American society . . . the in-group reaction will be very frequent and a revival of Italian culture will therefore appear.[21]

Half a century later, Mary Waters's study of the ethnic and racial identities adopted by second-generation West Indian and Haitian-origin adolescents in New York City also discerned a trio of adaptations, but in this case breaking out of the immigrant circle meant joining an African-American milieu, which was perceived by their parents as tantamount to downward assimilation. Waters describes the formation of three main identity types: a black American *racial* identity (among children who saw more racial discrimination and limited opportunities for blacks in the United States); an *ethnic*, or hyphenated-national, identity (among those who saw more opportunities and rewards for individual effort, had views consonant with their parents' outlook, and strongly distanced themselves from African Americans); and an unhyphenated *immigrant* identity (typical of more recently arrived teens who identified proudly with their birthplace and retained strong family roots in the islands). Parents' social class background and social networks, family structure, and the type of school the child attended were the main factors that, in interaction with the way race is defined in the United States, shaped the type of identity developed by these youths.[22]

Back west, on a related vein, fieldwork in the 1980s with Mexican-descent students in a California high school distinguished five different ethnic identity types. These ranged from recently arrived *Mexicanos* and longer-resident bilingual Mexican immigrants, who retained their attachment to their origins and did especially well in school, to assimilated U.S.-born Mexican Americans and the more troubled second- and third-generation Chicanos and *cholos*—all of whom differed profoundly in their achievement and aspirations.[23] Other field studies of Mexican-origin youths have observed that even in the same family, each child may resolve identity issues and conflicts differently and occupy a spectrum from *cholo* to anglicized, from conventionally conformist to gang member.[24]

In the remainder of this chapter, we examine factors shaping ethnic self-identification in our sample of second-generation youths in late adolescence. The way that these youths define themselves is significant, revealing much about their social attachments as well as how and where they perceive themselves to fit in the society of which they are the newest members. We expect that the processes of language learning and acculturation, discussed in the previous chapter, will be accompanied by changes in the character and salience of ethnicity—ranging from "linear" to "reactive" forms, from "thick" to "thin" identities—and hence by divergent modes of self-identification.

In particular, we address the following questions: What are their ethnic self-identities? How salient or important are they, and how have they shifted over time? What characteristics distinguish the different types of self-identities from each other? And among those characteristics, which are the main predictors of different types? In agreement with the theoretical model outlined in Chapter 3, we expect that modes of incorporation of parents, their socioeconomic achievements in the

United States, the composition of the family, and the types of acculturation undergone by these children will bear on their self-identification
and its changes over time.

Who Am I? Patterns of Ethnic Self-Identification

In both the 1992 and 1995–1996 surveys, an open-ended question was
asked to ascertain the respondent's ethnic self-identity.[25] No closed categories or checklists were provided, requiring the respondents to write
their answers in their own words and in their own hand. Those written
self-designations were then coded and quantified, and they have generated the main outcomes that we seek to describe and explain here. From
the variety of responses given, four mutually exclusive types of ethnic self-
identities became apparent, which accounted for over 95 percent of the
answers given in both surveys.[26] These four types were classified as follows: 1) a foreign national-origin identity (e.g., Jamaican, Nicaraguan,
Cambodian); 2) a hyphenated American identity, explicitly recognizing a
single foreign national origin (e.g., Cuban American, Filipino American,
Vietnamese American); 3) a plain American national identity, without a
hyphen; and 4) a panethnic minority-group identity (e.g., Hispanic,
Latino, Chicano, black, Asian).

The first two of these types identify with the immigrant experience
and original homeland, if at different degrees of closeness, whereas the
last two types are exclusively identities "made in the USA." The first
three also involve chiefly national identifications (past or present or a
bridging of both); the fourth reflects a denationalized identification
with racial-ethnic minorities in the U.S. and self-conscious differences in
relation to the white Anglo population. We focus the following analysis
on the distribution of the CILS sample across these four types and its
determinants.

Ethnic Identity Shifts

Figure 7.1 presents the frequency distribution of the results from both
surveys for the longitudinal sample as a whole.[27] In the 1992 survey,
when these youths were in the eighth and ninth grades, just over a quarter (27.5 percent) identified by foreign national origin, a plurality (40.8
percent) chose a hyphenated American identification, over a tenth (12.6
percent) identified as American, and one in six (15.8 percent) selected a

Figure 7.1   Ethnic Self-Identity Shifts among Children of Immigrants,
1992 to 1995–1996

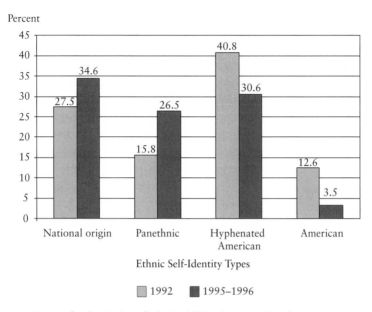

Percent

NOTE: See text for description of ethnic self-identity types. Not shown are mixed identities chosen by about 4 percent of the respondents in both surveys. *N* 5 4,288.

panethnic identity. By the 1995–1996 survey, as they were finishing high school, over a third (34.6 percent) of the same respondents now identified by national or ethnic origin; less than a third (30.6 percent) chose a hyphenated American identification, only 3.5 percent identified as American, and over a quarter (26.5 percent) selected a panethnic label.

Figure 7.2 breaks down the results for the specific types of panethnic identities reported in both surveys. Each type except Chicano[28] (which decreased from 2.2 percent to 0.8 percent) reflected increases during this period: Hispanic (or Hispanic American) was reported by 12 percent of the sample in the first survey and by 18 percent in the follow-up; a Latino self-designation was selected by a much smaller number of youths of Latin American origin, but it increased more rapidly from 0.5 to 1.4 percent.[29] While hardly any youth had identified as Asian or Asian American in the first survey (0.3 percent), that category grew noticeably to 4.5 percent in the second survey.

Figure 7.2   Percent of Children of Immigrants Selecting Various Types of
Panethnic Identities, 1992 and 1995–1996

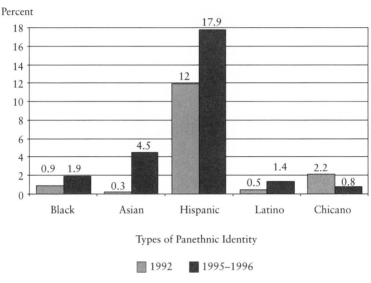

NOTE: See text for description of panethnic self-identity types.
N 5 4,288.

These results show substantial change over time, underscoring the malleable character of ethnicity. The magnitude of the change, however, is moderate: Nearly half (44 percent) of the youths reported exactly the same ethnic self-identity in their written responses to the open-ended question in the follow-up survey. This degree of stability takes on added significance when one considers that several years had passed between surveys, spanning a relatively volatile developmental period from middle to late adolescence in changing cultural contexts. If ethnic identity does not emerge here as a fixed characteristic, then neither is it so fluid as to fit what E. L. Doctorow's character Billy Bathgate called his "license-plate theory of identification"—the idea that "maybe all identification is temporary because you went through a life of changing situations."[30]

Still, the fact that over half of the respondents reported a change in their ethnic self-definitions in the span between surveys underscores the flexible character of this dimension. Moreover, the direction of the shift is noteworthy. If the rapid shift to English, documented in the previous chapter, was to have been accompanied by a similar acculturative shift in ethnic identity, then we should have seen an increase over time in the proportion of youths identifying themselves as American, with or without a hyphen, and a decrease in the proportion retaining an attachment to a foreign national identity. But as shown in Figure 7.1, results of the 1995 survey point in exactly the opposite direction. In 1992, over 53 percent identified as American or hyphenated American, but only 34.1 percent did so three years later—a net *loss* of nearly 20 percentage points. Meanwhile, both the foreign national–origin and panethnic identifications combined for a net *gain* of almost 20 percentage points. The shift, therefore, has not been toward mainstream identities but toward a more militant reaffirmation of the immigrant identity for some groups (notably Mexicans and Filipinos in California and Haitians and Nicaraguans in Florida) and toward panethnic minority-group identities for others. In the latter case, second-generation youths seemed to become increasingly aware of and adopt the ethnoracial markers in which they are persistently classified by the schools and other U.S. institutions. As will be seen next, how and why this occurred is a complex story.

Stability and Salience

Table 7.1 presents a detailed cross-tabulation of these results. For each of the identity types chosen in 1992, the table shows the proportion of respondents who reported exactly the same identity in 1995–1996 (a measure of the stability of that identity) as well as the proportions who shifted to a different type of ethnic self-identification. As Table 7.1 shows, 57.7 percent of the youths who identified by their own or their parents' foreign national origin in 1992 did so again three years later (the most stable and fixed type of self-identification), compared with 46.5 percent of those choosing panethnic identities, 44.6 percent of those reporting a hyphenated American identity, and a mere 14.8 percent of those who had identified as plain Americans. Of those shifting to other identities, Table 7.1 suggests the patterning of the shifts: They either added a hyphen or dropped the hyphen in favor of a panethnic or a foreign national identity. Very few shifted to a plain American self-label by the second survey; among those who had initially identified as American only, a third shifted to a hyphenated American identity, while another third adopted a panethnic identification.

In the follow-up survey, our respondents were asked how important their reported self-identity was to them. The responses, on a three-point scale from "very important" to "not important," provide a measure of

TABLE 7.1   CONTINUITY AND CHANGE IN THE ETHNIC
SELF-IDENTITIES OF CHILDREN OF IMMIGRANTS,
1992 AND 1995–1996

| Ethnic Self-Identity in 1992 | Ethnic Self-Identity in 1995–1996 | | | | | Total |
	National Origin	Panethnic	Hyphenated American	American	Mixed, Other	N in 1992 (%)
National origin	57.7	20.2	17.4	1.2	3.6	1,181 (27.5)
Panethnic	32.5	46.5	16.8	0.6	3.5	677 (15.8)
Hyphenated American	28.1	20.6	44.6	2.7	4.0	1,748 (40.8)
American	10.7	33.8	32.8	14.8	7.9	542 (12.6)
Mixed, other	22.9	27.9	26.4	3.6	19.3	140 (3.3)
Total N in 1995–1996 (%)	1,482 (34.6)	1,135 (26.5)	1,314 (30.6)	150 (3.5)	207 (4.8)	4,288 (100.0)

NOTE: Figures are row percentages, indicating the proportion of respondents who reported in the 1995–1996 survey the same or a different type of ethnic identity as that given in 1992. See text for a description of ethnic identity types.

the salience of the different identity types. Figure 7.3 compares these types by their degree of stability (the percent reporting the same identity years later) and salience (the percent reporting their identity as very important). Once again, foreign national identities command the strongest level of allegiance and attachment: Over 71 percent of the youths so identifying considered that identity to be very important to them, followed by 57.2 percent of the hyphenates, 52.8 percent of the panethnics, and only 42 percent of those identifying as plain American. The latter emerges as the "thinnest" identity, with the lowest stability and salience scores—fitting theoretical expectations for a highly accul-turated, majority-group self-image in socially supportive contexts. The foreign national identity, in contrast, emerges as the "thickest" type, with the highest stability and salience scores—fitting theoretical expectations for a less-acculturated, more acutely self-conscious image in socially challenging contexts. In the salience-stability hierarchy of eth-nic identities, the panethnic and hyphenated American types fall in between those two poles.

Figure 7.3   Stability and Salience of Ethnic Self-Identities, 1995–1996

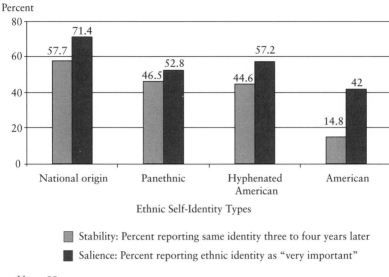

Percent

Stability: Percent reporting same identity three to four years later

Salience: Percent reporting ethnic identity as "very important"

N54,288.

Multivariate logistic regressions (not shown) were carried out to identify the factors most likely to predict ethnic identity stability (coded 1 if the same identity was reported in both surveys) and ethnic identity salience (coded 1 if assessed as very important). A large array of possible predictors was examined, although only a handful of variables emerged as significant determinants of stability and salience. Identities tended to be most stable (consistently adhered to in both surveys) among less acculturated respondents (i.e., who reported lesser preferences for English and for American ways of doing things) and those high in perceptions of discrimination (i.e., who reported experiences and expectations of unfair treatment because of their ethnicity or race). Identities were also more stable among those youths whose parents were both born in the same country and who spoke the parental language at home. Females were also more likely than males to have retained their identity over time.

Those same predictors also determined salience except that gender had no significant effect on this outcome, whereas a measure of family cohesion introduced in the analysis did.[31] In summary, thicker (stable and salient) ethnic self-identities were least likely to be found among second-generation youths who experienced little discrimination, had become more acculturated, and spoke English in homes with low family cohesion. Less stable ethnic identities thus correspond to a faster pace of acculturation and growing distance from immigrant parents' language and culture.

Ethnic Self-Identities by National Origin

How did these patterns of ethnic self-identification vary among the major nationalities in the sample? Table 7.2 provides a breakdown by national origin, showing both the percent selecting the four main ethnic identity types in the most recent survey as well as the percent change (1/2) in each identity since the initial survey. A number of points merit highlighting. First, a glance at Table 7.2 reveals that the patterns discussed so far do not apply equally to every nationality and that in fact there are very large discrepancies in some cases. For example, we found that 35 percent of the total sample identified by a foreign national origin in the latest survey, a gain of 7 percent from the first survey. However, that figure is an average that ranges from a high of 66.7 percent among the Lao and over 50 percent of Filipinos, Vietnamese, and Nicaraguans to a low of only 5.1 percent of Dominicans and 6.2 percent of the Cubans in private schools. The Mexicans and Filipinos in southern California registered the strongest gains in nonhyphenated foreign identities from the baseline survey (each increasing by about 24 percent), suggesting that the Proposition 187–induced process of reactive formation sketched in the opening vignette of this chapter was indeed widespread. Most of the Mexican shift came from youths who had identified as Chicano, Latino, or Hispanic in the 1992 survey.

Other groups registered significant losses in national-origin identification, especially Dominicans, West Indians, Chinese, and smaller Asian groups. All of these smaller groups instead posted very large increases in panethnic identities, with 71.8 percent of Dominicans choosing Hispanic or Latino self-identities, as did 62.7 percent of Colombians. The Hmong and Chinese, virtually none of whom had identified panethnically as Asian in 1992, made large inroads into this type of self-identification by 1995–1996. This result is clearly not explained by socioeconomic factors, since the Hmong had the lowest family SES of all the groups in the study, whereas the Chinese mostly came from professional families. By contrast, virtually none of the Filipinos identified in panethnic terms (less than 2 percent), as did only 4.4 percent of the Haitians. Filipinos and Haitians stand out from all other groups in that they almost entirely identified either by national origin or as hyphenated Americans, maintaining an explicit symbolic attachment to their parents' homeland.

Every group, with two exceptions, posted losses in plain American identities by the latest survey. Even private-school Cubans, over a third of whom had identified as American in 1992, abandoned that identity almost entirely by 1995–1996. The main—and telling—exceptions involve the Europeans and Canadians: not only were they the only groups who increased (by 15.8 percent) their proportion identifying as plain American, but by the last survey over half had adopted that mainstream identity as their own. All other groups were in the low single digits by comparison, marking a sharp segmentation of identities. Socioeconomic status alone would not explain this divergence; as noted, the high-status private-school Cubans dropped that identity, and another relatively high-status group—the Filipinos—consistently posted minuscule numbers identifying as unhyphenated Americans. In the following sections we attempt to untangle this puzzle.

Where Do I Come From? Nation, Family, and Identity

Ethnic identity is, in part, a way of answering the question, Where do I come from? The answers given are often expressed in a metaphorical language of kinship (e.g., *homeland, fatherland, mother tongue, blood ties*) with reference to a "birth connection"[32] to nation and family—to an imagined common origin or ancestry. Even the thinnest ethnicities tend to be rooted in such kinship metaphors. Thus, while ethnic identities may be socially and politically constructed, they are commonly experienced and expressed as natural. In this regard, nativity variables (where one was born, where one's parents were born) are clearly important to ethnic and national self-definitions. For children of immigrants, they are also variables that can significantly complicate a clear-cut answer to basic questions of ethnic self-definition, particularly when the parents' country of birth differs from that of the child and (in cases of interethnic marriage) from each other. The extent of such differences in the nativity patterns of our respondents and their parents is depicted in Table 7.3, broken down by national-origin groups.

Half of the children of immigrants in the CILS sample were born in the United States (the second generation), while the other half was foreign

TABLE 7.2   ETHNIC SELF-IDENTITIES OF CHILDREN OF IMMIGRANTS,
BY NATIONAL ORIGIN GROUPS, 1995–1996

Type of Ethnic Self-Identity

National-Origin Groups	National Origin		Panethnic Identities		Hyphenated American		American Identity	
	1995–1996 (%)	Percent Change since 1992	1995–1996 (%)	Percent change since 1992	1995–1996 (%)	Percent change since 1992	1995–1996 (%)	Percent change since 1992
Latin America								
Cuba (private school)	6.2	(+ 2.7)	19.2	(+15.1)	70.5	(+13.0)	2.1	(−32.9)
Cuba (public school)	16.5	(− 0.4)	31.5	(+23.2)	42.0	(−11.1)	6.1	(−14.6)
Dominican Republic	5.1	(−20.5)	71.8	(+44.9)	10.3	(−15.4)	2.6	(−16.7)
Mexico	41.2	(+23.5)	25.0	(−21.0)	28.9	(− 2.0)	1.2	(− 1.8)
Nicaragua	54.1	(+19.6)	25.6	(−13.2)	17.4	(+ 2.1)	0.4	(− 8.2)
Colombia	15.7	(− 7.6)	62.7	(+36.8)	13.0	(−17.3)	3.2	(−15.7)
Other Latin America	16.7	(−10.0)	43.3	(+33.2)	23.3	(− 7.1)	13.3	(−16.7)
Haiti and West Indies								
Haiti	37.8	(+ 6.7)	4.4	(− 7.4)	43.7	(+ 5.2)	0	(−14.1)
Jamaica	39.0	(−13.6)	15.3	(+10.2)	29.7	(+ 2.5)	2.5	(−10.2)
Trinidad/other W.I.	14.5	(−13.3)	55.4	(+47.0)	16.9	(−10.8)	2.4	(−24.1)

		Other	Asia	
Vietnam	52.6 (+ 5.9)	15.4 (+15.1)	31.7 (−17.6)	0.3 (−3.4)
Laos (Lao)	66.7 (+ 4.9)	11.8 (+ 9.0)	19.4 (− 9.7)	0.7 (+0.0)
Laos (Hmong)	48.0 (−14.0)	38.0 (+36.0)	12.0 (−14.0)	0 (−4.0)
Cambodia	48.3 (+ 7.9)	21.3 (+19.1)	30.3 (−15.7)	0 (−3.4)
Philippines	55.1 (+24.0)	1.9 (+ 1.2)	37.0 (−22.8)	1.7 (−3.6)
Chinese, other Asia	19.4 (−12.9)	43.9 (+42.6)	23.2 (−24.5)	5.8 (−8.4)
Middle East, Africa	18.8 (−15.6)	31.3 (+18.8)	25.0 (+ 9.4)	3.1 (−18.8)
Europe, Canada	8.8 (−14.0)	7.0 (− 3.5)	10.5 (−10.5)	57.9 (+15.8)
Totals	34.6 (+ 7.0)	26.5 (+10.7)	30.6 (−10.1)	3.5 (−9.2)

NOTE: See text for description of ethnic self-identity types. Not shown is a residual category of mixed identities chosen by 4.8 percent of the respondents in the 1995–1996 survey. Figures are row percentages.

TABLE 7.3   NATIVITY PATTERNS OF CHILDREN OF
IMMIGRANTS AND OF THEIR PARENTS

National Origin Groups	*Nativity of Children*		*Nativity of Father and Mother*		
	Foreign Born (1.5 generation) (%)	U.S. Born (Second generation) (%)	Both Born in Same Country (%)	Born in Different Countries (%)	One Parent Born in U.S. (%)
Latin America					
Cuba (private school)	8.9	91.1	85.6	9.6	4.8
Cuba (public school)	32.2	67.8	74.8	14.1	11.1
Dominican Republic	32.1	67.9	79.5	1.3	19.2
Mexico	38.2	61.8	73.0	9.5	17.5
Nicaragua	92.9	7.1	85.8	13.2	1.1
Colombia	48.1	51.9	64.9	25.9	9.2
Other Latin America	53.9	46.1	74.3	7.1	18.6
Haiti and West Indies					
Haiti	54.8	45.2	85.9	9.6	4.4
Jamaica	63.6	36.4	78.0	11.9	10.2
Trinidad/other W.I.	32.5	67.5	50.6	24.1	25.3
Asia					
Vietnamese	84.2	15.8	89.0	8.1	2.9
Laos (Lao)	98.6	1.4	95.1	4.9	0
Laos (Hmong)	94.0	6.0	90.0	10.0	0
Cambodia	96.6	3.4	80.9	19.1	0
Philippines	42.5	57.5	79.1	3.9	17.0
Other Asia	43.9	56.1	64.5	7.1	28.4
Other					
Middle East, Africa	34.4	65.6	56.3	28.1	15.6
Europe, Canada	14.0	86.0	22.8	3.5	73.7
Totals	49.9	50.1	76.8	10.4	12.9

NOTE: Figures are row percentages.

born (the 1.5 generation). However, as Table 7.3 shows, there are wide differences by nationality. Well over 90 percent of the Laotians, Cambodians, and Nicaraguans were foreign born, as were 84.2 percent of the Vietnamese. By contrast, over 90 percent of Cubans in private school were U.S. born, as were 86 percent of the Europeans and Canadians and well over half of Mexicans, Filipinos, and other Asians. Parental nativity patterns vary a great deal as well. Note that just three-fourths (77 percent)

Figure 7.4   Ethnic Self-Identities by Native Origin of Self and
Parents, 1995–1996

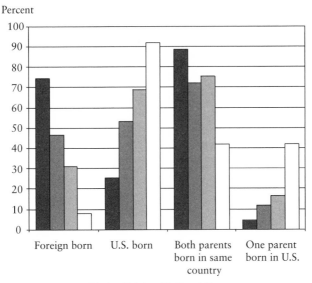

Percent

Native Origin of Self and Parents

Ethnic Identities

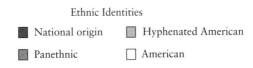

NOTE: Probability of differences being due to chance is less than 1 in 1,000
for all associations shown.

of the children in the sample had parents who were both born in the same
country—and hence who could transmit to their children a common
national origin. These rates of homogamy also vary widely by nationality,
with the highest proportions of endogamous conational parents (between
85 percent and 95 percent) found among Laotians, Vietnamese, Haitians,
Nicaraguans, and private-school Cubans, while less than one-fourth
(22.8 percent) of the Europeans and Canadians had conational parents—
indicative of high levels of interethnic marriage.

How do these nativity patterns affect ethnic self-identification? The
question is answered in Figure 7.4, which graphs each of the main types of
ethnic self-identity by the child's place of birth and those of his or her par-

ents. Among those who reported a foreign identity, 75 percent were foreign born, compared with 31 percent of those who reported a hyphenated American identity and a minuscule 8 percent of those identifying as plain American. Less than half (47 percent) of those identifying by panethnic categories were foreign born. In families where both parents came from the same country of birth, their offspring were much more likely to incorporate that national origin as part of their own identity (either wholly or as a hyphenated-American identity). In families where both parents were foreign born but came from different countries of birth, their offspring were more likely to simplify the complexity of mixed origins by adopting either a panethnic (minority) or plain American (majority) self-identity, thus resolving the conflict of identifying with one parent rather than the other.[33]

Asked how she identified, Rosa, the 15-year-old U.S.-born bilingual daughter of a Cuban-born father and a Salvadoran-born mother, paused and explained: "If I said I'm Cuban, that'd make my mom mad; and if I said I'm Salvadoran, my dad would get all upset, so I think I'm . . . Hispanic!" The panethnic identity label made sense for her as a simplified category that focused on shared traits (and was popular with her Spanish-speaking school friends as well) while avoiding the dilemma of privileging one or the other parental birth connection—to have done so would have been tantamount, to this offspring of a hybrid marriage, to an act of ethnic disloyalty to one or the other parent.[34]

Correlates of Self-Identities

Family Status, Composition, and Language

To flesh out the meaning of different types of ethnic identities, we examine their relationships with a set of other variables of an objective and subjective character. We start with the variables that have concerned us in previous chapters—parental status achievement, family composition, acculturation and its types—and then move on to examine other differences in psychosocial variables and subjective outlooks. An important consideration is the extent to which correlates change over time; that is, not only are self-identities malleable, but their *relationships* with other aspects of adaptation also change. For these purposes, we make use of the longitudinal feature of the study to examine these relations at both points in time.

Table 7.4 presents associations among various measures of parental status, family structure, acculturation, and subjective outlooks with ethnic identities. With a sample as large as ours, almost any bivariate association is statistically significant. For this reason, we focus on coefficients of strength of association and adopt a minimum cutoff point of .10 to define a relationship as noteworthy. Although arbitrary, this level of association is only achieved when differences across the various types of self-identification are clearly visible and substantial. A general result of interest is that while ethnic self-identities were closely related to a number of factors in 1992, several of these associations became insignificant by 1995–1996. In other words, ethnic identities in late adolescence became less patterned by individual demographic or family characteristics.

For instance, gender was closely related to self-labels in the first survey, with girls being less likely to label themselves plain Americans; that relationship disappears in the second survey. Similarly, the associations with parental status, education, and family composition pointed to a strong tendency for children who identified themselves with a panethnic or mixed label to come from less-advantaged backgrounds in 1992; those calling themselves American (hyphenated or not) tended to come from intact and higher-status families. These relationships disappeared or, in the case of parental status, were significantly reduced by late adolescence.

This result is congruent with our earlier observations concerning a significant shift in self-identifications during the teenage period and a strong move toward panethnic and national identifications in response to external events. Among associations that do *not* disappear, several deserve special mention. Length of U.S. residence and use of English at home continue to be strongly associated with a plain American identity in late adolescence. The relations become in fact stronger over time, indicating the resilient power of these acculturative factors. On the contrary, keeping most friendships within the ethnic circle—an indicator of selective acculturation—is strongly linked to preservation of an immigrant national identity and runs contrary to a shift to panethnic or plain American self-designations.

The language adaptation types discussed in Chapter 6 relate to ethnic identities as follows: bilingualism is most common among children identifying themselves with a panethnic label; English dominance is predominant among unhyphenated Americans; and limited bilingualism is associated with unhyphenated national identities. These patterns are reasonable, suggesting the greater exposure of bilinguals to a bicultural world, including awareness of how they are ethnically classified by mainstream institutions; the rapid shift of a minority of respondents into a

TABLE 7.4 CORRELATES OF ETHNIC SELF-IDENTITIES IN 1992 AND 1995–1996: PARENTAL STATUS, FAMILY COMPOSITION, AND ACCULTURATION

Correlates	National Origin	Pan-ethnic	Hyphenated American	American	Mixed	Total Sample	Strength of Association[1]
Gender (female) %							
1992	53.0	54.1	53.1	37.5	48.3	51.1	.11
1995–1996	50.7	53.7	51.8	44.7	52.7	51.7	ns[2]
Years of U.S. residence[3]							
1992	10.2	11.2	12.3	13.3	11.5	11.6	.29
1995–1996	10.6	11.8	12.8	13.8	12.3	11.6	.35
Parental status score[4]							
1992	85.0	65.9	102.8	122.8	81.1	93.7	.23
1995–1996	98.2	99.4	100.7	103.0	100.7	99.6	.16
Father is college graduate %							
1992	23.5	15.1	23.6	31.3	13.9	22.8	.11
1995–1996	21.9	23.2	24.7	31.3	23.2	23.5	ns
Mother is college graduate %							
1992	20.0	11.8	22.6	26.1	12.8	20.2	.12
1995–1996	21.7	17.7	23.4	20.0	23.2	21.2	ns

Intact family, %[5]							
1992	66.5	55.3	66.5	61.0	51.7	63.4	.10
1995–1996	66.3	61.8	66.6	62.7	59.9	64.8	ns
Language other than English at home, %							
1992	93.9	94.5	93.6	88.3	84.4	92.8	.10
1995–1996	94.9	92.1	93.0	76.7	79.7	92.2	.16
Language adaptation 1995–1996, %[6]							
Bilingual	24.8	36.3	28.8	18.0	17.4	28.5	.13
English dominant	42.6	42.8	54.5	72.7	64.3	48.4	
Limited bilingual	19.8	13.7	12.3	8.7	14.5	15.3	
Most friends are also children of immigrants, %							
1992	63.4	57.4	63.5	55.8	40.6	60.7	.10
1995–1996	65.1	58.2	59.5	36.7	36.7	59.2	.15
Expects to graduate from college, %							
1992	75.6	71.4	81.5	84.1	70.0	78.2	.11
1995–1996	78.9	81.2	86.7	82.6	79.2	82.11	ns
Self-esteem score[7]							
1992	3.24	3.27	3.31	3.42	3.21	3.30	.11
1995–1996	3.34	3.43	3.46	3.51	3.41	3.41	ns

(continued on next page)

TABLE 7.4 *(continued)*

Correlates	National Origin	Pan-ethnic	Hyphenated American	American	Mixed	Total Sample	Strength of Association[1]
				N			
1992	1,435	867	2,097	683	180	5,262	
1995–1996	1,482	1,135	1,314	150	207	4,288	

[1]Eta or Cramer's V coefficients of strength of association.
[2]Values below .10 are considered nonsignificant.
[3]Years of U.S. residence measured in 1995–1996.
[4]Standardized index of father's and mother's education, occupational status, and home ownership. Original index values multiplied by 10 and added to 100 to eliminate negative values.
[5]Percent of respondents living with both biological parents.
[6]The category of "Foreign dominant" is omitted from the analysis. Its values are equivalent to 100 minus the sum of the three language categories presented herein.
[7]Scores in Rosenberg's Self-esteem Scale; range is 1–4.

fully American, English-speaking world; and the continuous attachment of foreign-born children experiencing difficulties with English to their parents' national origin. Indicators of psychosocial adjustment such as self-esteem and educational ambition—to be explored at length in the next chapter—correlated with ethnic identities in early adolescence but not by the time of high school graduation, again pointing toward the less-patterned character of self-identities in this later period.

The Influence of Parental Self-Identities

How do parents affect their children's self-identities? Again the longitudinal character of CILS allows us to explore this relationship in detail. Two open-ended questions in the first survey asked the respondent to write in how their father and mother self-identified. Those responses were coded and correlated with the children's own ethnic identities in the 1992 and 1995–1996 surveys. Table 7.5 presents the associations for the main identity types over time, which effectively provide a measure of the degree of consonant identification of youths with their parents. It is noteworthy that the strongest correlations in the table are consistently between the same ethnic labels. That is, children were more prone to see themselves in the same terms as they perceived their parents' own self-definitions. This mirroring process endured over time, especially for those choosing an unhyphenated immigrant identity, although correlation co-efficients were again attenuated by the time of the second survey.

Region, Schools, and Discrimination

The story of the forging of an ethnic self-identity in the second generation, however, plays out on a much larger stage than that of the family. We began this chapter by focusing attention on social forces outside the family that shape both the creation of racial-ethnic categories and of ethnic self-definitions, particularly those involving discrimination and the politics of reactive ethnicity and those involving acculturation and the psychology of linear ethnicity. We return here to those concerns.

Regional location (in southern California or southern Florida) and the type of school these youths attended (inner-city or suburban, public or private schools) are two such extrafamilial contextual factors. They delimit the youths' exposure to different social worlds, shape differential associations with peers in those contexts, and influence ethnic socialization. As

TABLE 7.5 CORRELATIONS OF ETHNIC SELF-IDENTIFICATIONS OF PARENTS AND CHILDREN, 1992 AND 1995–1996

Parents' Identity as Perceived by Child in 1992

Children's Ethnic Self-Identities	Time of Survey	National Origin	Hyphenated American	American	Panethnic	Mixed Identity
National origin	1992	.373	–.229	–.202	–.058	–.024 (ns)
	1995–1996	.206	–.085	–.167	–.032 (ns)	.020 (ns)
Hyphenated American	1992	–.192	.280	.005 (ns)	–.066	–.045
	1995–1996	–.120	.131	.059	–.043	–.053
American	1992	–.201	.015 (ns)	.251	–.028 (ns)	–.023 (ns)
	1995–1996	–.089	–.002 (ns)	.128	–.031 (ns)	–.016 (ns)
Panethnic	1992	.015 (ns)	–.088	–.019 (ns)	.186	.050
	1995–1996	–.029 (ns)	–.034 (ns)	.030 (ns)	.083	.022
Mixed identity	1992	–.063	–.045	.063	.002 (ns)	.123
	1995–1996	–.063	–.021 (ns)	.072	.020 (ns)	.039

NOTE: Except where noted, probabilities of correlations being due to chance is less than 1 in 100.
ns: nonsignificant correlation.

Table 7.6 shows, slightly over half of the sample (54 percent) was located in southern Florida, and slightly less than half (46 percent) was in the San Diego area. But more than two-thirds (67.3 percent) of those identifying by a foreign national origin were in San Diego by the time of our second survey, while about four-fifths (78.7 percent) of those identifying as plain Americans were in southern Florida. The relationship between ethnic identity and regional location became stronger over time because of the disproportionate shift of our Florida sample toward panethnic and mixed labels and away from plain immigrant identities, the modal category in California. These regional differences naturally have to do with the nationalities that concentrate in each area and their different experiences of settlement and incorporation, as reflected in children's eyes. Whether there is something unique to common regional experiences transcending the effect of other factors is a question requiring more complex analysis and reserved for the final section.

The school experiences of our respondents and their outlooks on American society were closely associated with their self-identities in junior high school. These relationships followed a predictable pattern in which students in better suburban schools were more likely to adopt a plain American identity, while panethnic labels—primarily black and Hispanic—were more commonly adopted by children in inner-city schools. Similarly, those who saw themselves as Americans had a far more positive view of the United States than students who clung to their parents' nationality or adopted a racialized panethnicity.

But by senior high school, these tendencies had weakened significantly, again pointing to the less-patterned character of ethnicity in this late period: many more adolescents shifted to a panethnic self-definition, including a number who had attended suburban schools; the positive outlook toward American society increased for all groups, while differences between various ethnic categories became attenuated. Thus, a panethnic identity ceased to be a clear sign of an underprivileged condition, as in early adolescence, to become an indicator of growing awareness of externally defined ethnic categories in the entire sample.

This process of ethnic awareness is also evident in our respondents' perceptions and experiences of discrimination. By the second survey, 87 percent of the sample agreed that there is racial discrimination in economic opportunities in the United States, 88 percent agreed that there is much conflict between ethnic and racial groups, and 82 percent said that Americans feel superior to foreigners. This high level of sensitivity to ethnic differences and ethnic inequality is also evident in the fact that

TABLE 7.6 CORRELATES OF ETHNIC SELF-IDENTITIES IN 1992 AND 1995–1996: REGION, SCHOOLS, AND DISCRIMINATION

Ethnic Identities

Correlates	National Origin	Pan-ethnic	Hyphenated American	American	Mixed	Total Sample	Strength of Association[1]
Region, 1992 (%)							
South Florida	45.9	53.9	51.2	85.2	33.9	54.0	.25[2]
Southern California	54.1	46.1	48.8	14.8	66.1	46.0	
Region, 1995–1996 (%)							
South Florida	32.7	71.0	52.4	78.7	61.8	51.9	.32
Southern California	67.3	29.0	47.6	21.3	38.2	48.1	
Attended Inner-City School (%)[3]							
1992	39.2	53.2	32.0	26.1	35.6	36.8	.17
1995–1996	37.4	40.0	30.4	26.7	34.8	35.4	ns
Agrees that "The United States Is the Best Country to Live In" (%)							
1992	51.8	54.6	64.6	69.8	60.8	60.0	.14
1995–96	67.7	70.8	76.0	78.0	63.3	71.3	ns

Expects Discrimination in the Future (%)[4]

1992	36.8	31.4	30.5	23.3	38.3	31.7	ns
1995–1996	39.7	29.5	35.3	27.3	37.2	35.1	ns

Experienced Discrimination (%)

1992	62.3	57.7	54.2	39.1	58.8	55.2	.14
1995–1996	66.4	56.0	62.0	52.7	73.4	62.2	.10

N

1992	1,435	867	2,097	683	180	5,262
1995–1996	1,482	1,135	1,314	150	207	4,288

[1] Eta or Cramer's V coefficients of strength of association.
[2] Values below .10 are considered nonsignificant.
[3] In junior high school.
[4] Expects discrimination no matter how much education he or she manages to achieve.

about a third of respondents expected discrimination against themselves "no matter how much education [they] manage to achieve." As shown in Table 7.6, this dismal expectation did not vary significantly among ethnic identity categories. Only direct experiences of discrimination have a lasting relationship to ethnic self-identification. Reported discrimination increased significantly between both survey years. Table 7.6 shows that though attenuated, these experiences were much less common among students maintaining a plain American identity in senior high school and more common among those who retained or shifted to their parents' national identification.

In summary, results of this analysis again point to the shift in self-definitions of second-generation youths during adolescence. This shift corresponds to a process of growing ethnic awareness that weakened the close association in early adolescence between American identities and higher-status parents and better schools. The symbolic abandonment of ethnicity by many of our respondents in junior high school turned out to be premature. They returned to it three years later, either embracing their parents' origin as a form of national reaffirmation or a panethnic label as a recognition of their place in the American ethnic hierarchy. Still, length of residence in the United States and the type of home environment and circle of friendships, along with the settlement experiences of different nationalities in the two study sites, kept resilient associations with the self-identities adopted by these youths. We will seek to untangle these various influences to arrive at a clearer sense of the principal forces shaping ethnicity over time. First, however, it is necessary to consider a related but crucial dimension of self-identification, namely, second-generation definitions of race.

The Race Question

Near the end of the second survey, respondents were asked to answer a semistructured question about their race. They were given the option (following recent U.S. Census usage) to check one of five categories: white, black, Asian, multiracial, or other; if the latter was checked, they had to write in their own words what that other race was. The results are revealing. Less than half of the total sample checked the conventional categories of white (14 percent), black (7 percent), or Asian (26 percent); another 11 percent reported being multiracial; and over 40 percent checked other. When those other self-reports were coded, it turned out that nearly a quarter of the sample (24 percent) wrote down Hispanic or Latino as their race, and another 14 percent gave their nationality as their race. Among those youths adopting panethnic identities, there was an obvious convergence of race and ethnicity in the way they define their identities: Of those who identified ethnically as Asian, 92 percent also gave that as their race, as did 85 percent of those who identified as black. Fifty-eight percent of those who identified as Hispanic or Latino extended racial meaning to that label as well.

The explicit racialization of the Hispanic-Latino category, as well as the substantial proportion of youths who conceived of their nationality of origin as a fixed racial category, are noteworthy both for their potential long-term implications in hardening group boundaries and for their illustration of the arbitrariness of racial constructions. The latter point is made salient by directly comparing the youths' notions of their race with that reported by their own parents (the same race item was used in the parental interviews of 1995–1996). These results are synthesized in Table 7.7, broken down by national origin.

The closest match in racial self-perceptions between parents and children is evident among Haitians, Jamaicans, and other West Indians (most of whom self-report as black); among Europeans and Canadians (most of whom self-report as white); and among Asian-origin groups, except for Filipinos. The widest mismatches occur among Latin-origin groups. For example, 93.1 percent of Cuban parents identify themselves as white, compared with only 41.2 percent of their children; 67.7 percent of Nicaraguan parents see themselves as white, but only 19.4 percent of their children agree; and the same is the case among all other Latin-origin groups except Mexicans. Among Mexicans, the children preponderantly racialize their national origin, whereas Mexican parents are more likely to use other (mestizo) and multiracial descriptors.

These remarkable results point to the force of the acculturation process and its impact on children's self-identities. Parents are not only unable to transmit their own language to their children in most cases, as seen in Chapter 6, but they are also ineffective in conveying a sense of who they are in racial terms. Parents seldom confuse race and nationality in their own self-definitions and seldom accept "made in the U.S.A." categories such as Hispanic. Fully exposed to American culture and its racial definitions, children learn to see themselves more and more in these terms and even to racialize their national origin.

TABLE 7.7   SELF-REPORTED RACE OF CHILDREN OF IMMIGRANTS AND THEIR
PARENTS, BY NATIONAL ORIGIN GROUPS, 1995–1996

National Origin	Respondent	White (%)	Black (%)	Asian (%)	Multiracial (%)	Hispanic, Latino (%)	National Origin (%)	Other (%)
				Latin America				
Cuba	Child	41.2	0.8	—	11.5	36.0	5.5	4.9
	Parent	93.1	1.1	0.3	2.5	1.1	0.5	1.4
Mexico	Child	1.5	0.3	—	12.0	25.5	56.2	4.5
	Parent	5.7	—	2.1	21.6	15.9	26.1	28.5
Nicaragua	Child	19.4	0.5	1.6	9.7	61.8	2.7	6.5
	Parent	67.7	—	—	22.0	5.4	0.5	2.2
Other Latin America	Child	22.8	1.9	—	14.7	52.9	4.6	3.1
	Parent	69.5	4.6	0.8	17.8	2.3	1.9	3.1
				Haiti and West Indies				
Haiti	Child	—	75.9	—	8.4	—	9.6	6.0
	Parent	—	85.5	1.2	—	—	6.0	7.2
Jamaica, West Indies	Child	3.4	66.4	7.6	15.1	—	—	—
	Parent	8.4	65.5	5.0	8.4	—	6.7	5.9

Asia

Philippines	Child	1.1	—	61.6	13.2	—	23.0	1.1
	Parent	0.3	0.5	44.1	11.1	—	41.4	2.7
Vietnam	Child	—	—	89.8	1.6	—	7.0	1.6
	Parent	0.4	—	99.6	—	—	—	0.4
Laos, Cambodia	Child	—	—	87.8	3.4	—	7.2	1.1
	Parent	—	—	74.9	—	—	23.6	1.5
Other Asia	Child	1.5	—	82.4	13.2	—	2.9	—
	Parent	2.9	1.5	76.5	1.5	—	8.8	8.8
Middle East, Africa	Child	33.3	11.1	22.2	33.3	—	—	—
	Parent	44.4	22.2	33.3	—	—	—	—
Europe, Canada	Child	76.0	—	—	8.0	12.0	—	4.0
	Parent	84.0	—	—	8.0	4.0	—	4.0
Totals	Child	12.1	6.5	32.1	10.3	20.3	15.5	3.2
	Parent	30.2	7.4	29.2	9.6	3.2	14.2	6.3

NOTE: Figures are row percentages.

Figure 7.5   Correlates of Racial Self-Identification

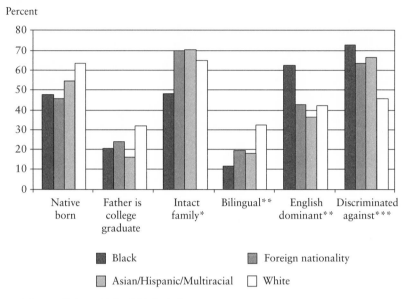

Percent

* Percent living with both biological parents, 1992.
** In 1992.
*** In 1995–1996.

Key correlates of children's racial identifications are summarized in Figure 7.5. Children who see themselves as white are significantly more likely to be native born, to have college-educated fathers, and to maintain bilingual skills. These results are due in part to the fact that most of these youths are offspring of Cuban and European/Canadian parents who have been in the United States for a longer period of time, identify themselves as white, and in the case of Cubans, have made sustained efforts to preserve their language. Respondents who self-identify as black are significantly more likely to be monolingual in English and to come from split families. Both results are a reflection of the West Indian origin of most of these children. By contrast, respondents who conflate their nationality with their race tend to have the least-educated fathers but come from stable families, a result of the Mexican origin of many of these youths.

The most poignant differences in Figure 7.5 pertain to experiences of discrimination. By late adolescence, less than half of children who self-defined as white reported having suffered any such experiences. In contrast, two-thirds of those who defined their race in pannational (Latino, Hispanic, Asian) or exclusively national terms had endured discrimination. The figure climbs to 73 percent among blacks—mostly the children of Haitians, Jamaicans, and other West Indians. These differences support results presented in previous chapters concerning growing perceptions of discrimination among all second-generation youths, along with a wide gap in such reports among various nationalities. The data in Figure 7.5 show that children who see themselves racially as black, Hispanic, or Asian are much more likely to associate such identities with a hostile outside environment.

Determinants of Ethnic and Racial Identities

In this section, we seek to bring together the various strands of the preceding analysis into a coherent portrait of the factors determining self-identities, ethnically and racially. We speak here of determinants rather than correlates since we seek to establish the variables that make a difference causally by considering all their potential effects simultaneously and identifying a temporal order between predictors and consequences. For this purpose, potential determinants are limited to those measured in the first survey, while their effects are established through self-identifications measured three years later. Although this temporal order does not prove causality, it establishes at least a prima facie case for it by eliminating the possibility that identities in late adolescence actually affect their alleged predictors.

Models presented in Tables 7.8 and 7.9 bring together the different factors affecting second-generation adaptation and its early outcomes, as seen in earlier chapters. They include parental socioeconomic status and family composition, including nativity of parents; measures of acculturation, beginning with nativity, length of U.S. residence, and citizenship of the respondent; and different types of linguistic adaptation. While we limit predictors mostly to objective characteristics of youths and their families, we make two exceptions. The first is children's experiences of discrimination, as reported in 1992; the second is the extent to which the child's and parents' self-identities were perceived to be identical in that year. We believe that these subjective perceptions in early adolescence can bear on the development of subsequent self-identities.

The dependent variables in Tables 7.8 and 7.9 are neither dichotomous nor continuous but categorical. To analyze them in a multivariate

TABLE 7.8 DETERMINANTS OF ETHNIC SELF-IDENTIFICATION, 1995–1996

Predictors, 1992[1]	Panethnic[2]			Hyphenated American			Plain American		
	Coefficient	Z	p[3]	Coefficient	Z	p	Coefficient	Z	p
Demographic[4]									
Region (S. California)	-1.72	16.90***	-.17	-.84	8.84***	-.12	-2.11	9.09***	-.03
Family									
Parental socioeconomic status	-.17	2.47*	-.03						
Intact family	.25	2.62*	.05						
One U.S.-born parent				.83	3.89**	.18	.67	2.17*	.03
Both parents born in same country	-1.20	8.34**	-.14				-1.42	5.20***	-.02
Acculturation									
Native born	.68	4.94***	.14	1.37	10.16***	.32	1.51	3.84**	.09
Foreign born, 10 years or more of U.S. residence[5]				.55	4.61**	.12			
No second-generation friends[6]				-.45	2.23*	-.07			
U.S. citizen	.46	3.89**	.09	.66	5.71***	.14	1.74	3.81**	.12
Language[7]									
Foreign language spoken at home				.47	2.48*	.10			

School

			Perceptions			
Attended inner-city school	.39	3.90*	.07	.21	2.08*	.04
Experienced discrimination	−.20	2.28*	−.03			
Parents' identity same as self	−.25	2.87*	−.04	−.25	2.92*	−.04
Constant	.85		−1.17			−6.74
Log likelihood chi square (degrees of freedom)				1,408.60# (57)		
Pseudo R^2				.14		
N				4,080		

[1]All independent variables were measured during the first survey. Predictors lacking any significant effect are excluded. Nonhyphenated national self-identities is the reference category for estimation of effects.

[2]Asian, black, Hispanic, Latino, and related terms.

[3]Net increase/decrease in the probability of each type of ethnic identification, controlling for other variables.

[4]Age and sex were included in the model. They are excluded from presentation because no significant effect was associated with either variable.

[5]Foreign born with less than 10 years of U.S. residence is the omitted category.

[6]"Many or most second-generation friends" is the omitted category. The intermediate category, "Some second generation friends," was also included in the model, but lacked any significant effect.

[7]The model included dummy variables representing types of language adaptation. They are excluded from presentation because no significant effects were associated with them.

*Moderate effect (coefficient doubles its standard error).

**Strong effect (coefficient quadruples its standard error).

***Very strong (coefficient sextuples its standard error).

#Probability that model improvement is due to chance is less than 1 in 10,000.

TABLE 7.9 DETERMINANTS OF RACIAL SELF-IDENTIFICATION, 1995–1996

Predictors, 1992[1]	Black			Pannational[2]			Immigrant Nationality		
	Coefficient	Z	p[3]	Coefficient	Z	p	Coefficient	Z	p
Demographic									
Age				-.19	3.07*	-.05	-.17	2.18*	-.02
Sex (Female)	.55	3.32*	.04				-.42	3.16*	-.05
Region (S. California)				3.16	15.54***	.35	4.48	19.40***	.79
Family[4]									
Parental socioeconiomic status							-.44	4.19**	-.05
Intact family	-.61	3.66**	-.03						
One U.S.-born parent	-.73	2.31*	-.04	-.67	3.51**	-.16			
Acculturation[5]									
Native-born[6]	-.74	2.79*	-.04						
No second generation friends	1.23	4.01**	.13	-.52	2.12*	-.13			
Some second generation friends[7]	.81	4.60**	.07	-.38	2.56*	-.09			
Language									
Foreign language spoken at home	-1.70	7.54***	-.06						
Limited bilingual							-.86	3.01*	-.08
Fluent bilingual							-.91	3.40*	-.09
English dominant[8]	1.22	3.01	.13						

School

Perceptions[9]

	b	z	Effect	b	z	Effect	b	z	Effect
Attended inner city school	.94	5.30**	.09						
Experienced discrimination	1.32	7.86***	.15	.52	5.08**	.11	.78	5.78***	.13
Constant	−.54			−4.19			1.24		
Log likelihood chi square (degrees of freedom)				1,863.66# (57)					
Pseudo R^2				.22					
N				4,132					

[1] All independent variables were measured during the first survey. Predictors lacking any significant effect are excluded. Racial identification as white is the reference category for estimation of effects.

[2] Asian, Hispanic, Latino, and related terms.

[3] Net increase/decrease in the probability of each type of racial identification, controlling for other variables.

[4] Conational parents were included in the model but lacked any significant effect.

[5] U.S. citizenship was included in the model, but lacked any significant effect.

[6] "Foreign-born with less than 10 years of U.S. residence" is the omitted category. "Foreign-born with 10 years or more of U. S. residence" was included in the model but lacked any significant effect.

[7] "Many or most second-generation friends" is the omitted category.

[8] "Foreign language dominant" is the omitted category.

[9] Parent-child convergence in ethnic self-identities in 1992 was included in the model but lacked any significant effect.

*Moderate effect (coefficient doubles its standard error).

**Strong effect (coefficient quadruples its standard error).

***Very strong (coefficient sextuples its standard error).

#Probability that model improvements is due to chance is less than 1 in 10,000.

framework, we make use of multinomial logistic regression, a procedure that allows simultaneous analysis of determinants of the different categories of ethnic and racial identification. Results of interest are the strength of the coefficients, as measured by the Z-statistic, the direction of significant effects, and the associated probabilities. To avoid clutter, the tables only report significant coefficients. Multinomial logistic regression requires that one meaningful category of the dependent variable be selected as the reference point. Effects are then computed relative to this category. For ethnic identities, we select unhyphenated national origin as the base. This is logical since first-generation nationalities were the original immigrant identities from which second-generation variants evolved.

Results in Table 7.8 make clear that ethnic identities are closely tied to the nationality and place of birth, both of parents and of children themselves. The strong negative effects associated with residence in southern California reflect the concentration there of groups whose children tend to identify with their parents' national origin, either because of recency of arrival or reactive formation. As seen at the beginning of the chapter, California was the site of a contentious struggle around Proposition 187 just prior to CILS's second survey. The anti-immigration campaign unleashed by supporters of this measure triggered a countermobilization that involved both immigrants and their offspring. Reactive formation among many second-generation youths, especially Mexican Americans, seemingly took the form of a resolute embracing of their parents' unhyphenated nationality; while other factors may be at play, this embracing corresponds well with this model's coefficients.

Controlling for region, U.S. nativity and U.S. citizenship lead away from immigrant self-identities and toward American identities. Foreign-born children—members of the 1.5 generation—are understandably more likely to retain their parents' nationality as their own self-identification. This is especially true if both parents were born in the same country. Based on model coefficients, a foreign-born child with less than 10 years in the United States and parents born in the same country is 28 percent less likely to identify panethnically than nationally and 11 percent less likely to adopt a plain American label. Conversely, having one U.S.-born parent significantly heightens the probability of calling oneself American, with or without the hyphen.

The final results of interest in the table pertain to the effects of having attended inner-city schools in early adolescence and having experienced discrimination at that age. Inner-city schools lead away from immigrant identities and toward American ones, primarily panethnic categories. The school coefficients reflect a process of socialization in which second-generation youths attending inner-city, mostly minority schools learn to apply to themselves the labels with which their native peers identify—Hispanic, Latino, black, and Asian. Children who attended nonminority suburban schools are much less likely to adopt these commonly stigmatized labels.

Effects of discrimination support the reactive formation argument advanced in connection with Mexican youths in California. Like collective consequences of the anti-immigration campaign in that state, direct experiences of discrimination trigger a reaction away from things American and toward reinforcement of the original immigrant identities. Thus, the process identified by Irvin Child among Italian Americans more than 50 years ago, and cited earlier in this chapter, is as valid then as it is now: Groups subjected to extreme discrimination and derogation of their national origins are likely to embrace them ever more fiercely; those received more favorably shift to American identities with greater speed and less pain.

The same model is applied to race self-identifications in late adolescence, although the interpretation of coefficients varies here. To begin with, nationality cannot be used as the base category since this is not the original racial identification of immigrants. Calling one's race Mexican or Laotian is not something that adult immigrants usually do but is learned by their children in the process of acculturation. In part for this reason, we adopt a racial identification as white as the norm. White is the modal racial identification of the American population and the one that comes closer to the social mainstream. The question then is how second-generation children who identify themselves in this manner differ from those who see themselves as part of racial minorities.

Evaluated against this standard, black-identified children differ in a number of dimensions. In this case, many of the significant coefficients do not so much signal causal effects as they signal social dimensions linked to a black identity in our sample. For example, the positive effect of English monolingualism and the negative ones of living in intact, foreign-speaking homes on black identification do not indicate that English usage or broken homes lead to black self-identities but that most of these children have West Indian parents with the linguistic and family traits described previously. The same is true of the strong effect of experiences of discrimination in middle school; it is less likely that such experiences "caused" a black identity than that they form an integral part of it, under the influence of pervasive racism in the outside environment.

Still, some net effects are worthy of attention as they indicate significant causal influences. Respondents who had none or few second-generation friends and those who attended inner-city schools in early adolescence are more likely to self-identify as black, controlling for other factors. These coefficients reflect the socialization effects of relating exclusively to native-born peers who, in inner-city schools, are mostly other minorities. These learning effects combined lead predictably to heightened awareness of a racial minority status. Thus, as in the case of ethnic identities seen previously, the school environments that children experience early in life play a distinct role in the formation of their racial self-images.

The causal profile of youths who define their race pannationally (that is, as Hispanic, Latino, or Asian) or according to their national origin is similar, again pointing to the impact of acculturation in the development of these identities. These children are older and reported more frequent experiences of discrimination in 1992. In this instance, a case can be made that such experiences play a causal role as they may have led children, who in other circumstances may have self-defined as white, to call themselves Hispanic or Mexican. The strong regional effects point in the same direction, as it is in California that children of Mexican and Asian origin concentrate. These are the groups that, as seen previously, are most prone to define their race pannationally or nationally. The southern Florida sample concentrates groups that, in contrast, are more likely to define themselves as white or black.

Parental status significantly reduces the tendency to conflate one's nationality with one's race, but being native born increases it. This is a telling result because it again signals the learned character of racial identification. In other words, it is not recently arrived foreign children who call their race Mexican or Filipino but American-born youths for whom their parents' country of birth is but a distant memory. The constructed character of race is evident in these results, as is the "made-in-the-U.S.A." character of racialized national origins. Lastly, claiming white as a racial self-identification, as opposed to a pannational racial identity, is more frequent among children with one U.S.-born parent and those having no second-generation friends. As in the case of black-identified youths, this last effect points to the significance of early socialization that leads, in this instance, to a stronger tendency toward a white self-identity among children who have left their ethnic circle behind. Based on model coefficients, a child with one American parent and no immigrant friends in junior high school is about 30 percent more likely to call himself/herself white than Hispanic or some other pannational label; that probability increases to 65 percent if the family happens to live in southern Florida.

Overall, these multivariate models fit the data rather well, accounting for a substantial proportion of the variance in both ethnic and racial identification. They point to the importance of nativity, region of settlement, and family composition as well as to the multiple influences of early acculturation. Parental and children's places of birth and citizenship emerge as major determinants of self-identities, as do the early schools that these youths attend. Experiences of discrimination are powerfully associated with subsequent racial identification either as a potential determinant or as an integral component of a racial minority status. All but the white-identified respondents had significantly endured these experiences by an early age.

Conclusion: From Translation Artists to Living Paradoxes

During the mass immigration to the United States from southern and eastern Europe in the early twentieth century, it was a common experience—or so it has been presented in national lore—for immigrants' last names to be Americanized upon arrival in Ellis Island. Members of the same family sometimes came out of Ellis Island with different surnames.[35] And many more during that era of hegemonic Americanization felt compelled to change their foreign names to fit more familiar American forms—and to avoid saddling their children with names that were tongue twisters for English speakers and could make them targets for ridicule.[36] Whether those sudden name changes stand as examples of symbolic violence against powerless immigrants or as the strategic choices of ambitious newcomers, the fact is that they often initiated immigrants in a path toward integration into American society. Symbolic acceptance of a new identity could lead the way for entry into a new culture and for learning the ropes of its social hierarchy.

In an era of civil rights and ethnic revivals, today's immigrants are treated more leniently. Their family names are spared, and often they do not even feel the need to anglicize their first names. Indeed, in California and Texas—the two most populous states in the country—the most popular baby boy's name in 1998 was no longer John, Michael, or David but José.[37] Instead, today's newcomers are recategorized in broad racial-ethnic clusters that the host society deems appropriate for those sharing (or imagined to share) a particular language or phenotype. Although the state, the school system, the media, and the society at large may insist on redefining today's immigrants into panethnic labels such as Hispanics and Asians, the children themselves are quite plural in their self-definitions. Challenged to incorporate what is "out there" into what is "in here" and to crystallize a sense of who they are, they translate themselves and construct a variety of self-identities. Some cling tenaciously to their parents' national loyalties and retain their national identities, with or without a hyphen. Others shift to an unhyphenated American self-image and identify symbolically with the mainstream. Still others internalize the racial and panethnic categories into which they are constantly classified and identify symbolically with national minorities.

The paths to those different forms of ethnic self-definition are, as we have seen, shaped by a variety of social and psychological forces. The results of our surveys show major differences in patterns of self-identification among teenage children of immigrants from scores of countries growing up in two distinct corners of the United States. They also suggest some of the complex, often incongruous, and unexpected ways in which race and class, discrimination and acculturation can complicate their sense of who they are. If for some the search for identity may with time and acceptance blur into the "twilight of ethnicity," as suggested by Alba,[38] for others it may lead with heightened salience into the high noon of ethnicity, as reactive formation remolds their self-image into a new reassertive stance. But the underlying process is one in which all children of immigrants are inescapably engaged and of which they are acutely aware: making sense of who they are and finding a meaningful place in the society of which they are the newest members.

Indeed, in this process of translating themselves, some gain in translation, while others may be lost in it. As Pérez Firmat writes of the 1.5 generation of Cuban Americans: "One-and-a-halfers are translation artists. Tradition bound but translation bent, they are sufficiently immersed in each culture to give both ends of the hyphen their due."[39] But, in the absence of racial discrimination and reactive formation, the process of acculturation may well "thin" ethnicity and take its inevitable generational toll:

My children, who were born in this country of Cuban parents and in whom I have tried to inculcate some sort of *cubanía,* are American through and through. They can be "saved" from their Americanness no more than my parents can be "saved" from their Cubanness. . . . Like other second-generation immigrants, they maintain a connection to their parents' homeland, but it is a bond forged by my experiences rather than their own. For my children Cuba is an enduring, perhaps an endearing, fiction. Cuba is for them as ethereal as the smoke and as persistent as the smell from their grandfather's cigars.[40]

In another context, the experience of self-translation and the quandaries of identity can take on a quite different meaning, as synthesized in these reflections on race and marginality by Caroline Hwang, the daughter of Korean immigrants. Her testimony also serves as a prelude to the analysis of ambition and self-esteem in the following chapter:

My identity is hardly clear-cut. To my parents, I am all American, and the sacrifices they made in leaving Korea pale in comparison to the opportunities those sacrifices gave me. They do not see that I straddle two cultures, nor that I feel displaced in the only country I know. I identify with Americans, but Americans do not identify with me. I've never known what it's like to belong to a community. I know more about Europe than the continent my ancestors unmistakably came from. By making the biggest move of their lives for me, my parents indentured me to the largest debt imaginable—I owe them the fulfillment of their hopes for me.

Children of immigrants are living paradoxes. We are the first generation and the last. When my parents boarded the plane, I don't think they imagined the rocks in the path of their daughter who can't even pronounce her own name.[41]

Chapter 8

THE CRUCIBLE WITHIN

Family, Schools, and the Psychology of the Second Generation

I wish I knew some other way to render the mental life of the immigrant child of reasoning age. . . . What the child thinks and feels is a reflection of the hopes, desires, and purposes of the parents who brought him overseas, no matter how precocious and independent the child may be.
— Mary Antin, *The Promised Land*, pp. 198

In his coming-of-age memoir *The Rice Room: Growing up Chinese-American*, Ben Fong-Torres recalls a childhood spent in the rice room behind his family's Chinese restaurant, working with his siblings in the family business while attending both public and Chinese school, learning Chinese calligraphy while yearning for all things American:

> [My parents] wanted me to do only two things: get the best grades possible and help out at the Bamboo Hut. . . . We were raised on work. Sometimes it got unhealthy, so that we felt guilty staying away from the restaurant one weekend, forcing more work onto Mom or a sister or brother. Our thinking—at least mine—got so twisted that I not only accepted the obligations of our family but even wanted them at the same time that I was fighting for freedom. 'What kind of son,' I'd ask myself in a demanding tone, 'would desert his parents?'[1]

Pushed to earn high grades, assist his father in the restaurant, and date Chinese girls rather than "foreign devils," second son Ben was pulled instead into the rock 'n' roll culture. It is a familiar story. A major theme in the psychology of the second generation is that children of immigrants perceive that they are a main, if not *the* main, reason for the immigration of their parents. Seeing the sacrifices made by parents, ostensibly on their behalf, not a small amount of guilt tinges the children's sense of obligation—a dynamic that, in turn, can give parents a degree of psychological leverage. This is a theme that recurs again and again in our interviews, as it does in Fong-Torres's account here and in Caroline Hwang's sense in the previous chapter of being not indebted but "indentured" to her parents' hopes for her.

Alongside this common feature of second-generation adaptation, there is another side: that of Irvin Child's "rebel" reaction of embarrassment and resentment, of role reversal and dissonant acculturation—a dynamic that gives the children, in turn, a measure of psychological leverage over their parents. Historian Marcus Lee Hansen describes this other facet of generational relations, what he calls "the psychology of the second generation," eloquently:

> Forget it all! Forget the language that had given them an accent that their schoolmates loved to mock. Forget the family and community customs that the sons of the Yankees and often the Yankees themselves had delighted to ridicule. Forget everyone and everything that antedated the moment when the foreign-born father first stepped upon American soil. . . . The participants in any great historic event or development never tire of talking about what they saw. Their sons, however, tire of listening and are as anxious to forget as their parents are to remember.[2]

Immigrant families must contend with the generational gaps and the stress of acculturation. It is a complex process, full of fault lines and reducible neither to the motto of "obey it all" nor to its opposite, "forget it all." At the heart of it are the relationship between immigrant parents and their children and the contradictions that are often engendered in the process of seeking to fulfill the hopes and desires of both. In Chapter 5, we examined the parents' own definitions of their situation, fears, and hopes. Here, we focus attention on the children's perceptions of their families, as part of our continuing analysis of the psychology of the second generation, leading to their own aspirations and self-esteem.

As we have seen, intergenerational relations in immigrant families are managed and shaped within divergent contexts of incorporation and within divergent sets of resources and vulnerabilities. Still, even after taking into account the objective circumstances within which they are coming of age, there is substantial variance in the children's intergenerational and subjective responses. Just as ethnic and racial identities vary significantly but along patterned lines as seen in Chapter 7, we seek to examine here how family orientations and various dimensions of psychological well-being vary by nationality, family status and composition, and patterns of language adaptation. That mix of psychosocial factors—in particular self-esteem and ambition—will be used, in turn, as predictors of educational achievement in the following chapter. Prior to the presentation of numerical results, however, we present four stories drawn from our fieldwork in San Diego and illustrative of the forms that daily relations between immigrant parents and their children can take.

San Diego Families

Within a few miles of each other in San Diego's sprawling inner city live some of the most impoverished immigrant families in the region, including southeast Asian refugees from Cambodia, Laos, and Vietnam and undocumented immigrants from Mexico. At the time of our interviews in the mid-1990s, most of the refugees were receiving some mix of cash and noncash public assistance, while most of the Mexican families were ineligible and did not. All clustered in co-ethnic neighborhoods, although some remained very isolated from their compatriots. Given their location, their children typically attended the same handful of area high schools. Still, despite their common poverty and the evident similarity in their families' objective circumstances, the youths' motivation for achievement and the manner in which they made subjective sense of their situations and their own selves varied. Consider the following cases:[3]

- Mrs. Chea lives in a small, one-bedroom apartment with her four youngest children in a complex inhabited entirely by Cambodians. The father has long been absent; her four oldest children are now married and living outside the home. The family spent seven years in refugee camps in Thailand before being resettled to the United States. A teacher who befriended the family has had a major influence on her youngest daughter Ranny, now a junior in high school who aspires to become a teacher as well, despite her middling GPA. But her mother, who seems anxious about her children growing up and leaving the home, is against her daughter going away to college. Girls who leave the home before getting married are perceived to be in some kind of trouble; besides, she says, it is customary for the youngest daughter to stay at home and take care of her mother. While the family speaks Khmer in the house, Mrs. Chea feels that Ranny is losing her ability to speak it well because she spends more time in school than at home. Her daughter, for her part, says that "when I'm at home I act Cambodian; at school I act American." She adds that she has had to develop a dual personality to cope with the conflict between her mother's desire for her to stay close to home and maintain her cultural traditions, and her own aspirations in school and in the wider society.

• In an ethnically mixed, working-class neighborhood in southeast San Diego lives Mr. Namvong and his wife and all nine of their children. He had been an air force pilot in Laos during the war but then was imprisoned in a "re-education camp" for more than a decade before the family arrived in the United States in the late 1980s. The parents are unemployed, receive SSI from the government, and worry about their family's financial situation in the future (the children over 18 have already been cut off public assistance). But their son Khamphay is doing very well in high school, having received straight A's in his last report card and planning on taking advanced placement courses in his senior year. He speaks Lao at home with his large family as well as with his friends at school. The family regularly attends a Buddhist temple nearby, which is also a center of social life for local Laotians. Mr. Namvong encourages his children to read aloud to him from Lao newspapers and magazines, of which there are many in the home, but also to be "flexible" in adapting to America, which he sees as their permanent home. "We are Lao American," he says. He wants Khamphay to become an engineer and feels confident that his son can achieve this goal.

• Alberto Díaz goes to the same high school as Khamphay. He lives with his mother and father and an older sister in a small wooden house that the family rents in a poor, mostly African American neighborhood shared uneasily with a scattering of Mexican families. His father, who works as a gardener, came alone years before from Jalisco and labored as a farm worker until he was able to secure his legal residency. Mrs. Díaz and Alberto joined him thereafter, but they are still in the process of getting their green cards. His mother said of Alberto that because he doesn't have his papers, *"no cree que él tiene valor"*—his illegal status undercuts his sense of self-worth. Still, both parents are supportive of his aspirations and would like him to finish college and to be more than his parents. *"Si él le echa ganas, puede lograr lo máximo"*—if he has the desire, he can achieve anything—said Mr. Díaz, adding that, in terms of future jobs, he wished for his son *"cualquiera menos cortar zacate como yo"*—anything but cutting grass like me. But Alberto is becoming dispirited; he feels the economic pressure on the family. Until recently he was working nights, and his schooling suffered.

In our first survey Alberto aspired to be an engineer; now he has downsized his hopes and says he wants to be a small-motor mechanic. Both Alberto and his older sister have been assaulted walking to and from school and also at school. Once he was robbed on the trolley. His sister said that another time a group of black girls "grabbed me and took me to the bridge and pulled a knife on me and were calling me names." After that incident the school said they would provide bus transportation for them. The parents said they "worry about drugs and gangs, because it's much easier here than in Mexico to get caught up in these dangers." Yet they can do little about it. They do not have the income to move to a better area and no one to turn to.

• The family discourse is very different in the home of Mr. and Mrs. Ngo, who live with three of their teenage daughters in an integrated working-class neighborhood a few miles to the north. Four older children had already moved out of the household and are doing well, three of them attending different campuses of the University of California. Neither Mr. Ngo nor his wife have worked since arriving in the United States in the mid-1980s; they live on government assistance, which Mr. Ngo describes as "retirement." However, that assistance has enabled them to focus on organizing family life around the education of their children. A strict disciplinarian, Mr. Ngo is a proud man who carries himself like the military officer he was in South Vietnam. He speaks virtually no English—his wife a little more—and in the home only Vietnamese is spoken. They have high aspirations for their daughters and want them to go into the medical field "without forcing them"—although the daughters report getting a lot of pressure on that score. They are otherwise expected to continue living with their parents until they are married, following Vietnamese custom. Mr. Ngo feels that American schools are too open and the laws are too lenient.

The family has heard of affluent Vietnamese who are sending their children to postnormalization Vietnam for the summers to "vaccinate them against Americanization" and give them a boost with their Vietnamese language skills, but the Ngos do not have the means to pay for their daughters' travel; they make do instead with what they have. Posted by the parents around the house are handmade signs in Vietnamese with rules or aphorisms; the mother explained that they don't like to nag the kids, so in this way the rules are always present without having to be spoken. Samples are "If you don't salt a fish, it will rot" (a variation on "Spare the rod, spoil the child"); "First come manners, then comes education"; and "If you talk back, you are doomed forever." The kids laugh as they translate these, especially the last one, and say that all the children in the family are stubborn and make their own rules. But the parents say that the "sole purpose of their lives" is to raise their daughters and are totally dedicated to that goal.

Family Cohesion, Conflict, and Change

The 5,262 young people we interviewed in 1992 lived in households in which over 25,000 persons resided, of whom 98 percent were family members. In terms of their relationship to the respondents, these included over 9,000 parents and stepparents; over 9,000 brothers and sisters (not counting many older siblings who had already moved out of the household); over 1,000 grandparents; and over 1,000 aunts, uncles, cousins, and other relatives. While the average household comprised only the nuclear family, as noted in Chapter 4, household size ranged from as few as 2 or 3 people to more than 15 persons. Noting the variety of these family forms and arrangements, our focus here will be on the nature of the relations between second-generation adolescents and their parents as the complement of the parental outlooks examined in Chapter 5, with an emphasis on how these relations bear on family solidarity and children's psychological well-being and aspirations.

Table 8.1 presents a summary of several objective and subjective indices of family composition, cohesion and conflict broken down by national origin, parental socioeconomic status, and the children's type of language adaptation. In the years between the initial and follow-up surveys, substantial changes took place in some of these families, including the parents' divorce or separation (11 percent of the sample), remarriage (8 percent), or even the death of a parent (3 percent). *Stressful family life events* occurring during the previous three years were measured by a summated index of seven types of such events reported by our respondents. These included the divorce, separation, remarriage or death of a parent; a

TABLE 8.1   STRESSFUL FAMILY EVENTS AND
PERCEPTIONS OF FAMILY RELATIONSHIPS, BY
NATIONAL ORIGIN, PARENTAL SOCIOECONOMIC
STATUS, AND LANGUAGE ADAPTATION, 1995–1996

Variables	Stressful Family Events[1] (% Two or more)	Family Cohesion[2] (% High)	Parent-Child Conflict[3] (% High)	Embarrassed by Parents[4] (%)	Familism[5] (% High)
Total	18.1	34.0	39.9	29.3	28.2
National origin					
Cuba (private school)	13.0	41.1	35.6	26.7	24.0
Cuba (public school)	22.1	35.8	38.3	28.9	24.3
Dominican Republic	21.8	38.5	35.9	14.1	24.4
Mexico	20.7	38.6	32.2	14.2	31.2
Nicaragua	17.8	42.0	31.7	21.7	25.6
Colombia	19.5	37.3	35.1	23.2	28.6
Other Latin America	21.4	40.4	33.9	28.9	24.3
Haiti	31.1	22.2	57.0	41.5	31.1
Jamaica	18.6	28.8	39.8	22.0	24.6
Other West Indies	30.1	30.1	41.0	38.6	20.5
Vietnam	10.3	27.7	49.4	38.1	43.9
Laos (Lao)	14.6	32.6	42.4	30.6	50.0
Laos (Hmong)	8.0	30.0	66.0	48.0	46.0
Cambodia	15.7	24.7	55.1	43.8	33.7
Philippines	14.2	28.6	46.7	33.7	24.3
Chinese, other Asia	7.7	34.2	37.4	52.3	21.9
Europe, Canada	10.5	28.1	26.3	35.1	21.0
p^*	<.001	<.001	<.001	<.001	<.001

parent's job loss (reported by almost 24 percent of the sample); a family member being the victim of crime (22 percent); a sibling dropping out of school (nearly 8 percent); or a serious illness or disability suffered by the respondent (7 percent). Almost half of our sample (49 percent) reported experiencing no such disruption in their families during the previous three years, a third reported one such event, and nearly a fifth (18 percent) experienced two or more such negative life change events.

In addition to this objective indicator of family stability, Table 8.1 provides information on four subjective dimensions of parent-child relationships: family cohesion, parent-child conflict, embarrassment over parents' ways, and attitudes of familial obligation. These psychosocial

TABLE 8.1   (*continued*)

Variables	Stressful Family Events[1] (% Two or more)	Family Cohesion[2] (% High)	Parent-Child Conflict[3] (% High)	Embarrassed by Parents[4] (%)	Familism[5] (% High)
Socioeconomic status[6]					
Bottom tertile	19.5	34.8	41.0	25.9	35.1
Middle tertile	19.9	31.5	40.7	30.0	27.4
Upper tertile	15.1	35.9	38.2	31.7	22.6
*p**	<.002	ns	ns	<.002	<.001
Language dominance[7]					
Fluent bilingual	18.1	47.0	30.6	21.3	23.0
English dominant	18.2	27.9	43.1	36.1	23.5
Foreign lang. dominant	19.2	42.7	33.3	17.4	42.1
Limited bilingual	17.5	26.3	48.6	31.3	37.8
*p**	ns	<.001	<.001	<.001	<.001

[1]Two or more stressful events occurring during past year. See text for explanation.
[2]High score (> 4.0) in three-item family cohesion index; items measured from 1 to 5.
[3]High score (> 2.0) in four-item parent-child conflict index; items measured from 1 to 4.
[4]Embarrassed or ambivalent over parents' ways.
[5]High score (> 2.0) in three-item familial obligations index; items measured from 1 to 4.
[6]Composite index of father's and mother's education, occupational prestige, and home ownership, in 1992 tertiles.
[7]Based on scores in English proficiency and foreign language proficiency indices in 1995–1996. See Chapter 6.
* Probability of differences being due to chance. ns: Not significant.

indices provide a means to examine the inner workings of immigrant families. Earlier we suggested that systematic differences can exist among families and groups along a continuum ranging from situations where parental authority is fully preserved to those where it is thoroughly undermined by generational gaps in acculturation—particularly in English knowledge and the extent to which second-generation youth retain their parents' language. This is the basis for the typology of consonant, selective, and dissonant acculturation. In empirical terms these types should be reflected in the degree of intergenerational cohesion or conflict between parents and children, the extent to which these youths report being embarrassed by their parents' ways or attached to them by filial duty.

Family cohesion was measured by a scale composed of three items administered in the follow-up survey: "Family togetherness is important," "Family members feel close to each other," and "Family members like to spend free time with each other." To each item, respondents were asked to record how frequently each sentence applied to their own family, on a scale from 1 (never) to 5 (always). The data in Table 8.1 indicate the percent of youths who scored high on this scale (mean scores above 4.0). Parent-child conflict is a scale composed of four items also administered during the follow-up survey and identified through factor analysis as forming a single factor: "My parents and I often argue because we don't share the same goals"; "My parents are usually not very interested in what I say"; "My parents do not like me very much"; and "[I] get in trouble because my way of doing things is different from that of my parents." These are scored on a scale from 1 to 4, with mean scores above 2.0 reflecting a high degree of conflict, as indicated in Table 8.1.[4] The parent-child conflict index represents a follow-up extension and refinement of the single-item measure of dissonant acculturation used in Chapter 6 as a correlate of language adaptation. Not surprisingly, family cohesion and intergenerational conflict are negatively related (r 5 2.41) although they represent different dimensions of family dynamics. Similarly, the single item measuring embarrassment with parents' cultural ways is positively correlated with parent-child conflict (.28) and negatively with family cohesion (2.22).

Factor analyses of a separate battery of attitudinal items also identified a three-item familism scale.[5] The three items, answered on a four-point scale, were "One should find a job near his or her parents even if it means losing a better job somewhere else"; "When someone has a serious problem, only relatives can help"; and "In helping a person get a job, it is always better to choose a relative rather than a friend." The same questions were asked in both surveys. Table 8.1 shows the percent of respondents who scored high (mean scores above 2.0) on this measure in the second survey. This scale is weakly correlated with family cohesion (.08) but not with generational conflict or embarrassment, suggesting that it constitutes a different psychosocial dimension altogether.

Several points are worth highlighting from results presented in Table 8.1. Asian-origin families are less likely to experience family change events over time; Hmong and Cambodian refugees are the main exceptions, in part as a result of a greater proportion of widowed mothers. Among Latin Americans, the most advantaged in this regard are middle-class Cubans whose children attend private schools in Miami. Without exception, Latin American nationalities have the most cohesive families as well as the lowest levels of parent-child conflict. Most Latin groups also have lower proportions of youths who report being embarrassed by their parents, with the lowest (14 percent) found among two groups of modest socioeconomic status—Mexicans and Dominicans.

We saw in Chapter 6 that a Latin background was a strong predictor of bilingualism, indicative not only of the significant advantage of Spanish speakers but also of its likely association with a selective form of acculturation. High levels of cohesion and low levels of intergenerational conflict among Latin families in Table 8.1 confirm this finding. By contrast, all Asian, European/Canadian, and black Caribbean groups fall below the average in their reported levels of family cohesion. Nearly all Asian and black Caribbean groups also score above the sample average in terms of reported intergenerational conflict. Lowest family cohesion was found among Haitians and Cambodians, and highest parent-child conflict was found among the Hmong, Haitian, and Cambodian families. Those same three groups—along with Chinese and other Asians—also showed the highest percentage of youths reporting feeling embarrassed by their parents.

Recall from Chapter 6 that children from these nationalities were likely to abandon their parental languages and, hence, were least represented among fluent bilinguals. The association between parental language loss and dissonant acculturation advanced in that chapter is confirmed by these results. This relationship gains further support when we relate our measures of family cohesion and parent-child conflict directly to language types. As shown in the bottom rows of Table 8.1, fluent bilinguals are the least likely to report persistent conflict with their parents and the most likely to indicate high levels of family cohesion. Along with more recent arrivals in the foreign language–dominant category, they are also the least embarrassed by their parents' ways. By contrast, and in agreement with earlier results, English monolinguals and limited bilinguals exhibit the strongest tendencies toward dissonant acculturation.

The familism scale clearly measures a different dimension indicative of more traditional family attachments. It is negatively associated with SES and English acquisition. Fluent bilinguals are among the least likely to score high in this measure. Children who display the strongest attachment to traditional family obligations are Mexican Americans and offspring of southeast Asian refugees. Most other nationalities tend to steer away from these traditional orientations and toward more individualistic forms.[6]

Figure 8.1   Family Orientations by Length of U.S. Residence

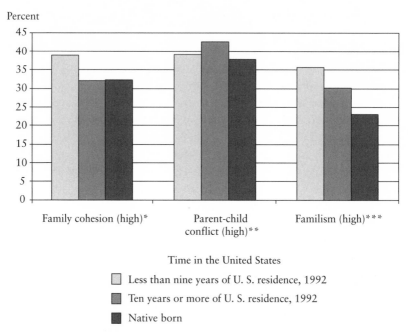

Percent

Time in the United States

▢ Less than nine years of U. S. residence, 1992

◩ Ten years or more of U. S. residence, 1992

■ Native born

* Scores higher than 4 in 1–5 scale. Probability of relationship being due to chance is less than 1 in 1,000.
** Scores of 2 or more in 1–4 scale. Relationship is not significant.
*** Scores higher than 2 in 1–4 scale. Probability of relationship being due to chance is less than 1 in 1,000.

Figure 8.1 presents graphically the relationships between our family orientation indices and length of U.S. residence as an indicator of general acculturation. Family cohesion and familism are highest among the most recent arrivals. The latter relationship is particularly strong, indicating the prevalence of traditional family orientations among recent immigrants. Acculturation weakens these family values and leads toward more individual-centered orientations. By contrast, there is no observable relation between length of U.S. residence and parent-child conflict. This result suggests that it is not acculturation per se but the *form* that it takes that leads to different degrees of estrangement between immigrants and their children.

School Environments and Peer Groups

Until completing their formal schooling, children and adolescents spend more time in schools than in any other setting outside their homes. As such, schools play a critical role in their development, shaping what they learn as well as their motivation and aspirations to learn. Indeed, for children of immigrants, American public schools since the last century have served as quintessential agencies of acculturation. It is in school settings that immigrant youths come most directly in contact with their native peers—whether as role models or close friends, as distant members of exclusionary cliques, and as sources of discrimination or of peer acceptance.

Table 8.2 presents a set of selected characteristics of the schools attended by CILS respondents, as they perceived them at the time of the 1995–1996 survey. The School Condition Index consists of four items, scored on a four-point scale: "I don't feel safe at this school"; "There are many gangs in school"; "Fights occur between different racial or ethnic groups"; and "Disruptions by other students get in the way of my learning." Table 8.2 shows the percent reporting a high sense of unsafe conditions at school (mean scores above 2.0) as well as the percent reporting the presence of gangs, frequent fights between ethnic or racial groups, and drugs at school.[7] The Teaching Quality Index is another composite, scored 1 to 4, and formed by the following items: "The teaching in my school is good"; "Teachers are interested in students"; "Students are graded fairly"; and "Discipline is fair." Table 8.2 shows the percentages reporting a high quality of teaching (mean scores above 3.0.)[8]

Overall, 3 out of 10 students (29.5 percent) reported a high degree of unsafe and disruptive conditions at their school. In particular, 4 out of 10 perceived that there were many gangs and frequent fights between racial-ethnic groups. These results support the high concern for dangerous school conditions voiced by parents of our respondents in Chapter 5. Even the rank order of nationalities reporting or experiencing these conditions is similar. Thus, students of Laotian and Cambodian origin reported by far the most unsafe conditions, including a high prevalence of gang activity and violent fights, followed by the Vietnamese—all in San Diego high schools. At the other extreme are Cuban students in Miami private schools, who experienced by far the safest learning environment as well as the highest quality of teaching. These differences reflect, in part, the importance of parental socioeconomic resources and access to the type of schools that such resources can make available.

Variables	Unsafe conditions at school[1] (% High)	Many gangs at school[2] (% Agree)	Many fights between race-ethnic groups[2] (% Agree)	Drugs at school[3] (%)	High quality of teaching[4] (%)
Total	29.5	38.9	41.8	26.5	25.9
National Origin					
Cuba (private school)	6.2	6.2	10.3	19.2	34.3
Cuba (public school)	27.1	36.1	37.3	34.2	22.7
Dominican Republic	30.8	21.8	42.3	20.5	14.1
Mexico	27.7	37.9	44.1	29.2	32.1
Nicaragua	23.8	31.0	33.1	23.1	30.6
Colombia	24.9	35.7	36.2	42.7	19.5
Other Latin America	27.9	32.5	36.4	32.5	22.5
Haiti	24.4	16.3	36.3	11.9	28.2
Jamaica	20.3	17.8	35.6	13.6	17.8
Other West Indies	24.1	27.7	37.4	19.3	25.3
Vietnam	36.5	49.7	55.8	17.4	25.2
Laos (Lao)	53.5	62.5	71.5	16.7	27.8
Laos (Hmong)	62.0	78.0	78.0	10.0	22.0
Cambodia	50.6	59.6	66.3	10.1	21.4
Philippines	34.5	54.1	44.6	28.2	26.4
Chinese, other Asia	23.2	36.8	34.8	17.4	27.7
Europe, Canada	28.1	28.1	45.6	35.1	26.3
p*	< .001	< .001	< .001	< .001	< .001
Socioeconomic status[5]					
Bottom tertile	33.8	42.5	47.8	21.1	27.8
Middle tertile	29.3	37.0	40.8	28.4	24.8
Upper tertile	25.8	37.4	37.3	29.6	25.3
p*	< .001	< .004	< .001	< .001	ns

TABLE 8.2   (*continued*)

Variables	Unsafe conditions at school[1] (% High)	Many gangs at school[2] (% Agree)	Many fights between race-ethnic groups[2] (% Agree)	Drugs at school[3] (%)	High quality of teaching[4] (%)
Close friends who will attend a 4-year college[6]					
None	33.9	40.0	47.5	37.5	22.8
Some	32.0	41.0	44.5	31.6	23.4
Many	26.2	36.6	38.1	19.2	29.1
p^*	< .001	< .02	< .001	< .001	< .001
Close friends who dropped out of school[6]					
None	26.1	36.4	38.3	17.3	29.6
Some	32.6	41.0	44.8	36.0	21.8
Many	40.9	49.5	55.6	46.0	20.7
p^*	< .001	< .001	< .001	< .001	< .001

[1]High mean score (> 2.0) in four-item index; items measured from 1 to 4. See text for explanation.
[2]Percent who agreed with the statement as characterizing the respondent's school.
[3]Percent who reported being offered drugs for sale during current school year.
[4]High mean score (> 3.0) in four-item index; items measured from 1 to 4. See text for explanation.
[5]Composite index of father's and mother's education, occupational prestige, and home ownership, in 1992 tertiles.
[6]School plans of close friends, reported in the 1995–96 survey.
*Probability of differences being due to chance.
ns: not significant.

As Table 8.2 documents, different types of peer groups are closely associated with school conditions. Youths whose close friends plan to attend college tend to be enrolled in safer schools and report a significantly higher quality of teaching. Conversely, as Figure 8.2 also illustrates, students who reported that many of their close friends had dropped out of school attended institutions perceived as much more unsafe and plagued by interracial fights. This association is predictable as it points to the higher probability of dropping out from poorer schools and the lesser chance to find peers with firm college plans in these environments.

Reported exposure to illegal drugs at school yields several noteworthy results. Students were asked how many times in the current year someone offered to sell them drugs at school. While the question is discreet

Figure 8.2   School Indices and Dropout Status of Close
Friends, 1995–1996

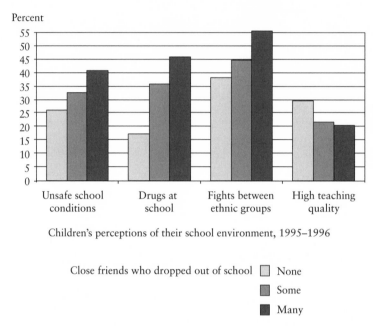

Children's perceptions of their school environment, 1995–1996

Close friends who dropped out of school ☐ None
                                          ■ Some
                                          ■ Many

NOTE: Probability of differences being due to chance is less than 1 in 1,000 for
all associations shown. All variables measured in 1995–1996 survey when most
respondents were completing high school.

and does not ask about personal drug use, it is indicative of an atmosphere where drugs and the drug trade are present. A fourth of the sample (26.5 percent) reported at least one or more such incidents with drug
sellers. Among national-origin groups, Colombians in Miami reported
by far the most frequent exposure (43 percent)—confirming the fears
about drugs expressed by Mr. Restrepo, the Colombian father profiled in
Chapter 4.

In this instance, parental socioeconomic status again plays a significant role but ironically, in a negative sense: As Table 8.2 shows, the
higher the family SES, the more likely it is that students have been
approached to buy illegal drugs. This anomalous association is weak,
but it suggests that even high-status children are not insulated form the
pervasive influence of the drug trade. Indeed, it may be their greater
wealth that turns them into more attractive targets to purveyors. Be that

as it may, the data also show a stronger relationship between the presence of drugs at school and the number of peers who have given up on education. That is, the greater the level of exposure to the drug scene, the more likely a respondent's close friends are to have dropped out of school and the fewer the number who are planning to attend college.[9]

Psychological Well-Being: Self-Esteem and Depressive Affect

Over the course of the study, we examined two key aspects of the children's psychological well-being: self-esteem and depressive affect. To measure the first, we administered the 10-item Rosenberg Global Self-Esteem Scale to the students in both surveys.[10] It is scored on a scale from 1 to 4. To measure depressive symptoms, we used the 4-item Center for Epidemiological Studies-Depression (CES-D) short-form scale. Respondents were asked how often during the past week they "felt sad," "could not get going," "did not feel like eating," and "felt depressed." Responses were scored from 1 to 4 on a scale from "rarely (less than once a week)" to "most of the time." The two measures get at different cognitive and affective dimensions of psychological well-being, although they are inversely related: The correlation between self-esteem and depression was 2.392 in the 1992 survey and 2.445 in 1995–1996.[11] The correlation of self-esteem scores from one survey to the other was .456; that of depression scores .338, indicating significant change in these measures over the three years.

Table 8.3 summarizes the principal results. Nearly half of the total sample (47.8 percent) showed high self-esteem (mean scores above 3.5) in the follow-up survey, an increase of 10 percentage points over the level measured three years earlier. By contrast, nearly a third of the sample exhibited a relatively high level of depressive symptoms (defined as CES-D mean scores above 2.0), about the same proportion as was observed in junior high school. The data show significant differences by national origin. All groups, without exception, went up in self-esteem in the span between both CILS surveys, showing normal and positive developmental adjustment in the movement from early to late adolescence. As Table 8.3 spells out, groups with the highest levels of self-esteem were Cubans and other Latin Americans (with the notable exception of Mexicans), West Indians, and Europeans/Canadians. Those with the lowest self-esteem scores were the children of southeast Asian refugees—Vietnamese, Lao, Hmong, and Cambodians. The same

Variables	High Self-Esteem[1] (%)	High Depressive Symptoms[2] (%)	N
Total	47.8	30.0	4,288
National origin			
Cuba (private school)	67.8	17.1	146
Cuba (public school)	58.1	26.9	822
Dominican Republic	61.5	34.6	78
Mexico	42.4	28.4	599
Nicaragua	55.5	32.0	281
Colombia	56.0	33.2	185
Other Latin America	55.7	24.7	280
Haiti	49.6	36.3	135
Jamaica	59.3	32.2	118
Other West Indies	63.9	27.7	83
Vietnam	25.8	34.6	310
Laos (Lao)	25.7	25.0	144
Laos (Hmong)	24.0	34.0	50
Cambodia	25.8	32.6	89
Philippines	39.8	32.7	724
Chinese, other Asia	47.1	36.8	155
Europe, Canada	57.9	21.1	57
p^*	<.001	<.001	
Sex			
Female	46.5	36.5	2,219
Male	49.2	22.9	2,069
p^*	N. S.	<.001	
Socioeconomic status[3]			
Bottom tertile	39.7	31.4	1,372
Middle tertile	50.0	30.1	1,445
Upper tertile	53.2	28.4	1,471
p^*	<.001	ns	

TABLE 8.3 *(continued)*

Variables	High Self-Esteem[1] (%)	High Depressive Symptoms[2] (%)	N
Stressful life events[4]			
None	50.2	25.6	2,091
One	47.4	31.2	1,419
Two or three	43.1	38.2	736
Four or more	26.2	61.9	42
p^*	<.001	<.001	
Family cohesion[5]			
Low	35.8	40.4	1,397
Middle	45.2	28.8	1,417
High	61.8	21.0	1,460
p^*	<.001	<.001	
Parent-child conflict[6]			
Low	64.2	17.3	1,531
Middle	46.3	29.6	1,478
High	30.0	45.5	1,279
p^*	<.001	<.001	
Language type[7]			
Fluent bilingual	63.7	25.8	1,105
English dominant	50.4	30.6	1,859
Foreign lang. dominant	35.0	29.3	454
Limited bilingual	28.9	34.3	870
p^*	<.001	<.001	

[1]Rosenberg self-esteem scale; high self-esteem (>3.5). See Appendix C for items and psychometric properties of scale.

[2]Center for Epidemiological Studies-Depression (CES-D); high depressive symptoms (>2.0). See Appendix C.

[3]Index of father's and mother's education, occupational prestige, and home ownership, in 1992 tertiles.

[4]Number of family stressful life events occurring during past year, reported in follow-up survey.

[5]Mean score in family cohesion index, measured in follow-up survey. Low <3.0; Medium 3.0–4.0; High >4.0

[6]Mean score on parent-child conflict index, measured in follow-up survey. Low <1.5; Medium 1.5–2.0; High >2.0.

[7]Based on scores in English and foreign language proficiency scales; see Chapter 6 for additional details.

* Probability of differences being due to chance.

ns: not significant.

rank order was not observed for depressive symptoms, however. Cubans in private school and the Europeans/Canadians fared best in this respect (with only about a fifth reporting high depression scores), followed by almost all of the other groups.

There is a marked divergence by gender with respect to psychological profiles. While the advantage in self-esteem by the latest survey was only marginally higher for males over females, there remained a sharp gender difference in depressive symptoms. Over a third of the females (36.5 percent) reported high depression scores, compared to less than a fourth of the males—a difference that remained essentially the same over time.[12] Family change, family cohesion, and conflict also correlated with both psychological measures. The greater the number of stressful family life-change events experienced by respondents in the years between the original and follow-up surveys, the lower their self-esteem and the higher the level of depression.

Differences in psychological well-being are still wider between respondents in low-conflict versus high-conflict families, underscoring the psychological costs of dissonant acculturation. This finding has both theoretical and practical implications because it shows that intergenerational dissonance not only reduces parental control but is also linked to a diminished sense of self-worth and well-being among children. If this conclusion is correct, effects of acculturative dissonance should also be reflected in strong relationships between measures of psychological well-being and types of language adaptation. This is just what the results in the bottom rows of Table 8.3 show. These findings confirm those presented in Chapter 6 indicating that fluent bilinguals tend to have significantly better psychological profiles, while limited bilinguals—a common product of forced language acculturation—have the worst. Nonconflictual family relations, parental language preservation, and positive psychological outcomes thus come together in a coherent whole, indicating the benefits of selective acculturation.

Finally, school environments and experiences also show strong associations with these psychological outcomes. Students attending schools reported as unsafe and plagued with gangs reported significantly lower self-esteem and higher depressive symptoms. The reverse pattern is seen with regard to students' perceptions of school quality: higher psychological well-being is correlated with good teaching and a fair and supportive learning climate. Figure 8.3 illustrates some of these relationships with respect to self-esteem outcomes.

Figure 8.3   Level of Self-Esteem by Family and School Indices, 1995–1996

Percent

Family and School Indices, 1995–1996

Self-Esteem   ■ Low
               ▨ Mid
               ▢ High

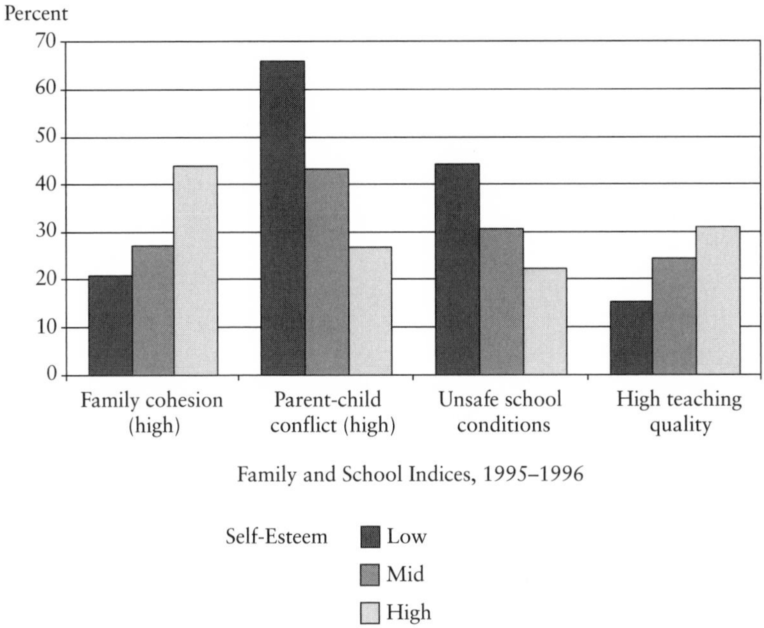

NOTE: Probability of differences being due to chance is less than 1 in 1,000 for all associations shown. Level of self-esteem is measured from scores in the Rosenberg 10-item scale administered in the 1995–1996 survey.

School Engagement and Effort

Lia Thao, a Hmong senior at Hoover High School in San Diego's central city, lives with her parents and five siblings in a small apartment near her school. As her family is very poor, she has found jobs at a local restaurant and as a classroom aide to help ends meet. Despite those demands, she spends hours on homework each night, and with the second-highest GPA among Hoover seniors, she plans to attend the University of California as a premed student. For her achievements, she gives credit to her family, especially her father, who fought in the war in Laos and now delivers produce. "One of the things he taught me is that a pen is heavier than a sword."[13]

School success and failure are influenced by a complex of objective and subjective factors, but among the most fundamental are those that involve the youths' motivation to learn and their willingness to expend the requisite effort to achieve educational goals. Indeed, the evidence

TABLE 8.4

SCHOOL ENGAGEMENT AND SCHOOL WORK
DISCIPLINE, BY SELECTED VARIABLES,
1992–1996

Variables	School Engagement[1] (% high)	Homework: Over Two Hours Daily[2] (%)	N
Total	56.2	26.0	4,288
	National Origin		
Cuba (private school)	50.7	17.1	146
Cuba (public school)	50.2	16.4	822
Dominican Republic	47.4	16.8	78
Mexico	52.4	14.4	599
Nicaragua	57.3	21.4	281
Colombia	44.3	16.8	185
Other Latin America	53.2	18.2	280
Haiti	52.6	22.2	135
Jamaica	70.3	36.4	118
Other West Indies	68.7	25.3	83
Vietnam	58.7	44.8	310
Laos (Lao)	68.6	38.2	144
Laos (Hmong)	62.0	48.0	50
Cambodia	59.6	36.0	89
Philippines	64.0	40.8	724
Chinese, other Asia	61.3	38.1	155
Europe, Canada	56.1	17.5	57
p^*	<.001	<.001	
	Sex		
Female	60.5	31.4	2,219
Male	51.7	20.2	2,069
p^*	<.001	<.001	

from the research literature indicates that high academic expectations
successfully predict subsequent educational performance and occupational choice.[14] Table 8.4 presents two preliminary indicators from our
longitudinal data: a measure of school engagement and the number of
hours spent daily on homework. School engagement is operationalized
as responses to an attitudinal item asking how important grades are to

TABLE 8.4   *(continued)*

Variables	School Engagement[1] (% high)	Homework: Over Two Hours Daily[2] (%)	N
Family cohesion[3]			
Low	48.1	21.3	1,397
Middle	56.6	27.6	1,417
High	63.9	29.1	1,460
p*	<.001	<.001	
Close friends who dropped out of school[4]			
None	61.5	32.0	2,288
Some	51.2	19.8	1,802
Many	41.4	13.1	198
p*	<.001	<.001	
Close friends who will attend a four-year college[4]			
None	43.8	12.9	333
Some	52.1	20.6	2,027
Many	62.8	34.0	1,928
p*	<.001	<.001	

[1]Percent who indicated that "grades are very important" to them in both 1992 and 1995–1996.
[2]Percent who reported over two hours spent daily on school homework, in both surveys.
[3]Score in family cohesion index, measured in follow-up survey. See cutoff points in Table 8.3.
[4]School plans of close friends, reported in follow-up survey.
*Probability of differences being due to chance.
ns: not significant.

the student. *High engagement* is defined as responses of "very important" in both surveys. Schoolwork discipline is measured by the percent who reported that they spent over two hours daily on homework in both surveys—an indicator of persistent effort well above the national average of one hour or less among all public high school students.

Table 8.4 breaks down these indicators by nationality and other key variables. Over half of CILS's follow-up sample reported high school engagement, and about one-fourth put a serious level of effort in their schoolwork. As with other psychosocial indicators, there are significant differences by nationality. Haitians and Latin Americans show the low-

Figure 8.4   School Engagement and School Work Effort, by Year of
Arrival in the United States

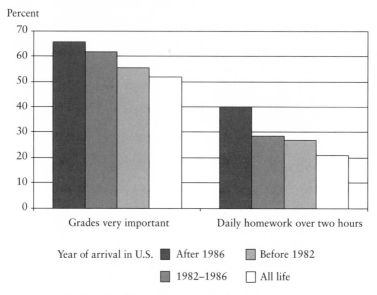

NOTE: Probability of differences being due to chance is less than 1 in 1,000 for all
associations shown. See text for explanation of measurement of variables.

est levels of school engagement, and West Indians plus all Asian groups
show the highest. On schoolwork, intergroup differences become much
wider, with all Asian groups putting in at least twice the amount of time
on homework as Latin Americans, Europeans/Canadians, and others.
Hmong students averaged almost three hours of reported homework
per day, a pattern that Lia Thao's story helps illustrate. All other Asian
groups came close to this figure, while only about one-sixth of Cubans,
Colombians, Dominicans, and Mexicans devoted two or more hours
daily to school homework.[15]

Notice the disjuncture between the association of national origin
with dissonant/selective acculturation and school engagement and
effort. In general, Latin children exhibit the highest levels of fluent bilingualism, high levels of family cohesion, and low intergenerational conflict. These positive outcomes do not translate, however, into extraordinary school effort but are associated instead with a more relaxed
attitude toward schoolwork. By contrast, Asian-origin children, despite
greater difficulties in retaining their parental languages and higher lev-

els of intergenerational conflict, are strongly driven to succeed in school. In their case, different dynamics seem to be at play, guiding their orientation toward achievement.

It is likely that in this case, selective acculturation is manifested less in fluent bilingualism than in the intergenerational transmission of a strong achievement drive. It is also possible that many of the reported discrepancies with parents have to do with the latter's extraordinary pressure on children to achieve, a pattern rendered plausible by many of our qualitative interviews. In any case, these results reveal a broad divergence in intergenerational relations and individual drive by national origin. We will see in the following section how these dynamics play themselves out in the development of educational expectations, and in the following chapter we will examine their bearing on actual academic achievement.

As with full bilingualism, discussed in Chapter 6, gender has a significant relationship to school engagement and discipline, with girls showing significantly higher levels of interest and work effort. These results are in line with our theoretical discussion in Chapter 3 concerning expected gender differences in adaptation. Acculturation, as indexed by length of U.S. residence, relates to these variables in a by-now-predictable pattern, namely, to *reduce* engagement and effort. Thus, the longer a child of immigrants has lived in this country, the lower the importance he or she attributes to school grades and the more his or her schoolwork habits approach the (low) average of the general student population. The achievement drive common among many immigrant children, especially those of Asian origin, declines steadily over time. Figure 8.4 illustrates this notable relationship between school engagement and the advance of the acculturation process.

Educational Expectations

A second and still more central aspect of subjective drive consists of the aspirations and expectations that children have for their future. These dimensions have been shown to affect positively and consistently subsequent educational and occupational achievement. This causal relation has been identified both in national samples and among specific ethnic minorities.[16] Aspirations and expectations are not the same thing. *Aspirations* refer to desired levels of future performance (what people want to happen); *expectations* are beliefs about a probable future state of affairs (what people think will happen). Aspirations are less realistic than expectations, since what people subjectively desire typically exceeds what they rationally expect. As such, expectations constitute the fundamental blocks on which future behavioral choices are made.[17]

In both surveys we asked respondents about their educational aspirations—"What is the highest level of education you would *like* to achieve?"—as well as their expectations—"And *realistically speaking, what is the highest level of education that you think you* will *get?"* Each of these items was scored 1 to 5 ("less than high school," "finish high school," "some college," "finish college," and "finish a graduate degree"). Table 8.5 summarizes the results for students who in 1995–1996 aspired to an advanced degree and those who realistically expected to earn such a degree. As the table shows, the percentage aspiring to an advanced degree (66.5 percent) is much higher than the percentage who realistically expected to attain it (44 percent)—although both figures reflect a very high overall level of ambition.

Further, the data point to the resilience of aspirations and expectations over time. For the sample as a whole, these variables remained virtually identical from junior high to the end of high school. For the sample as a whole, the proportion aspiring to an advanced degree changed less than 1 percent during this period (67.0 to 66.5), and expectations changed less than 2 percent. Similarly small changes occur when these variables are broken down by gender, parental SES, and national origin, with exceptions noted as follows.

In both surveys, significant differences in aspirations and expectations emerged among nationalities. The most ambitious groups were Cubans in bilingual private schools in Miami and Chinese and other Asians (mostly Japanese, Koreans, and Indians). Along with the Vietnamese, these were the groups that showed the most significant *increases* in educational expectations over time. Realistic expectations for an advanced degree increased by 9 percent among Cuban and Vietnamese students and by a remarkable 15 percent among Chinese and other Asians. At the bottom of the distribution were Dominicans, Mexicans, Laotians, and Cambodians.

The Hmong, who come from the poorest immigrant group in the country, are perhaps the most poignant example of the gulf that can open between educational aspirations and realities. We just saw in the previous section how Hmong-origin students display the highest level of schoolwork effort. In their own perceptions, however, this is not enough: While 54 percent of Hmong youths aspired to an advanced degree, a minuscule 6 percent realistically expected that they would be

Variables[1]	Aspires to an Advanced Degree, 1995–1996 (%)	Expects an Advanced Degree, 1995–1996 (%)	N
Total	66.5	44.0	4,288

National Origin

Cuba (private school)	84.9	75.3	146
Cuba (public school)	69.2	46.6	822
Dominican Republic	47.4	34.6	78
Mexico	48.4	24.9	599
Nicaragua	76.9	49.5	281
Colombia	68.1	47.0	185
Other Latin America	68.6	45.4	280
Haiti	67.4	54.8	135
Jamaica	75.4	54.2	118
Other West Indies	74.7	56.6	83
Vietnam	68.7	48.1	310
Laos (Lao)	50.7	22.2	144
Laos (Hmong)	54.0	6.0	50
Cambodia	51.7	22.5	89
Philippines	71.4	44.5	724
Chinese, other Asia	74.8	65.2	155
Europe, Canada	68.4	57.9	57
p^*	<.001	<.001	

Sex

Female	73.0	48.9	2,219
Male	59.6	38.8	2,069
p^*	<.001	<.001	

Socioeconomic status

Bottom tertile	54.7	29.5	1,372
Middle tertile	65.7	43.5	1,445
Upper tertile	78.3	58.1	1,471
p^*	<.001	<.001	

(continued on next page)

TABLE 8.5   (*continued*)

Variables[1]	Aspires to an Advanced Degree, 1995–1996 (%)	Expects an Advanced Degree, 1995–1996 (%)	N
	Family cohesion		
Low	63.2	37.1	1,397
Middle	66.1	43.7	1,417
High	70.3	51.0	1,460
p*	<.001	<.001	
	Parent-child conflict		
Low	70.4	53.2	1,531
Middle	66.5	43.2	1,478
High	61.9	34.1	1,279
p*	<.001	<.001	
	Language type		
Fluent bilingual	74.8	54.3	1,105
English dominant	70.1	47.7	1,859
Foreign lang. dominant	56.6	32.6	454
Limited bilingual	53.7	29.2	870
p*	<.001	<.001	
	Parents' perceived aspirations for child[2]		
Less than college degree	28.8	15.2	1,692
Finish 4-year college	34.0	20.0	1,463
Advanced degree	85.1	57.9	1,111
p*	<.001	<.001	

[1]See text and previous tables for description of variables and cutoff points.
[2]Respondents' perceptions of their parents' educational aspirations for them, reported in 1995–1996.
*Probability of differences being due to chance.

able to attain it. That figure actually reflects a decline of 6 percent since junior high school. The Hmong, along with other second-generation southeast Asians, thus exhibit a notable combination of subjective traits characterized by high school discipline and engagement along with poor self-esteem and a pessimistic view of their future chances in life. The question remains of how these contradictory trends affect their actual educational achievement.

Predictably, advanced career goals increase with family socioeconomic status, the differentials across status categories becoming wider in the youths' expectations of what they will actually achieve. Female students aim much higher than males, with half of the females expecting to earn an advanced degree. Although not shown in Table 8.5, these gender differentials are reflected in occupational aspirations as well. The difference is most telling with respect to aspirations to become physicians—the top-status career choice of 18 percent of the sample in the latest survey. Across almost all nationalities, female students voiced this career aspiration significantly more often than males. This is in line with our analysis in Chapter 3 that points to distinct gender complexes, in which females combine higher goals and school effort with persistent lower levels of psychological well-being.

The importance of patterns of acculturation is again made clear by the next three breakdowns in the table. Dissonant acculturation reduces ambition, and consonant or selective acculturation increases it. Thus, both educational aspirations and expectations rise significantly with family cohesion and decline with parent-child conflict. As seen in Chapter 6, high educational expectations are most common among fluent bilinguals. Along the same lines, the importance of parental goals on children's own ambition is evident in the bottom rows of Table 8.5. Only 28.8 percent of students whose parents held less than college aspirations for them aspired to an advanced degree; the figure increases to a remarkable 85 percent among those who saw their parents as having high goals for them.

The relationship between educational expectations and other psychosocial dimensions examined previously is illustrated in Figure 8.5. For the sample as a whole, self-esteem and educational expectations are strongly and positively correlated; the same is true with indicators of school engagement and effort. Thus, at the bivariate level, a series of mutually supportive relations emerges that is generally congruent with our initial theoretical framework. Consonant/selective acculturation, including fluent bilingualism, relate positively to key psychosocial outcomes. These subjective variables, including self-esteem and ambition, in turn relate strongly to each other, suggesting a "virtuous cycle" of cumulative development. The opposite downward cycle is associated with acculturative dissonance. This general trend registers some notable exceptions by gender and by southeast Asian nationalities, as discussed previously. We examine next how these diverse factors come together as actual determinants of psychological well-being and ambition.

Figure 8.5   Educational Expectations and Its Correlates, 1995–1996

Percent

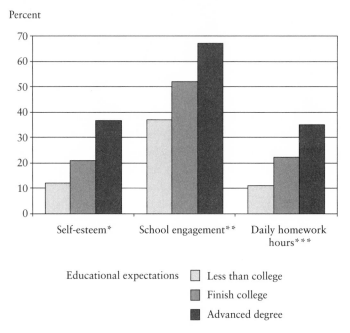

NOTE: Probability of differences being due to chance is less than 1 in 1,000 for all associations shown. Predictors are scores from composite indices measured in both the 1992 and 1995–1996 surveys. Educational expectations are those reported in 1995–1996.
* Percent scoring high (>3.5) in Rosenberg's self-esteem scale.
** Percent indicating that "grades are very important to me" in both surveys.
*** Percent who reported two or more daily homework hours in both surveys.

Determinants of Psychosocial Outcomes

Self-Esteem and Depression

As in the analysis of ethnic and racial identities in Chapter 7, we seek to predict major psychosocial outcomes in late adolescence on the basis of mostly objective individual and family traits measured three years earlier. To these we add subjective reports, also measured in junior high school, that indicate types of acculturation and early experiences of discrimination. As in past models, we do not include all possible predictors but seek to develop parsimonious models on the basis of the framework outlined in Chapter 3. By establishing a clear separation in time between psychosocial variables and their predictors, we seek to avoid, at least partially, the strong tendency of these variables to be causally ambiguous—affecting various adaptation outcomes and being affected by them in turn.

For the sake of brevity, we do not examine determinants of every dimension discussed previously but only the most theoretically important. Models of self-esteem and psychological depression are presented next, followed by educational aspirations and expectations. Rosenberg's self-esteem and the CES-D depression scales are continuous measures lending themselves to multivariate least-squares regression analysis. Rosenberg's scale, where higher scores indicate greater self-esteem, is skewed to the left; the opposite happens with the CES-D scale, where higher scores indicate greater depression. For this reason, both variables were transformed.[18] Table 8.6 presents results of the analysis in three successive columns: The first includes individual and family characteristics; the second adds national communities of origin; and the third includes the autoregression effect of the dependent variable, measured three years before.

Self-esteem in late adolescence is very responsive to length and types of acculturation, as shown in the first column of the table. Length of acculturation, as indexed by U.S. nativity and long-term U.S. residence, increases self-esteem, but dissonant acculturation, measured by higher parent-child conflict and feelings of embarrassment toward parents, reduces it significantly. So do higher experiences of discrimination, a reasonable result in light of the impact that such episodes can have on the self-images of the young. The effects of language adaptation support these results and offer strong evidence for the positive influence of selective acculturation, as reflected in fluent bilingualism, on psychosocial outcomes. The effect is very strong, exceeding eight times its standard error. By contrast, limited bilingualism—another indicator of dissonance—significantly reduces self-esteem.

Gender has a major effect on this outcome, with girls exhibiting lower scores after controlling for other variables. In Chapter 6 we saw that female students were significantly more likely to be fluent bilinguals, an effect that should improve their self-esteem. With language adaptation controlled, however, the gender effect runs in the opposite direction. Early academic performance also has a strong influence on self-esteem, with higher school grades leading to a more positive self-image. Controlling for this array of variables, family characteristics—parental SES and intact families—have positive but

TABLE 8.6   DETERMINANTS OF SELF-ESTEEM AND PSYCHOLOGICAL DEPRESSION, 1995–1996

Predictors[1]	Self-esteem[2] I	II[4]	III[4]	Depression[3] I	II[4]	III[4]
Demographic						
Age	.38[5]			.00[5]		
Sex (Female)	-1.93**	-1.97**		.13***	.13***	
Region (S. California)	-5.14***		-.88*	.01		.09***
Family						
Parental SES	.88*	.81*		.01		
Intact family	.53			-.06**	-.06**	-.04*
Length of acculturation						
U.S. born	1.58*	1.25*		.00		
Long-term U.S. resident[6]	1.57*	1.76*		-.01		
Type of acculturation						
Limited bilingual	-2.63**	-2.13*		-.02		
Fluent bilingual	4.51***	4.20***	2.98**	-.05**	.04**	-.04*
Parent-child conflict	-1.14**	-1.07*		.04***	-.04***	.02*
Embarrassed by parents	-1.48**	-1.35**		.03**	.03**	.02*
Experienced discrimination	-1.08	-1.09*		.06**	.05**	.03*
School						
Grade Point Average	1.33**	1.60***	.67*	-.00		

Nationality

Chinese/Korean				−.07*
Colombian				
Cuban, private school				
Cuban, public school				
Filipino		−3.37*		
Haitian				
Laotian/Cambodian		−4.43**	−2.25*	
Mexican				
Nicaraguan				
Vietnamese		−6.45**	−3.74*	
West Indian				
Auto-regression				
Self-esteem		.07	.39#	−.02
Depression		.07	−.05	.28#
Constant	40.48	35.34	21.42	.03
R^2	.11	.12	.23	.14
N	4,321	4,321	4,321	4,321

[1]All predictors measured in first survey, 1992. See text for explanation.
[2]Exponential transformation of Rosenberg's self-esteem scale. Positive values indicate higher self-esteem.
[3]Logarithmic transformation of CES-D scale. Positive values indicate higher depression.
[4]Statistically insignificant effects omitted.
[5]Non-asterisked coefficients are statistically insignificant.
[6]Ten or more years in the U.S. Less than ten years in the reference category.
*Moderate effect (exceeds twice its standard error).
**Strong effect (exceeds four times its standard error).
***Very strong effect (exceeds six times its standard error).
#Auto-regression effect (exceeds 10 times its standard error).

relatively weak effects. This indicates that the influence of early parental outcomes on children's self-esteem is mediated through the latter's own acculturative experiences, including language adaptation and school achievement.

One of the strongest effects in the table is that of region of residence, which suggests that living in California depresses self-esteem. That result is, however, spurious because it reflects the concentration in San Diego of nationalities with strong propensities toward lower self-esteem, controlling for other variables. Southeast Asian refugees and Filipinos belong in this category. Since these groups were favorably or neutrally received in the United States, some having been recipients of generous government assistance, these effects cannot be attributed to their negative mode of incorporation. In the case of Filipinos, this finding also contradicts original expectations that predicted better psychosocial adjustment among nationalities with high levels of parental human capital.[19]

The third column of Table 8.6 introduces the autoregression effect of self-esteem. This modifies the interpretation of coefficients that now indicate the bearing of each predictor on *change* in self-esteem over the adolescent years. The autoregression effect is very strong. Since limited change occurred over time, the number of significant effects is reduced accordingly. Fluent bilingualism and high GPAs improve self-esteem over time; a southeast Asian refugee background continues to reduce it, even after controlling for the lower self-esteem of these students three years earlier. No other variable affects this changed definition of the dependent variable, indicating that most observed relationships were already present in early adolescence.[20] The remarkable effect of southeast Asian origin suggests that in this case, Rosenberg's scale could be partially invalid because of these children's cultural peculiarities. However, the observed result is congruent with other findings for these groups, including their generally low parental education, traumatic experiences of flight and resettlement, and mostly low expectations for the future. These factors converge in a distinct psychological complex that affects children's self-esteem.

The last three columns of Table 8.6 show results of regressing the logarithm of CES-D depression scores on the same set of predictors. With some exceptions, results are quite similar to those just reviewed. The strongest effect is that of gender in a pattern akin to that noted earlier:

Girls exhibit higher depression levels, congruent with their lower self-esteem. Length of acculturation has no effect on depression, but dissonant acculturation, as indexed by levels of parent-child conflict and feelings of embarrassment of parents, leads to significantly higher levels, as do past experiences of discrimination. Selective acculturation, reflected in fluent bilingualism, has the opposite effect, sharply reducing depression. In this instance, unlike preceding models, family composition retains a significant independent influence, with intact families protecting their children against maladjustment.

These combined effects indicate that strong family and ethnic community affiliations support the psychosocial adaptation of second-generation children, while acculturative dissonance threatens it. These findings are in line with our theoretical expectations. On the other hand, the lower self-esteem and higher depression levels observed among female students reflect broader sociocultural processes that transcend the second generation, as similar results have been reported by several national samples.[21] They indicate that among children of immigrants as among those of native parentage, the traumas of adolescence and adult socialization have a stronger negative effect among young females. Controlling for these individual and family characteristics, no nationality retains an independent influence, showing that the earlier bivariate associations between national origin and depression are entirely accounted for by the factors just discussed.

The introduction of the autoregression effect of CES-D scores leaves these conclusions unaltered but strengthens the plausibility of the observed causal effects. That is, with early depression controlled, gender plus measures of selective and dissonant acculturation continue to influence significantly the dependent variable, indicating an unambiguous causal pattern. The same is the case for family structure. As indicators of psychosocial adjustment, self-esteem and depression represent important outcomes of the adaptation process, and they are expected to affect later dimensions. The bearing of self-esteem on these dimensions, including academic achievement, will be examined in the following chapter.

Ambition

> All brains are, in essence, anticipation machines.
> **—Daniel C. Dennett, *Consciousness Explained***

> These questions about what education I'd like to get and what educa-
> tion I will really get are silly. Like I mean, if this is what I really want,
> that's what I'll get. No question about it.
> **—Angel, student at Belén Jesuit Prep, Miami, 1995**

In modeling determinants of educational aspirations and expectations, we follow past theories of the status attainment process that define ambition as an outcome of family variables, especially parental SES and past academic performance.[22] To these variables, we add age and sex, measures of length and type of acculturation, and national background. As in past analyses, we seek to establish the independent effect of individual and family variables plus the extent to which they account for intergroup differences. Significant net nationality effects are indicative of the durable influence of an immigrant group's sociocultural characteristics and modes of incorporation.

Both educational aspirations and expectations are highly skewed variables, with most respondents clustered toward the high end. Over 60 percent in the follow-up survey indicated that they aspired, and over 40 percent expected, to reach an advanced postgraduate degree. Since both variables were originally measured as ordinal scales, we opt to dichotomize them and to examine determinants through logistic regression. For this analysis, postcollege aspirations and expectations are coded one. Table 8.7 presents results in two panels for each variable, the first including national origin and all individual and family predictors and the second adding autoregression effects as a means to establish changes in ambition over time. In addition to regression coefficients, the table includes Wald statistics as measures of their respective strength. Statistically significant coefficients are translated into probabilities that indicate the net change in the chances of aspiring or expecting an advanced degree associated with each predictor.

The models do a good job of accounting for each dependent variable, correctly predicting over 75 percent of the cases in each specification. For the sake of brevity, we focus on significant effects on educational expectations, noting differences with aspirations where relevant. Results in Table 8.7 confirm the dominant effects of parental SES and academic grades, as posited by status attainment theory. These effects are positive and very strong, each exceeding 10 times its standard error. Each unit increase in the Parental SES index raises the probability of aiming at an advanced degree by a net 9 percent; each higher grade point increases it by 17 percent. The strength of these coefficients dwarfs those of most other predictors, although other effects deserve mention. Female students have significantly higher educational goals than males, a pattern that contrasts sharply with girls' lower self-esteem and higher levels of depression. The distinct role of gender in adaptation is reflected in this finding: Second-generation females combine greater adherence to their parents' language and ambitions for the future with a more problematic psychological profile, reflecting their socialization into distinct gender roles.[23]

Length of acculturation has no effect on educational expectations, but indicators of types of acculturation have the predicted consequences. Early parent-child conflict and limited bilingualism reduce ambition, reflecting the influence of dissonant acculturation. The pattern is confirmed with the opposite effect of fluent bilingualism: Controlling for other variables, children who managed to preserve their home languages along with English in early adolescence exhibit significantly higher ambition later on in life. Thus, it is not the length but the type of acculturation that children undergo that emerges as a main determinant of their future orientations.

Controlling for these factors, only a few nationalities continue to retain an independent effect. But the contrast between dreams and realities is very apparent in these findings. Children of Nicaraguan immigrants and Vietnamese refugees, for example, have grand aspirations, but these lofty goals are greatly reduced when asked what they realistically expect to achieve. The independent effects of both nationalities on expectations remain positive, but are insignificant. This contrast reflects the perceived impact of a challenging outside environment and modest family resources. In the Nicaraguan case, the gap between aspirations and expectations is well illustrated by the family of Milagros Fernández-Rey, whose story is sketched in Chapter 1.

The notable exception to this trend is reflected in Cuban-American students in private schools, who retain strong positive effects on both measures of ambition. As the remark of Angel at the beginning of this section illustrates, many of these children could not understand the difference in survey questions about aspirations and expectations since they perceived no serious obstacles to the fulfillment of their goals. Controlling for other variables, Cuban students in private schools have a 16 percent greater probability of expecting an advanced degree. This figure reflects the privileged situation of these youths, who are mostly descendants of the early and economically successful waves of Cuban exiles.[24]

A major contrast is apparent between these Cuban-American students and Mexican Americans who continue to voice much humbler goals, even

TABLE 8.7 DETERMINANTS OF EDUCATIONAL ASPIRATIONS AND EXPECTATIONS, 1995–1996

	Aspirations					Expectations				
	I			II[2]		I			II[2]	
Predictors[1]	Coefficient[3]	Wald Statistic[4]	p[5]	Coefficient	Wald Statistic	Coefficient[3]	Wald Statistic[4]	p[5]	Coefficient	Wald Statistic
Demographic										
Age	-.13	-9.75*	-.03	-.12	-7.00*	-.10	-3.8*	-.02		
Sex (Female)	.50	45.98**	.10	.36	21.36**	.32	12.36*	.04	.30	10.22*
Region (S. California)	-.43	-5.16	-.10			-.24	-.91[6]			
Family										
Parental SES	.42	51.95***	.09	.28	21.84**	.63	72.11***	.09	.50	43.3 ***
Intact family	-.01	-.04[6]				.00	.00			
Length of Acculturation										
U.S. born	.07	.55				.20	2.97*			
Long-term U.S. resident[7]	-.14	-2.13				.07	.33			
Type of Acculturation										
Limited bilingual	-.28	-8.55*	-.06			-.26	-5.09*	-.04		
Fluent bilingual	.40	17.23**	.08	.30	9.36*	.31	6.34*	.04		
Parent-child conflict	-.05	-1.02				-.18	-9.16*	-.03	-.19	-8.87*
Embarrassed by parents	-.02	-.14				-.03	-.35			
Experienced discrimination	.13	3.22				.08	.74			
School										
GPA, 1992	.66	197.32***	.13	.54	121.53***	.83	204.33***	.10	.70	137.09***

Nationality

Nationality[1]								
Chinese/Korean	.36	1.30				.26	.31	
Colombian	.15	.56				.21	.66	
Cuban, private school	.90	9.74*	.16	.76	6.56*	2.56	6.69*	.16
Cuban, public school	.22	2.63				.20	1.21	2.33
Filipino	.31	2.30				-.25	-.86	
Haitian	.25	1.17				-.06	-.06	
Laotian/Cambodian	.16	.47				-.18	-.35	
Mexican	-.34	-5.7*	-.10			.53	-4.14*	-.10
Nicaraguan	.67	12.42*	.13	.59	9.01*	.36	2.25	
Vietnamese	.53	5.25*	.11	.59	6.05*	.42	1.83	
West Indian	.38	3.49				-.21	-.75	5.51*
Autoregression								
Aspirations		1.32#						1.29#
Expectations						1.40		
Constant	.51	-.06				1.40	.65	
Model chi square (degrees of freedom)	686.33## (24)	978.83## (25)				690.75## (24)	862.02## (25)	
N	4,225	4,232				4,232		

[1] All predictors measured in first survey. See text for explanation.
[2] Statistically insignficant effects omitted.
[3] Logistic regression coefficients predicting the log-odds of aspiring or expecting a postgraduate degree.
[4] Coefficient of strength of association.
[5] Net increase/decrease in the probability of aspiring or expecting a postgraduate degree per unit change of each predictor variable.
[6] Nonasterisked coefficients are statistically insignificant.
[7] Ten years or more in the U.S. Less than 10 years is the reference category.
* Moderate effect (coefficient exceeds twice its standard error).
** Strong effect (coefficient exceeds four times its standard error).
*** Very strong effect (coefficient exceeds six times its standard error).
**** Very strong effect (coefficient exceeds ten times its standard error).
# Autoregression effect exceeds six times its standard error.
Probability of model improvement being due to chance is less than 1 in 10,000.

after controlling for age, sex, parental SES, and acculturation. The bearing of the history and negative modes of incorporation of Mexican immigrants on the adaptation of their young is evident in these findings where, independent of other factors, Mexican origin reduces educational aspirations and expectations by almost 10 percent. As the case of Alberto Díaz at the beginning of this chapter shows, Mexican parents also voice high aspirations for their children and encourage them to achieve in schools. But the self-reinforcing web of objective disadvantages that they face—an often insecure legal status, persecution by immigration authorities, poor and dangerous neighborhoods—takes a definite toll, making the goal of a college education an unrealistic dream for the children.

Introducing the autoregression effects of educational expectations leaves the preceding results largely intact, except that language ceases to be a significant predictor. This means that the effect of language adaptation type on ambition operates on the stable component of the latter rather than on change over time. By the same token, it leaves open the possibility of a two-way causal effect. In Chapter 6 and earlier in this chapter, we presented figures showing educational ambition to be a strong correlate of fluent bilingualism. The present results confirm this finding but do not firmly establish causal direction, implying that both variables may be mutually reinforcing. In contrast, the effects of early grades and parent-child conflict, as an indicator of dissonance, remain strong after taking autoregression into account, further validating their causal influence.

Conclusion

> We began to develop a taste for the American good teenage life and soon Island was old hat, man . . . By the end of a couple of years, we had more than adjusted. And, of course, as soon as we had, Mami and Papi got all worried that they were going to lose their girls to America . . . The next decision was obvious—we four girls would be sent summers to the Island so we won't lose touch with la familia.
>
> **—Julia Alvarez, *How the García Girls Lost their Accent***

To avoid losing her daughter Thuy to America, Mrs. Huyhn sings karaoke in Vietnamese with her. Mrs. Huyhn was a seamstress in Vietnam, but she now lives alone with Thuy in San Diego. Their source of income is "a check that comes in the mail." Although a single parent and at a loss in her new world, she struggles indefatigably to push her girl ahead. She buys the Vietnamese karaoke videos and decorates her otherwise bare living room with photos of Thuy and mementos of her achievements. Exceptionally, Thuy has managed to retain her Vietnamese, which she speaks daily with her mother. One of the living room plaques recognizes Thuy for achieving the highest GPA in her school during the preceding year. Like the Ngo family, described in a story at the beginning of this chapter, Mrs. Huyhn does not have the means to send Thuy back to Vietnam during the summers. Unlike the Ngos, she does not bombard her daughter with written proverbs from the old country but has instead turned her tiny apartment into a shrine to her daughter and her ancestral past. The karaoke sessions are paying off: Thuy wants to be a gynecologist, and her high grades position her well for a scholarship; she is firmly set on achieving this goal.

As we complete our tour of the psychology of the second generation, two apparently contradictory trends stand out. The first is the *lawfulness* of the process of adaptation as successive outcomes build on each other, leading to predictable consequences. Hence, parental success in opening the doors to the American middle class translates into higher educational ambitions among children and greater confidence in reaching these goals. Higher parental status and unbroken families support fluent bilingualism and other manifestations of selective acculturation that, in turn, increase self-esteem, reinforce aspirations, and lower psychological distress. A favorable mode of incorporation and early academic achievement in school also set the grounds for an optimistic outlook on the future.

But amidst these predictable trends, we also discern other paradoxical outcomes that involve both individuals and collectivities.[25] At the collective level, certain nationalities manifest unexpected results that are at times incompatible with their known histories. The low self-esteem of Filipinos fits into this category, as it endures after taking family characteristics into account and cannot be attributed to a negative context of reception. The humble aspirations of Mexican Americans are a reflection of the negative incorporation of their parents but are noteworthy because they persist regardless of parental achievement, language preservation, or type of acculturation. This is a telling demonstration of the power of social context.

At the individual level, there are surprising stories of children's lack of ambition despite parental achievement and, conversely, of willpower and determination in the face of adverse circumstances. The case of Yvette Santana (Chapter 1) is an example of the first outcome, and those of Aristide Maillol (Chapter 1), Roberto Santos (Chapter 4), and Thuy Huyhn represent noteworthy instances of the second. Throughout, we have relied on these individual cases both to help guide the analysis and to emphasize variability and exceptions to statistical averages. For the García sisters, for example, traveling to the Dominican Republic in the summers was the usual thing to do, as their parents sought to slow down their acculturation to America, but they could not know that their experience was exceptional.[26]

Most immigrant parents cannot or will not send their children back home. They rely instead on the strength of their community or of their family to help preserve some connection with the old country and, through these, some semblance of parental authority. They take their children to church or temple, surround them with relatives, pepper them with proverbs in the home language, and sing karaoke with them in an effort to stem dissonant acculturation. The successive outcomes documented in our data, though predictable on the average, clearly show the manifold results that such efforts produce and the divergent ways in which children adapt to the chances and challenges of their situation.

Chapter 9

SCHOOL ACHIEVEMENT AND FAILURE

Van Le was born into a North Vietnamese family that emigrated south after the partition of their country. The family reemigrated again after the fall of Saigon, so that by age 15 Van found himself a refugee in the United States along with nine siblings and a widowed mother. Van spoke no English at the time although his father spent considerable time teaching him math and other basic subjects before he died. Now, as the older brother, it was Van's obligation to pass this information along to his younger siblings.

Five years later, Van was a medical student at the University of California with a GPA of 3.95. He explains his academic success as the result of the pressures suffered in his country: "If you fail a class, you go into the military. And that's for life. Don't get out until you die or lose your arm or leg. So that's a very strong pressure on the man in Vietnam. In Vietnam, exam only once a year. You fail exam, you fail class. That's why Vietnamese of my generation work harder in school, because we went through that kind of environment."[1]

Coming from that environment, Van marveled at how easy school was in America and, particularly, at the obvious tie between effort and reward: "So every time I think about that I work harder. The nice thing about the U.S. is the harder I work, the more I can advance. Not like in Vietnam. It was not sure there whether you can advance even if you work harder."

Charged with instructing his younger brothers and sisters, Van laments what he sees as rapid signs of "Americanization." One of his younger sisters "even studies like an American. Waits till the night before the exam to study, instead of like us steady for a week in advance. And then she comes up and complains that she got a B on a paper. And she wrote it last night!" The change is obviously linked in his mind to the changes in early life experiences: "The younger ones see the easy life in America. They don't have to go through the time that they starve to death and hungry and didn't have money . . . and they have no problem with the English. But it turns out that they use that to just relax and work less."

Unlike the adult first generation, for whom success or failure is largely determined by performance in the labor market, for the second generation the key outcomes are linked to academic achievement. How well they do and how far they go in school will govern their eventual position in the American status system. This applies both individually and collectively. One of the most noteworthy features of this process is that in addition to family status and related variables, the experiences that the child and the family bring from their country of origin condition their perceptions and attainment in American schools. As the case of Van Le illustrates, difficult experiences of flight and resettlement often provide a spur to greater effort, as children compare their present lot with what they left behind. In other instances, longer periods of U.S. residence and a more secure stake in the country lead to a less driven attitude, as immigrant youths learn to imitate their American peers.

Our analysis of academic achievement pays close attention to these contextual factors while building on the set of results described previously. In other words, we wish to know how the structure of the family and the achievements of the first generation, the presence or absence of bilingualism, the extent of dissonant or selective acculturation, and the levels of ambition and self-esteem of the children themselves condition their performance in school and their chances for securing their degrees.

Early Educational Achievement

Preliminary Results

We focus first on academic test scores and GPAs in the junior high school years, both because of their intrinsic interest and as a point of reference for subsequent educational outcomes. Chapter 3 makes certain predictions concerning the effects of parental SES, family composition, acculturation, and types of school environment on attainment. Before considering them, it is important to see how this outcome varies by nationality and length of U.S. residence. Nationality differences in attainment reflect the combined weight of parental status and human capital, family composition, and intergenerational acculturation in addition to the collective history and experiences of each group. Length of U.S. residence is the prime indicator of children's acculturation, although its bearing on educational attainment is ambiguous: On the one hand, longer residence in the country leads to better knowledge of English, as shown in Chapter 6; on the other, its positive effect on grades and test scores can be countermanded by a less-driven attitude toward achievement, as indicated by the negative association of this variable with indicators of school effort in Chapter 8. The case of Van Le's siblings and other earlier stories illustrate this pattern.

Table 9.1 presents the relevant results. For this analysis, Chinese and Korean students are combined in a single category, based on common cultural backgrounds, contexts of reception, and generally high levels of parental human capital. Laotian and Cambodian students were also joined in a single group because of their similar histories of exit and incorporation, as discussed previously. The large Cuban sample is divided, in turn, into students attending public and private schools in Miami in order to examine differences in patterns of achievement and their determinants in both groups. Table 9.1 shows wide differences in academic test scores and GPAs. Topping the national rankings in the Stanford math and reading tests are Cuban Americans in private school and students of Chinese and Korean origin, closely followed by other Asians. Filipinos, Vietnamese, and Nicaraguans have middling average scores, while children of Mexican immigrants and Laotian and Cambodian refugees bring up the rear of the respective distributions.

The GPA rankings are quite different. Mexican students remain at the bottom and are joined there by Haitians and by Cubans in public schools. The top is occupied exclusively by Asian nationalities, including Chinese/Koreans, Vietnamese, Filipinos, *and* Laotians/Cambodians. This contrasting pattern is partially attributable to the different content of the three indicators of academic achievement. School grades reflect not only actual knowledge but also teacher's evaluations influenced by proper student conduct, demeanor, and work habits. In this respect, a noteworthy difference exists between children of Asian immigrants,

Predictors	Math Score[1]	Reading Score[1]	GPA
National origin			
Chinese-Korean	77.38	61.66	3.34
Colombian	58.35	44.66	2.34
Cuban, private school	79.52	68.52	2.68
Cuban, public school	56.24	45.10	2.23
Filipino	59.11	51.07	2.93
Haitian	45.03	30.40	2.27
Laotian-Cambodian	37.87	18.33	2.83
Mexican	31.87	26.54	2.24
Nicaraguan	55.45	38.04	2.32
Vietnamese	60.30	37.45	3.03
West Indian	52.78	45.62	2.40
Other Asian	70.31	62.39	3.09
Other Latin	55.33	42.85	2.30
Other nationalities[2]	66.04	58.81	2.79
E[3]	.385***	.403***	.363***
Length of U.S. residence			
U.S. born	56.01	47.05	2.47
10 years or more	50.18	39.06	2.50
9 years or less	50.80	32.87	2.64
E[3]	.073*	.198**	.072*
Totals	53.16	41.55	2.52
N = 5,262			

[1]Percentile scores in standardized Stanford achievement tests administered in the eighth and ninth grades.
[2]Canadian, European, Middle Eastern, and other smaller nationalities.
[3]Eta coefficient of strength of association.
*Probability that differences are due to chance is less than 5 in 100.
**Probability that differences are due to chance is less than 1 in 100.
***Probability that differences are due to chance is less than 1 in 1,000.

who consistently exceed the average sample GPA, and Latin youths who, with the exception of Cubans in private schools, fall below it. Hence, despite their very modest family status and low achievement scores, Laotian and Cambodian children manage to maintain relatively high GPAs. Cubans in public school represent the opposite situation, coming from more advantaged backgrounds and doing acceptably in standardized tests but falling behind in school grades.

It is important to note at this point that these comparisons are internal to our sample. Relative to school district norms, average grades for most national groups and for the sample as a whole are higher. For example, in San Diego, only 29 percent of all ninth graders had GPAs above 3.0 (better than a B average) in the 1992–1995 period, as compared with 44 percent of those from immigrant families in our San Diego CILS sample. At the other extreme, 36 percent of ninth graders district-wide had GPAs under 2.0 (less than a C average), while only half as many (18 percent) of second-generation students in the CILS sample performed as poorly. These findings indicate that, taken as a whole, second-generation students are performing well in school. This result corresponds with and reinforces the strong current of optimism among immigrant parents, reported in Chapter 5.

School district data also show, however, that native-immigrant differences in academic attainment decline over time so that by the end of high school, the mean advantage in favor of children of immigrants is reduced to insignificance. This result is further supported by data in Table 9.1 indicating that length of U.S. residence is associated with significantly higher reading scores but *lower* GPAs. Hence, congruent with results presented in Chapter 6, length of acculturation leads to greater English proficiency; at the same time, and in agreement with results presented in Chapter 8, it is also associated with lesser school effort and, hence, lower grades.

These preliminary results are useful in illustrating gross differences between nationality and nativity groups that reflect the combined influence of a diverse set of causal factors. These differences provide an appropriate background to tease out what these factors are and how they bear on our original predictions. While plausible from a theoretical standpoint, the observed intergroup differences, the overall superior academic performance of second-generation youths, and their declining advantage over time require additional analysis if these results are to yield valid conclusions about the process of educational attainment.

Determinants of Early Achievement

In agreement with the theoretical literature on academic achievement, we expect family SES to play a major role in children's school performance. For reasons outlined in Chapter 3, family structure in the form of intact families can also be expected to play an important causal role. As just seen, length of acculturation has a problematic relationship with academic achievement. To clarify this effect, we consider simultaneously the effects of U.S. nativity and of long-term U.S. residence among the foreign born, with more recently arrived respondents as the reference category. We supplement these measures with indicators of the *type* of acculturation that children and their parents have undergone. Fluent and limited bilingualism are brought into the analysis as measures of selective and dissonant acculturation, as discussed in Chapter 6. Other more direct indicators of intergenerational acculturation introduced in the same chapter, such as parent-child conflict, are also included.

Finally, the argument about the influence of school and street environments as potential barriers to successful adaptation, presented in Chapter 3, is represented here by the types of school that children attend. We anticipate that respondents who attend schools located in inner-city areas and where most students come from low-status backgrounds will perform significantly worse after controlling for individual factors. This prediction is based on the lower quality of instruction in these schools and the expected character of peer influences in them.[2]

The following multivariate analysis enters predictors in a two-step sequence: first, effects of individual, family, and school variables and second, the same array of predictors plus national origin. We control for average differences between school systems by entering region (southern Florida versus southern California) into the equation. The values, range, and mean of all variables used in this analysis are presented in Appendix C. In the interest of brevity, we focus the following discussion on the final regressions for each dependent variable, although the reader is invited to explore the first set of equations in the table. Results of interest are the regression coefficients, which indicate the net increase/decrease in test scores or grades associated with a unit increase in each predictor, and the relative strength of each effect, symbolized here by the number of asterisks. The R^2 coefficients in the bottom rows indicate the amount of variance in each dependent variable explained by the model.

Results in Table 9.2 correspond closely with our theoretical predictions while revealing a number of new and interesting findings. Parental SES exercises a consistent and strong influence on second-generation achievement. For example, each unit change in the parental SES index raises math and reading test scores by 6 to 7 points.[3] This figure indicates that immigrant human capital affects not only the economic achievement of parents but carries into second-generation attainment as well. Family composition has a similar set of effects, with children from intact families enjoying a significant academic advantage, especially in grades. The role of family variables for motivating and guiding children during early adolescence is reflected quite clearly in these coefficients.

On the other hand, the ambiguous effect of length of acculturation is also made explicit by these results: Both U.S. nativity and long-term residence among the foreign-born increase English skills but significantly lower grades. Since these are net effects controlling for all other variables, they lend support to the qualitative evidence at the start of the chapter. Taken jointly with results presented in earlier chapters, these findings strongly suggest that second-generation children gradually lose their achievement drive with increasing acculturation. The effect is also in line with the previously noted disappearance of immigrant-native differences in school grades in senior high school.

The next set of predictors make clear that not only the passage of time but also the type of acculturation that children undergo has a major influence on academic achievement. Dissonant acculturation, as indexed by limited bilingualism, has a consistent, powerful, and negative effect on early academic achievement. As seen in Chapter 6, limited bilingualism is a common outcome of forced language immersion, leading to the rapid loss of parental languages and associated strongly with other indicators of dissonance. One of these, the frequency of parent-child cultural conflict, also has a consistently negative and powerful influence on achievement.

Conversely, selective acculturation, as indexed by fluent bilingualism, has a significant positive effect. Notice that this effect is nil in the first columns of each model and only emerges when national origin is controlled. The reason is that many of the high-achieving national groups come from Asia and, as seen in Chapter 6, they are *not bilingual* on the average. Their superior performance is due to other factors, as will be discussed shortly. Once these national differences are taken into account, the positive net association of bilingualism with achievement emerges clearly. A second indicator of the role of selective acculturation is provided by children's friends. Students who have kept most of their

TABLE 9.2   MODELS OF EARLY (MIDDLE SCHOOL) EDUCATIONAL ATTAINMENT, 1992

Predictors[1]	Math[2]		Reading[2]		GPA	
	I[3]	II[3]	I[3]	II[3]	I[3]	II[3]
Demographic						
Age	-4.49***	-4.10***	-3.55***	-3.24***	-.11***	-.10***
Sex (female)	1.44	1.62*	2.55*	2.63*	.33***	.33***
Region (S. California)	-5.37***	-8.46**	-.46	3.85*	.45***	.27
Family						
Parental SES	7.52***	5.80***	9.03***	6.88**	.21***	.18***
Intact family	4.48**	3.45**	1.15	.90	.22***	.18***
Length of Acculturation						
U.S. Born	-2.16*	.56	6.06***	6.84***	-.25***	-.16***
Long-term U.S. resident[4]	-.10	.02	6.23**	6.64***	-.11*	-.12*
Type of Acculturation						
Fluent bilingual	-.19	1.93*	1.17	2.30*	.01	.06*
Limited bilingual	-5.85**	-7.14***	-12.73***	-12.14***	-.14**	
Parent-child conflict	-2.80***	-3.12***	-2.03**	-2.15**	-.15***	-.16***
Second-generation friends	4.62***	3.84**	2.29**	1.88	.08**	-.06**

School

Inner city	−6.04**	−6.21**	−2.46*	−2.07*	.01	.00
Average student SES	.14***	.10**	.20***	.18*	−.04	−.06
Nationality						
Chinese/Korean		23.22***		12.97**		.76***
Colombian		−.45		.07		−.05
Cuban, private school		5.60		7.14*		.25**
Cuban, public school		−3.48*		−1.64		−.14*
Filipino		3.39		−1.69		.17*
Haitian		−7.18*		−8.29**		.00
Laotian/Cambodian		2.10		−12.41**		.47***
Mexican		−11.52**		−14.70***		−.25**
Nicaraguan		−2.62		−3.71*		−.10
Vietnamese		15.79***		−3.20		.51***
West Indian		−4.94*		1.07		−.01
Constant	113.02	117.10	76.38	72.36	3.10	3.37
R^2	.19	.25	.26	.29	.18	.24
Number of Cases[5]		4,420		4,518		5,153

[1] See Appendix C for description of variables used in this analysis.
[2] Scores in standardized Stanford achievement tests administered in the eighth and ninth grades.
[3] Unstandardized ordinary regression coefficients. Non-asterisked coefficients are statistically insignificant.
[4] Foreign-born with 10 years or more of U.S. residence. Less than 10 years is the reference category.
[5] Cases with missing data are excluded. Missing data are mostly due to unavailable test scores or grades from the respective school system.
* Moderate effect (coefficient doubles its standard error).
** Strong effect (coefficient quadruples its standard error).
*** Very strong effect (coefficient sextuples its standard error).

close friendships within the ethnic circle do consistently better, indicating once again that rapid, full acculturation is not necessarily the best path to achievement. A selective path, guided by strong family and friendship ties, yields better results on the average.

The schools that children attend also influence academic performance. Second-generation youths who attend minority inner-city schools do consistently worse, leading to a net two-point drop in reading scores and a six-point drop in math scores. The average SES of the student body has the opposite effect. Our measure of average school SES is the obverse of the proportion of students eligible for the federally subsidized lunch program. The lower the proportion of such students, the higher the average status of the student population. Based on model coefficients, a student who attended a suburban school where less than 10 percent of the students were poor (i.e., eligible for subsidized meals) had a major advantage in both math and reading scores: Attending these schools leads to an approximately 20 percentile point gain in both test scores, regardless of individual and family characteristics.

Among control variables, age is associated with lower achievement, and sex (female) is associated with significantly higher grades and reading scores. The lower performance of older students and the superiority of females, especially in GPAs, are consistent with results obtained by prior national student samples.[4] The female advantage is also congruent with girls' superior preservation of fluent bilingualism and with their higher educational expectations, as shown in earlier chapters. The overall pattern of results is in line with the theoretical argument in Chapter 3 concerning the distinct role of gender in the socialization process and in the adaptation of the second generation.

The final question for the analysis is the extent to which this array of individual, family, and school factors explains the initial observed differences among national groups. The basic answer is no. Many significant nationality effects remain, and they run consistently in the direction expected from the history and modes of incorporation of each immigrant nationality. For example, children of Mexican and Haitian parents do much worse in school, even after controlling for family SES, family composition, and types of acculturation. Conversely, children of Chinese and Korean immigrants and of Vietnamese refugees—groups that have benefited from strong preexisting ethnic communities or extensive resettlement assistance—perform much better on the average.[5]

Cuban Americans, descendants of another favorably received refugee group, are bifurcated between those attending private schools, who have consistently high achievement scores, and those in public schools, who perform below average. The anomaly posed by Cuban Americans in public schools will receive additional attention later in this chapter. A last telling result pertains to Laotians and Cambodians, who perform poorly in terms of standardized achievement scores but have average grades that exceed the norm when controlling for other factors. In Chapter 4, we saw how adults from these countries had a net earnings advantage despite very low levels of education, a pattern attributable to the strong official support they received upon arrival. In Chapter 8, we noted the superior school effort and engagement of children from these nationalities, despite their generally low expectations for an advanced education. Until junior high school at least, their efforts do pay off.

Grades are a somewhat different measure of achievement than test scores because they are influenced by student demeanor, effort, and self-discipline. It is in these areas that children of southeast Asian refugees excel, reflecting the influence of strong families and co-ethnic networks. The remaining southeast Asian group—the Vietnamese—also follows this pattern, with net negative reading scores but high school marks.

Summarizing this complex set of results, our analysis of academic achievement by middle school yields the following highlights:

The influence of parental human capital carries across generations, with children of high-status parents doing much better in all measures of academic performance. Family structure in the form of intact families plays a similar role.

Length of acculturation, as indexed by both U.S. nativity and long-term U.S. residence, has contradictory effects on achievement. However, measures of dissonant and selective acculturation behave consistently, the first strongly lowering achievement and the second increasing it.

Language adaptation has the expected effects, with fluent bilinguals performing better than average when other variables are controlled and limited bilinguals doing much worse. These results indicate the value of selective preservation of linguistic ties to families and co-ethnic communities.

School contexts are also important predictors of achievement. Inner-city and low-status schools lead to a sharp drop in test scores, net of all individual and family predictors.

The combination of all these factors reduces, but does not eliminate, national effects on achievement. As in the case of parental socioeconomic achievement, these effects run consistently in agreement to the known history and modes of incorporation of each group.[6]

Figures 9.1 and 9.2 graphically summarize these results by showing grades and reading scores for selected nationalities and adjusted scores after controlling for individual, family, and school variables. Groups included are those that retain significant effects in each dependent variable, with these effects evaluated at the mean of the respective distribution. The graphs show that a sizable portion of the original advantage of groups such as Chinese/Koreans and private-school Cubans in reading and Chinese/Koreans and Filipinos in school grades is due to the effect of other predictors.

However, the achievement gap remains in all cases, indicating the resilient influence of immigrant communities. The Laotian/Cambodian group presents a unique situation in which not only would its (low) reading scores be higher if parental human capital were equivalent to the sample's average, but its already superior grades would still be higher in that contingency as well. The role of a favorable mode of incorporation in compensating for low parental endowments is strongly highlighted by these results.

Educational Achievement in Late Adolescence

Happens all the time. They finish, get their diploma, and go to work for Seven-Eleven. What's the point? Next year, I'll go to work for Tío Chucho. He never finished high school and already owns three car washes and an auto parts store.

— Fermín, 16, Cuban-American student, Miami Senior High[7]

The secret is all at the start. If a kid gets into his head that he wants to be a doctor or a computer programmer, then he'll work harder and, if he gets good grades, that'll spur him to more effort. Those who drift at the start just keep on drifting and sometimes drop out. Some parents lean hard on their kids, the Jamaicans, the Chinese; others just let them do their own thing.

— Tony F., school counselor, Lauderhill High, Ft. Lauderdale

The key thing to doing well academically is not whether you're gifted or really bright, but it's more just how studious you are. I think sheer ability

Figure 9.1   Gross and Net Effects of Nationality on Grade Point
Average, 1992

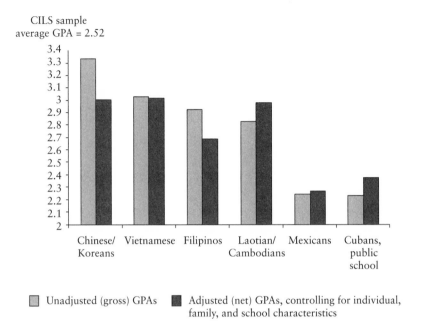

CILS sample
average GPA = 2.52

◻ Unadjusted (gross) GPAs   ◼ Adjusted (net) GPAs, controlling for individual,
family, and school characteristics

matters only to a very small extent, but everything else comes down to
that you have to work at it.

— Quy, 19, Vietnamese student, San Diego

I wanted to be a physical therapist and worked hard at it. Then Marcel
got me pregnant, and I had to leave the house. My parents are very
Catholic. Haitian parents are very strict on these things. So to get an
abortion, I had to leave. So now I am living with Marcel and his family
and have to work part-time to help with the bills. I am still in school, but
my energy is gone. Somehow, I still hope to finish.

— Antoinette, 17, Edison High School, Miami

Grades in Senior High School

The adolescent years are a time of profound transformations in the lives
of children, where identities and plans often change rapidly and where
key formative experiences determine the course of future lives. Second-

Figure 9.2   Gross and Net Effects of Nationality on Reading Scores, 1992

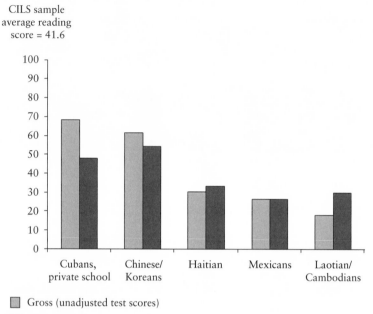

CILS sample average reading score = 41.6

Gross (unadjusted test scores)

Net (adjusted scores controlling for individual, family, and school characteristics)

generation youths are no exception and, as seen in previous chapters, their self-identities, language abilities, and outlooks on their social environment also evolve markedly during this period. This is the time when dissonant acculturation appears in full force and when the first signs of segmented assimilation become established as some children leave school prematurely because of unexpected pregnancies or economic need and others seek outside job opportunities and fall behind in school.

From our previous indicators of achievement, only one remains by the late high school years—GPA. Lamentably, school systems during this period opted for optional achievement tests so that standardized test scores are available only for a fraction of the sample in the follow-up survey. Even for those students for whom scores are available, they become unusable as dependent variables because the optional nature of the test introduces a clear element of selectivity—only the most motivated can be expected to undergo this extra effort.[8]

TABLE 9.3   CORRELATIONS BETWEEN
INDICATORS OF EDUCATIONAL ACHIEVEMENT

	GPA (1992)	GPA (1995)
GPA, 1992	1.000[1]	.804
Math test scores, 1992	.516	.480
Reading test scores, 1992	.390	.374
Active in school, 1995–1996[2]	.184	.143
Not a dropout, 1995–1996[2]	.140	.133

[1]The probability of all correlations being due to chance is less than 1 in 1000.
[2]From school records.

As seen previously, grades are less than a perfectly valid indicator of academic achievement because they are influenced by other factors. Grading scales are not universalistic in different types of schools, and they vary significantly by school systems. Yet despite these limitations, GPAs possess certain characteristics that render them useful as an indicator of school performance. First, they are quite stable over time; second, they correlate positively and significantly with other indicators of achievement. This is evident in Table 9.3, which presents intercorrelations between average grades in both survey years with achievement test scores and school retention. The correlation between grades in 1992 and 1996 is .80; the corresponding rank-order correlation by national origin reaches .95. The correlations of math and reading standardized scores with GPAs are almost identical in both years, being positive and of moderate size in each case. Overall, grades by the end of secondary schooling can be interpreted as an indicator of educational attainment that combines actual knowledge with motivation and adjustment to institutional routines.

Two additional predictors are introduced in our analysis of late educational attainment: educational expectations and self-esteem. These variables are representative of key dimensions of psychosocial adjustment, as seen in chapter 8. They were omitted from the analysis of middle-school achievement because their causal effect on educational outcomes was ambiguous. In other words, since expectations, self-esteem, and grades were all measured in 1992, it is impossible to tell whether psychosocial variables led to higher achievement or whether the latter produced higher expectations and self-esteem. For the present analysis, we use the 1992 psychosocial indicators to predict achievement in 1995, thus establishing

TABLE 9.4   DETERMINANTS OF GRADE POINT
AVERAGE IN LATE HIGH SCHOOL

Predictors[1]	GPA (1995)		GPA (1995) Controlling for Autoregression[2]	
	I	II	III	IV
Demographic				
Age	−.05*	−.05*		
Sex (female)	.30***	.31***	.07**	.07**
Region (S. California)	.58***	.47***	.17***	.24***
Family				
Parental SES	.17***	.16***	.05**	.05**
Intact family	.19***	.16***		
Length of Acculturation				
U.S. born	−.18**	−.11*		
Long-term U.S. resident[3]	−.09*	−.09*		
Type of Acculturation				
Fluent bilingual	−.07*	−.01		
Limited bilingual	−.05	−.13**		
Parent-child conflict	−.09***	−.10***		
Second-generation friends	.03	.03		
Psychosocial				
Educational expectations	.20***	.18***		
Self-esteem	.20***	.21***	.04*	.04*

a clear time order between alleged cause and effects. Expectations are the educational levels that respondents realistically thought they would attain in 1992, categorized in a five-point hierarchy. Self-esteem are scores in Rosenberg's 10-item self-esteem scale. As in the previous analysis, measurement characteristics of all variables are presented in Appendix C.

The first two columns of Table 9.4 present nested regressions of senior-year GPA on individual and family predictors (first column) plus national origin (second). The total number of cases on which the model was estimated exceeds the size of the follow-up survey because data on

TABLE 9.4   (*continued*)

Predictors[1]	GPA (1995)		GPA (1995) Controlling for Autoregression[2]	
	I	II	III	IV
School				
Inner city	.04	.00	−.07**	−.06*
Average School SES	.004**	.002*	.003***	.003***
GPA, 1992			.81#	.80#
Nationality				
Chinese/Korean		.81***		.22*
Colombian		−.09		
Cuban, private school		.20*		
Cuban, public school		−.14*		
Filipino		.02		−.13*
Haitian		−.02		
Laotian/Cambodian		.33**		
Mexican		−.23*		
Nicaraguan		−.10		
Vietnamese		.43**		
West Indian		−.01		
Constant	.35	.59	−.56	−.60
R^2	.22	.26	.68	.68
N		4,899		4,899

[1]See Appendix C and Table 9.2 for description of variables and coefficients.
[2]Insignificant effects omitted.
[3]Foreign born with 10 years or more of U.S. residence. Less than 10 years is the reference category.
*Moderate effect (coefficient doubles its standard error).
**Strong effect (coefficient quadruples its standard error).
***Very strong effect (coefficient sextuples its standard error).
#Autoregression effect exceeds 50 times its standard error.

senior GPAs did not come from the survey but from school records, while all predictors were measured during the first survey. As in the middle school years, average grades in San Diego tend to be higher than in southern Florida, a main-effect discrepancy that is controlled by including region in the equation.

The principal results of interest pertain to family SES and family structure, which continue to have strong and positive effects on grades, reinforcing earlier results. Similarly, length of acculturation, measured by nativity and long-term U.S. residence, maintains its persistent negative effect, giving additional weight to this key finding. Measures of selective acculturation—fluent bilingualism and co-ethnic friendships—fade away, its effects mediated by the newly introduced psychosocial variables. However, dissonant acculturation, indexed by limited bilingualism and parent-child conflict, maintains its consistently strong negative effects on achievement. This implies that a child who spoke neither language well in middle school and who grew increasingly apart from his or her family during that period is much less likely to do well academically in later years.

The most novel findings in the table pertain to the effects of the two psychosocial predictors. Educational expectations and personality adjustment, as indexed by self-esteem scores, influence school achievement strongly and positively. Hence, psychosocial outcomes of the adaptation process, like linguistic acculturation earlier on, are not isolated but build on each other, leading to subsequent significant effects.[9]

The question of the extent to which this set of predictors explains interethnic group differences in school achievement receives the same negative answer as before. Again, a number of ethnic group effects persist, ranging from the remarkably strong performance of Chinese and Korean students to the persistent and serious disadvantage of Mexican Americans. We see again the notable bifurcation between Cuban-American students in public and private schools, while children of southeast Asian refugees perform consistently better than expected. Recall that many of these children come from poor families with low human capital endowments, that they seldom retain their parental languages, and that they commonly have low self-esteem and modest expectations for the future. The positive Vietnamese and Laotian/Cambodian effects seem thus exclusively attributable to the strong social capital provided by their ethnic communities. These results again impress upon us the importance of broader contextual forces that do not disappear after controlling for individual, family, and even school variables.

Change over Time

The last columns of Table 9.4 introduce the autoregression effect of grades over time. As in previous analyses, the addition changes the meaning of other coefficients to effects on *change* in the dependent variable. The stability of grades during the high school years, shown by their high intercorrelation in Table 9.3, means that there is little residual variance to explain, reducing most effects to insignificance. This does not negate the validity of prior causal effects but indicates that they apply to the stable component of grades and not to their increase/decrease over time. Results in Table 9.4 show that females and children of high-status parents not only do better academically but also increase their advantage over the high school years. The same is true for Chinese/Korean students, reinforcing the evidence of their extraordinary drive for achievement.

The coefficient associated with self-esteem is noteworthy because it establishes unambiguously the causal significance of this variable. With middle school grades controlled, it cannot be argued that the influence of self-esteem on late achievement is just a function of the early correlation between both variables. The same is not the case for educational expectations, causing some doubt as to the actual direction of this effect.[10] Lastly, these results highlight the durable influence of early school contexts. The type of middle school that these children attended bears heavily on their subsequent academic performance. The causal direction of school effects is unambiguous, providing strong support for the role of external factors on children's educational adaptation. Based on model coefficients, a female student of high-status parents who attended a middle-class school in her early teens is expected to improve her GPA by about half a point, in addition to the early advantage conferred by the same variables.

Overall, the analysis strongly supports our initial theoretical expectations indicating that educational achievement is a predictable process governed by family and school contextual influences as well as by earlier adaptation outcomes, including types of acculturation and personality adjustment. The adaptation process of children of immigrants does not consist of a set of disparate outcomes but instead builds on itself, with earlier results affecting subsequent ones. The strong influence of gender on achievement and the persistent advantages or disadvantages linked to specific national origins are also apparent in these results. Nationality effects reflect the enduring influence of immigrant modes of incorporation, with this influence being much stronger among some groups than others. We will return to this central point in the final section.

Dropping Out of School

When Arcadia High School sophomore Johnson Lee gets home, his mother has vegetable sushi and egg rolls waiting on the kitchen table. When he stays up late before a big exam, she brews a pot of coffee to keep him going. And when there is no room in his backpack for a hefty advanced placement biology textbook, no problem—she copies the chapters he needs in the machine outside his bedroom. These are the courses he plans to take in his junior year: advanced placement English, advanced placement U.S. history, advanced placement calculus, Spanish 3, and advanced placement physics. In this household, failure is spelled B. The thought of leaving school is simply inconceivable.[11]

Down at San Diego's Hoover High, one of the schools in our sample, there's a group that calls itself the Crazy Brown Ladies. They wear heavy makeup—"ghetto paint" they call it—and reserve special derision for classmates striving for grades—"school girls" is the Ladies' label for these lesser beings.[12] Petite Guatemalan-born Iris de la Puente never joined the Ladies, but again, she never made it to senior year at Hoover. The daughter of a gardener and a seamstress, she has lived with her mother alone for several years after her father was deported and did not return. Mrs. de la Puente kept exhorting Iris to stay in school, but her message was empty. The pressure of work kept the mother away from home for many hours, and her own modest education and lack of English did not give her a clue how to help Iris. By ninth grade, the girl's GPA had fallen to a C, and she was just hanging in there, hoping for a high school diploma. When junior year rolled around, it was all over. "Going to college would be nice, but it became clear that it was not for me," Iris said. Getting a job, no matter how poorly paid, became the only option.[13]

Even more than grades, a key dimension of educational achievement is whether children actually stay in school. Even if grades are low, graduating from high school gives adolescents a range of future options closed to dropouts. In terms of segmented assimilation, this is the most significant outcome for second-generation youths at this stage of life. By late adolescence, the set of factors conditioning the early adaptation process has begun to distill into a few behavioral and psychosocial characteristics that determine, in turn, future outcomes. Early school grades, ambition, and self-esteem emerge as important predictors affecting who finally gets the diploma and who falls behind. Family composition and the type of school attended in junior high also play a role. Together, they mold different social environments where, for children like Johnson Lee, the possibility of leaving school does not exist, while for Iris de la Puente it becomes the only thing to do "for people like her."

In examining school attrition and its determinants, we benefit again from the longitudinal nature of the CILS data, which allows us to establish causal effects unambiguously. Indicators of attrition consist of a pair of school-supplied measures: students known to have dropped out of school and those who have become inactive. Neither variable is a perfectly valid measure: The first probably underestimates it by excluding students who have actually left school, even if they were not officially recorded as dropping out. The second errs in the opposite direction by inflating the estimate with students who became "inactive" because they graduated early or moved to another school system. Our data allow a partial correction of this problem by adjusting the school-reported figures with information on the actual status of students collected during CILS' second survey.

Figure 9.3 presents the distribution of both variables by major national groups in the sample. Dropping out of high school ranges from a low of 3 percent among Asian children to a high of 10 percent among Cuban Americans in public school. That last figure adds to the anomalous school performance of this group, which will require additional analysis. Inactivity rates also vary widely—from a high of 25 percent among Mexican Americans to just 14 percent among Chinese and Korean students. Haitian Americans also have low inactivity rates, a result at variance with other measures of school performances and that points to the different character of this measure of achievement. As in prior analyses, we ask whether these intergroup differences are explainable by other factors or persist after controlling for them.

Table 9.5 presents results based on the same models used for school grades in Table 9.4. Since the outcomes of interest are dichotomous—dropping out or becoming inactive—we estimate these models using logistic regression. As in prior analyses, we also estimate the net probabilities of each outcome associated with significant effects. Positive coefficients in this case indicate poorer outcomes since the dependent variables are coded in agreement with their labels (1 for dropouts and inactives). Figures in Table 9.5 reveal two major results at variance with those obtained for grades: First, very few predictors have reliable effects on either measure of school attrition; second, after controlling for these factors, *no* significant nationality effects remain, indicating that intergroup differences on these variables are due to individual, family, and school characteristics.

The absence of effects from either nationality or parental status suggests that by late adolescence, many of these early influences on the process of adaptation are already mediated by children's own experiences. For 17- and 18-year-olds, the decision to stay in school or quit is

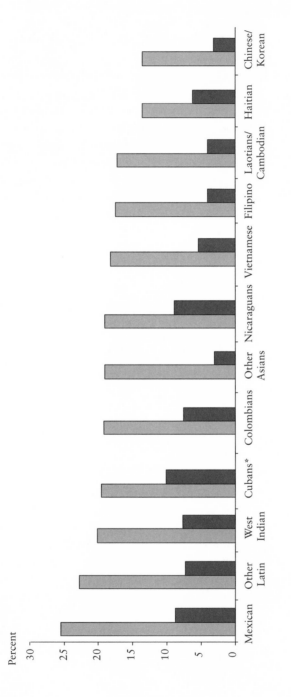

Figure 9.3 Indicators of School Attrition by Nationality, 1995

Percent

Mexican · Other Latin · West Indian · Cubans* · Colombians · Other Asians · Nicaraguans · Vietnamese · Filipino · Laotians/ Cambodian · Haitian · Chinese/ Korean

■ Percent inactive in school
■ Percent dropout

*Cuban students in public schools only; no data for those attending private schools.

conditioned by what happened to them earlier on. Among these early outcomes, type of school attended, grades in middle school, and the educational goals and self-image that they developed at that time play key roles. Only 7 percent of the sample was officially classified as dropouts, but among students who attended a middle-class junior high school, had an A average there, and planned to graduate from college, the probability of leaving school drops to zero. Conversely, those who attended an inner-city school and had a below-B average and no college plans were about 20 percent more likely to become inactive.

Among the few significant effects on attrition, two stand out. First, indicators of length of acculturation do not affect dropping out but reduce the inactivity rate. This effect is partially attributable to the lower residential mobility of established immigrant families. Many students are declared "inactive" when they leave the school system and cannot be located elsewhere. The residential mobility that leads to this outcome is more common among recent immigrants than among families long settled in the United States. Of greater theoretical importance is the strong influence of family structure on both dependent variables. Living in an intact family reduces the probability of dropping out to just 5 percent and the inactivity rate to less than 10 percent. The latter effect is quite strong statistically, exceeding eight times its standard error. These results demonstrate the enduring effect of intact families in motivating children to higher educational achievement. Of all the early parental effects on second-generation adaptation, this is the one that persists, unmediated, through late adolescence.

The high ambition displayed by immigrant parents and the high goals that they voice for their children are not just empty words. These beliefs carry forth in the form of higher grades and higher probabilities of graduation. The significance of the immigrant drive for achievement is especially apparent when we compare our results with those for the student population as a whole. School systems publish dropout rates for their respective populations that can be directly compared with those in the CILS sample. Results show that *in every category,* children of immigrants have lower dropout rates than the reference population. The multiyear dropout rate for grades 9 through 12 in Miami-Dade public schools was 17.6 percent in 1996, or more than double the reported number in the CILS sample. On the other coast, the differential was still greater since the San Diego system-wide dropout rate of 16.2 percent almost tripled that of second-generation students (5.7 percent).

TABLE 9.5 DETERMINANTS OF SCHOOL ATTRITION

Predictors[1]	Dropout (1995)			Inactive (1995)		
	Coefficient[2]	Wald Statistic[3]	P[4]	Coefficient[2]	Wald Statistic[3]	P[4]
Demographic						
Age				.21	18.2***	.04
Sex (female)				.56	7.2*	.10
Region (S. California)						
Family						
Parental SES						
Intact Family	−.42	−11.6*	−.02	−.66	−65.6***	−.08
Length of Acculturation						
U.S. Born				−.27	−7.1*	−.04
Long-term U.S. Resident				−.20	−3.7*	−.03
Type of Acculturation						
Fluent bilingual						
Limited bilingual						
Parent-child conflict						
Second generation friends						
Psychosocial						
Educational expectations	−.16	−5.3*	−.01	−.11	−4.9*	−.02
Self-esteem	−.30	−6.5**	−.02			

School

	School		Nationality			
Inner city	−.01		−.001	.20		.03
Average school SES	−.45	−10.0**	−.03	−.47	3.1	−.06
GPA, 1992		−35.0***			−84.5***	
Chinese-Korean						
Colombian						
Cuban[5]						
Filipino						
Haitian						
Laotian/Cambodian						
Mexican						
Nicaraguan						
Vietnamese						
West Indian						
Constant	−.03			−3.49		
Model chi square (degrees of freedom)		148.83#(26)		301.14#(26)		
N[6]		4,449		4,490		

NOTE: Insignificant effects omitted from the table.
[1] See Appendix C for description of variables.
[2] Logistic regression coefficients indicating net effects on the log-odds of each dependent variable.
[3] Coefficient of strength of association.
[4] Net increase/decrease in the probability of dropping out or becoming inactive evaluated at the mean of the sample distribution.
[5] Sample restricted to Cuban-origin students in public school. No attrition data for those attending private schools.
[6] Cases with missing data were excluded from the analysis. Such cases are due to no information on student status on school district records.
*Moderate effect (coefficient doubles its standard error).
**Strong effect (coefficient triples its standard error).
***Very strong effect (coefficient quintuples its standard error).
#Probability that model improvement is due to chance is less than 1 in 10,000.

Figure 9.4 shows that children of immigrants have lower dropout rates among both males and females and in every racial/ethnic category including non-Hispanic whites. In Miami, the highest percentage of dropouts was found among non-Hispanic black students (20.2 percent), but the rate among black Haitians and West Indians in the CILS sample was only 7.5 percent. In San Diego, the highest attrition among children of immigrants was for those classified as Hispanic (including an 8.8 percent rate for Mexican-origin students), but even this figure was a fraction of the 26.5 percent dropout rate for Hispanics district-wide.

These comparisons indicate that in the real world, immigrant parents' drive carries greater weight than their voiced fears of the streets and drugs. Signs of dissonant acculturation are common, and our analysis shows that they significantly lower academic performance, but they have not led so far to mass school desertion. Children of immigrants do better in this respect than children of natives of any ethnic background. This positive assessment must be qualified immediately by two important considerations: First, the passage of time lessens the achievement drive. This was shown by the results just presented on educational ambition and performance. It is also congruent with the fact that third-generation and higher native groups, including Hispanics and blacks, have lower average grades and much higher dropout rates than second-generation students. These results offer no grounds for believing that additional time in the country and further acculturation will improve present second-generation averages.

Second, as Figure 9.3 indicates, there are major variations among immigrant nationalities in rates of school completion. Our analysis shows that these differences reflect the cumulative effects of living in different types of families, attending different types of schools, and having different expectations for the future. Children of specific national minorities, such as Mexicans, Nicaraguans, and Cubans, are still at significant risk of leaving school prematurely. This fact should temper the optimism prompted by sample averages in comparison to the native-parentage population.

Two Achievement Paradoxes

Southeast Asians

Despite the overall predictability of academic achievement, two distinct ethnic patterns stand out. The first is the notable academic performance of students of Vietnamese and especially of Laotian and Cambodian origins whose families' human capital, generally low self-esteem scores,

Figure 9.4   School Dropout Rates of Student Population and Children of Immigrants, 1992–1996[1]

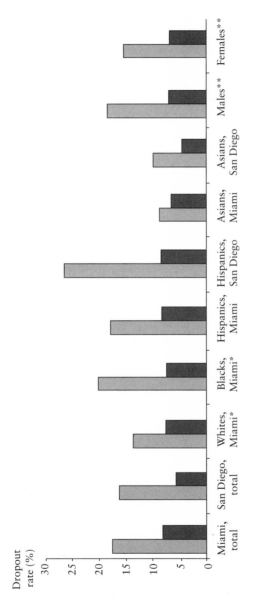

* Insufficient number of white and black immigrant students in the CILS San Diego sample for comparison.
** Unweighted average of rates in both school systems.
[1] Percentages refer to multiyear (grades 9–12) dropout rates.

and low expectations for the future would lead exactly to the opposite prediction. In Chapter 8 and earlier in this chapter, we noted the paradoxical profile of these students, who combine high school engagement and unusually strong schoolwork effort with a rather pessimistic assessment of their own future. In the end, however, they do not leave school in great numbers and do better than their peers academically.

In search of an explanation for this paradox, we look first at the cultural background of these groups. Some authors have invoked the so-called Confucian ethic as a possible cause for the extraordinary success of Asian students. They have gone to describe how socialization into this disciplined, pragmatic religion can affect the outcome and performance of children.[14] On the face of it this would be a plausible explanation, except that the majority of these families are not Confucian but come from very different cultural traditions. They do not even share a common religion to which these habits of school discipline and achievement could be imputed. The Vietnamese are mostly Mahayana Buddhists, with a strong minority of Roman Catholics; the Cambodian and Lao immigrants are predominantly Theravada Buddhists, a contemplative, otherworldly oriented form of Buddhism, and typically adhere to beliefs in reincarnation; the Hmong are mainly animists, with a strong component of ancestor worship, although notable numbers joined Mormon and Christian churches after resettlement in the United States. Additional minorities among all of these groups subscribe to a mix of other religions, and about 1 in 10 reports no religious commitment at all.[15] If a unique ethic were to be attributed to each of these rather diverse religious backgrounds to explain a common outcome, we would have a rather untidy explanation.

One might go a step further and look for a causal explanation in a common racial origin. According to such a view, Asians perform better, regardless of their religion or socioeconomic backgrounds, because of their superior genetic endowment. Apart from the obvious difficulty of determining who is a true Asian in racial terms because of the enormous intermix of people in that continent, it turns out that not all Asian nationalities have the same effect, as this interpretation would lead us to expect. Thus, there is no net Filipino effect on senior high school grades after controlling for individual and family predictors, and the Filipino effect on change in grades during high school is actually negative. More importantly, the Laotian/Cambodian net effect on math test scores is insignificant and on reading scores, it is strongly negative (see Table 9.2), results that contradict any supposition of innate racial superiority.

We are left with one possible explanation, and that is the character of the ethnic communities, molded in turn by these groups' histories and modes of incorporation. In Chapter 4, we saw how the favorable reception experienced by southeast Asians enabled these refugees to achieve an economic situation superior to what their human capital profile would lead us to expect. The same contextual forces favored the unification of families and the emergence of tightly knit communities that can act favorably on children's school behavior and performance. This also explains why consistently positive southeast Asian effects are present only on *grades,* the one measure of achievement most dependent on self-discipline and personal demeanor. These are precisely the normative patterns that can be readily instilled by southeast Asian refugee families and communities on their young.[16]

Cuban Americans

The paradox posed by Cuban Americans in public schools in southern Florida is the opposite of that posed by southeast Asians. Despite a favorable reception and relatively high levels of family human capital, Cuban-American students in public schools perform significantly worse than average in grades and have a higher propensity to drop out of school. Noteworthy is the persistently negative Cuban effect on GPAs even after controlling for other predictors. These results run contrary to our initial theoretical model, which would predict positive outcomes in school adaptation and achievement for this group.

A possible explanation is the longer residence of Cuban immigrants in the United States and the consequent larger proportion of native-born Cuban Americans relative to other nationalities. As already noted, longer periods in the country are associated with greater acculturation and partial loss of the original achievement drive. This explanation goes some way in accounting for results but is incompatible with two other findings in the data. First, with length of U.S. residence controlled, Cuban public school students continue to have significantly lower grades. Second, Cuban students in private schools have much better levels of performance, even when they are mostly native born and their parents have been in the country for a long time.

In trying to elucidate this paradox, we draw on knowledge of the history of Cubans in the United States and, in particular, the characteristics of their Miami ethnic enclave. Cubans are not only the largest national group in the sample but also the only one whose history has been marked by a decisive shift in modes of incorporation.[17] Other immigrant groups have experienced a relatively uniform context of reception, either because they are recent arrivals, like Nicaraguans and Southeast Asian refugees, or because the stance taken toward them by governmental authorities and society at large has not changed significantly, as is the case for Mexicans. Cuban exiles, on the other hand, went from being one of the most favorably received groups in American immigration history to becoming one of the least popular.

The earlier waves of refugees coming in the immediate aftermath of Castro's communist takeover were composed of educated professionals and businesspeople who were welcomed in the United States as opponents of communism and allies of America in the struggle to contain it. After the defeat at the Bay of Pigs and other events that led to the abandonment of the armed struggle against Castro, Cubans proceeded to build a large ethnic economy in Miami that gave employment to new arrivals and facilitated their entrepreneurial ambitions.[18] Cuban exiles continued to arrive in southern Florida and benefit from the same favorable context of reception until the momentous events associated with the Mariel exodus of 1980.

The Cuban government's decision to open the port of Mariel to all Cubans wishing to leave the island triggered a chaotic exodus that brought over 125,000 refugees in a six-month period, more than the sum total of the preceding eight years. The image of the Mariel boats bringing thousands of ragged refugees onto American shores was transmitted nationwide by the media and instantly altered public opinion about Cubans. The Castro government deliberately reinforced this negative perception by placing aboard the boats common criminals, mental patients, and others labeled the scum of Cuban society.[19] Levels of education and professional skills among Mariel refugees were significantly lower than among earlier waves of Cuban immigrants.[20]

As a consequence, Cuban exiles went from being a "model minority" helping to build southern Florida's future to becoming one of the foreign groups viewed with greatest suspicion. This public perception was soon followed by a change in federal policies that limited the previously unrestricted welcome granted to these refugees. For administrative purposes, Mariel Cubans were lumped together with Haitian boat people seeking entry in Florida during the same period. The increasingly restrictive official policy culminated in the 1994 decision by the Clinton administration to turn back all Cuban boats and rafts found at sea. This drastic shift in public and official attitudes was accompanied by a parallel change within the older Cuban community itself. This settled and successful population came to regard new arrivals as different and less desirable. They were blamed for the fast decline of Cubans' public image and for increasing crime and insecurity in Miami. Mariel refugees, in particular, were subjected to growing discrimination in their own community, compounding the effects of a negative official reception.[21]

We reason that this change in modes of incorporation, added to the more modest skills of recent refugees, should have a significant impact on the adaptation patterns of Cuban families and, in particular, their children. Offspring of the first well-received exiles had access to material and moral resources that Mariel and post-Mariel children did not. Accordingly, we divided the large CILS Cuban sample into students whose parents arrived prior to the Mariel exodus and those who arrived during it and afterwards. Results on our measures of academic performance are presented in Table 9.6. They agree with this expectation by showing a wide gap between these two groups on all variables. It is noteworthy that students who provided no information on their parents' year of arrival score very close to the Mariel/post-Mariel averages. Further analysis suggests that these are also mostly children of post-1979 refugees.[22]

More telling are the net effects associated with this division of the Cuban-American sample, controlling for individual, family, and school predictors. For brevity's sake, we do not present results of the full linear regressions but only the Cuban effects split according to year of arrival. These can be directly compared with coefficients presented in Tables 9.2 and 9.4. Results in the bottom rows of Table 9.6 show that early Cuban origin has a significant positive effect on math scores but no effect on other indicators of achievement. This is consistent with the expectation that the influence of a positive mode of incorporation among children of older exiles would be mediated by high parental occupational status, high educational expectations, and other intervening factors. On the contrary, the net effect of Mariel and post-Mariel family background is negative on all dependent variables.[23] Since parental SES and related variables are controlled, these coefficients add weight to the argument that the principal reason for the observed gap is the sharp break in contexts of reception experienced by these refugees and its influence on their children.[24]

This shift is not, however, the only factor at play in the propensity of Cuban youths to drop out of school. A second important consideration

TABLE 9.6   TIME OF ARRIVAL AND ACADEMIC
PERFORMANCE OF CUBAN AMERICANS IN MIAMI

Outcome	Year of Parental Arrival in U. S.[1]			
	Before 1980	1980 and After	No Information	E^2
Math scores, 1992	66.51	50.97	53.97	.258**
Net effect[3]	3.37*	−4.14**	—[4]	
Reading scores, 1992	53.14	40.55	46.20	.22**
Net effect[3]	2.78 (ns)	1.95 (ns)	—[4]	
GPA, 1992	2.43	2.20	2.19	.132**
Net effect[3]	0.031 (ns)	−0.103*	—[4]	
GPA, 1995	2.36	2.07	2.07	.160**
Net effect[3]	0.024 (ns)	−0.140**	—[4]	
N	547	290	299	

[1]If both parents are Cuban born or the father is Cuban born, this is the year of father's arrival. If the mother only is Cuban born, this is the year of her arrival.
[2]Eta coefficient of strength of association.
[3]Effect of Cuban origin and time of arrival controlling for all individual, family, and school predictors in the original models.
[4]Cases added to post-1979 category. See text for explanation.
*Moderate association or effect. (p < .05).
**Strong association or effect (p < .01).
ns: Nonsignificant association or effect.

is outside employment. Students who take paid jobs are more likely to get lower grades and leave school earlier than those who are fully dedicated to academic pursuits. The effect is not significant among those whose outside work requires only a few hours per week but can become quite strong for those holding serious jobs that demand large amounts of time. Only a minority of CILS respondents held such jobs in 1995. One reason is the priority assigned by parents and children themselves to school tasks; another is the difficulty that inexperienced teenagers have in finding employment. Even those wanting to trade schoolwork for paid jobs often find that the opportunities available to them are undesirable or nonexistent.[25] Young Cuban Americans are in a uniquely favorable situation in this respect because they are surrounded by a large co-ethnic enclave that offers just such opportunities.

The proliferation of Cuban-owned businesses in Miami has been a source of economic advancement for the proprietors and of employment for new arrivals and younger people at the same time.[26] The enclave gives Cuban students greater options for outside employment than those available to other second-generation youths. Naturally, those in a more precarious economic situation, including children of Mariel and

TABLE 9.7   STUDENT OUTSIDE EMPLOYMENT,
BY NATIONALITY, 1995

National Origin	Percent of Students Working 15 Hours or More per Week[1]	N
Mariel and Post-Mariel Cubans[2]	44.5	533
Nicaraguans	36.6	281
West Indians	33.8	201
Pre-Mariel Cubans[3]	32.9	435
Colombians	31.9	185
Haitians	26.7	135
Mexicans	22.1	598
Filipino	21.4	724
Vietnamese	18.4	310
Chinese/Koreans	15.3	85
Laotians/Cambodians	15.2	283
Total[4]	28.4	4,288

[1]No job or uncertain hours coded as 0 hours.
[2]Parents arrived in 1980 or after, or no data on year of arrival. See text and endnote 22 for explanation. Restriction of figures to respondents for which data are available changes the reported figure by less than 1 percent.
[3]Parents arrived before 1980.
[4]Full sample figure; smaller nationalities grouped in "other" categories are omitted from the table.

post-Mariel arrivals, are more likely to avail themselves of these opportunities. This expectation is confirmed by results in Table 9.7, which show that Cuban-American students whose parents came during or after 1980 are those most frequently employed in jobs requiring many hours a week. In 1995, almost half of children of Mariel and post-Mariel Cubans were employed in such jobs, as compared with less than a third for the CILS sample and just 15 percent among Laotians/Cambodians, the group least likely to hold outside employment.

The figures in Table 9.7 are actually an undercount because they exclude Cuban students who had dropped out of the sample by the time of the follow-up survey and who were mostly working in 1995. Since we have data on their parents' year of arrival from CILS' first survey, it is possible to assign most of them unambiguously to the pre- and post-1980 entry groups and to examine their academic performance by senior high school. Results are presented in Figure 9.5. They reveal major differences between children of earlier Cuban exiles who managed to remain outside of the labor market and the rest of the Cuban sample, especially children of more recent arrivals who became employed.[27] The

Figure 9.5   Effects of Outside Employment and Parental Year of Arrival:
Cuban Americans in Southern Florida, 1995

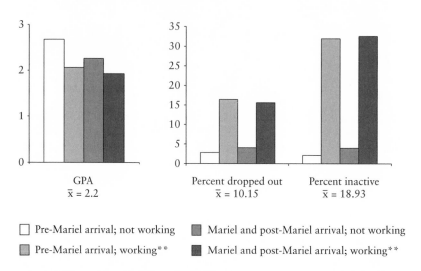

GPA
x̄ = 2.2

Percent dropped out
x̄ = 10.15

Percent inactive
x̄ = 18.93

☐ Pre-Mariel arrival; not working   ▨ Mariel and post-Mariel arrival; not working

▨ Pre-Mariel arrival; working**   ■ Mariel and post-Mariel arrival; working**

*Probability that differences are due to chance is less than 1 in 1,000. N=1,177.
**Fifteen hours or more per week. Follow-up sample dropouts added to this category according to known year of parents' arrival.

1995 GPA of the latter group is below 2.00, or almost one full grade point below that of students whose parents came before Mariel and remained full time in school. Differences in school attrition are still more significant, with the major gap being between students who are and are not working. Dropout and inactivity rates among Cuban students who were not employed are very low, contradicting the original impression of uniformly high attrition rates. These rates are extremely high, however, among students with outside jobs, more than doubling the CILS sample average.

These findings clarify the Cuban-American paradox as the outcome of two forces. First, favorable modes of incorporation benefited Cuban exiles who came early but not more recent arrivals; the lower human capital and the unfavorable reception accorded to Mariel and post-Mariel refugees had intergenerational consequences, affecting children's orientations and achievement. Second, Cuban-American students are also affected by an unexpected consequence of the successful economic performance of the earlier exile generation. Cuban entrepreneurship in Miami produced both successful businesses and employment opportunities for young people. By creating such opportunities, the Cuban ethnic economy paradoxically facilitated school attrition, especially among children whose families confronted a more difficult economic situation.

When placed side by side, these two ethnic paradoxes have significant implications for theory and policy. First, they support the influence of early modes of incorporation that lead to divergent paths of adaptation and achievement even *within* the same nationality. Second, they indicate that high rates of immigrant entrepreneurship do not necessarily translate into higher educational achievement in the second generation. Laotian/Cambodian refugees are the *least* entrepreneurial groups in our parental sample; in part because of this, their children have next to no opportunities for early employment mediated through ethnic networks. This second effect requires additional clarification. It is not the case that children of successful entrepreneurs are themselves dropouts. Among Cuban Americans, these children have a high probability of attending bilingual private schools and, consequently, of finding themselves in an upward-mobility. Instead, it is the children of more recent and generally poorer arrivals who respond to the opportunities for early employment available in the community. In so doing, they compromise their chances for school graduation and future professional careers.

Conclusion

Despite individual exceptions and unexpected effects, the basic conclusion that emerges from our analysis is that of a patterned sequence of adaptation conditioned by predictable social forces: immigrant human and social capital, first, and opportunities and barriers in the host society, second. These sets of factors play themselves out over time, conditioning the socioeconomic achievement and family stability of first-generation immigrants and, later, the career horizons and academic performance of their offspring.

Our findings give a partial lie to the proverb "When there's a will, there's a way," at least in its social policy implications. It is true that many exceptional individuals prevail despite adverse circumstances, weak family resources, and cultural dissonance. The stories that we have covered of disadvantaged but courageous youths seeking to make the best of their poor endowments can be multiplied by the hundreds. But on the whole, the environments created by the combination of immigrants' human and social capital and the context that receives them dominate the process of adaptation and its prospects of success. Placed in an impoverished community and surrounded by a hostile world, even the most motivated individuals flounder, despite brave declarations to the contrary. This is what the consistently negative effects associated with disadvantaged nationalities tell us.

On the whole, the new second generation seems to be achieving and adapting well, as indicated by its superior academic performance relative to native-parentage students. Common stories of success support immigrant parents' goals and give reason to anticipate that most, if not all, members of this emerging population will successfully join the American mainstream in the future. Set against this outcome is the passage of time, which diminishes the early immigrant drive, especially among children experiencing dissonant acculturation, and bad schools and weak families that make others abandon their educational goals as unattainable dreams. This combination of factors means that while the second generation as a whole is moving ahead and thus providing grounds for general optimism, some children are doing much better than others. Adapting and achieving in a new society cannot be attributed to any single factor; it is the way that individual and contextual forces are joined in a particular time and place that affects individual outcomes in a manner that is complex but not chaotic. This joining of forces underlies the place that different immigrant communities take in the process of segmented assimilation and, hence, their eventual standing in the American hierarchies of wealth, status, and power.

Chapter 10

CONCLUSION

Mainstream Ideologies and the Long-Term Prospects of Immigrant Communities

Ronald Unz, the Jewish-American millionaire who spearheaded California's successful Proposition 227, the so-called English for the Children initiative, explained his support for the measure as follows: "As a strong believer in American assimilationism, I had a long interest in bilingual education. Inspired in part by the example of my own mother, who was born in Los Angeles into a Yiddish-speaking immigrant home but had quickly and easily learned English as a young child, I had never understood why children were being kept for years in native-language classes, or why such programs had continued to exist and even expand after decades of obvious failure."[1]

As we saw in Chapter 6, the supposedly bilingual programs against which Unz railed are not bilingual education at all but a potpourri of efforts to gradually mainstream foreign students into English-only classes. There is actually a dearth of certified bilingual teachers in a state where well over one million students speak a language other than English at home, and for many of these languages, there are no bilingual teachers at all. Furthermore, because of bureaucratic inertia and perhaps the interest of some school administrations in continuing to receive funds, these programs ended up keeping many students in second-rate remedial classes, especially at the secondary level. Not surprisingly, English for the Children garnered the support of many immigrant parents, tired of such inferior instruction. Some of the parents had actually picketed the schools to force them to teach their children exclusively in English.

A thoughtful conservative, Unz sought to distance his initiative from the anti-immigrant activists capitalizing on the fears of white, middle-class voters in California. He read well the mood of these descendants of earlier European immigrants in the wake of the 1992 Los Angeles riots: "Terrified of social decay and violence, and trapped by collapsed property values, many whites felt they could neither run nor hide. Under these circumstances, attention inevitably began to focus on the tidal force of foreign immigration. . . . Public sentiment was [however] quite confused on the matter. . . . To most people, "illegal immigrant" was simply a synonym for 'poor immigrant' or 'bad immigrant' or perhaps even 'Mexican immigrant.'"[2]

This was the frame of mind that led white Californian voters to support overwhelmingly Proposition 187, the so-called Save our State proposal. That measure conveyed a direct message to immigrants that they were less than welcome in the Golden State. Accordingly, as seen in Chapter 7, it triggered a strong reactive formation among the foreign born and their children that produced levels of political mobilization and ethnic reassertiveness seldom seen before. Unz apparently wished to avoid the mean-spiritedness of 187 since his English for the Children proposal did not aim at excluding immigrants but at incorporating them as rapidly as possible into the American mainstream. This goal is to be accomplished by abandoning foreign-language instruction and immersing immigrant children into English-only classes.[3]

Two Mainstream Ideologies

The politics surrounding Propositions 187 and 227 in California are useful to give us a glimpse into the way the mainstream native population understands migration and its consequences. Throughout the preceding chapters, we have delved into the worlds of immigrant parents and their children, seeking to understand how they cope with the challenges of their new environment and how they struggle to carve a niche in it. In this final chapter, we turn the tables, exploring the dominant views among the native citizenry and how they affect the chances for success of immigrant adaptation efforts.

The experiences of California are strategic because they provide a blueprint for the reaction of the electorate elsewhere in the country as the number of immigrants inevitably grows. The political environment leading to the vote in these two referenda was marked by three key features: first, the central importance attributed to immigration by native voters as they became increasingly aware of its power to transform the state demographically and culturally; second, the growing fears expressed by or on behalf of white voters and crystallized in such expressions as the "end of white America" and California becoming a "minority white" state[4]; and third, the fact that neither of the main ideological positions that competed for support among this electorate offers a viable blueprint for successful immigrant adaptation. In other words, the political stances that appear understandable and appealing among middle-class suburbanites would not lead to successful solution of the immigration "problem" but to its exacerbation. Instead of a viable process of integration of the foreign born, policies derived from these ideologies would lead exactly to the opposite outcome.

The first ideology, represented by the drafters of Proposition 187, can be labeled "intransigent nativism." It seeks to stop all or most immigration, send unauthorized immigrants back as quickly as possible, and put immigrants who remain in the United States on notice that they occupy an inferior position, ineligible for the privileges of citizens. The second ideology, represented by Unz and supporters of Proposition 227, can be labeled "forceful assimilationism." It seeks to mainstream immigrants and their children as far and as swiftly as possible, in the model of Yiddish-speaking mothers who left everything behind in their quest for English fluency and social acceptance. According to its proponents, this policy will reunify anew the state and the nation, avoiding the fractious influence of multiple languages and cultures.

Supporters of intransigent nativism look mainly to the present. They give expression to the growing discomfort of a settled, middle-class citizenry that sees itself increasingly surrounded and even outnumbered by foreigners. Advocates of this position seldom stop to reflect on the origins of contemporary immigration. They do not know or care to know that these origins are closely intertwined with the activities of U.S. corporate capitalism or the colonialist ventures of the U.S. government. The deliberate recruitment of workers by American interests in the interior of the Mexican republic since the nineteenth century, the creation and repeated extension of the Bracero labor contract program during the twentieth century, and the creation of numerous legal loopholes by Congress to give employers uninterrupted access to this flow of foreign workers after the end of the Bracero Program do not figure high in the nativists' story.[5] And neither does the colonialist occupation of the Philippines by U.S. forces at the beginning of the twentieth century or U.S. interventions in southeast Asian internal conflicts that set the stage for massive refugee outflows.[6]

Intransigent nativism pays attention only to the present consequences of these processes as they give rise to fear and discomfort among the white suburban population. Accordingly, it lashes out not against the sources of these outflows—U.S. agribusiness, corporate interests, and the framers of U.S. foreign policy—but against the immigrants themselves, seeking to eliminate their presence. The restoration of social peace, from the perspective of the framers of the Save Our State proposition, requires rendering the foreign element once again invisible.

The second ideological position is less irrational. Forceful assimilationism does look at the past but less to find the origins of contemporary immigrant flows than to search for ways in which prior waves were separated from their cultures and integrated into the American mainstream. The nation's success in absorbing so many foreigners in the past is attributed to its relentless hostility to the perpetuation of cultural enclaves and the immersion of foreign children into an English-only environment that made Americans out of them in the course of a single generation.[7] Assimilationists want the future to mirror this past as a proven way to restore cultural unity and peace. Just as Yiddish-speaking mothers had to leave their culture and language behind, so should Mexican immigrants and Vietnamese refugees today.

Both positions have consequences for immigrant families and their children. To the extent that it is translated into policy, intransigent nativism yields heightened discrimination and new barriers to successful adaptation. It also triggers a defensive reaction in which self-identities and political mobilizations are structured in opposition to a native mainstream perceived as hostile. As demonstrated by numerous historical examples, nativism is likely to produce both self-fulfilling and self-defeating prophecies.[8] Self-fulfilling prophecies arise because discrimination and external barriers encourage labor market failure, poverty, weaker communities, and the rise of an oppositional stance among foreign groups who could have adapted successfully in a less hostile environment. Self-defeating prophecies come about because the effort to "put immigrants in their place" and return society to its culturally integrated past results in exactly the opposite situation—greater ethnic polarization, greater conflict, and the emergence of impoverished and embittered groups at the bottom of society.

The preceding chapters have presented consistent evidence of how a mode of incorporation marked by a hostile governmental and societal reception yields negative outcomes both for immigrant adults and children. Adults are unable or less able to put their human capital to use; it becomes more difficult to forge solidary communities that can support parental control and promote high expectations for the future. Children's perceptions of the surrounding society become more threatening, their academic aspirations and achievements suffer, and they become more preoccupied with issues of ethnic identity and reassertiveness than with the achievement of high goals through individual effort.

Although less traumatic, forceful assimilationism also has negative consequences, both individual and collective. Policies derived from this ideology delegitimize the culture and language of parents, thus promoting dissonant acculturation. By instilling in children the sense that their parents' language is inferior and should be abandoned in favor of English, schools help drive a wedge across generations, weakening parental efforts to preserve a common cultural memory. As seen in Chapter 6, immersion programs can prove highly traumatic and lead to maladaptive outcomes. A common result is limited bilingualism, in which immigrant children move away from their parents' language and culture without having acquired full command of English. Self-esteem, educational expectations, and academic achievement suffer accordingly.

By remaining fixed on the past, assimilationists neglect the major changes that have taken place in the world and in the U.S. economy during the last twenty-five years. A century ago, immigrants came from remote lands to fill the labor needs of a rapidly industrializing country. Few other ties linked sending nations with the United States. At present, sending countries are increasingly part of a single global web with the United States at its center.[9] In this new world order where multiple economic, political, and cultural ties bind nations more closely to one another, it is not clear that the rapid extinction of foreign languages is in the interest of individual citizens or of the society as a whole. In an increasingly interdependent global system, the presence of pools of citizens able to communicate fluently in English plus another language and to bridge the cultural gap among nations represents an important collective resource.

Despite being grounded on thoughtful reflection on immigration history, Unz's Proposition 227 is designed to accomplish exactly the opposite. Despite its moderation, its vision is ultimately reactionary. It wants an America as it was in the 1920s, a relatively isolated society, not as it must be in the new millennium, after it successfully emerged as the core of the global system. In the process, old-line assimilationism undermines the very forces of parental authority and ambition that can overcome the barriers to successful adaptation and forge productive and self-respecting citizens out of the new second generation.

A Third Way: Selective Acculturation and Bilingualism

The findings from our longitudinal study consistently point to the benefits of selective acculturation. This path is closely intertwined with preservation of fluent bilingualism and linked, in turn, with higher self-esteem, higher educational and occupational expectations, and higher academic achievement. From a theoretical standpoint, these relationships are reasonable. Children who learn the language and culture of their new country without losing those of the old have a much better understanding of their place in the world. They need not clash with their parents as often or feel embarrassed by them because they are able to bridge the gap across generations and value their elders' traditions and goals. Selective acculturation forges an intergenerational alliance for successful adaptation that is absent among youths who have severed bonds with their past in the pursuit of acceptance by their native peers.[10]

By the same token, members of the second generation who are American without having abandoned their roots are in a position to make a significant contribution to society by dint of their ability to communicate in other languages and comprehend other cultures. In global cities, such as New York, Los Angeles, and Miami, bilingualism is commonly a prerequisite for employment. The same is true for global corporations. Still, as seen in Chapter 6, selective acculturation, as indexed by fluent bilingualism, is exceptional; the normative path continues to be monolingualism and monoculturalism.

Despite its advantages, selective acculturation has no political constituency. For nativists and assimilationists alike, anything that reeks of preservation of foreign ways is suspicious and should be made to disappear. For assimilationists, this is accomplished by the surrender of immigrants' language and cultures; for nativists, by the removal of the immigrants themselves. The reactive formation process triggered by nativist policies does not represent selective acculturation but marks the start of a far more problematic outcome. As seen in Chapter 7, children of immigrants can abandon hyphenated identities that incorporate their past and present (i.e., Mexican-*American*) in favor of a purely nationalist stance (i.e., Mexican) in response to attacks against their origins and culture. Subsequent ethnic mobilizations under foreign flags are part of the self-fulfilling prophecy prompted by nativist policies. In turn, the spectacle of thousands marching under these banners adds to the fears of middle-class suburbanites in a vicious spiral.[11]

Selective acculturation requires a socially and politically supportive environment where learning of English and American culture takes place in a paced fashion, without losing valuable cultural resources in turn. In addition to other shortcomings of American public education documented by the recent literature, public schools tend to discourage rather than support selective acculturation.[12] In the absence of such support, achievement of this outcome is at present in the hands of immigrant families and co-ethnic communities. A good example, revisited in previous chapters, is the pre-1980 Cuban exile community in southern Florida. This group was able to construct a solidary and institutionally diversified ethnic community that includes a well-developed system of bilingual private schools. Children attending such schools are most likely to remain fluent bilinguals, and this outcome is accompanied by high levels of self-esteem, high ambition, and a solid academic record.

The type of education imparted by these schools is worth attention as a viable model for the institutional promotion of selective acculturation. However, as seen in Chapter 9, not all Cuban children attend bilingual private schools. In fact, only a minority do, and these are mostly children of older exiles. Those whose parents came during or after the Mariel boatlift are more likely to enroll in the public school system. Conditions for selective acculturation are weakened accordingly. Ironically, it is children attending public schools who are most likely to remain trapped within the Cuban ethnic enclave as they drop out of school in search of early employment.

Asian parents have not been able to create bilingual school systems, and the smaller size of their communities has made collective support for second-generation bilingualism more difficult. While fewer Chinese, Korean, or Vietnamese children turn out fluent bilinguals, there are signs of selective acculturation in the support that tight ethnic communities provide to parental authority, the transmission of a strong achievement drive across generations, and the remarkable academic performance of these youths. As Nghi Van Nguyen stated in Chapter 4, the Vietnamese family is "like a corporation," and their mutual assistance, coupled with the decisive support from the community, leads to sustained academic effort even when bilingual skills are dissipated.

Assimilationism sustains a vision of an integrated society composed of well-behaved citizens who share key values and normative commitments. There is nothing wrong with that vision, but the proposed way of achieving it is mistaken. One does not get there by pressuring immigrants and their children into a uniform mold but by making use of the values and resources that they themselves have brought. These are the resources that provide second-generation youths with the necessary sense of self-worth and normative guidance to succeed in the face of multiple external challenges. The irony of the situation is that many immigrant families are doing for American society what it will not do for itself: raising law-abiding, achievement-oriented, and bilingual citizens in the teeth of the obstacles stemming from intransigent nativism and forceful assimilation.

The Mexican Case

> The first girl born in California in 2000 was born to Mexican parents. She was named Anayeli de Jesús. Her parents, Elena and Javier, came from Mexico in the 1990s looking for a better life and hope the same for their daughter: "To be a good student and to go to the university."
> — Kate Folmar and Scott Martelli, "The New Faces of Orange County's Future," p. 1.

"If one takes out the Mexicans, there will be no evidence for segmented assimilation." This is a statement often heard among immigration specialists. It is buttressed by the size of the Mexican-origin population, by far the largest among contemporary immigrant groups, and by its low human capital. Some observers believe that signs of dissonant acculturation, low ambition, and the emergence of oppositional attitudes concentrate mainly among second-generation Mexicans.[13] As seen in the preceding chapters, this is erroneous since other groups that have experienced negative modes of incorporation are also at risk. In different contexts, we have examined evidence to that effect among other sizable immigrant minorities, including Nicaraguans, Haitians, and post-Mariel Cubans.

Nevertheless, the Mexican immigrant population is defined by several attributes that make it unique and deserving of special attention. In this final chapter, it is worth reviewing what these are and how they affect the second generation, particularly in the context of the ideological battles just discussed. In California, in particular, nativist and assimilationist policies have been directed primarily at Mexicans and their offspring with consequences that, as just seen, have been the opposite of those intended. The Mexican population of the United States is marked by three characteristics that make it unique:

It is the product of an uninterrupted flow lasting more than a century. Mexicans are the *only* foreign group that has been part of both the classic period of immigration at the beginning of the twentieth century and the present movement. Accordingly, Mexicans are also the only group among today's major immigrant nationalities to have spawned an earlier second and even third generation.[14]

Mexicans come from the only less-developed country sharing a land border with the United States. This geographical contiguity has facilitated both labor recruitment and subsequent mass labor displacements, mediated by social networks. The facility of such movements across a land border accounts for the lower average human capital of Mexican immigrants relative to other groups, who come from even poorer but more distant countries.

Because of their numbers, poverty, and visibility, Mexican immigrants were targets of repeated waves of nativist hostility throughout the twentieth century. These attacks included organized government campaigns aimed at their repatriation or at forcefully preventing their settlement.[15] Mexican immigrants have thus experienced a negative mode of incorporation not only at present but for over 100 years. Demand for Mexican migrant labor has been equally persistent, but the conditions under which it has been employed have been marked by the social inferiority and political vulnerability created by this negative context.

Results of our study offer abundant evidence of the consequences of these features. Mexican immigrants represent *the* textbook example of theoretically anticipated effects of low immigrant human capital combined with a negative context of reception. It is worth summarizing these results for what they tell us about the specific experiences of the group and, by extension, of those to be anticipated for other disadvantaged foreign minorities:

Adult Mexican immigrants not only receive low earnings, but their economic disadvantage also endures even after controlling for their human capital. Net of human capital factors, Mexican parents in our sample earn $1,910 less per year than other adult immigrants (Chapter 4).

This economic disadvantage is compounded because whatever human capital Mexican immigrants possess has a lower return than that among more successful groups. Thus, years of U.S. residence do not increase incomes for Mexican parents in our sample, and knowledge of English yields a lower payoff than for immigrants from other countries (Chapter 4).

Mexican parents are significantly more likely to report low bonds of solidarity and low levels of support from their co-ethnics, reflecting the weak communities that have emerged under their precarious conditions of arrival and settlement. Aspirations for their children are also significantly lower than for other groups (Chapter 5).

Mexican-American children are the only Latin group in the sample to lack a positive nationality effect on fluent bilingualism, and they have the lowest average self-esteem. Controlling for other factors, Mexican origin makes no positive contribution to either adaptation outcome (Chapters 6 and 8).

Mexican-American children are the most likely to have shifted self-identities away from any American label and toward an unhyphenated national (i.e., Mexican) identity. They are also the group most prone to racialize their national origin. Both trends reflect a strong process of reactive formation to perceived external hostility (Chapter 7).

Reflecting their parents' low aspirations, Mexican-American children have significantly lower educational expectations than the CILS average and the lowest among Latin-origin groups. This disadvantage persists after controlling for other factors. Net of them, second-generation Mexican students are still 10 percent less likely to believe that an advanced college degree is within their reach than other students (Chapter 8).

Corresponding to these low aspirations and cumulative disadvantages, Mexican-origin students are less likely to perform well in school. Their lower-than-average grades and test scores cannot be explained by individual, family, or school predictors. In junior high school, Mexican students fell behind a net 12 points in standardized math scores and 15 points in reading scores, after controlling for these predictors; they also had a significant net disadvantage in grades. This inferior performance continues in late high school, where Mexican-American students suffer a significant handicap after controlling for a wide array of individual and family factors.

These cumulative results clearly point to a difficult process of adaptation and to the likelihood of downward assimilation in many cases. The high optimism of parents and the superior school performance and lower dropout rates of second-generation Mexicans relative to their native-parentage peers only qualify this conclusion. This optimism and relatively better academic record reflect a residual immigrant drive that weakens with the passage of time under the continuous influence of an adverse social environment. It is worth emphasizing that the second-generation Mexican advantage is only observable in comparison with their native counterparts, that is, third-generation and higher Hispanics who perform even worse than the more recent arrivals.[16] This comparison offers no grounds for expecting that academic performance will improve and dropout rates will decline over time.

Hence, while the likelihood of downward assimilation is not exclusive to Mexican-American adolescents, the condition of this group does deserve special attention. Given the size of the Mexican immigrant population and its all-but-certain continuing growth in future years, the cumulative disadvantages under which its second generation struggles should be of prime practical concern. As López and Stanton-Salazar put it:

> The Mexican-American case stands apart. They and their parents lack many of the resources that have allowed other recent groups of newcomers to thrive. A rather large proportion of children of Mexican immigrants do poorly in school and their occupational prospects are bleak. If Mexican-origin youths were just another in the vast array of new second generation groups, there would only be modest room for concern regarding their below average achievement and future prospects. But, in California and the Southwest, *Mexicanos* and their children are not "just another" immigrant-based ethnic group. They are instead by far the largest "minority" and are rapidly becoming the single largest ethnic group.[17]

The danger of downward assimilation for Mexican-American youths is only compounded by the policies that have captured the imagination of mainstream voters. For reasons already examined, nativism and forceful assimilationism yield programs that undermine successful adaptation by increasing dissonant acculturation or provoking an adversarial reaction. In light of the present evidence, there is no second-generation group for which selective acculturation is more necessary than for Mexican Americans. This would entail educational programs that combine learning of English and acculturation with preservation of Spanish and understanding and respect for the parents' culture. In particular, there should be ample external support for the immigrant family and for its incipient attempts at building strong community bonds. In many Mexican families, the *only* thing going for the children is the support and ambition of their parents. These aspirations should be strengthened rather than undermined.

From a long-term perspective, policies toward Mexican immigration advocated by the two mainstream ideologies discussed previously verge on the suicidal. Demand for Mexican migrant labor continues unabated, and its arrival is guaranteed by various legal loopholes and the strong social networks created over a century. Once here, however, migrant workers and their children are heavily discriminated against, blamed for their poverty, and subjected either to nativist ire or pressures toward immediate assimilation. The results are not hard to discern in the spectacle of the impoverished barrios of Los Angeles, San Diego, Houston, and other large southwestern cities and in consistent results from our study. The same evidence points to an alternative and more enlightened path applicable to all children of immigrants but with particular urgency to Mexican Americans.

Theoretical Reprise

We refer the reader back to the theoretical models in Chapter 3 that have framed the analysis of successive adaptation outcomes. Overall, they stand well in light of the evidence. In particular, the analysis has shown the significance of types of acculturation in confronting the challenges to successful adaptation (Figure 3.1) and the cumulative character of the process with outcomes "building on each other" to define alternative assimilation paths (Figure 3.3). As just seen, one of these paths—downward assimilation—constitutes a real possibility for children growing up in poverty and lacking the support of strong and solidary communities. The significance of modes of incorporation comes through repeatedly as they condition the chances for such communities to emerge and the opportunities for socioeconomic achievement in the first generation.

The contexts of reception that greet different immigrant groups are not determined solely by their human capital. While better-educated groups should elicit a more positive governmental and societal response in theory, this is not always the case. As we saw in previous chapters, a relatively well-educated group such as Nicaraguans in Miami experienced a hostile context of reception, their claims for asylum and assistance being routinely denied. In contrast, southeast Asians, although having much poorer human capital endowments, were well received and granted refugee status with generous resettlement aid. The decisive variable in all these cases had to do with the geopolitical interests of the U.S. government and its particular relationship with countries of origin. A second important factor in the case of the groups just mentioned is that neither Nicaraguans nor southeast Asians had strong preexisting ethnic communities to host them and, hence, their modes of incorporation were largely determined by governmental policy.

Time and Acculturation

There are, however, several significant results and some anomalies that are not captured in our original models. The most important is the passage of time. Time in the United States increases opportunities for immigrant economic progress although, for reasons just seen, these opportunities vary with individual endowments and contexts of reception. Some foreign groups move effortlessly into the American middle class, while others are stuck, seemingly forever, in a subordinate social and economic status. Above all, the passage of time brings about greater acculturation and, with it, the weakening of the original immigrant drive. At some point, immigrants become like natives in terms of their work effort, motivation, and social networks. The question then is at what level of the socioeconomic hierarchy are families and entire ethnic communities found when this seemingly inexorable shift takes place.

The evidence of an immigrant achievement drive is documented by multiple results in our analysis. They include the strong ambition and optimism of immigrant parents (Chapter 5); the high expectations, school commitment, and work effort of children that consistently exceed those of the general student population (Chapter 8); and the superior grades and lower dropout rates of every second-generation group relative to their third-generation-and-higher peers (Chapter 9). The evidence of a dampening effect with increasing acculturation is equally strong: the diminishing school commitment and effort of native-born students, especially among some groups who, like Cuban Americans, managed to reach middle-class status in the first generation (Chapters 4 and 8); the consistently negative effect of length of acculturation on educational expectations and grades (Chapters 8 and 9); *and* the lower academic performance and higher dropout rates of native-parentage minority students relative to their respective second generations (Chapter 9).

Taken together, this evidence points to a race, as it were, between original immigrant ambition and the passage of time. Results of that race will determine the long-term character of the ethnic groups created by today's immigration. The point is illustrated by the inter-generational outcomes portrayed in Figure 10.1: Riding on the strength of their human capital and a favorable mode of incorporation, some groups manage to make it into the middle classes in the first generation; their children are guaranteed the resources for a good education and, in some instances, entrepreneurial opportunities. They can afford to adopt a more relaxed, native-like stance toward schools and the future. By the third generation, ethnic ties and identities weaken as these groups become fully integrated into the American mainstream.

Other immigrants manage to reach middle-class status in the second generation, drawing resources from strong families and ethnic communities. The following are some of the activities that poor but motivated parents have been known to engage in to ensure that this transition takes place:

Working two or three jobs to buy a home in a neighborhood with good schools or pay tuition in a bilingual private school

Sending their children to their home country to be educated under the care of grandparents and other kin

Moving to cities where their co-ethnics concentrate to increase social ties and external influences supportive of parental authority

Keeping grandparents at home and supporting extended families to reinforce parents' control and use of their language[18]

From the perspective of these immigrant families, selective acculturation can be redefined as a strategy to preserve the original achievement drive and transmit it across generations. Otherwise, offspring of poor immigrants would be no better off than native-minority youths, whose fate parents seek at all costs to avoid.

Other groups fail to move upward in the second generation, the children having educational credentials and occupational opportunities no

Figure 10.1   Paths of Mobility across Generations

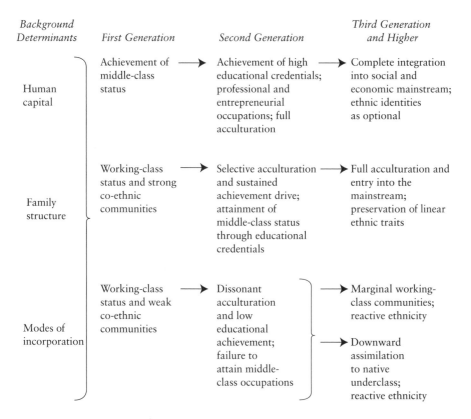

Background Determinants	First Generation	Second Generation	Third Generation and Higher
Human capital	Achievement of middle-class status	Achievement of high educational credentials; professional and entrepreneurial occupations; full acculturation	Complete integration into social and economic mainstream; ethnic identities as optional
Family structure	Working-class status and strong co-ethnic communities	Selective acculturation and sustained achievement drive; attainment of middle-class status through educational credentials	Full acculturation and entry into the mainstream; preservation of linear ethnic traits
Modes of incorporation	Working-class status and weak co-ethnic communities	Dissonant acculturation and low educational achievement; failure to attain middle-class occupations	Marginal working-class communities; reactive ethnicity / Downward assimilation to native underclass; reactive ethnicity

better than their parents'. This situation has two consequences: First, it significantly increases the chances for assimilation into the native underclass for reasons already explained in Chapter 3. Second, it defines the long-term character of the respective ethnic community. A thoroughly acculturated third generation lacks the drive and social resources of their immigrant ancestors and, hence, their position in the American hierarchies of wealth and power is conditioned by what happened to their parents and grandparents. There is no empirical evidence at present to expect that groups confined to the working class or that have moved downward into the native underclass would miraculously rise during the third generation to alter their collective status. There is, on the other hand, strong evidence on the intergenerational transmission of both privilege and disadvantage.[19] This is why long-term prospects of the ethnic groups created by today's immigration will be conditioned by what happens to these immigrants' children.

Reactive Ethnicity and Its Aftermath

A second significant issue not covered by the theoretical models of Chapter 3 is that of the rise and effects of reactive ethnicity. As seen in Chapter 7, reactive ethnicity is the product of confrontation with an adverse native mainstream and the rise of defensive identities and solidarities to counter it. In contrast to the deliberate preservation of immigrant languages and cultures brought about by selective acculturation, reactive ethnicity is a "made-in-America" product. The discourses and self-images that it creates develop as a situational response to present realities. Even when the process involves embracing the parents' original national identities, this is less a sign of continuing loyalty to the home country than a reaction to hostile conditions in the receiving society.

As seen earlier in this chapter, the Mexican case represents the most significant example of this process because of the group's size, continuity over time, and persistent disadvantage. Along the lines predicted in Figure 10.1, reactive ethnicity is common in children and grandchildren of Mexicans. Terms such as *the Nation of Aztlán* or *La Raza* did not exist in the immigrants' original lexicon but were coined by their descendants.[20] The process is perfectly understandable as a defense to threatened self-images and collective dignity. However, as a vehicle for collective upward mobility, reactive identities are a double-edged sword. In these final lines, we review these implications both to round out the theoretical discussion of earlier chapters and to advance concrete proposals for immigrant minorities at risk.

Reactive formation processes provide a viable basis for collective solidarity and political mobilization in defense of ethnic group interests. This is what happened among Mexican Americans during the 1960s and 1970s when the term *Chicano* was coined and a number of militant organizations such as the Brown Berets and La Raza Unida Party emerged.[21] As we have seen, the process repeated itself in the 1990s in response to California's Proposition 187. Political mobilization has a series of positive *collective* consequences in terms of empowering an ethnic minority and bringing attention to its plight. The mobilizations of the 1960s and 1970s did increase the representation of Mexican Americans in Congress and state legislatures and brought about a number of governmental programs favorable to the group.[22] Similarly, the Mexican-American mobilizations of the late 1990s spelled the end of the political careers of several of the most ardent California nativists.

Consequences of reactive formation at the *individual* level are less positive, especially among the young. Youthful solidarity based on opposition to the dominant society yields an adversarial stance toward mainstream institutions, including education. This is the situation that, in Matute-Bianchi's words, creates a forced-choice dilemma for the young between doing well in school and staying loyal to one's ethnic group. In the process, many minority students "learn not to learn."[23] This dismal outcome can be defined as an instance of the downward effects of social capital; that is, bonds of solidarity that, among other immigrant groups, represent a powerful resource for advancement lead, in this case, to downward-leveling norms. Instead of the peer group supporting the achievement efforts of its own, it pushes them to conform to the status quo under threat of being ostracized.[24]

The process was discussed in Chapter 3 as one of the major challenges to successful adaptation of today's second generation. The question here is what to do about third-generation-and-higher minorities caught in this situation. The logical answer lies in *reversing* the sign of the social capital created by the reactive formation process. Ethnic role models with credibility among the young are best situated to convey the message about the self-destructive consequences of downward-leveling norms and the need to support individual achievement.[25] A number of minority leaders have become actively involved in this task among their own student populations. To be successful, such efforts must be supported by school programs that accord attention to the history and culture of the respective minority.

In the film *Stand and Deliver,* actor Edward James Olmos impersonates famed teacher Jaime Escalante, who had remarkable success in teaching advanced math to impoverished minority students in East Los Angeles. This rousing tale need not be isolated but can furnish a blueprint for the reorientation of minority youths' social capital. Such a policy toward students who have been the victims of downward assimilation in the past has elements in common with that advanced previously to ward off this threat among the second generation. Referring to Figure 10.1, the promotion of selective acculturation among children of immigrants is based on group solidarity and support of a common collective memory as sources of self-esteem and ambition. For children of minorities that have been marginalized in the past, the same elements are needed for countering downward-leveling norms and constructing an empowerment-for-achievement orientation.

Tragically, the ideologies that hold sway among broad segments of the white middle-class electorate yield exactly the opposite results, imperiling the future of today's second generation and perpetuating the condition of the existing minority underclass. Results of this study point to the urgent need to enlighten the dominant majority as to where its real self-interests lie in the long run and thus build a constituency for an alternative set of policies. The future of the metropolitan areas where immigrants concentrate and of American society as a whole may well hang in the balance.

Appendix A

CHILDREN OF IMMIGRANTS LONGITUDINAL STUDY

Follow-up Questionnaire

Case Number _____

YOUTH ADAPTATION AND GROWTH QUESTIONNAIRE (II)

For each question, please check the correct answer or write neatly in the space provided.

1. What is your full name? _____
   (Please print clearly)   Last (Family) Name   First   Middle

2. Where do you live?

   _____
   Address   Apt. No.

   _____
   City   State   Zip Code

3. What is your telephone number? _____

4. What is the name of your school? _____

5. What grade are you in? _____

6. What is your sex?   1. Male _____   2. Female _____

How much do you agree with each of the following statements about your current school and teachers?

	1. Agree a lot	2. Agree a little	3. Disagree a little	4. Disagree a lot
7. There is real school spirit	_____	_____	_____	_____
8. Students make friends with students of other racial and ethnic groups	_____	_____	_____	_____
9. The teaching is good	_____	_____	_____	_____
10. Teachers are interested in students	_____	_____	_____	_____

	1. Agree a lot	2. Agree a little	3. Disagree a little	4. Disagree a lot
11. I don't feel safe at this school	_____	_____	_____	_____
12. Disruptions by other students get in the way of my learning	_____	_____	_____	_____
13. Fights often occur between different racial or ethnic groups	_____	_____	_____	_____
14. There are many gangs at school	_____	_____	_____	_____
15. Students are graded fairly	_____	_____	_____	_____
16. Discipline is fair	_____	_____	_____	_____

During the current school year how many times did any of the following things happen to you at school?

	1. Never	2. Once or twice	3. More than twice
17. I had something stolen from me at school	_____	_____	_____
18. Someone offered to sell me drugs at school	_____	_____	_____
19. Someone threatened to hurt me at school	_____	_____	_____
20. I got into a physical fight at school	_____	_____	_____

21. (If you were born in a foreign country) In what year did you come to the United States?

Year: _____   Never came (I was born in U.S.): _____

22. How long have you lived in the United States?

1. All my life _____   2. Ten years or more _____

3. Five to nine years _____   4. Less than five years _____

23. Are you a U.S. citizen?

    1. Yes _____   2. No _____   3. Don't know _____

24. How well do you speak English?

    1. Not at all _____   2. Not well _____

    3. Well _____   4. Very well _____

25. How well do you understand English?

    1. Not at all _____   2. Not well _____

    3. Well _____   4. Very well _____

26. How well do you read English?

    1. Not at all _____   2. Not well _____

    3. Well _____   4. Very well _____

27. How well do you write English?

    1. Not at all _____   2. Not well _____

    3. Well _____   4. Very well _____

We would like to learn a little more about your family. Here are a few questions about them.

28. Which of the following best describes your present situation (Please read the whole list, then check the category that applies to you):

    1. I live with my (biological or adoptive) father and mother. _____

    2. I live with my father and stepmother (or other female _____ adult).

    3. I live with my mother and stepfather (or other male adult). _____

    4. I live with my father alone. _____

    5. I live with my mother alone. _____

    6. I alternate living with my father and mother who are _____ divorced or separated.

    7. I live with other adult guardians. _____

    8. Other. Please explain: _____ _____

29. Which of the following people, *in addition to your parents or guardians,* live with you, that is in the house where you spend most of the time? (Check all that apply)

    a. Brothers or step-brothers   _____   How many? _____

    b. Sisters or step-sisters   _____   How many? _____

    c. Grandfather or grandmother _____   How many? _____

    d. Uncles or aunts   _____   How many? _____

    e. Other relatives   _____   How many? _____

    f. Non-relatives   _____   How many? _____

30. In total, how many people, beside you, live in the same house with you?   Number: _____

31. In total, how many older brothers (or stepbrothers) and sisters (or stepsisters) do you have?   Number: _____

*Please describe the present or most recent job of your **father, stepfather, or male guardian:***

32. Is he currently working, unemployed, retired, or disabled?

    1. Currently working _____   2. Unemployed _____

    3. Retired _____   4. Disabled _____

If your father is unemployed, retired, *or* disabled, *answer the following questions for his most recent job.*

Also, if your father works more than one job, *please answer for the job you consider to be his major activity.*

33. What kind of work does he normally do? That is, what is his job called?

    Name of Occupation: _____

34. What does he actually do in that job? What are some of his main duties?

    _____

    _____

35. Describe the place where he works; what does the company make or do?

_____

_____

_____

36. What is the highest level of education that he completed?

    1. Elementary school or less   _____

    2. Middle school graduate or less   _____

    3. Some high school   _____

    4. High school graduate   _____

    5. Some college or university   _____

    6. College graduate or more   _____

    7. Other _____   Explain _____

Please describe the present or most recent job of your **mother, step-mother, or female guardian:**

37. Is she currently working, unemployed, retired, or disabled?

    1. Currently working _____   2. Unemployed _____

    3. Retired _____   4. Disabled _____

If your mother is unemployed, retired, or disabled, answer the following questions for her most recent job.

Also, if your mother works more than one job, please answer for the job you consider to be her major activity.

38. What kind of work does she normally do? That is, what is her job called?

    Name of Occupation: _____

_____

39. What does she actually do in that job? What are some of her main duties? _____

_____

40. Describe the place where she works; what does the company make or do? _____

_____

41. What is the highest level of education that she completed?

    1. Elementary school or less   _____

    2. Middle school graduate or less   _____

    3. Some high school   _____

    4. High school graduate   _____

    5. Some college or university   _____

    6. College graduate or more   _____

    7. Other _____   Explain _____

42. Do your parents (or adult guardians) own or rent the house or apartment where you now live?

    1. Own _____   2. Rent _____   3. Other _____

    (Please explain) _____

43. Compared to **three** years ago, do you think that your family's economic situation now is:

    1. Much better _____   2. Better _____

    3. About the same _____   4. Worse _____   5. Much worse _____

44. And three years from now, do you think that your family's economic situation will be?

    1. Much better _____   2. Better _____

    3. About the same _____   4. Worse _____   5. Much worse _____

45. Do you have a paying job at present? 1. Yes _____   2. No _____

46. If yes, what is your job? (Please describe clearly, *including the place where you work*) _____

_____

47. How many hours *per week* do you work at it? _____

48. Approximately how much do you earn per week in this job? $____

Let's talk about the language that you speak at your home:

49. Do you know a language other than English?

    1. Yes _____   2. No _____

50. (If yes) What language is that? (If more than one, please list first the language you know best) _____

_____

51. How well do you speak that language? (Or the foreign language that you know best)

    1. Very little _____   2. Not well _____

    3. Well _____   4. Very well _____

52. How well do you understand that language?

    1. Very little _____   2. Not well _____

    3. Well _____   4. Very well _____

53. How well do you read that language?

    1. Very little _____   2. Not well _____

    3. Well _____   4. Very well _____

54. How well do you write that language?

    1. Very little _____   2. Not well _____

    3. Well _____   4. Very well _____

55. Do people in your home speak a language other than English?

    1. Yes _____   2. No _____

56. (If yes) What language is that? (If more than one please list first the language that they use most often) _____

    _____

57. How often do the people who live in your home use this language when they are talking to each other? (Or the language they use most often)

    1. Seldom_____   2. From time to time _____

    3. Often _____   4. Always   _____

58. When you talk to your parents (or guardians), what language do you most often use? (Write in) _____

59. In what language do you prefer to speak most of the time? (Write in) _____

About your plans for the future:

60. What is the **highest** level of education that you would like to achieve?

    1. Less than high school _____   2. Finish high school _____

    3. Finish some college   _____   4. Finish college   _____

    5. Finish a graduate degree (masters, doctor, etc.)   _____

61. And **realistically speaking,** what is the highest level of education that you think you will get?

    1. Less than high school _____   2. Finish high school _____

    3. Finish some college   _____   4. Finish college   _____

    5. Finish a graduate degree (masters, doctor, etc.)   _____

62. What is the highest level of education that your parents want you to get?

    1. Less than high school _____   2. Finish high school _____

    3. Finish some college   _____   4. Finish college   _____

    5. Finish a graduate degree (masters, doctor, etc.)   _____

63. What job would you like to have as an adult? (Please write clearly)

_____

_____

64. Among the following job categories, which is the one that comes closest to the job that you would like to have as an adult?

    1. Factory worker   _____

    2. Office clerk   _____

    3. Salesperson   _____

    4. Technician/computer programmer   _____

    5. Nurse/physical therapist/dietitian   _____

    6. Business executive/manager   _____

    7. Engineer   _____

    8. Teacher/professor   _____

    9. Lawyer   _____

    10. Doctor (Physician)   _____

    11. Other (write in)   _____

65. And **realistically speaking,** how do you see your chances of getting this job?

    1. Very poor _____   2. Poor   _____

    3. Good   _____   4. Very good _____

66. (a) If you plan to attend college, which is the college that you would *like* to attend?

Name of College   _____

No plans to attend college   _____

Don't know   _____

66. (b) And **realistically speaking,** which is the college you think you *will* attend?

Name of College   _____

No plans to attend college   _____

Don't know   _____

66. (c) If you do not go to college, what is the main reason why you do not plan to go?

_____

_____

How important is each of the following to you in your life?

	1. Not Important	2. Somewhat Important	3. Very Important
67. Having lots of money	_____	_____	_____
68. Having strong friendships	_____	_____	_____
69. Being able to find steady work	_____	_____	_____
70. Living close to parents and relatives	_____	_____	_____
71. Getting away from this community	_____	_____	_____

72. How many close friends do you have in school? (Write number) ___

73. How many of these close friends have parents who came from foreign countries, that is who were not born in the United States?

1. None _____   2. Some _____   3. Many or most_____

74. How many of your friends have:

	1. None	2. Some	3. Many or most
a. Dropped out of school without graduating	_____	_____	_____
b. No plans to go to college	_____	_____	_____
c. Plans to get a full-time job after high school?	_____	_____	_____
d. Plans to attend a 2-year community college?	_____	_____	_____
e. Plans to attend a 4-year college or university?	_____	_____	_____

75. In talking with your friends at school, do you sometimes use a language other than English?

    1. Yes _____   2. No _____

76. (If yes) What language is this? (Please write) _____

77. How often do you use this language when talking with your school friends?

    1. Seldom   _____   2. From time to time _____

    3. Often   _____   4. Always   _____

78. (a) How do you identify, that is, what do you call yourself? (Examples: [used in Miami survey; different ones were used in San Diego] Asian, Hispanic, American, Latino, African-American, Black, Cuban, Cuban-American, Haitian, Haitian-American, Nicaraguan, Nicaraguan-American, Jamaican, Jamaican-American, etc.) _____

78. (b) And how important is this identity to you, that is what you call yourself?

    1. Not important _____   2. Somewhat important _____

    3. Very important _____

Please indicate how much do you agree or disagree with the following statements (mark the right line):

	1. Agree a lot	2. Agree a little	3. Disagree a little	4. Disagree a lot
79. There is racial discrimination in economic opportunities in the U.S.	_____	_____	_____	_____
80. The American way of life weakens the family.	_____	_____	_____	_____
81. There is much conflict between different racial and ethnic groups in the U.S.	_____	_____	_____	_____
82. Non-whites have as many opportunities to get ahead economically as whites in the U.S.	_____	_____	_____	_____
83. There is no better country to live in than the United States.	_____	_____	_____	_____
84. Americans generally feel superior to foreigners.	_____	_____	_____	_____

85. Have you ever felt discriminated against?   1. Yes ___ 2. No ___

86. (If yes) And by whom did you feel discriminated? (Check all that apply)

    a. Teachers   _____

    b. Students   _____

    c. Counselors   _____

    d. White Americans in general   _____

    e. Latinos in general   _____

    f. Black Americans in general   _____

    g. Others _____ (Write in)   _____

87. What do you think was the main reason for discriminating against you? (Please write clearly) _____

How often is each of the following true about your immediate family (the people you live with)?

88. Family members like to spend free time with each other.

    1. Never _____   2. Once in a While _____

    3. Sometimes _____   4. Often _____   5. Always _____

89. Family members feel very close to each other.

    1. Never _____   2. Once in a While _____

    3. Sometimes _____   4. Often _____   5. Always _____

90. Family togetherness is very important.

    1. Never _____   2. Once in a While _____

    3. Sometimes _____   4. Often _____   5. Always _____

Please indicate how you feel about the following statements:

	1. Agree a lot	2. Agree a little	3. Disagree a little	4. Disagree a lot
91. If someone has the chance to help a person get a job, it is always better to choose a relative rather than a friend.	_____	_____	_____	_____
92. When someone has a serious problem, only relatives can help.	_____	_____	_____	_____
93. When looking for a job a person should find a job near his/her parents even if it means losing a better job somewhere else.	_____	_____	_____	_____

94. During the typical **weekday,** how many hours do you spend studying or doing school homework?

    1. Less than one _____   2. One to two _____

    3. Two to three _____   4. Three to four _____

    5. Four to five _____   6. Five or more _____

95. Who helps you most with your homework when you need help? (Pick one)

    1. My father or mother _____   2. My brother or sister _____

    3. My friend(s) _____   4. My teacher(s) _____

    5. My counselor(s) _____   6. Other _____

    7. No one _____

    Write in_____

96. During the typical **weekday,** how many hours do you spend watching television or playing video games?

    1. Less than one _____   2. One to two _____

    3. Two to three _____   4. Three to four _____

    5. Four to five _____   6. Five or more _____

97. Linda and Luis are both students whose parents are foreign-born. Linda says: "I am sometimes embarrassed because my parents don't know American ways." Luis says: "I am never embarrassed by my parents. I like the way they do things."
Which one comes closest to how you feel?

    1. Linda _____   2. Luis _____

    3. Neither (explain)_____

98. How often do you prefer American ways of doing things?

    1. All the time _____   2. Most of the time _____

    3. Sometimes _____   4. Never _____

99. How often do your parents (or adults with whom you live) prefer American ways of doing things?

    1. All the time _____   2. Most of the time _____

    3. Sometimes _____   4. Never   _____

100. And how often do you get in trouble because your way of doing things is different from that of your parents?

    1. All the time _____   2. Most of the time _____

    3. Sometimes _____   4. Never   _____

Please indicate if you agree or disagree with the following statements:

	1. Agree a lot	2. Agree a little	3. Disagree a little	4. Disagree a lot
101. I feel that I am a person of worth, at least on an equal basis with others.	_____	_____	_____	_____
102. I feel that I have a number of good qualities.	_____	_____	_____	_____
103. All in all, I am inclined to feel that I am a failure.	_____	_____	_____	_____
104. I am able to do things as well as most other people.	_____	_____	_____	_____
105. I feel I do not have much to be proud of.	_____	_____	_____	_____
106. I take a positive attitude toward myself.	_____	_____	_____	_____
107. On the whole, I am satisfied with myself.	_____	_____	_____	_____
108. I wish I could have more respect for myself.	_____	_____	_____	_____

	1. Agree a lot	2. Agree a little	3. Disagree a little	4. Disagree a lot
109. I certainly feel useless at times.	_____	_____	_____	_____
110. At times I think I am no good at all.	_____	_____	_____	_____
111. I am satisfied with how I look.	_____	_____	_____	_____
112. I am not very popular with members of the opposite sex.	_____	_____	_____	_____
113. I am seen as a trouble maker by other students.	_____	_____	_____	_____

Below is a list of feelings that people sometimes have. For each answer, how often have you felt this way during the past week?

	1. Rarely (less than once a week)	2. Some of the time (1 or 2 days a week)	3. Occasionally (3 or 4 days a week)	4. Most of the time (5 to 7 days a week)
114. I felt sad.	_____	_____	_____	_____
115. I could not get "going."	_____	_____	_____	_____
116. I did not feel like eating; my appetite was poor.	_____	_____	_____	_____
117. I felt depressed.	_____	_____	_____	_____

Now, this is another list that describes young people. Please answer how true each statement is for you.

	1. Very True	2. Partly True	3. Not Very True	4. Not True at All
118. My parents do not like me very much.	_____	_____	_____	_____
119. It is very important to me to get good grades.	_____	_____	_____	_____

	1. Very True	2. Partly True	3. Not Very True	4. Not True at All
120. My parents and I often argue because we don't share the same goals.	_____	_____	_____	_____
121. My parents are usually not very interested in what I say.	_____	_____	_____	_____
122. No matter how much education I get, people will still discriminate against me.	_____	_____	_____	_____

123. Which of the races listed do you consider yourself to be?

1. White _____   2. Black _____   3. Asian _____

4. Multi-racial _____   5. Other _____

(If other race, which race is that?) _____

124. Lots of things happen in families that may affect young people. In the last 3 years, have any of the following happened to your family?

(Circle one in each line)

	Yes	No
a. My family moved to a new home	1	2
b. My parents got divorced or separated	1	2
c. One of my parents got married or remarried	1	2
d. One of my parents lost his/her job	1	2
e. I became seriously ill or disabled	1	2
f. One of my parents died	1	2
g. One of my brothers or sisters dropped out of school	1	2
h. A member of my family was the victim of a crime	1	2
i. One or both of my parents became a U.S. citizen	1	2
j. I became a U.S. citizen	1	2

125. Finally, how important is each of the following to you in your life?

	1. Not Important	2. Somewhat Important	3. Very Important
a. Having children	____	____	____
b. Having leisure time to enjoy my own interests	____	____	____
c. Getting away from my parents	____	____	____
d. Becoming an expert in my field of work	____	____	____
e. Getting a good education	____	____	____

126. What is your social security number?_____

Thank you very much for your cooperation.

Appendix B

CHILDREN OF IMMIGRANTS LONGITUDINAL STUDY
Parental Questionnaire

Parental Interview

Interview No. _____

Name of Interviewee:_____

Address: _____
         Street and No.   Apt. No.

_____
         City   State   Zip Code

Telephone Numbers: Home: _____ Work: _____

Relationship to child: _____ Name of Child: _____

Interviewer:_____

Date and Hour of Interview:_____

Duration of Interview: _____

Comments: _____

_____

_____

Interview Completed _____
               Signature   Date

Revision _____
               Signature   Date

Field Supervision _____
               Signature   Date

Coding Completed_____
               Signature   Date

Coding Revised _____
               Signature   Date

Case Number _____

I. Demographic Characteristics

1. What is your full name? _____
   (Please print clearly)

2. Where do you live? _____

   _____
                    City   Zip Code

3. What is your telephone number? _____

4. Sex: Male _____   Female _____

5. In what year were you born? _____

6. Where were you born?   _____

   _____
                    City   Country

7. What was your last place of residence before coming to live permanently in the United States?

   _____
                    City   Country

8. In what year did you arrive to live permanently in the United
   States? _____

9. In what city did you live when you first arrived in the United
   States? _____

10. In how many cities (including the present one) have you lived in
    the United States? _____

    _____

11. In how many different states have you lived in the United States?

    _____

12. Are you a U.S. citizen?

    1. Yes _____   2. No _____

13. What is your marital status? (Read alternatives)

    1. Married   _____   (To question 14)

    2. Lives with a partner   _____   (To question 14)

    3. Divorced or separated _____   (To question 15)

    4. Widowed   _____   (To question 16)

    5. Other   _____   Specify: _____

14. What is the relationship of your spouse/partner to your child *(name of child)*?

    1. Biological father or mother (To question 18)

    _____

    2. Step-father or step-mother (To question 15)

    _____

    3. Other _____   Specify: _____

15. Where does your child's *(name)* other biological parent currently live?

    1. Same city   _____

    2. Other city in same state   _____

    3. Other state   _____

    4. Other country   _____

    5. Deceased   _____

    6. Don't know   _____

16. Where was your child's *(name)* other biological parent born?

_____

            City   Country

17. How long is it since the last time your child *(name)* saw him or her?

    1. Less than a week   _____

    2. Less than a month   _____

    3. Less than six months   _____

    4. Less than a year   _____

    5. One year or more   _____

    6. Don't know   _____

[If divorced, separated, or widowed, skip to question 21]

18. How long have been living together with your present spouse/ partner?

    1. Less than a year   _____

    2. One to three years   _____

    3. Four to six years   _____

    4. Seven to ten years   _____

    5. Eleven years or more   _____

19. Where was she/he born?

_____

                City   Country

20. Is she/he a U.S. citizen?   1. Yes ____   2. No ____   3. D.K. ____

21. How many children in total do you have? (#)_____

22. Please give me the age and sex of the children who currently live with you including *(name of child)*.

Age   Sex

    1. _____ (eldest)   _____

    2. _____   _____

    3. _____   _____

Age   Sex

4. _____   _____

5. _____   _____

6. _____   _____

7. _____   _____

8. _____   _____

23. In total, how many people live in this residence? (#) _____

24. How many of your child's *(name)* grandparents live in this residence?

   (#)_____

25. How many other adult relatives live in this residence? (#) _____

II. Language, Education, Occupation

26. What is the language spoken mostly in this residence?

   1. English _____

   2. Other   _____   Specify language: _____

   3. Mixed   _____   Specify languages: _____

27. In what language do you mostly speak to your child?

   1. English _____

   2. Other   _____   Specify language: _____

   3. Mixed   _____   Specify languages: _____

28. I would like you to tell me about your knowledge of English:

	1. Not at all	2. A little	3. Well	4. Very well
1. How well do you speak English?	_____	_____	_____	_____
2. How well do you understand English?	_____	_____	_____	_____

	1. Not at all	2. A little	3. Well	4. Very well
3. How well do you read English?	____	____	____	____
4. How well do you write English?	____	____	____	____

[Skip to question 30 if divorced, widowed or separated]

29. And now please tell me about your spouse or partner's English knowledge.

	1. Not at all	2. A little	3. Well	4. Very well
1. How well does she/he speak English?	____	____	____	____
2. How well does she/he understand English?	____	____	____	____
3. How well does she/he read English?	____	____	____	____
4. How well does she/he write English?	____	____	____	____

30. How do you identify, that is what do you call yourself? (Examples: American, Hispanic, Asian, Black, African-American, Latino, Mexican, Mexican-American, Vietnamese, Vietnamese-American).

_____

31. What is the highest level of education that you completed?

1. Eighth grade or less   _____

2. Beyond eighth grade, but not high   _____
   school graduation

3. High school graduation   _____

   Vocational, trade or business school after High School:

   4. Less than one year   _____

5. One to two years   _____

6. Two years or more   _____

College program:

7. Less than two years   _____

8. Two or more years   _____

9. Finished a four or five-year program   _____

10. Master's degree or equivalent   _____

11. Ph.D., M.D., or other advanced degree   _____

32. Did you have a regular job in your country of birth before coming to the United States?

1. Yes _____   2. No _____

33. (If yes) Please tell me what was that occupation and who was your employer.

a. Occupation (describe clearly)   _____

_____

_____

b. Employer (Name of company, government agency, or other institution. Indicate if self-employed.) _____

_____

_____

34. Which one of these best describes your present situation?

1. Employed full-time   _____

2. Employed part-time   _____

3. Unemployed and looking for work   _____

4. Unemployed and not looking for work   _____

5. Attending school full-time   _____

6. Retired   _____

7. Disabled   _____

8. Keeping house (homework)   _____

9. Other _____   Specify: _____

[Skip to question 44 if not presently employed]

35. (If employed, full or part-time) please tell me what is your present occupation? (Describe clearly).

_____

_____

36. Which of the following categories comes closest to describing your present job?

   1. Clerical such as bank teller, bookkeeper, secretary,   _____ typist, mail carrier, ticket agent

   2. Craftsperson such as baker, automobile mechanic,   _____ machinist, painter, plumber, telephone installer, carpenter

   3. Farmer, Farm Manager   _____

   4. Homeworker (without other job)   _____

   5. Laborer such as construction worker, car washer,   _____ sanitary worker, farm laborer

   6. Manager, Administrator such as sales manager, office _____ manager, school administrator, buyer, restaurant manager, government official

   7. Military such as career officer, enlisted man or   _____ woman in the Armed Forces

   8. Operative such as meat cutter, assembler, machine   _____ operator, welder, taxicab, bus or truck driver

9. Professional such as accountant, artist, registered _____
nurse, engineer, librarian, writer, social worker, actor,
actress, athlete, politician, but not including school teacher

10. Professional such as clergyman, dentist, physician, _____
lawyer, scientist, college teacher

11. Proprietor or Owner such as owner of a small _____
business, contractor, restaurant owner

12. Protective Service such as detective, police officer _____
or guard, sheriff, fire fighter

13. Sales such as salesperson, advertising or insurance _____
agent, real estate broker

14. School teacher such as elementary or secondary _____

15. Service such as barber, beautician, practical nurse, _____
private household worker, janitor, waiter

16. Technical such as draftsman, medical or dental _____
technician, computer programmer

37. (If employed) Are you mostly self-employed or do you work for
someone else?

1. Self-employed _____

2. Working for someone else _____

3. Other _____   Specify: _____

38. (If working for someone else) Are the Owner(s) of the place where
you work American or foreign born?

1. American _____

2. Foreign-born _____

3. Not/applicable _____

4. D.K. _____

39. (If foreign-born) What country(ies) did they come from?

_____

40. Are the Managers of the place where you work mostly American or foreign-born?

   1. American   _____

   2. Foreign-born   _____

   3. D.K.   _____

41. (If foreign-born) What country(ies) did they come from?

_____

42. Are most Co-workers in the place where you work American or foreign-born?

   1. American   _____

   2. Foreign-born   _____

   3. D.K.   _____

43. (If foreign-born) What country(ies) did they come from?

_____

[Skip to question 47 if employed]

44. Did you ever work in the United States?

   1. Yes _____   2. No _____

45. (If yes) Please tell me what was your last occupation and who was your employer.

   a. Occupation (describe clearly)

_____

_____

b. Employer (company, agency, etc. Indicate if self-employed)

_____ _____

_____

46. Which of the following categories comes closest to describing that job:

1. Clerical such as bank teller, bookkeeper, secretary,   _____
   typist, mail carrier, ticket agent

2. Craftsperson such as baker, automobile mechanic,   _____
   machinist, painter, plumber, telephone installer, carpenter

3. Farmer, Farm Manager   _____

4. Homeworker (without other job)   _____

5. Laborer such as construction worker, car washer,   _____
   sanitary worker, farm laborer

6. Manager, Administrator such as sales manager, office _____
   manager, school administrator, buyer, restaurant
   manager, government official

7. Military such as career officer, enlisted man or   _____
   woman in the Armed Forces

8. Operative such as meat cutter, assembler, machine   _____
   operator, welder, taxicab, bus or truck driver

9. Professional such as accountant, artist, registered   _____
   nurse, engineer, librarian, writer, social worker, actor,
   actress, athlete, politician, but not including school teacher

10. Professional such as clergyman, dentist, physician,   _____
    lawyer, scientist, college teacher

11. Proprietor or Owner such as owner of a small   _____
    business, contractor, restaurant owner

12. Protective Service such as detective, police officer   _____
    or guard, sheriff, fire fighter

13. Sales such as salesperson, advertising or insurance   _____
    agent, real estate broker

14. School Teacher such as elementary or secondary   _____

15. Service such as barber, beautician, practical nurse,   _____
    private household worker, janitor, waiter

16. Technical such as draftsman, medical or dental   _____
    technician, computer programmer

[Skip to question 52 if divorced, widowed or separated]

47. What is the highest level of education that your spouse/partner
    completed?

    1. Eighth grade or less   _____

    2. Beyond eighth grade, but not high   _____
       school graduation

    3. High school graduation   _____

    Vocational, trade or business school after High School:

        4. Less than one year   _____

        5. One to two years   _____

        6. Two years or more   _____

    College program:

        7. Less than two years   _____

        8. Two or more years   _____

    9. Finished a four or five-year program   _____

    10. Master's degree or equivalent   _____

    11. Ph.D., M.D., or other advanced degree   _____

48. Which one of these best describes her/his present situation?

    1. Employed full-time   _____

    2. Employed part-time   _____

3. Unemployed and looking for work   _____

4. Unemployed and not looking for work   _____

5. Attending school full-time   _____

6. Retired   _____

7. Disabled   _____

8. Keeping house (homework)   _____

9. Other _____   Specify: _____

49. (If employed, full or part-time) please tell me what is her/his present occupation? (Describe clearly)

_____

_____

_____

50. (If employed) Is she/he mostly self-employed or do you work for someone else?

1. Self-employed   _____

2. Working for someone else   _____

3. Other _____   Specify: _____

51. Which of the following categories comes closest to describing her/his job:

1. Clerical such as bank teller, bookkeeper, secretary,   _____
   typist, mail carrier, ticket agent

2. Craftsperson such as baker, automobile mechanic,   _____
   machinist, painter, plumber, telephone installer, carpenter

3. Farmer, Farm Manager   _____

4. Homeworker (without other job)   _____

5. Laborer such as construction worker, car washer,   _____
   sanitary worker, farm laborer

6. Manager, Administrator such as sales manager, office _____
   manager, school administrator, buyer, restaurant
   manager, government official

7. Military such as career officer, enlisted man or   _____
   woman in the Armed Forces

8. Operative such as meat cutter, assembler, machine   _____
   operator, welder, taxicab, bus or truck driver

9. Professional such as accountant, artist, registered   _____
   nurse, engineer, librarian, writer, social worker, actor,
   actress, athlete, politician, but not including school teacher

10. Professional such as clergyman, dentist, physician,   _____
    lawyer, scientist, college teacher

11. Proprietor or Owner such as owner of a small   _____
    business, contractor, restaurant owner

12. Protective Service such as detective, police officer   _____
    or guard, sheriff, fire fighter

13. Sales such as salesperson, advertising or insurance   _____
    agent, real estate broker

14. School Teacher such as elementary or secondary   _____

15. Service such as barber, beautician, practical nurse,   _____
    private household worker, janitor, waiter

16. Technical such as draftsman, medical or dental   _____
    technician, computer programmer

52. Is there any other person that has a paid occupation living in this
    house?

    1. Yes _____   2. No _____

53. (If yes) Which of the above categories comes closest to describing
    their jobs?

    [Same categories as in question 51]

Person (Relationship to Respondent)	Job Category
1st _____	_____
2nd _____	_____
3rd _____	_____
4th _____	_____

54. Are you satisfied with your present earnings?

    1. Yes _____   2. No _____

    3. Other _____   Specify: _____

55. Approximately, how much do you earn per month from all sources? $ _____

56. And what was the total income of your family from all sources last year? (Include the sum of all earned and unearned incomes from self, spouse, and all other family members).

    1. None   _____

    2. Less than $1,000   _____

    3. $1,000–$2,999   _____

    4. $3,000–$4,999   _____

    5. $5,000–$7,499   _____

    6. $7,500–$9,999   _____

    7. $10,000–$14,999   _____

    8. $15,000–$19,999   _____

    9. $20,000–$24,999   _____

    10. $25,000–$34,999   _____

    11. $35,000–$49,999   _____

    12. $50,000–$74,999   _____

13. $75,000–$99,999 _____

14. $100,000–$199,999 _____

15. $200,000 or more _____

57. Does your family have health insurance at present?

1. Yes _____   2. No _____

3. Other _____   Specify: _____

III. Early Settlement and Discrimination

58. During your first year of residence in the United States, did you or your family receive any kind of economic assistance from a government or private agency?

1. Yes _____   2. No _____

3. Other _____   Specify: _____

59. (If yes) Please tell us which agencies were these and what type of assistance did you receive?

	Agency	Type of Assistance
1.	_____	_____
2.	_____	_____
3.	_____	_____
4.	_____	_____
5.	_____	_____

60. During your first year of residence, did you have any contact with agencies or departments of the U.S. government?

1. Yes _____   2. No _____

61. Would you say that these contacts helped you or made it harder for you to adapt to life in the United States?

1. Helped _____   2. Neither_____

3. Made it harder _____

62. Do you or any other member of your family currently receive any of the following?

	1. Yes	2. No
1. Food stamps	_____	_____
2. Aid to Families with Dependent Children	_____	_____
3. Supplemental Security Income	_____	_____
4. Disability Payments	_____	_____
5. MediCal/Medicaid	_____	_____
6. Other public assistance of any kind	_____	_____

63. (If self-employed—See Question 37) Did you receive any kind of government assistance, such as a loan or a training course to start your business?

   1. Yes _____   2. No _____

64. (If yes) What kind of assistance was this?

   _____

   _____

65. What is your race? (For example: white or Caucasian, black or Negro, Asian, mulatto, mestizo. Note ethnicity is NOT race)

   _____

66. Do you feel that you have been discriminated against because of your race or your ethnicity in the United States?

   1. Yes _____   2. No _____

   3. Other _____   Specify: _____

   [If not discriminated, skip to question 69]

67. (If yes) How often have you been discriminated against?

   1. Often _____   2. Occasionally _____

   3. Rarely _____

68. And what group has mostly discriminated against you? (For example: whites, blacks or African-Americans, Cubans or Cuban-Americans, Asians, or Asian-Americans. (Try to obtain a single response).

_____

_____

[Skip to question 72 if respondent does not have a job]

69. Compared to people of other races or nationalities, how many opportunities for job advancement do you get at your work?

A Lot Less	A Little Less	The Same as Others	A Little More	A Lot More
1. _____	2. _____	3. _____	4. _____	5. _____

70. Because of your race or nationality, how often do people in your work place treat you as less competent than you deserve to be treated?

Almost Never	At least Once a Year	At least Once a Month	At least Once a Week	Almost Daily
1. _____	2. _____	3. _____	4. _____	5. _____

71. How often do you hear people in your workplace make rude remarks or negative comments about people of your race or nationality?

Almost Never	At least Once a Year	At least Once a Month	At least Once a Week	Almost Daily
1. _____	2. _____	3. _____	4. _____	5. _____

72. Because of your race or nationality, how often do you receive poor service, for instance in stores or restaurants?

Almost Never	At least Once a Year	At least Once a Month	At least Once a Week	Almost Daily
1. _____	2. _____	3. _____	4. _____	5. _____

73. Because of your race or nationality, how often do you feel out of place or unwelcome in public places?

Almost Never	At least Once a Year	At least Once a Month	At least Once a Week	Almost Daily
1. _____	2. _____	3. _____	4. _____	5. _____

74. Which of these words best describe the relations between your own ethnic group and white Americans according to your experience?

a. 1. Cordial _____   2. Cold _____   3. D.K. _____

b. 1. Close _____   2. Distant _____   3. D.K. _____

c. 1. Friendly _____   2. Hostile _____   3. D.K. _____

75. Do you think your child *(name)* will experience opposition in the future if he or she wants to:

	1. Yes	2. No	3. D.K.
1. Join a club of white Americans	_____	_____	_____
2. Move into a white American neighborhood	_____	_____	_____
3. Marry a white American	_____	_____	_____

76. Do you think that white Americans consider themselves:

1. Superior   _____

2. Equal   _____

3. Inferior to your own group?   _____

4. D.K.   _____

Now let us return to your early experiences when you arrived in the United States.

77. How many relatives (other than spouse and children) were already living in the United States when you arrived? (#) _____

78. And how much help did you receive from your relatives when you arrived?

    0. No relatives   _____

    1. None   _____

    2. Little   _____

    3. Much   _____

79. How many friends did you have in the United States when you arrived? (#) _____

80. And how much help did you receive from your relatives when you arrived?

    0. No relatives   _____

    1. None   _____

    2. Little   _____

    3. Much   _____

81. Who helped you get your first job in the United States?

    0. Never worked   _____

    1. Got it himself/herself   _____

    2. Relative(s)   _____

    3. Friend(s)   _____

    4. Other compatriot   _____

    5. Government agency   _____

    6. Private agency   _____

    7. Other _____   Specify: _____

82. Were the Owners of the place where you first worked in the United States American or foreign-born?

    1. American   _____

    2. Foreign-born   _____

    3. D.K.   _____

83. (If foreign-born) What country(ies) did they come from?

_____

84. Were most Co-workers in the place where you first worked American or foreign-born?

   1. American   _____

   2. Foreign-born   _____

   3. D.K.   _____

85. (If foreign-born) What country(ies) did they come from?

_____

IV. Social Networks and Ethnicity

86. Apart from those who live in this house, how many relatives of yours live now near you (in the same city or county)? (#) _____

87. Do you have relatives who live in the United States, but not in this area?

   1. Yes _____   2. No _____

88. (If yes) How many?_____

89. How many friends do you have in this city or county? (#) _____

90. How many of them did you know before you came to the United States? (#)_____

91. How many of these friends were NOT born in your country of birth? (#) _____

92. In general, do you socialize mainly with (read categories):

   1. Other persons born in my own country of birth   _____

   2. Other foreign-born persons   _____

   3. White Americans   _____

   4. Black Americans   _____

5. Hispanic-Americans   _____

6. Asian-Americans   _____

7. Other _____   Specify: _____

93. The people in your neighborhood are mostly (read categories):

    1. From my own country   _____

    2. Immigrants from other countries   _____

    3. White Americans   _____

    4. Black Americans   _____

    5. Hispanic-Americans   _____

    6. Asian-Americans   _____

    7. Other _____   Specify: _____

Now I am going to ask you a few questions about your national background.

	1. Not at all	2. A little	3. Somewhat	4. Very
94. How much do people from your country help each other in the United States?	_____	_____	_____	_____
95. How important is it for you to keep in contact with other people from your country living here?	_____	_____	_____	_____
96. How proud are you of your country?	_____	_____	_____	_____
97. How important is it for (child's name) to know about your country?	_____	_____	_____	_____

98. How often do you
    talk to (child's name)
    about your country?   _____ _____ _____ _____

99. How often do you
    celebrate any special
    days connected with
    your country?   _____ _____ _____ _____

How true are the following statements?

	1. True	2. False	3. D.K.
100. Many people from my country live in this neighborhood.	_____	_____	_____
101. People from my country who live in this neighborhood do not help each other.	_____	_____	_____
102. I have a close community of friends among people from my country.	_____	_____	_____
103. People from my country are usually very supportive of each other.	_____	_____	_____
104. People from my country have NOT been very successful economically in the United States.	_____	_____	_____
105. I prefer to buy in stores owned by people from my own country.	_____	_____	_____
106. If I needed a loan, I would rather borrow from people from my own country than from Americans.	_____	_____	_____

V. Neighborhood, School, and Rules

107. How long have you lived in this neighborhood?

       Years _____ Months _____

108. How satisfied are you with your neighborhood? (Read categories)

    1. Very satisfied   _____

    2. Satisfied   _____

    3. Neither satisfied nor dissatisfied   _____

    4. Dissatisfied   _____

    5. Very dissatisfied   _____

Please tell us if you think each of the following is not a problem, somewhat a problem or a big problem in your neighborhood.

In your neighborhood, how much of a problem is . . .	1. Not a Problem	2. Somewhat of a Problem	3. A Big Problem
109. Different racial or cultural groups who do not get along with each other?	_____	_____	_____
110. Little respect for rules, laws, and authority?	_____	_____	_____
111. Assaults or muggings?	_____	_____	_____
112. Delinquent gangs or drug gangs?	_____	_____	_____
113. Drug use or drug dealing in the open?	_____	_____	_____

Do you think that the people in your neighborhood would intervene (do something) in the following situations?

	1. Very Unlikely	2. Unlikely	3. Likely	4. Very Likely
114. If there was a fight in front of your house and someone was being beaten?	____	____	____	____
115. If someone were trying to sell drugs to one of your children in plain sight?	____	____	____	____

116. If your kids were getting   _____   _____   _____   _____
      into trouble?

The following statements are about the people who live in your neighborhood. Please tell us how much you agree or disagree with each statement.

	1. Strongly Disagree	2. Disagree	3. Neither Agree Nor Disagree	4. Agree	5. Strongly Agree
117. There are a lot of adults around that my children can look up to.	____	____	____	____	____
118. My neighbors have similar views about how to raise children.	____	____	____	____	____
119. I can count on people in in the neighborhood to let me know about opportunities for my kids.	____	____	____	____	____

120. Do you and your spouse/partner do any of the following at your child's school?

	1. Yes	2. No
a. Belong to a parent-teacher organization	____	____
b. Attend meetings of a parent-teacher organization	____	____
c. Act as a volunteer in the school	____	____

121. Do you know the first name or nickname of any of *(child's name)* close friends?

    1. Yes _____   2. No _____

122. (If yes) How many? _____

123. Do you know the parents of any of these children?

    1. Yes _____   2. No _____

124. (If yes) How many? _____

125. Are there family rules about any of the following television-related activities?

	1. Yes	2. No
a. What program he/she may watch	_____	_____
b. How early or late he/she may watch television	_____	_____
c. How many hours he/she may watch television overall	_____	_____

126. Are there family rules for your child about any of the following activities?

	1. Yes	2. No
a. Maintaining a certain grade average	_____	_____
b. Doing homework	_____	_____
c. Doing household chores	_____	_____

127. Parents differ in how much they talk to their children about what they do in school. How often do you or your spouse/partner talk with your child about his or her experiences in school?

1. Not at all   _____

2. Rarely   _____

3. Occasionally _____

4. Regularly   _____

128. How often do you or your spouse/partner talk with your child about her or his educational plans for after high school?

1. Not at all   _____

2. Rarely   _____

3. Occasionally _____

4. Regularly _____

129. How often do you or your spouse/partner help your child with his or her homework?

    1. Seldom or never _____

    2. Once or twice a month _____

    3. Once of twice a week _____

    4. Almost every day _____

130. Are any of the following people at home when your child returns home from school?

	1. Usually	2. Sometimes	3. Rarely	4. Never
a. Mother or female guardian	_____	_____	_____	_____
b. Father or male guardian	_____	_____	_____	_____
c. Other adult relative	_____	_____	_____	_____
d. Adult neighbor	_____	_____	_____	_____
e. Older brother or sister	_____	_____	_____	_____

131. How satisfied are you with the education that your child has received up to now?

    1. Very satisfied _____

    2. Somewhat satisfied _____

    3. Not satisfied at all _____

132. How far in school do you expect your child to go?

    1. Eighth grade or less _____

    2. Beyond eighth grade, but not high school graduation _____

3. High school graduation   _____

Vocational, trade or business school after High School:

    4. Less than one year   _____

    5. One to two years   _____

    6. Two years or more   _____

College program:

    7. Less than two years   _____

    8. Two or more years   _____

   9. Finished a four or five-year program   _____

  10. Master's degree or equivalent   _____

  11. Ph.D., M.D., or other advanced degree _____

133. Have you or your spouse/partner done anything specific in order to have some money for your child's education after high school?

    1. Yes _____   2. No _____   3. D.K. _____

134. About how much money have you set aside for your child's future educational needs?

    0. None   _____

    1. Less than $1,000   _____

    2. $1,000–$3,000   _____

    3. $3,001–$6,000   _____

    4. $6,001–$10,000   _____

    5. $10,001–$15,000   _____

    6. More than $15,000 _____

135. The following statements are about financial aid for education beyond high school. Indicate which statement is true or false for your family.

	1. True	2. False	3. Have not thought about this
a. My child will be able to earn most of the money he or she will need for schooling beyond high school	_____	_____	_____
b. We can pay for our child's further education without getting any outside assistance	_____	_____	_____
c. The family is not willing to go into debt for schooling	_____	_____	_____
d. The family income is too high to qualify for a loan or scholarship	_____	_____	_____

	1. Not at All	2. A Little	3. Somewhat	4. Very	5. D.K.
136. How worried are you about negative influences on (child's name) from other students in her/his school?	____	____	____	____	____
137. How worried are you about negative influences on (child's name) from her/his own close friends?	____	____	____	____	____
138. How different are your views and ideas from those of (child's name) friends?	____	____	____	____	____

	1.Not at All	2. A Little	3. Somewhat	4. Very	5. D.K.
139. How different are the messages she/he is getting from you and from her/his friends about becoming a successful person?	____	____	____	____	____

140. Do you want your child *(name)* to be raised according to the customs of your own country or according to American customs?

   1. Own country customs   _____

   2. American customs   _____

   3. Other _____   Specify: _____

   4. D.K. _____

141. In general, how satisfied are you from having come to the United States to live?

   1. Very satisfied   _____

   2. Somewhat satisfied   _____

   3. Dissatisfied   _____

   4. Very dissatisfied   _____

142. Do you plan to stay in the United States or return to your own country?

   1. Stay in U.S.   _____

   2. Return   _____

   3. Other _____   Specify: _____

   4. D.K. _____

Thank you very much for your cooperation!

VARIABLES USED IN MULTIVARIATE ANALYSES
Chapters 6 to 9

I. VARIABLES USED IN ANALYSIS OF BILINGUALISM (CHAPTER 6)

Variable	Measurement	Range	Mean
	Independent		
Age	Years (in 1992)	12 to 18	14.23
Sex	Dichotomous	1 = Female 0 = Male	.51
Latin American National Origin	Dichotomous	1 = Latin Origin 0 = Not Latin Origin	.57
Length of U.S. Residence	Years, 1992	1 = Less than 5 2 = 5 to 9 3 = 10 or more 4 = All life, native born	3.12
Parental Nativity	Dichotomous	1 = One parent U.S. born 0 = Both parents are foreign born	.14
Parental SES	Standardized unit-weighted sum of father's and mother's education, occupational status, and home ownership, 1992	–2.00 to +2.00	.00

Foreign Language Used at Home (in families with both biological parents present)	Dichotomous, 1992	1 = "Always" or "often"
		    use foreign language
		    at home
		0 = Infrequent home use
		    of foreign language
			.51

Second-Generation Friends	Number of friends who are also children of immigrants, 1992	1 = None 2 = Some 3 = Many or most	2.55
GPA, 1992	Grade point average in school (grades eighth and ninth), weighted for honors or advanced placement (AP) courses	0 to 5	2.52
Percent Latin Students in School	Pecentage, 1992	4 to 99	.46
Percent Asian Students in School	Pecentage, 1992	0 to 45	.15
Private Bilingual School	Dichotomous, 1992	1 = Attends private bilingual school 0 = Does not	.04

Variable	Measurement	Range	Mean
	Independent		
Fluent Bilingual	Dichotomous, measured in 1992	1 = English Knowledge Index score of 3.75 or higher (up to 4.0) (speaks, understands, reads, and writes very well), and Foreign Language Index score of 3.25 or higher 0 = Other	.24
	Dependent		
Fluent Bilingual	Dichotomous, measured in 1995–1996	1 = English Knowledge Index score of 3.75 or higher (up to 4.0) (speaks, understands, reads, and writes very well), and Foreign Language Index score of 3.25 or higher 0 = Other	.28

2. VARIABLES USED IN THE ANALYSIS OF ETHNIC AND RACIAL SELF-IDENTIFICATION (CHAPTER 7)

Variable	Measurement	Range	Mean
	Independent		
Region	Dichotomous	1 = Southern California 0 = Southern Florida	.46
Age	Years (in 1992)	12 to 18	14.23
Sex	Dichotomous	1 = Female 0 = Male	.51
Parental SES	Standardized unit-weighted sum of father's and mother's education, occupational status, and home ownership, 1992	−2.00 to +2.00	.00

Variable	Measurement	Range	Mean
		Independent	
Intact Family	Dichotomous, measured in 1992	1 = Both biological parents present in the household 0 = Other family arrangements	.63
Parental Nativity (U.S. born)	Dichotomous	1 = One parent U.S. born 0 = Both parents are foreign born	.14
Parental Nativity (same country of birth)	Dichotomous	1 = Both parents born in same country 0 = Parents born in different countries	.76
Respondent's Nativity (U.S. born)	Dichotomous	1 = U.S. born 0 = Foreign born	.50
Respondent's Nativity (foreign born length of U. S. residence as of 1992)	Dichotomous	1 = Foreign born, with 10 years or more of U.S. residence 0 = Other	.27
U.S. Citizenship	Dichotomous, 1992	1 = U.S. citizen 0 = Not a U.S. citizen	.63
Second-generation Friends	Number of friends who are also children of immigrants, 1992	1 = None 0 = Some or most	.05
		1 = Some 0 = None, or most	.38
Foreign Language Use at Home	Dichotomous, 1992	1 = Yes 0 = No (English only)	.93
Language Proficiency Types	Dichotomous, 1992	1 = Fluent Bilingual 0 = Other	.24
		1 = English Dominant 0 = Other	.42
		1 = Limited bilingual 0 = Other	.18
Inner-City School	Dichotomous, measured in 1992	1 = School located in inner-city area 0 = Suburban school	.37
Experienced Racial or Ethnic Discrimination	Dichotomous, measured in 1992	1 = Yes 0 = No	.55
Perceived Ethnic Identity of Parent	Dichotomous, 1992	1 = Same as self 0 = Different from self	[Varies by identity type]

Variable	Measurement	Range	Mean
		Dependent	
Ethnic Self-Identity	Dichotomous, measured in 1995–1996	1 = Panethnic (Asian, Black, Hispanic, etc.) 0 = Other	.27
		1 = Hyphenated American 0 = Other	.31
		1 = Plain American 0 = Other	.04
Racial Self-Identity	Dichotomous, measured in 1995–1996	1 = Black 0 = Other	.07
		1 = Pannational (Asian, Latin, Hispanic, etc.) 0 = Other	.61
		1 = Nationality as Race 0 = Other	.15

3. VARIABLES USED IN THE ANALYSIS OF SELF-ESTEEM, DEPRESSION, AND EDUCATIONAL ASPIRATIONS AND EXPECTATIONS (CHAPTER 8)

Variable	Measurement	Range	Mean
		Independent	
Region	Dichotomous	1 = Southern California 0 = Southern Florida	.46
Age	Years (in 1992)	12 to 18	14.23
Sex	Dichotomous	1 = Female 0 = Male	.51
Parental SES	Standardized unit-weighted sum of father's and mother's education, occupational status, and home ownership, 1992	−2.00 to +2.00	.00
Intact Family	Dichotomous, measured in 1992	1 = Both biological parents present in the household 0 = Other family type	.63

Length of U.S. Residence	Years, 1992	1 = Less than 5 2 = 5 to 9 3 = 10 or more 4 = All life, native born	3.12
Parent-Child Conflict (single item)	Frequency of intergenerational clashes because of "different ways of doing things," 1992	1 = Never 2 = Sometimes 3 = Most of the time 4 = All the time	2.03
Embarrassed by Parents	Dichotomous, measured in 1992	1 = Yes 0 = No	.17
Experienced Racial or Ethnic Discrimination	Dichotomous, measured in 1992	1 = Yes 0 = No	.55
GPA, 1992	Grade point average in school, weighted for honors or AP courses	0 to 5	2.52
Limited Bilingual	Dichotomous, measured in 1992	1 = Does not speak English very well and does not speak a foreign language at least well 0 = Other	.18
Fluent Bilingual	Dichotomous, measured in 1992	1 = Speaks English very well and a foreign language at least well 0 = Other	.24
Self-Esteem	Rosenberg 10-Item Self-Esteem Scale, 1992	1 to 4	3.30
Depression	CES-D 4-Item Short-Form Depression Scale, 1992	1 to 4	1.65
Educational Aspirations	Level of schooling that student wants to attain, 1992	1 = Less than high school 2 = Finish high school 3 = Finish some college 4 = Graduate college 5 = Graduate degree	4.51
Educational Expectations	Level of schooling that student expects to complete, 1992	1 = Less than high school 2 = Finish high school 3 = Finish some college 4 = Graduate college 5 = Graduate degree	4.10

Dependent

Self-Esteem	Rosenberg 10-Item Self-Esteem Scale, 1995–1996	1 to 4	3.41
Depression	CES-D 4-Item Short-Form Depression Scale, 1995–1996	1 to 4	1.66

Educational Aspirations	Level of schooling that student wants to attain, 1995–1996	1 = Less than high school 2 = Finish high school 3 = Finish some college 4 = Graduate college 5 = Graduate degree	4.59
Educational Expectations	Level of schooling that student expects to complete, 1995–1996	1 = Less than high school 2 = Finish high school 3 = Finish some college 4 = Graduate college 5 = Graduate degree	4.19

4. VARIABLES USED IN THE ANALYSIS OF EDUCATIONAL ATTAINMENT (CHAPTER 9)

Variable	Measurement	Range	Mean
	Independent		
Age	Years (in 1992)	12 to 18	14.23
Sex	Dichotomous	1 = Female 0 = Male	.51
Region	Dichotomous	1 = Southern California 0 = Southern Florida	.46
Parental SES	Standardized unit-weighted sum of father's and mother's education, occupational status, and home ownership, 1992	−2.00 to +2.00	.00
Intact Family	Dichotomous, measured in 1992	1 = Both biological parents present in the household 0 = Other family arrangements	.63
Length of U.S. Residence	Years, 1992	1 = Less than 5 2 = 5 to 9 3 = 10 or more 4 = All life, native born	3.12
Fluent Bilingual	Dichotomous, measured in 1992	1 = Speaks English very well and a foreign language at least well 0 = Other	.24
Limited Bilingual	Dichotomous, measured in 1992	1 = Does not speak English very well and does not speak a foreign language at least well 0 = Other	.18

Parent-Child Conflict (single item)	Frequency of intergenerational clashes because of "different ways of doing things," 1992	1 = Never 2 = Sometimes 3 = Most of the time 4 = All the time	2.03
Second-Generation Friends	Number of friends who are also children of immigrants, 1992	1 = None 2 = Some 3 = Many or most	2.55
Educational Expectations	Level of schooling that student expects to complete, 1992	1 = Less than high school 2 = Finish high school 3 = Finish some college 4 = Graduate college 5 = Graduate degree	4.10
Self-Esteem	Rosenberg 10-Item Self-Esteem Scale, 1992	1 to 4	3.30
Inner-City School	Dichotomous, measured in 1992	1 = School located in inner-city area 0 = Suburban school	.37
Average Student SES	One hundred minus percentage of students in school who are eligible for federally subsidized lunches, measured in 1992	8 to 100	54.55

Dependent

Math Scores	Percentile scores in the Stanford standardized achievement test, 1992	0 to 99	53.16
Reading Scores	Percentile scores in the Stanford standardized achievement test, 1992	0 to 99	41.55
GPA, 1992	Grade point average in school (grades eighth and ninth), weighted for honors or AP courses	0 to 5	2.52
GPA, 1995	Grade point average in Senior high school (grades eleventh and twelfth), weighted for honors or AP courses	0 to 5	2.46
Dropout	Dichotomous, from school records, 1995	1 = Student dropped out of school 0 = Student in school or graduated	.07
Inactive	Dichotomous, from school records, 1995	1 = Student inactive in school 0 = Student active in school or graduated	.20

NOTES

Chapter 1

1. Unless otherwise indicated, the following accounts come from unpublished interviews conducted by the authors or their assistants as part of the Children of Immigrants Longitudinal Study (CILS), a project described in Chapter 2.

2. Adapted from Fernández-Kelly and Schauffler, "Divided Fates" (p. 37), where the original interview as conducted by those authors was published.

3. Adapted from Rumbaut and Ima, *The Adaptation of Southeast Asian Refugee Youth* (ch. 6), where the original interview as conducted by those authors was published.

4. Adapted from Rumbaut and Ima, *The Adaptation of Southeast Asian Refugee Youth* (ch. 6), where the original interview as conducted by those authors was published.

5. Adapted from Rumbaut and Ima, *The Adaptation of Southeast Asian Refugee Youth* (ch. 6), where the original interview as conducted by those authors was published.

Chapter 2

1. For detailed descriptions of the new immigration, see Portes and Rumbaut, *Immigrant America;* and Pedraza and Rumbaut, eds., *Origins and Destinies.*

2. See Gans, "Second Generation Decline"; Portes and Zhou, "The New Second Generation."

3. Passel and Edmonston, "Immigration and Race," Table 2, p. 25.

4. Rumbaut, "Origins and Destinies," Table 1.

5. Rumbaut, "Transformations," Table 1. The figure is based on the combined 1997 and 1996 March Current Population Survey (CPS) data files. See also U.S. Census Bureau, *Profile of the Foreign-Born Population in the United States: 1997*.

6. Rumbaut, "Transformations"; Rumbaut, "Assimilation and Its Discontents." See also Landale, Oropesa, and Gorman, "Immigration and Infant Health."

7. Hirschman, "Studying Immigrant Adaptation from the 1990 Population Census." When referring to the *first generation,* immigration scholars commonly have in mind persons socialized in another country who immigrate as adults, while *second generation* refers to their U.S.-born offspring. Neither term accurately captures the experience of youths who fall between these generations or their different developmental contexts at the time of immigration. Thomas and Znaniecki, in *The Polish Peasant,* refer in passing to the "half-second generation" to describe foreign-born youths coming of age in the United States. Warner and Srole, in *The Social Systems of American Ethnic Groups,* distinguish the foreign-born—which they call the "parental" or "P" generation—from the U.S.-born generations—dubbed the "filial first" or "F1" generation (the offspring of the immigrants). The immigrant generation, in turn, is divided into those who entered the United States after the age of 18 (labeled the P1 generation) versus those who entered at age 18 or younger (the P2 generation). The P2 concept is akin to the terms *one-and-a-half* or *1.5 generation,* coined by Rumbaut in studies of Cuban and southeast Asian youths, especially those who had come to the United States after reaching school age but before reaching puberty. Adolescents and preschool immigrant children are at different developmental stages at arrival and closer to the experience of the first and second generations, respectively. See Rumbaut and Ima, *The Adaptation of Southeast Asian Refugee Youth;* and Rumbaut, "The Agony of Exile."

8. Hirschman, "Studying Immigrant Adaptation"; Rumbaut, "Origins and Destinies"; Rumbaut, "A Legacy of War."

9. Findings from these surveys have been published in a number of articles and books. See Portes and Zhou, "The New Second Generation"; Portes and Rumbaut, *Immigrant America,* Ch. 7; Portes and MacLeod, "What Shall I Call Myself?"; Portes and Schauffler, "Language and the Second Generation"; Portes and MacLeod, "The Educational Progress of Children of Immigrants"; Rumbaut, "The Crucible Within"; Rumbaut, "The New Californians"; Rumbaut, "Ties That Bind"; Rumbaut, "Coming of Age in Immigrant America"; Rumbaut, "Passages to Adulthood"; Rumbaut, "Profiles in Resilience"; Fernández-Kelly and Schauffler, "Divided Fates"; Pérez, "The Households of Children of Immigrants." Several of these articles appeared in a collection published as a special issue of *International Migration Review* and reprinted subsequently as a book; see Portes, ed., *The New Second Generation.* For examples of journalistic articles based on the study, see Sontag, "A Fervent 'No' to Assimilation"; Sharp, "English: Kids' Language of Choice"; Viglucci and Marks, "Family and Community Ties"; Fulwood, "Children of New Arrivals"; Judson, "How to Stir the Melting Pot"; de Vise, "Children of Immigrants Get High

Marks"; Woo, "School Success of Immigrants' Children Tracked"; Dugger, "Among Young of Immigrants, Outlook Rises"; Miller, "Scholars of Immigration Focus on the Children"; Feldman, "Double Exposure"; and Viadero, "Generation Gap."

10. Both regional samples exceed two thousand cases. With such samples, correlations as small as .06 are significant at the .01 level, conveying an erroneous impression of the real size of the relationship. For this reason, an absolute criterion of strength is preferable.

11. This relative absence of differences in the original survey does not mean, however, that the situation of dropouts and respondents in the follow-up survey would be the same. In particular, second-survey dropouts are now likely to be employed or in a situation with direct effects on their educational preference and likelihood to remain in school. These relationships are analyzed in later chapters.

12. Since 1994, the annual (March) Current Population Surveys conducted by the U.S. Census Bureau with national samples have asked respondents about the birthplace of their parents, a key question no longer asked in the decennial census. The CPS thus allows estimates of the size and characteristics of the first and second generations, but the samples are too small to permit reliable analyses beyond a breakdown by a few variables, such as parental nativity, national origin, and year of arrival. The CPS was used to generate the data in Table 2.1.

13. Hirschman, "Studying Immigrant Adaptation."

14. Oropesa and Landale, "In Search of the New Second Generation."

15. Jensen and Chitose, "Today's New Second Generation."

16. The relevant research literature on the role of aspirations and expectations dates back to David McClelland's analysis of achievement motivation and the work of Wisconsin researchers on the status attainment process to contemporary research in the sociology of education. See McClelland, *The Achieving Society;* Haller and Portes, "Status Attainment Processes"; Sewell and Hauser, *Education, Occupation, and Earnings;* Portes, MacLeod, and Parker, "Immigrant Aspirations."

17. See Mintz and Price, eds., *Caribbean Contours;* and Knight and Palmer, *The Modern Caribbean.* See also Waters, "Immigrant Families at Risk."

18. Interview by Alejandro Portes (conducted as part of a related project on the development of transnational communities), transcript, Los Angeles, California, April 1997.

Chapter 3

1. Alba and Nee, "Rethinking Assimilation Theory."

2. Alba and Nee, "Rethinking Assimilation Theory"; Gordon, *Assimilation in American Life.*

3. Warner and Srole, *The Social Systems of American Ethnic Groups,* p. 2.

4. For earlier European immigrants, see Kraut, *The Huddled Masses;* Rosenblum, *Immigrant Workers.* For contemporary immigrants, see Portes and Rumbaut, *Immigrant America.*

5. Jensen and Chitose, *The New Immigration;* Portes and Zhou, "Self-Employment and the Earnings of Immigrants."

6. Gold, *Refugee Communities;* Zolberg, Shurke, and Aguayo, "International Factors in the Formation of Refugee Movements"; Rumbaut, "The Structure of Refuge"; Rumbaut, "A Legacy of War."

7. By 1945, Warner and Srole were already able to design a hierarchy of American ethnic groups with white English-speaking Protestants at the top. They predicted that the more ethnic groups departed from this standard, the longer they would take to assimilate in American society. See Warner and Srole, *The Social Systems.* See also Portes and Rumbaut, *Immigrant America,* ch. 4.

8. Portes and Rumbaut, *Immigrant America,* ch. 4; Waters, "West Indian Immigrants, African Americans, and Whites in the Workplace"; Tienda and Stier, "The Wages of Race."

9. Stepick, *Pride against Prejudice;* Tumulty, "When Irish Eyes Are Hiding."

10. On the role of social networks in the onset and adaptation process of immigrants, see Massey, "Understanding Mexican Migration"; Roberts, "Socially Expected Durations"; Zhou, *Chinatown.*

11. Rumbaut, "Origins and Destinies"; Mahler, *American Dreaming.*

12. Portes, "The Social Origins"; Gold, *Refugee Communities.*

13. Fernández-Kelly, CILS project interview in southern Florida, 1995.

14. Child, *Italian or American?;* Alba, *Italian Americans;* Gans, "Second Generation Decline."

15. Gordon, *Assimilation in American Life;* Rumbaut, "Assimilation and Its Discontents"; Rumbaut, "Ties That Bind."

16. This typology has been presented and discussed in greater detail in Portes and Rumbaut, *Immigrant America,* ch. 7.

17. Waters, "Ethnic and Racial Identities"; Waldinger and Bozorgmehr, "The Making of a Multicultural Metropolis;" Rumbaut, "Origins and Destinies."

18. Portes and Zhou, "The New Second Generation."

19. Jensen and Chitose, "Today's New Second Generation"; Passel and Edmonston, "Immigration and Race."

20. On this point, see Waters, "Ethnic and Racial Identities"; Fernández-Kelly and Schauffler, "Divided Fates"; Rumbaut, "The Crucible Within."

21. Rosenblum, *Immigrant Workers;* Marks, *Farewell—We're Good and Gone;* Fligstein, *Going North.*

22. Sassen, *The Mobility of Labor and Capital;* Romo and Schwartz, "The Structural Embeddedness of Business Decisions"; Bluestone and Harrison, *The Deindustrialization of America.*

23. Gans, "Second Generation Decline"; Alba and Nee, "Rethinking Assimilation Theory."

24. Harrison and Bluestone, *The Great U-Turn,* p. 8.

25. Harvey, *The Limits to Capital.*

26. Gereffi, "The Organization of Buyer-Driven Global Commodity Chains"; Fernández-Kelly, *For We Are Sold;* Schoepfle and Pérez-López, "Employment Implications of Export Assembly Operations in Mexico and the Caribbean Basin."

27. U.S. Census Bureau, *U.S. Employment Data, 1950–1997.*

28. Karoly, "The Trend in Inequality among Families, Individuals, and Workers."

29. Title of *Money Magazine* lead story, May 1999.

30. Updegrave, "Assessing Your Wealth."

31. Bean, Van Hook, and Fossett, "Immigration, Spatial and Economic Change, and African American Employment"; Wilson, "Ethnic Concentrations."

32. Gans, "Second Generation Decline," p. 182.

33. On this point, see Zhou and Bankston, "Social Capital and the Adaptation of the Second Generation"; Portes and MacLeod, "The Educational Progress of Children of Immigrants."

34. While there is disagreement between advocates of mismatch theory and other positions, there is widespread consensus that the decline of America's inner-city areas is closely linked to the disappearance of industrial job opportunities in them. See Massey and Denton, *American Apartheid*; Wilson, *The Truly Disadvantaged*; Fitzpatrick, *Puerto Rican Americans*; Bonilla and Campos, "A Wealth of Poor"; Nelson and Tienda, "The Structuring of Hispanic Ethnicity."

35. Wacquant and Wilson, "The Cost of Racial and Class Exclusion."

36. Field interview conducted for an earlier project on Miami's ethnic composition. Final results of this study are reported in Portes and Stepick, *City on the Edge*.

37. Matute-Bianchi, "Ethnic Identities and Patterns of School Success"; Bourgois, *In Search of Respect*; Waters, "Ethnic and Racial Identities."

38. Matute-Bianchi, "Situational Ethnicity."

39. Suárez-Orozco, "Towards a Psychosocial Understanding," p. 164.

40. Portes and Sensenbrenner, "Embeddedness and Immigration"; Bourgois, *In Search of Respect*.

41. Stepick, "The Refugees Nobody Wants"; Fernández-Kelly and Schauffler, "Divided Fates."

42. Waters, "Ethnic and Racial Identities," p. 191.

43. Matthei and Smith, "Women, Households, and Transnational Migration Networks"; Rother, "Island Life Not Idyllic."

44. McLanahan and Sandefur, *Growing Up with a Single Parent*; Rumbaut, "Ties That Bind"; Waters, "Immigrant Families at Risk."

45. The Indian Sikh community of California, studied by Margaret Gibson, offers a good example of this pattern of gender socialization. See Gibson, *Accommodation without Assimilation*.

46. On the significance of gender in the origins of migration and the adaptation process of immigrant families, see Hondagneu-Sotelo, *Gendered Transitions*; Grasmuck and Pessar, *Between Two Islands*; Kibria, *Family Tightrope*; Fernández-Kelly and García, "Informalization at the Core."

47. *Social capital* is defined in the literature as the ability to gain access to resources by virtue of membership in social networks and other social structures. See Coleman, "Social Capital in the Creation of Human Capital"; Portes, "Social Capital: Its Origins and Applications."

48. Bailey and Waldinger, "Primary, Secondary, and Enclave Labor Markets"; Portes, "The Social Origins."

49. Burt, *Structural Holes*.

50. This argument has been developed at greater length in Portes and Rumbaut, *Immigrant America*, ch. 7.

51. Fernández-Kelly and Schauffler, "Divided Fates."

52. Field interview conducted by Patricia Fernández-Kelly and Richard Schauffler in Miami, summer 1993.

53. Zhou and Bankston, "Social Capital and the Adaptation of the Second Generation."

54. Ibid., p. 207.

Chapter 4

1. CILS project interview. Names are fictitious.

2. CILS project interview. Names are fictitious.

3. Portes and Rumbaut, *Immigrant America,* ch. 3.

4. Portes and Zhou, "Self-Employment and the Earnings of Immigrants."

5. The more common alternative is to use the natural log of earnings as the dependent variable to correct for a skewed earnings distribution. Replication of this analysis using the log form of the dependent variable yields comparable results. For clarity of presentation, we prefer to present findings in terms of actual dollars.

6. See Bielby and Baron, "Men and Women at Work"; England, "Wage Appreciation and Depreciation."

7. Portes and Stepick, *City on the Edge,* ch. 6; Zhou, *Growing up American.*

8. CILS project interview, 1996. Names are fictitious.

9. Models are computed on cases with valid data for all variables. There are not enough Chinese and Korean cases with valid data for reliable estimation. These cases are incorporated into the Other Asian category.

10. See Mintz and Price, *Caribbean Contours;* Anderson and Witter, "Crisis, Adjustment, and Change."

11. Bach and Gordon, "The Economic Adjustment of Southeast Asian Refugees"; Rumbaut, "The Structure of Refuge"; Rumbaut, "A Legacy of War"; Smith-Hefner, *Khmer-American.*

12. Stepick, *Pride against Prejudice.*

Chapter 5

1. CILS project interview. Names are fictitious.

2. Martí is considered the greatest Cuban patriot. He was the organizer and leader of the War of Independence against Spain (1895–1898) and died in combat during its early days.

3. CILS project interview. Names are fictitious.

4. A partial exception to this trend is found among black immigrants from Haiti and the West Indies. A significantly higher proportion of parents from these groups believe that their children will experience discrimination. Even among black immigrants, however, majorities are optimistic that their children will be able to move ahead in U.S. social circles.

5. All of these quotes are excerpts from CILS interviews with immigrant parents.

6. Rother, "Island Life Not Idyllic."

7. See the chapters on New York Jews and Italians in Glazer and Moynihan, *Beyond the Melting Pot*. Also see Alba and Nee, "Rethinking Assimilation Theory."

8. See Perlmann and Waldinger, "Second Generation Decline?"

9. On the Cambodian flight experience and its consequences for immigrant mental health, see Smith-Hefner, *Khmer American;* Rumbaut and Ima, *The Adaptation of Southeast Asian Refugee Youth;* Rumbaut, "Mental Health and the Refugee Experience"; Rumbaut, "Migration, Adaptation, and Mental Health."

10. CILS project interview, 1995. Names are fictitious.

11. See Fernández-Kelly and Schauffler, "Divided Fates"; Stepick, *Pride against Prejudice;* Rumbaut, "The Agony of Exile."

12. Fernández-Kelly and Schauffler, "Divided Fates," pp. 38–39, based on CILS parental interviews conducted in 1993.

13. Zhou and Bankston, "Social Capital and the Adaptation of the Second Generation," pp. 208–209.

14. Interviewer's field notes. CILS interview in San Diego, August 3, 1995. Names are fictitious.

15. CILS project interview, San Diego, 1996. Names are fictitious.

Chapter 6

1. Cited in Brumberg, *Going to America*, p. 7

2. The classic statement on language and the self in social psychology remains George Herbert Mead's *Mind, Self, and Society*. See also Leopold, *Speech Development;* Hakuta, *Mirror of Language;* Bialystock and Hakuta, *In Other Words*.

3. Lieberson, Dalto, and Johnston, "The Course of Mother Tongue Diversity"; Dillard, *Toward a Social History of American English;* Marckwardt, *American English;* Fishman, *Language Loyalty in the United States;* Laponce, *Languages and their Territories*. Glazer, "Ethnic Groups in America"; Portes and Schauffler, "Language and the Second Generation."

4. In recent years, U.S. English has been the most visible movement advocating linguistic unity. It has spearheaded campaigns in various states to declare English the official language of the land as well as a constitutional amendment to that effect. See Portes and Rumbaut, *Immigrant America*, ch. 6. See also Crawford, *Hold Your Tongue;* Crawford, *Language Loyalties*.

5. Lieberson, Dalto, and Johnston, "The Course of Mother Tongue Diversity."

6. López, *Language Maintenance and Shift*.

7. Fishman, *Language Loyalty in the United States;* Veltman, *Language Shift in the United States*.

8. Hakuta, *Mirror of Language,* ch. 1.

9. Brigham, *A Study of American Intelligence*, pp. 194–195.

10. Smith, "Some Light on the Problem of Bilingualism," p. 253; Hakuta, *Mirror of Language*, p. 31.

11. Dillard, *Toward a Social History of American English*.

12. Malzberg and Lee, *Migration and Mental Disease,* pp. 7–8.

13. U.S. English policy statement, 1993.

14. Peal and Lambert, "The Relation of Bilingualism to Intelligence;" Hakuta, *Mirror of Language;* Bialystock and Hakuta, *In Other Words.*

15. Leopold, *Speech Development of a Bilingual Child.*

16. Cummins, "Metalinguistic Development of Children," p. 127.

17. Rumbaut, *Immigrant Students in California Public Schools;* Rumbaut, "The New Californians."

18. Hakuta and Diaz, "The Relationship between Degree of Bilingualism and Cognitive Ability."

19. Sassen, *The Global City;* Sassen, *The New Labor Demand.*

20. Portes and Stepick, *City on the Edge;* Nijman, "The Paradigmatic City."

21. Mears, "Miami Hispanics"; Fradd, "The Economic Impact of Spanish-Language Proficiency in Metropolitan Miami."

22. Lamm and Imhoff, *The Immigration Time Bomb;* Brimelow, *Alien Nation.*

23. Past studies have shown that language self-reports are generally highly reliable. The items used to measure English proficiency are identical to those used by the U.S. Census. See Fishman and Terry, "The Validity of Census Data on Bilingualism"; Fishman, "A Sociolinguistic Census." The index is constructed as the mean score of four items measuring each language skill and ranges from 1 to 4.

24. The Foreign Language Index is constructed in a manner identical to the English Knowledge Index and has an identical range, 1–4.

25. *Fluent bilinguals* are defined as respondents who speak English very well (English Index score of 3.75) and a foreign language well (Foreign Language Index score of 3.25 or above).

26. Balmaseda, "The Issue Is Power, Not Language," p. A1.

27. Rumbaut, "The Agony of Exile"; Smith-Hefner, *Khmer American.*

28. Fernández-Kelly and Schauffler, "Divided Fates"; Rumbaut, "The Crucible Within."

29. Navarro, "Bilingual Parents Dismayed by English's Pull."

30. Immigrant informant reporting his experience with English immersion in the 1960s. Interview, May 11, 1998.

31. Immigrant informant reporting on his early university experiences in the 1970 Interview, April 24, 1998.

32. Bronner, "Bilingual Education Facing Push toward Abandonment"; Trillin, "Policy by Anecdote."

33. Dorfman, "If Only We All Spoke Two Languages."

34. Authors' fieldwork, Miami, Florida, Summer 1995.

35. Beck, "Don't Wait until High School." See also Lenneberg, *Biological Foundations of Language;* and Penfield, "Conditioning the Uncommitted Cortex for Language Learning."

36. See Portes and Hao, *"E Pluribus Unum:* Bilingualism and Language Loss."

37. Ibid.

38. Based on net probabilities computed at the mean of the dependent variable. See Petersen, "A Comment of Presenting Results from Logit"; Portes and Stepick, "Unwelcome Immigrants."

39. Notice that not all causal effects are subject to this challenge. For example, children's language ability will not change their national origin, and neither is it likely to determine parental status. The language spoken at home is similarly decided by adult parents rather than the children. In these instances, causal effects identified in Table 6.6 are unambiguous.

40. Based on net probabilities computed at the mean of the dependent variable.

41. Replication of the analysis with a less strict definition of bilingualism (limited to ability to speak and understand a foreign language) yielded results that reproduce, in all their essentials, those presented herein. There are no significant differences in the pattern of effects of individual and family predictors. The single difference lies in the effects of school context. In this model, a larger proportion of Latin students in school has no effect on bilingualism, while a larger proportion of Asian students has a moderately negative effect. This finding reinforces the point that the absence of a common language among Asian students not only fails to strengthen bilingual fluency but actually leads to a faster shift toward monolingualism.

42. Quoted in Mears, "Miami Hispanics," pp. 1–2.

43. Quoted in Zhou and Bankston, "Social Capital and the Adaptation of the Second Generation," p. 218.

44. "Statement on California Proposition 227," U.S. Department of Education, April 27, 1998. http://www.ed.gov/PressReleases/04-1998/unzst.html.

45. Smith-Hefner, *Khmer American*, p. 141.

46. Recent empirical evidence shows that the key factor affecting second-generation achievement is the ability of parents to communicate fluently with their children and hence guide them, whether in English or in their native tongue. See Mouw and Xie, "Bilingualism and the Academic Achievement of Asian Immigrants."

47. Smith-Hefner, *Khmer American*.

Chapter 7

1. Pyle and Romero, "Prop 187 Fuels a New Campus Activism," p. B1.

2. Pyle and Romero, "Prop 187 Fuels a New Campus Activism." See also McDonnell, "Complex Family Ties Tangle Simple Premise of Prop. 187"; Navarrette, "At the Birth of a New—and Younger—Latino Activism."

3. Pyle and Romero, "Prop 187 Fuels a New Campus Activism," p. B-1.

4. Proposition 187 was not implemented after its passage but landed in federal court. The measure—including the section regarding public education, which would have forced hundreds of thousands of children out of California public schools—was declared unconstitutional in 1998 by a U.S. district judge. That ruling was appealed by then-Governor Pete Wilson, a primary sponsor of the initiative. Newly elected Governor Gray Davis, who had opposed Proposi-

tion 187, inherited the appeal in 1999 but decided not to pursue it, killing the enactment of these measures.

5. On the characteristics and determinants of "thick" and "thin" ethnic identities, see Cornell and Hartmann, *Ethnicity and Race*. On the related concept of "thick" and "thin" types of citizenship, see Tilly, "Citizenship, Identity, and Social History," p. 8.

6. The distinction between reactive and linear ethnicity is elaborated in Portes and Rumbaut, *Immigrant America*, ch. 4. See also Aleinikoff and Rumbaut, "Terms of Belonging"; Zolberg, "Modes of Incorporation." Identity-defining reactive-formation processes in situations of ethnic conflict have their parallel in the way national self-definitions have been forged in international conflicts and particularly wars. See Howard, "War and Nations." Similarly, on the influence of catastrophe on identity in the second generation, focusing on post-Holocaust Jewish identity, see Berger, "Job's Children"; Prince, *The Legacy of the Holocaust*.

7. As many as 30,000 persons participated in a solidarity rally held in Koreatown on the day after the rioting ended, making it the largest Korean meeting ever held in the United States. See Min, "Korean Americans." See also Bozorgmehr, Sabagh, and Light, "Los Angeles: Explosive Diversity."

8. A 1982 national Gallup poll, conducted nearly two years after the Mariel exodus, dramatically depicted the extent of the Cubans' unpopularity: Cubans ranked dead last in the public's view of the contributions made by 15 different ethnic groups to American national welfare. See Portes and Stepick, *City on the Edge*, p. 31. Fifteen years later the same question was asked in a 1997 national poll, and again it showed Cubans coming in last place; see Zaldívar, "Cubanos en último lugar de sondeo." See also Simon, "Old Minorities, New Immigrants"; García, *Havana USA*.

9. Portes and Stepick, *City on the Edge*, ch. 2. See also Alejandro Portes, "The Rise of Ethnicity." In their much earlier study of New York City's ethnic groups, *Beyond the Melting Pot*, Glazer and Moynihan made the observation that "the point about the melting pot . . . is that it did not happen. . . . The American ethos is nowhere better perceived than in the disinclination of the third and fourth generation of newcomers to blend into a standard, uniform national type" (p. xcvii).

10. Alba, *Ethnic Identity;* Gans, "Symbolic Ethnicity"; Waters, *Ethnic Options*.

11. Alba, *Italian Americans: Into the Twilight of Ethnicity.*

12. Gordon, *Assimilation in American Life*. See also Warner and Srole, *The Social Systems of American Ethnic Groups*.

13. Nahirny and Fishman, "American Immigrant Groups," p. 266.

14. Ibid., p. 267.

15. Since 1977, these categories have been set by Statistical Directive 15 of the U.S. Office of Management and Budget (OMB), the agency responsible for determining standard classifications of racial and ethnic data on all federal forms and statistics, including the census. OMB Directive 15 fixed the identities of Americans in five broad categories (the other three are American Indian or Alaskan Native, Black, and White) for statistical purposes, but through wide-

spread public use, these categories soon began to shape ethnic identities and evolved into political entities with their own constituencies and lobbies. See Wright, "One Drop of Blood"; Nagel, "The Political Construction of Ethnicity"; Espíritu, *Asian American Panethnicity;* Portes and MacLeod, "What Shall I Call Myself?"

16. See Veerasarn, "The Faces of Asian America," p. 48; Escobar, "Dominicans Face Assimilation," p. A-1.

17. Tajfel, *Human Groups and Social Categories.*

18. Deaux, "Social Identification."

19. Rosenberg, *Conceiving the Self.*

20. Child, *Italian or American?*

21. Child, *Italian or American?* pp. 196–97. William F. Whyte, in *Street Corner Society,* a classic ethnography written at about the same time as Child's book but set in Boston's Italian "slum district," describes the divergent trajectories of "college boys," who assimilated out of the ethnic colony and into the larger society, and "corner boys," who were loyal above all to their peers and stayed behind. For a parallel recent ethnography of ethnic fates in an inner-city neighborhood, see MacLeod, *Ain't No Making It.*

22. Waters, "Ethnic and Racial Identities."

23. Matute-Bianchi, "Ethnic Identities and Patterns of School Success and Failure." See Chapter 3 for a brief discussion of the oppositional identities represented by the latter two types.

24. Suárez-Orozco and Suárez-Orozco, "The Cultural Patterning of Achievement Motivation"; Vigil, *Barrio Gangs.*

25. The wording of the question was: "How do you identify, that is, what do you call yourself?" It was followed in parentheses by a wide array of illustrative national and ethnic designators appropriate to each research site.

26. In the remaining cases (3.3 percent in the 1992 survey, 4.8 percent in the 1995–1996 survey), respondents gave a variety of mixed identities not classifiable into the four main types. Typically they consisted of a combination of two or more national origins, most often mirroring the different national origins of parents.

27. There were no statistically significant differences in the distribution of ethnic identity types reported in the baseline survey between the 4,288 youth who were reinterviewed three years later and the 974 who were not, suggesting no bias as a result of sample attrition with respect to this variable. In this chapter, accordingly, we focus only on results for the longitudinal sample of 4,288. For analyses of cross-sectional results from the full baseline survey, see Rumbaut, "The Crucible Within"; Portes and MacLeod, "What Shall I Call Myself?"

28. For an analysis of the characteristics and determinants of a Chicano ethnic identity based on results from the 1992 CILS survey in San Diego, see Rumbaut, "The Crucible Within," pp. 781–782.

29. Douglas Massey, in "Latinos, Poverty, and the Underclass," has observed that "there is no 'Hispanic' population in the sense that there is a black population. Hispanics share no common historical memory and do not comprise a single, coherent, community. . . . Saying that someone is Hispanic or

Latino reveals little or nothing about likely attitudes, behaviors, beliefs, race, religion, class, or legal situation in the United States. The only thing reasonably certain is that either the person in question or some progenitor once lived in an area originally colonized by Spain" (p. 454). Notwithstanding, with some key exceptions, a substantial and growing segment of the population of U.S.-reared children of Latin American immigrants appears to be self-consciously internalizing that label as a minority-group identity. See also Rumbaut, "The Americans."

30. Doctorow, *Billy Bathgate*, as quoted in Deaux, "Social Identification," p. 792.

31. The family cohesion measure is a scale composed of three items: "Family togetherness is important," "Family members feel close," and "Family members like to spend time together." For each item, the respondents were asked to record how frequently that was the case in their own family, on a scale from 1 (never) to 5 (always).

32. Cornell and Hartmann, *Ethnicity and Race*, p. 54; Horowitz, *Ethnic Groups in Conflict*.

33. Most respondents in this situation did not identify by both of their parents' national origins although, as noted earlier, a small number did explicitly recognize mixed ethnic origins. Just over 10 percent of respondents in this category reported a mixed self-identity.

34. Subjective identification with a country of origin was not associated with objective knowledge about basic aspects of that country's history or geography. In the 1992 survey, respondents were asked to write down the name of the capital and of the political leader of their parents' native country as well as to give an estimate of the population of their country. Two-thirds of the total sample (65 percent) knew the capital of their country correctly, less than half (47 percent) knew the name of its political leader, and fewer than a tenth (9 percent) could hazard even a ballpark estimate of its population. Although differences were not significant, respondents who identified as American and who were U.S. born were somewhat more knowledgeable; less knowledgeable were those respondents who identified by that foreign nationality or by panethnic categories and who were foreign born.

35. Portes and MacLeod, "What Shall I Call Myself?"; Kraut, *The Huddled Masses*.

36. For example, Meyer R. Schkolnick, born in the slums of South Philadelphia in 1910 to working-class Eastern European Jewish immigrants, changed his name at the age of 14 to Robert K. Merton because "it seemed 'more American' back then in the 1920s." That invention of an Americanizing second-generation youngster has since become the most cited name in the history of American sociology. See Merton, "A Life of Learning," p. 9. See also Berrol, *Growing Up American*.

37. See Garvey and McDonnell, "José Moves into Top Spot in Name Game"; Pitts, "José Is Just as American as Baseball."

38. Alba, *Italian Americans*.

39. Pérez Firmat, *Life on the Hyphen*, p. 7.

40. Ibid., p. 5.

41. Hwang, "The Good Daughter," p. 16.

Chapter 8

1. Fong-Torres, *The Rice Room*, pp. 101, 259.

2. Hansen, "Who Shall Inherit America?" pp. 207, 209.

3. The following case histories are based on CILS project interviews with immigrant families in San Diego in 1994. The names are fictitious.

4. The reliability coefficient (Cronbach's alpha) for the three-item cohesion scale is .85; the alpha for the four-item conflict scale is .71. Both figures are based on responses to items in the 1995–1996 survey (N 5 4,288). The items for the family cohesion scale are derived from the work of Olson et al., *Families*, and have been applied in recent research with immigrant families. See, in particular, Gil and Vega, "Two Different Worlds."

5. This scale was developed by J. Cuellar and has been widely used. See Cuellar, Harris, and Jasso, "An Acculturation Scale"; Szapocznik et al., "Theory and Measurement of Acculturation"; Vega et al., "Cohesion and Adaptability"; Gil and Vega, "Two Different Worlds." See also García-Coll and Magnuson, "The Psychological Experience of Immigration"; Fuligni, "The Academic Achievement."

6. For a related study examining differences and effects of such attitudes toward familiar duty in a northern California sample of tenth and twelfth graders of Asian, Latin American, and European backgrounds, see Fuligni, Tseng, and Lam, "Attitudes toward Family Obligations." See also Baca-Zinn, "Adaptation and Continuity in Mexican-American Families"; Goldscheider and Goldscheider, *Leaving Home before Marriage;* Bertaux-Wiame, "The Pull of Family Ties"; Rumbaut and Rumbaut, "The Family in Exile"; Rumbaut, "Ties That Bind."

7. In one high school, students distinguished among cliques called Preps, Freaks, Goths, Skaters, Jocks, Greasers, Nerds, and Brainiacs, among others—not including gangs, which all had their own distinctive names, norms, rituals, and rigid membership boundaries. For a study of immigrant students in a northern California high school, see Olsen, *Made in America*.

8. The two indices were identified via factor analyses of a battery of school-related items adapted from the National Educational Longitudinal Study (NELS).

9. In San Diego we obtained data on the number of times that CILS students were suspended from school for any reason between 1991 and 1995. Suspending a student from school for one or more days is, except for expulsion, the most severe official reaction to student disciplinary infractions. Children of immigrants overall had a lower suspension rate than the district-wide average. About 17 percent of the CILS sample in San Diego schools were suspended at least once during that four-year period, for an average of 0.34 suspensions per student. Male students were suspended far more often than females (0.53 to 0.17). See Rumbaut, "Profiles in Resilience."

10. See Rosenberg, *Society and the Adolescent Self-Image;* Rosenberg, *Conceiving the Self.* Note that our focus here is on global self-esteem; for an analysis of its distinction from specific self-esteem, see Rosenberg et al., "Global Self-esteem and Specific Self-esteem." See also Rosenberg, Schooler, and Schoenbach, "Self-Esteem and Adolescent Problems"; Owens, "Two Dimen-

sions of Self-Esteem"; Yabiku, Axinn and Thornton, "Family Integration and Children's Self-Esteem"; Mecca, Smelser, and Vasconcellos, *The Social Importance of Self-Esteem;* Coopersmith, *The Antecedents of Self-Esteem.*

11. The reliability coefficients (Cronbach's alpha) for the 10-item self-esteem scale are .81 and .83, respectively, for the initial and follow-up surveys; the respective alphas for the 4-item depression scale are .74 and .76.

12. Studies have reported declines in self-esteem and sharp increases in depressive symptomatology among girls in early adolescence and during the transition to junior high school in particular. See, for example, Simmons et al., "The Impact of Cumulative Change in Early Adolescence"; Hirsch and Rapkin, "The Transition to Junior High School." Among adults, national as well as regional studies have consistently documented higher depression rates for women than men, in both majority and minority ethnic groups. For a review of the evidence, see Vega and Rumbaut, "Ethnic Minorities and Mental Health." See also Mirowsky and Ross, *Social Causes of Psychological Distress.* Two volumes by the National Research Council review recent research on the health and mental health of immigrant youth; see Hernández and Charney, *From Generation to Generation;* Hernández, *Children of Immigrants.*

13. Woo, "Home Life Plays a Crucial Role," p. A-1.

14. See, for example, Eccles and Wigfield, "Schooling's Influences on Motivation and Achievement"; Zimmerman, Bandura, and Martinez-Pons, "Self-Motivation for Academic Attainment"; Eccles et. al., "Expectancies, Values, and Academic Behaviors." For a comparison of sociological models in status attainment research, focusing on social psychological dynamics mediating interpersonal influences on individual attainment, see Haller and Portes, "Status Attainment Processes"; Kao and Tienda, "Optimism and Achievement"; Kao and Tienda, "Educational Aspirations of Minority Youth."

15. In 1998, the Los Angeles Times conducted a statewide poll in California that found that almost 50 percent of Asian-origin parents reported two hours or more on homework every night by their children, compared with 33 percent of blacks, 27 percent of whites, and 18 percent of Latins. These are virtually the same proportions we found in CILS for Asian and Latin American groups. See Woo, "Home Life Plays A Crucial Role."

16. See, for example, Haller and Portes, "Status Attainment Processes"; Griffin and Alexander, "Schooling and Socio-Economic Attainments"; Kao and Tienda, "Educational Aspirations of Minority Youth."

17. Olson, Roese, and Zanna, "Expectancies." Social psychologists distinguish between probabilistic expectancies and normative expectancies. The latter refer to obligations or prescriptions that individuals perceive for themselves or others (what should happen); the items composing the Familism index discussed earlier illustrate such normative expectancies.

18. The skewness of the self-esteem scale measured in the follow-up is 2.86. An exponential transformation reduces it to 2.02. The skewness of the CES-D scale is 1.17. Transforming it into natural logarithms reduces it to .43.

19. The strong pressure brought by many Filipino and southeast Asian parents on their children to achieve academically may be related to this outcome.

Recent ethnographic studies report a great deal of distress among Filipino children because of the seemingly endless expectations of their parents. However, this explanation runs into problems because other Asian parents—Chinese and Koreans, in particular—are also known to engage in similar practices without their children suffering significant declines in self-esteem as a result. On the case of Filipino children, see Wolf, "Family Secrets." See also Lau, "Filipina Girls Pondering Suicide"; Kann et al., "Youth Risk Behavior Surveillance—United States, 1993."

20. This raises the question of the potential ambiguity of some effects, in particular those of subjective indicators. For example, the coefficient associated with perceptions of discrimination may indicate a causal effect on self-esteem or show, alternatively, that students with lower self-esteem are more prone to perceive and report discrimination. Within the limits of our data and the relatively straightforward style of statistical analysis that we selected for readability, the question cannot be fully elucidated. Note that this objection does not apply to more objective predictors such as gender or national origin. And neither, of course, does it apply to those predictors that do affect change over time, in particular, GPA and bilingualism. In these cases, the claim of a causal effect is better established.

21. Simmons et al., "The Impact of Cumulative Change in Early Adolescence"; Hirsch and Rapkin, "The Transition to Junior High School." Cf. also Phinney, "Ethnic Identity in Adolescents and Adults."

22. Haller and Portes, "Status Attainment Processes"; Sewell, Haller, and Portes, "The Educational and Early Occupational Attainment Process"; Kao and Tienda, "Educational Aspirations."

23. For further analyses of gender effects based on the longitudinal CILS sample in California, see Rumbaut, "Profiles in Resilience"; Rumbaut, "Passages to Adulthood." For analyses based on cross-sectional results of the baseline survey for the full CILS sample, see Rumbaut, "The Crucible Within"; Rumbaut, "Ties That Bind." For related findings based on the NELS national sample of 25,000 eighth graders, see Kao, "Psychological Well-Being and Educational Achievement among Immigrant Youth."

24. The significance of differences in modes of incorporation between earlier and late Cuban arrivals will become apparent when we examine the relative educational achievement of their offspring in the following chapter.

25. For a broader discussion of such paradoxes, see Rumbaut, "Assimilation and Its Discontents: Ironies and Paradoxes." Cf. also Harris, "The Health Status and Risk Behaviors of Adolescents in Immigrant Families."

26. There is a rapidly growing literature of memoirs and semi-autobiographical novels written by children of immigrants; see, for example, Rodríguez, *Hunger of Memory* and *Days of Obligation*; Pérez Firmat, *Next Year in Cuba*; Fong-Torres, *The Rice Room*; Hoffman, *Lost in Translation*; Lee, *Native Speaker*; García, *Dreaming in Cuban*; Tan, *The Joy Luck Club*; Kingston, *The Woman Warrior*. For early-twentieth-century works in these genres, see Antin, *The Promised Land*; and the recently reprinted work by Roth, *Call It Sleep*.

Chapter 9

1. CILS project interview in San Diego, November 1987. Names are fictitious.

2. Strictly speaking, school contextual effects should be examined with methodologies other than ordinary least-squares regression because the clustered nature of the sample violates the statistical assumption of independence among cases drawn from the same school. We present results in this fashion to avoid the complexities of multilevel interaction analysis and because prior detailed analysis of these data on the basis of hierarchical linear methods did not reveal substantive departures from the pattern of contextual effects reported herein. See Portes and MacLeod, "The Educational Progress of Children of Immigrants."

3. This is the same index used in previous chapters and consisting of the unit-weighted standardized sum of the father's and mother's education and occupational status plus family home ownership. The index is highly reliable and has strong construct validity based on its correlations with related variables. A replication of results using family earnings for the subsample with complete parental data yields results substantively similar to those reported herein.

4. Similar findings concerning age and sex effects were found in an analysis of the National Educational Longitudinal Survey (NELS) of 1988, which includes samples of both second-generation and native-parentage youths. See Portes and MacLeod, "Educating the Second-Generation."

5. Earlier research reports also highlight the exceptional performance of Asian-origin students in American schools and its relationship to personal discipline and demeanor. See Hirschman and Wong, "The Extraordinary Educational Attainment of Asian Americans"; Rumbaut and Ima, *The Adaptation of Southeast Asian Refugee Youth;* Rumbaut, "The New Californians"; Zhou and Bankston, *Growing Up American;* Wolf, "Family Secrets."

6. It is worth recalling that the average education and occupational background of southeast Asian refugees is very low, thus negating the possibility that their positive reception in the United States was due to their desirable human capital characteristics. In general, there is only a loose relation between an immigrant group's average human capital and its mode of reception since the latter is dependent on other factors, including the political relationship between the United States and the sending country.

7. This and the following citations are based on CILS project interviews in San Diego and southern Florida. The names are fictitious.

8. In Chapter 6, we demonstrated how different types of language adaptation correlate with this selective feature, used as a measure of students' academic motivation.

9. In Chapter 8, we examined the positive relationship between fluent bilingualism and psychosocial adjustment. This relationship comes into play at present as the positive effect of fluent bilingualism on grades disappears after self-esteem and educational expectations are controlled. This result is subject to alternative causal interpretations. Given our earlier findings indicating a positive effect of bilingualism on these psychosocial variables, we interpret it as evidence of a causal chain where achievement of fluent bilingualism leads to higher ambition and self-

esteem that, in turn, influence school performance. This is the underlying rationale for the argument that adaptation outcomes build on each other.

10. There is additional evidence, however, indicating that early educational goals do have the expected positive effect on subsequent performance. This effect can be gauged indirectly by examining the influence of educational goals on academic tests in the late school years. For this analysis, we do not use actual test scores since, as explained earlier, only a minority of students took these tests. Since doing so was voluntary, the variable of interest becomes the *willingness* of students to put themselves through this effort. We reasoned that if educational ambition has an independent causal effect, it should lead to greater motivation to undertake additional academic tasks, including taking optional tests. That reasoning proved accurate. After controlling for other predictors, the logistic coefficients of early educational expectations on test taking in senior high school triples its standard error for both math and reading scores. The corresponding Wald coefficients are 12.5 and 15.0, both highly significant. Since early test scores were controlled, the observed effects are not attributable to higher early scores leading to higher expectations. Instead, they indicate a reliable effect of educational ambition on subsequent academic effort.

11. Woo, "Home Life Plays a Crucial Role."

12. Ibid.

13. CILS project interview in San Diego. Names are fictitious.

14. See Hirschman and Wong, "The Extraordinary Educational Attainment of Asian Americans"; Zhou and Bankston, *Growing Up American.*

15. Rumbaut and Ima, *The Adaptation of Southeast Asian Refugee Youth;* Rumbaut, "Portraits, Patterns and Predictors of the Refugee Adaptation Process."

16. See Zhou and Bankston, *Growing Up American;* Smith-Hefner, *Khmer American;* Rumbaut and Ima, *The Adaptation of Southeast Asian Refugee Youth.*

17. Bach, Bach, and Triplett, "The Flotilla 'Entrants'"; Portes and Stepick, *City on the Edge,* ch. 2.

18. Portes and Stepick, *City on the Edge;* Wilson and Martin, "Ethnic Enclaves"; David Rieff, *Going to Miami.*

19. Newspapers as far away as Columbus, Ohio, reported that "the 'Marielistas,' a society of Cuban criminals who came to this country on the Freedom Flotilla, are organizing in our town. This criminal syndicate, whose members advertise their specialties by tattoos, . . . have been seen around buying handguns." Cited in Martínez, "Mariel Myths Feed Venom across Nation," p. 31A. See also García, *Havana USA.*

20. Bach, Bach, and Triplett, "The Flotilla 'Entrants'"; Portes, Clark, and Manning, "After Mariel."

21. A 1986 survey of Mariel refugees interviewed in Miami found that 32 percent of respondents reported being discriminated against by white Americans but that fully 80 percent had suffered similar treatment by older (pre-Mariel) Cubans. See Portes and Clark, "Mariel Refugees."

22. The strong stigma associated with Mariel led many refugees who arrived at that time to conceal their year of arrival. We do not know to what extent this

was a factor inducing Cuban students in our sample to withhold information on their parents' date of arrival. For the case of their parents, see Portes and Clark, "Mariel Refugees"; Bach, Bach, and Triplett, "The Flotilla 'Entrants'."

23. Results presented in Table 9.6 are based on pooling together Cuban respondents whose parents arrived in 1980 or later and those who provided no information on their parents' date of arrival. This is justified by their very similar profile on a series of relevant variables. However, the pattern of results is not altered by limiting the sample to respondents with full information on this variable.

24. These results do not rule out the possible effect of selectivity of migration, especially given the different human capital profiles of Mariel and post-Mariel Cubans. Seeking to establish precisely the relative effects of selection and context is beyond the scope of this analysis. In our view, the latter factor played the stronger role because of the consistently hostile reception experienced by Mariel-era and later arrivals.

25. As noted by Granovetter, teenagers generally do not find jobs on their own; instead, jobs come to them through the mediation of kin and community networks. This pattern explains the differential propensity for full-time employment among youths from different ethnic origins. See Granovetter, *Getting a Job*; Sullivan, *Getting Paid*.

26. For analysis of the origins and dynamics of the Cuban enclave economy of Miami, see Portes and Bach, *Latin Journey,* ch. 6; Portes and Jensen, "The Enclave and the Entrants"; Wilson and Martin, "Ethnic Enclaves."

27. The same pattern of results is observable if students who dropped out of the CILS follow-up survey are excluded. The numbers are naturally smaller and the differences less substantial than those presented in Figure 9.5.

Chapter 10

1. Unz, "California and the End of White America," p. 24.

2. Ibid., p. 20.

3. Proposition 227 leaves room for a transitional period and for foreign language instruction in special cases, mostly at parents' request. Its thrust is, however, to abandon long-term instruction in any language other than English.

4. Unz, "California and the End of White America." For an alternative discussion of the growth of California's immigrant population and its political and educational effects, see Rumbaut, "The New Californians."

5. There are numerous detailed accounts of the political underpinnings of the Mexican immigrant flow from the nineteenth century to the present. Among the most important, see Barrera, *Race and Class in the Southwest;* Samora, *Los Mojados: The Wetback Story;* Massey, "Understanding Mexican Migration"; Massey, "March of Folly"; Cornelius, "The Structural Embeddedness"; Bach, "Mexican Immigration and the American State."

6. Espíritu, *Filipino American Lives;* Wolf, "Family Secrets"; Cariño, "The Philippines and Southeast Asia"; Smith-Hefner, *Khmer American;* Rumbaut and Ima, *The Adaptation of Southeast Asian Refugee Youth;* Rumbaut, "A Legacy of War."

7. Lieberson, Dalto, and Johnston, "The Course of Mother Tongue Diversity"; Handlin, *Boston's Immigrants;* Higham, *Strangers in the Land;* Alba, *Italian Americans;* Rumbaut, "Origins and Destinies."

8. The concepts of self-fulfilling and self-defeating prophecies were introduced to American sociology by Robert K. Merton, who elaborated their meaning and implications in a number of publications. See Merton, "The Unanticipated Consequences of Purposive Action"; "Unanticipated Consequences and Kindred Sociological Ideas"; *Social Theory and Social Structure,* ch. 13.

9. For historical overviews of the forces driving labor immigration to the United States in the nineteenth and early twentieth centuries, see Rosenblum, *Immigrant Workers;* Lebergott, *Manpower in Economic Growth;* Thomas, *Migration and Economic Growth.* For accounts of contemporary economic globalization and its effects on international migration, see Sassen, *The Mobility of Labor and Capital;* Cohen, *The New Helots;* Smith and Guarnizo, *Transnationalism from Below.*

10. In our typology of intergenerational outcomes in Chapter 3, consonant acculturation can be expected to produce similar effects except that in this case, it is based on the joint abandonment by parents and children of their culture and language to seek integration in the social mainstream. Though this pattern also reduces family tensions and is seen by assimilationists as desirable, it entails the loss of historical reference points and the psychological and economic benefits of being fluent in more than one language.

11. Lamm and Imhoff, *The Immigration Time Bomb;* Unz, "California and the End of White America."

12. For comments on current problems in American education and proposed solutions, see Lee, and Bryk, "A Multilevel Model of the Social Distribution of High School Achievement"; Bryk, Lee, and Holland, *Catholic Schools and the Common Good;* Coleman, "The Design of Organizations." See Chapter 6 for an extended comment on the role of public schools in language learning and loss. See also Portes and Schauffler, "Language and the Second Generation."

13. For a critical comment on the concept of segmented assimilation and a discussion of the central role of Mexican immigration in driving down human capital averages among the foreign born and their offspring, see Waldinger and Perlmann, "Second Generations."

14. See López and Stanton-Salazar, "The New Mexican Second Generation."

15. Barrera, *Race and Class;* Bach, "Mexican Immigration"; Portes and Bach, *Latin Journey,* ch. 3; Massey et. al., *Return to Aztlán.*

16. For ethnographic data on the origins and dynamics of Mexican-American educational decline, see Suárez-Orozco, "Towards a Psychosocial Understanding"; Matute-Bianchi, "Ethnic Identities and Patterns of School Success." See also Rumbaut, "The New Californians."

17. López and Stanton-Salazar, "The New Mexican Second Generation."

18. This list is based on qualitative interviews with CILS immigrant parents in 1993 and 1995 as well as on parental survey reports and interviewers' comments.

19. In an analysis of the educational attainment of 25 "religio-ethnic" groups in the United States, Hirschman and Falcón found that parental school-

ing, followed by the father's occupation, were the most important factors accounting for differences among groups. Immigrant generation did not significantly affect educational attainment. This result suggests that time in the United States does not compensate for low educational achievements in the first and second generations. Descendants of well-educated first- and second-generation immigrants continue to maintain a significant advantage in subsequent generations. See Hirschman and Falcón, "The Educational Attainment of Religio-Ethnic Groups."

20. Moore and Pachón, *Hispanics in the United States;* Barrera, *Race and Class;* Mirandé, *The Chicano Experience;* Estrada et. al., "Chicanos in the United States."

21. Moore and Pachón, *Hispanics in the United States;* Estrada et. al., "Chicanos in the United States."

22. Portes and Rumbaut, *Immigrant America,* pp. 127–129; Moore and Pachón, *Hispanics in the United States,* pp. 184–186; Gann and Duignan, *The Hispanics in the United States.*

23. Suárez-Orozco, "Towards a Psychological Understanding," p. 163.

24. Portes and Sensenbrenner, "Embeddedness and Immigration"; Bourgois, *In Search of Respect.*

25. For the case of African Americans, see Butler, *Entrepreneurship and Self-Help;* Green and Pryde, *Black Entrepreneurship in America.* For Mexican Americans, see Raijman, *Pathways to Self-Employment;* Raijman and Tienda, "Immigrants' Socio-economic Progress."

REFERENCES

Alba, Richard D. 1985. *Italian Americans: Into the twilight of ethnicity.* Englewood Cliffs, N.J.: Prentice Hall.

———. 1990. *Ethnic identity: The transformation of white America.* New Haven, Conn.: Yale University Press.

Alba, Richard D., and Victor Nee. 1997. Rethinking assimilation theory for a new era of immigration. *International Migration Review* 31 (Winter), pp. 826–874.

Aleinikoff, T. Alexander, and Rubén G. Rumbaut. 1998. Terms of belonging: Are models of membership self-fulfilling prophecies?" *Georgetown Immigration Law Journal* 13 (Fall), pp. 1–24.

Alvarez, Julia. 1991. *How the García girls lost their accent.* Chapel Hill, N.C.: Algonquin Books.

Anderson, Patricia, and Michael Witter. 1994. "Crisis, adjustment, and change: The case of Jamaica." In *Consequences of structural adjustment: A review of the Jamaican experience,* edited by Elsie Le Franc. Kingston, Jamaica: Canoe Press.

Antin, Mary. 1912. *The promised land.* New York: Houghton Mifflin.

Baca-Zinn, Maxine. 1994. "Adaptation and continuity in Mexican-origin families." In *Minority families in the United States,* edited by Ronald L. Taylor. Englewood Cliffs, N.J.: Prentice Hall.

Bach, Robert. 1978. Mexican immigration and the American state. *International Migration Review* 12 (Winter), pp. 536–558.

Bach, Robert, Jennifer B. Bach, and Timothy Triplett. 1981. The flotilla "entrants": Latest and most controversial. *Cuban Studies* 11 (July), pp. 29–48.

369

Bach, Robert, and Linda W. Gordon. 1984. "The economic adjustment of southeast Asian refugees in the United States." In *World Refugee Survey, 1983*. Geneva: United Nations High Commissioner for Refugees.

Bailey, Thomas, and Roger Waldinger. 1991. Primary, secondary, and enclave labor markets: A training system approach. *American Sociological Review* 56 (August), pp. 432–435.

Balmaseda, Liz. 1997. The issue is power, not language. *The Miami Herald*, 26 April, p. A1.

Banks, Sandy. 1994. Unflagging controversy. *Los Angeles Times*, 10 November, p. A1.

Barrera, Mario. 1980. *Race and class in the Southwest: A theory of racial inequality*. Notre Dame, Ind.: University of Notre Dame Press.

Bean, Frank D., Jennifer Van Hook, and Mark A. Fossett. 1999. "Immigration, spatial and economic change, and African American employment." In *Immigration and opportunity: Race, ethnicity, and employment in the United States*, edited by Frank D. Bean and Stephanie Bell-Rose. New York: Russell Sage Foundation.

Beck, Joan. 1997. Don't wait until high school to teach foreign tongue. *The Houston Chronicle*, 20 July.

Berger, Alan L. 1991. "Job's children: Post-Holocaust Jewish identity in second-generation literature." In *Jewish identity in America*, edited by David M. Gordis and Yoav Ben-Horin. Los Angeles: Wilstein Institute.

Berrol, Selma Cantor. 1995. *Growing up American: Immigrant children in America, then and now*. New York: Twayne.

Bertaux-Wiame, Isabelle. 1993. "The pull of family ties: Intergenerational relationships and life paths." In *Between generations: Family models, myths, and memories*, edited by Daniel Bertaux and Paul Thompson. New York: Oxford University Press.

Bialystok, Ellen, and Kenji Hakuta. 1994. *In other words: The science and psychology of second-language acquisition*. New York: Basic Books.

Bielby, William T., and James N. Baron. 1986. Men and women at work: Sex segregation and statistical discrimination. *American Journal of Sociology* 91 (January), pp. 759–779.

Bluestone, Barry, and Bennett Harrison. 1982. *The deindustrialization of America: Plant closings, community abandonment, and the dismantling of basic industry*. New York: Basic Books.

Bonilla, Frank, and Ricardo Campos. 1981. A wealth of poor: Puerto Ricans in the new economic order. *Daedalus* 110 (Spring), pp. 133–176.

Bourgois, Philippe I. 1995. *In search of respect: Selling crack in El Barrio*. Cambridge, U.K.: Cambridge University Press.

Bozorgmehr, Mehdi, Georges Sabagh, and Ivan Light. 1996. "Los Angeles: Explosive diversity." In *Origins and destinies: Immigration, race, and ethnicity in America*, edited by Silvia Pedraza and Rubén G. Rumbaut. Belmont, Calif.: Wadsworth.

Brigham, Carl Campbell. 1923. *A study of American intelligence*. Princeton, N.J.: Princeton University Press.

Brimelow, Peter. 1995. *Alien nation: Common sense about America's immigration disaster.* New York: Random House.

Bronner, Ethan. 1998. Bilingual education is facing push toward abandonment. *The New York Times,* 30 May, p. A-10.

Brown, Mary Elizabeth. 1994. "Parents and children: Fundamental questions about immigrant family life." In *Immigrant America: European ethnicity in the United States,* edited by Timothy Walch. New York: Garland.

Brumberg, Stephen F. 1986. *Going to America, going to school: The Jewish immigrant public school encounter in turn-of-the-century New York City.* New York: Praeger.

Bryk, A. S., V. Lee, and P. Holland. 1993. *Catholic schools and the common good.* Cambridge, Mass.: Harvard University Press.

Burt, Ronald S. 1992. *Structural holes: The social structure of competition.* Cambridge, Mass.: Harvard University Press.

Butler, John S. 1991. *Entrepreneurship and self-help among black Americans.* Albany: State University of New York Press.

Caplan, Nathan, Marcella H. Choy, and John K. Whitmore. 1991. *Children of the boat people: A study of educational success.* Ann Arbor: University of Michigan Press.

Cariño, Benjamin V. 1987. "The Philippines and southeast Asia: Historical roots and contemporary linkages." In *Pacific bridges: the new immigration from Asia and the Pacific Islands,* edited by J. T. Fawcett and B. V. Cariño. Staten Island, N.Y.: Center for Migration Studies.

Chávez, Leo R. 1992. *Shadowed lives: Undocumented immigrants in American society.* San Diego: Harcourt Brace Jovanovich.

Child, Irvin L. 1970 [1943]. *Italian or American? The second generation in conflict.* New York: Russell & Russell.

Cohen, Robin. 1988. *The new Helots: Migrants in the international division of labour.* Hants, U.K.: England's Gower.

Coleman, James S. 1961. Social capital in the creation of human capital. *American Journal of Sociology* 94 (Supplement), pp. 95–121.

————. 1993. The design of organizations and the right to act. *Sociological Forum* 8 (4), pp. 527–46.

Coopersmith, Stanley. 1967. *The antecedents of self-esteem.* San Francisco: W. H. Freeman.

Cornelius, Wayne. 1998. "The structural embeddedness of demand for Mexican immigrant labor: New evidence from California." In *Crossings: Mexican immigration in interdisciplinary perspectives,* edited by Marcelo Suárez-Orozco. Cambridge, Mass.: Center for Latin American Studies, Harvard University.

Cornell, Stephen, and Douglas Hartmann. 1998. *Ethnicity and race: Making identities in a changing world.* Thousand Oaks, Calif.: Pine Forge.

Crawford, James. 1992. *Hold your tongue: Bilingualism and the politics of English Only.* Reading, Mass.: Addison-Wesley.

Crawford, James, ed. 1992. *Language loyalties: A source book on the official English controversy.* Chicago: University of Chicago Press.

Cropley, A. J. 1983. *The education of immigrant children: A social-psychological introduction.* London: Croom Helm.

Cuellar, José, L. C. Harris, and R. Jasso. 1980. An acculturation scale for Mexican normal and clinical populations. *Hispanic Journal of Behavioral Sciences* 2, no. 3, pp. 199–217.

Cummins, Jim. 1978. "Metalinguistic development of children in bilingual education programs." In *The Fourth LACUS Forum: 1977,* edited by Michel Paradis. Columbia, S.C.: Hornbeam Press.

Deaux, Kay. 1996. "Social Identification." In *Social psychology: Handbook of basic principles,* edited by E. Tory Higgins and Arie W. Kruglanski. New York: Guilford Press.

Dennett, Daniel Clement. 1991. *Consciousness explained.* Boston: Little, Brown.

de Vise, Daniel. 1997. Children of immigrants get high marks. *San Diego Union-Tribune,* July 6, p. A1.

Dillard, Joey Lee. 1985. *Toward a social history of American English.* New York: Mouton.

Doctorow, E. L. 1989. *Billy Bathgate.* New York: Random House.

Dorfman, Ariel. 1998. If only we all spoke two languages. *The New York Times,* 24 June.

Dugger, Celia W. 1998. Among young of immigrants, outlook rises. *The New York Times,* 21 March, p. A-1.

Eccles, Jacquelynne S., Terry F. Adler, Robert Futterman, Susan B. Goff, Caroline M. Kaczala, Judith L. Meece, and Carol Midgley. 1983. "Expectancies, values, and academic behaviors." In *Achievement and achievement motivation: Psychological and sociological approaches,* edited by Janet T. Spence. San Francisco: W. H. Freeman.

Eccles, Jacquelynne S., and Allan Wigfield. 2000. "Schooling's influences on motivation and achievement." In *Securing the future: Investing in children from birth to college,* edited by Jane Waldfogel and Sheldon Danziger. New York: Russell Sage Foundation.

England, Paula. 1984. Wage appreciation and depreciation: A test of neoclassical economic explanations of occupational sex segregation. *Social Forces* 62 (March), pp. 726–749.

Escobar, Gabriel. 1999. Dominicans face assimilation in black and white. *The Washington Post,* 14 May, p. A-3.

Espíritu, Yen Le. 1992. *Asian American panethnicity: Bridging institutions and identities.* Philadelphia: Temple University Press.

———. 1995. *Filipino American lives.* Philadelphia: Temple University Press.

Estrada, Leobardo F., F. Chris García, Reynaldo Flores Macías, and Lionel Maldonado. 1988. "Chicanos in the United States: A history of exploitation and resistance." In *Latinos and the political system,* edited by F. Chris García. Notre Dame, Ind.: Notre Dame University Press.

Everybody is getting rich. 1999. *Money* 28, no. 5 (May).

Feldman, Claudia. 1999. Double exposure: Two homelands, two cultures shape view of future for second-generation teens. *The Houston Chronicle,* 3 October, p. D-1.

Fernández-Kelly, Patricia. 1983. *For we are sold, I and my people: Women and industry in Mexico's frontier.* Albany: State University of New York Press.

———. 1995. "Social and cultural capital in the urban ghetto: Implications for the economic sociology of immigration." In *The economic sociology of immigration: Essays in networks, ethnicity, and entrepreneurship,* edited by Alejandro Portes. New York: Russell Sage Foundation.

Fernández-Kelly, Patricia, and Ana M. García. 1989. "Informalization at the core: Hispanic women, homework, and the advanced capitalist state." In *The informal economy: Studies in advanced and less developed countries,* edited by Alejandro Portes, Manuel Castells, and Lauren Benton. Baltimore: Johns Hopkins University Press.

Fernández-Kelly, Patricia, and Richard Schauffler. 1996. "Divided fates and the new assimilation." In *The new second generation,* edited by Alejandro Portes. New York: Russell Sage Foundation.

Fishman, Joshua A. 1966. *Language loyalty in the United States: The maintenance and perpetuation of non-English mother tongues by American ethnic and religious groups.* The Hague: Mouton.

———. 1969. A sociolinguistic census of a bilingual neighborhood. *American Journal of Sociology* 75 (November), pp. 323–339.

———. 1978. *Language loyalty in the United States.* New York: Arno Press.

Fishman, Joshua A., and Charles Terry. 1969. The validity of census data on bilingualism in a Puerto Rican neighborhood. *American Sociological Review* 34 (October), pp. 636–650.

Fitzpatrick, Joseph P. 1987. *Puerto Rican Americans: The meaning of migration to the mainland.* Englewood Cliffs, N.J.: Prentice Hall.

Fligstein, Neil. 1981. *Going North: Migration of blacks and whites from the South, 1900–1950.* New York: Academic Press.

Folmar, Kate, and Scott Martelli. 2000. The new faces of Orange County's future: Reflecting changing demographics, immigrants give birth to year's first babies. *Los Angeles Times,* January 2, p. 1.

Fong-Torres, Ben. 1994. *The rice room: Growing up Chinese-American—From number two son to rock 'n' roll.* New York: Hyperion.

Fradd, Sandra H. 1996. *The economic impact of Spanish-language proficiency in metropolitan Miami.* Miami: School of Education, University of Miami.

Fuligni, Andrew J. 1997. The academic achievement of adolescents from immigrant families: The roles of family background, attitudes and behavior. *Child Development* 68 (April), pp. 261–273.

Fuligni, Andrew J., Vivian Tseng, and May Lam. 1999. Attitudes toward family obligations among American adolescents with Asian, Latin American, and European backgrounds. *Child Development* 70 (July-August), pp. 1030–1044.

Fullwood, Sam. 1993. Children of new arrivals avoid melting into the mainstream. *Los Angeles Times,* 7 September.

Gann, H. L., and Peter Duignan. 1986. *The Hispanics in the United States: A history.* Boulder, Colo.: Westview Press.

Gans, Herbert J. 1979. Symbolic ethnicity: The future of ethnic groups and cultures in America. *Ethnic and Racial Studies* 2 (January), pp. 1–20.

———. 1992. "Second generation decline: Scenarios for the economic and ethnic futures of the post-1965 America immigrants. *Ethnic and Racial Studies* 15 (April), pp. 173–192.

García, Cristina. 1992. *Dreaming in Cuban.* New York: Ballantine Books.

García, María Cristina. 1996. *Havana, USA: Cuban exiles and Cuban Americans in South Florida, 1959–1994.* Berkeley: University of California Press.

García-Coll, Cynthia, and Katherine Magnuson. 1997. "The psychological experience of immigration: A developmental perspective." In *Immigration and the family: Research and policy on U.S. immigrants,* edited by Alan Booth, Ann C. Crouter, and Nancy S. Landale. Mahwah, N.J.: Lawrence Erlbaum Associates.

Garvey, Megan, and Patrick J. McDonnell. 1999. José moves into top spot in name game: Favorite choice for boys in California, Texas last year marks major shift. *Los Angeles Times,* 8 January, p. A-1.

Gereffi, Gary. 1994. "The organization of buyer-driven global commodity chains: How use retailers shape overseas production networks." In *Commodity chains and global capitalism,* edited by Gary Gereffi and Miguel Korzeniewicz. Westport, Conn.: Praeger.

Gibson, Margaret. 1989. *Accommodation without assimilation: Sikh immigrants in an American high school.* Ithaca, N.Y.: Cornell University Press.

Gil, Andrés G., and William A. Vega. 1996. Two different worlds: Acculturation stress and adaptation among Cuban and Nicaraguan families. *Journal of Social and Personal Relationships* 13 (August), pp. 435–456.

Glazer, Nathan. 1954. "Ethnic groups in America." In *Freedom and control in modern society,* edited by Theodore Abel, Monroe Berger, and Charles H. Page. New York: Van Nostrand.

Glazer, Nathan, and Daniel Patrick Moynihan. 1970. *Beyond the melting pot: The Negroes, Puerto Ricans, Jews, Italians, and Irish of New York City.* Cambridge, Mass.: MIT Press.

Gold, Steven J. 1992. *Refugee communities: A comparative field study.* Newbury Park, Calif.: Sage Publications.

Goldscheider, Frances K., and Calvin Goldscheider. 1993. *Leaving home before marriage: Ethnicity, familism, and generational relationships.* Madison: University of Wisconsin Press.

Gordon, Milton M. 1971. *Assimilation in American life: The role of race, religion, and national origins.* New York: Oxford University Press.

Granovetter, Mark S. 1974. *Getting a job: A study of contacts and careers.* Cambridge, Mass.: Harvard University Press.

Grasmuck, Sherri, and Patricia Pessar. 1991. *Between two islands: Dominican international migration.* Berkeley: University of California Press.

Green, Shelly, and Paul Pryde. 1990. *Black entrepreneurship in America.* New Brunswick, N.J.: Transactions.

Griffin, Larry, and Karl L. Alexander. 1978. Schooling and socio-economic attainment: High school and college influences. *American Journal of Sociology* 84 (September), pp. 319–347.

Hakuta, Kenji. 1986. *Mirror of language: The debate on bilingualism.* New York: Basic Books.

Hakuta, Kenji, and Rafael M. Díaz. "The relationship between degree of bilingualism and cognitive ability: A critical discussion and some new longitudinal data." In *Children's Language, Vol. 5*, edited by Keith E. Nelson. Hillsdale, N.J.: Lawrence Erlbaum Associates, 1985.

Handlin, Oscar. 1941. *Boston's immigrants: A study of acculturation*. Cambridge, Mass.: Harvard University Press.

Hansen, Marcus Lee. 1990 [1937]. "Who shall inherit America?" In *American immigrants and their generations: Studies and commentaries on the Hansen thesis after fifty years*, edited by Peter Kivisto and Dag Blanck. Urbana: University of Illinois Press.

Haller, Archibald O., and Alejandro Portes. 1973. Status Attainment Processes. *Sociology of Education* 46 (Winter), pp. 51–91.

Harris, Kathleen Mullan. 1999. "The health status and risk behaviors of adolescents in immigrant families." In *Children of immigrants: Health, adjustment, and public assistance*, edited by Donald J. Hernández. Washington, D.C.: National Academy of Science Press.

Harrison, Bennett, and Barry Bluestone. 1988. *The great U-turn: Corporate restructuring and the polarizing of America*. New York: Basic Books.

Harvey, David. 1982. *The limits to capital*. Chicago: University of Chicago Press.

Hernández, Donald J., ed. 1999. *Children of immigrants: Health, adjustment, and public assistance*. Washington, D.C.: National Academy Press.

Hernández, Donald J., and Evan Charney. 1998. *From generation to generation: The health and well-being of children in immigrant families*. Washington, D.C.: National Academy Press.

Higham, John. 1955. *Strangers in the land: Patterns of American nativism, 1896–1925*. New Brunswick, N.J.: Rutgers University Press.

Hirsch, Barton J., and Bruce D. Rapkin. 1987. The transition to junior high school: A longitudinal study of self-esteem, psychological symptomatology, school life, and social support. *Child Development* 58 (October), pp. 1235–1243.

Hirschman, Charles. 1996. "Studying immigrant adaptation from the 1990 population census: From generational comparisons to the process of 'becoming American.'" In *The new second generation*, edited by Alejandro Portes. New York: Russell Sage Foundation.

Hirschman, Charles, and Luis Falcón. 1985. The educational attainment of religio-ethnic groups in the United States. *Research in Sociology of Education and Socialization* 5, pp. 83–120.

Hirschman, Charles, and Morrison G. Wong. 1986. The extraordinary educational attainment of Asian Americans: A search for historical evidence and explanations. *Social Forces* 65 (September), pp. 1–27.

Hoffman, Eva. 1989. *Lost in translation: A life in a new language*. New York: Penguin Books.

Hondagneu-Sotelo, Pierrette. 1994. *Gendered transitions: Mexican experiences of immigration*. Berkeley: University of California Press.

Horowitz, Donald L. 1985. *Ethnic groups in conflict*. Berkeley: University of California Press.

Howard, Michael. 1994. "War and nations." In *Nationalism,* edited by John Hutchinson and Anthony D. Smith, Oxford, U.K.: Oxford University Press.

Hwang, Caroline. 1998. The good daughter. *Newsweek,* 21 September, p. 16.

Jensen, Leif, and Yoshimi Chitose. 1989. *The new immigration: Implications for poverty and public assistance utilization.* New York: Greenwood Press.

———. 1996. "Today's new second generation: Evidence from the 1990 U.S. Census." In *The new second generation,* edited by Alejandro Portes. New York: Russell Sage Foundation.

Judson, Olivia. 1996. "How to stir the melting pot." *The Economist,* 17 February.

Kann, Laura, C. W. Warren, W. A. Harris, J. L. Collins, K. A. Douglas, M. E. Collins, B. I. Williams, J. G. Ross, and L. J. Kolbe. 1995. Youth risk behavior surveillance—United States, 1993. *Morbidity and Mortality Weekly Report* 44 (SS-1), pp. 1–56.

Kao, Grace. 1999. "Psychological well-being and educational achievement among immigrant youth." In *Children of immigrants: Health, adjustment, and public assistance,* edited by Donald J. Hernández. Washington, D.C.: National Academy Press.

Kao, Grace, and Marta Tienda. 1995. Optimism and achievement: The educational performance of immigrant youth. *Social Science Quarterly* 76 (March), pp. 1–19.

———. 1998. Educational aspirations of minority youth. *American Journal of Education* 106 (May), pp. 349–384.

Karoly, Lynn A. 1992. *The trend in inequality among families, individuals, and workers in the United States: A twenty-five-year perspective.* Santa Monica, Calif.: Rand.

Kibria, Nazli. 1976. *Family tightrope: The changing lives of Vietnamese Americans.* Princeton, N.J.: Princeton University Press.

Knight, Franklin W., and Colin A. Palmer. 1989. *The modern Caribbean.* Chapel Hill, N.C.: University of North Carolina Press.

Kingston, Maxine Hong. 1976. *The woman warrior: Memoirs of a girlhood among ghosts.* New York: Knopf.

Kraut, Alan M. 1982. *The huddled masses: The immigrant in American society, 1880–1921.* Arlington Heights, Ill.: Harlan Davidson.

Lamm, Richard D., and Gary Imhoff. 1985. *The immigration time bomb: The fragmenting of America.* New York: Dutton, 1985.

Landale, Nancy S., R. S. Oropesa, and Bridget K. Gorman. 1999. "Immigration and infant health: Birth outcomes of immigrant and native women." In *Children of immigrants: Health, adjustment, and public assistance,* edited by Donald J. Hernández. Washington, D.C.: National Academy of Science Press.

Laponce, Jean A. 1987. *Languages and their territories.* Buffalo, N.Y.: University of Toronto Press.

Lau, Angela. 1995. Filipina girls pondering suicide at highest rate in school survey. *San Diego Union-Tribune,* 11 February.

Lee, Chang Rae. 1995. *Native speaker.* New York: Putnam.

Lee, Valerie E., and Anthony S. Bryk, "A Multilevel Model of the Social Distribution of High School Achievement", *Sociology of Education* 62 (July 1989): 172–192.

Lebergott, Stanley. 1964. *Manpower in economic growth: The American record since 1800.* New York: McGraw-Hill.

Lenneberg, Eric H. 1967. *Biological foundations of language.* New York: Wiley.

Leopold, Werner F. 1970. *Speech development of a bilingual child: A linguist's record.* New York: AMS Press.

Lieberson, Stanley, Guy Dalto, and Mary Ellen Johnston. 1975. The course of mother tongue diversity in nations. *American Journal of Sociology* 81 (July), pp. 34–61.

López, David E. 1978. *Language maintenance and shift in the United States today: The basic patterns and their social implications.* Volumes 1–4. Los Alamitos, Calif.: National Center for Bilingual Research.

López, David E., and Ricardo Stanton-Salazar. 2001. "The new Mexican second generation." In *Ethnicities: Children of immigrants in America*, edited by Rubén G. Rumbaut and Alejandro Portes. Berkeley: University of California Press.

MacLeod, Jay. 1995. *Ain't no making it: Leveled aspirations in a low-income neighborhood.* 2d ed. Boulder, Colo: Westview.

Mahler, Sarah J. 1995. *American dreaming: Immigrant life on the margins.* Princeton, N.J: Princeton University Press.

Malzberg, Benjamin, and Everett Spurgeon Lee. 1956. *Migration and mental disease: A study of first admissions to hospitals for mental disease, New York, 1939–1941.* New York: Social Science Research Council.

Marckwardt, Albert Henry. 1980. *American English.* New York: Oxford University Press.

Marks, Carole. 1989. *Farewell—We're good and gone: The great black migration.* Bloomington: Indiana University Press.

Martínez, Guillermo. 1982. Mariel myths feed venom across nation. *Miami Herald*, 18 November, p. 31A.

Massey, Douglas S. 1987. Understanding Mexican migration to the United States. *American Journal of Sociology* 92 (May), pp. 1372–1403.

———. 1993. Latinos, poverty, and the underclass: A new agenda for research. *Hispanic Journal of Behavioral Sciences* 15 (November), pp. 449–475.

———. 1998. March of folly: U.S. immigration policy after NAFTA. *The American Prospect* 37 (March-April), pp. 22–33.

Massey, Douglas S., Rafael Alarcón, Jorge Durand, and Humberto González. 1987. *Return to Aztlán: The social process of international migration from western Mexico.* Berkeley: University of California Press.

Massey, Douglas S., and Nancy A. Denton. 1993. *American apartheid: Segregation and the making of the underclass.* Cambridge, Mass.: Harvard University Press.

Matthei, Linda M., and David A. Smith. 1996. "Women, households, and transnational migration networks: The Garifuna and global economic restructuring." In *Latin America in the world-economy*, edited by Roberto Patricio Korzeniewicz and William C. Smith. Westport, Conn.: Greenwood Press.

Matute-Bianchi, María Eugenia. 1986. Ethnic identities and patterns of school success and failure among Mexican-descent and Japanese-American students in a California high school: An ethnographic analysis. *American Journal of Education* 95 (November), pp. 233–255.

McClelland, David C. 1961. *The achieving society.* Princeton, N.J.: Van Nostrand.

McDonnell, Patrick J. 1994. Complex family ties tangle simple premise of Prop. 187. *Los Angeles Times,* 20 November, p. A-1.

McLanahan, Sara, and Gary D. Sandefur. 1994. *Growing up with a single parent: What hurts, what helps.* Cambridge, Mass.: Harvard University Press.

Mead, George Herbert. 1962. *Mind, self, and society: From the standpoint of a social behaviorist.* Chicago: University of Chicago Press.

Mears, Teresa. 1997. Miami Hispanics losing their Spanish. *The Miami Herald,* 5 October, p. A-1.

Mecca, Andrew M., Neil J. Smelser, and John Vasconcellos. 1989. *The social importance of self-esteem.* Berkeley: University of California Press.

Merton, Robert K. 1936. The unanticipated consequences of purposive social action. *American Sociological Review* 1, pp. 894–904.

———. 1968. *Social theory and social structure.* New York: The Free Press.

———. 1989. "Unanticipated consequences and kindred sociological ideas: A personal gloss." In *L'opera de R. K. Merton e la sociologia contemporanea,* edited by C. Mongardini and S. Tabboni. Genova, Italy: Edizioni Culturali Internazionali.

———. 1996. "A Life of Learning." In *Robert K. Merton: On social structure and science,* edited by Piotr Sztompka. Chicago: University of Chicago Press.

Miller, D. W. Scholars of immigration focus on the children. *Chronicle of Higher Education,* February 5, pp. 20–21.

Min, Pyong Gap. 1995. "Korean Americans." In *Asian Americans: Contemporary trends and issues,* edited by Pyong Gap Min. Thousand Oaks, Calif.: Sage.

Mintz, Sidney Wilfred, and Sally Price, eds. 1985. *Caribbean contours.* Baltimore: Johns Hopkins University Press.

Mirandé, Alfredo. 1985. *The Chicano experience.* Notre Dame, Ind.: Notre Dame University Press.

Mirowsky, John, and Catherine E. Ross. 1989. *Social causes of psychological distress.* New York: Aldine de Gruyter.

Moore, Joan, and Harry Pachon. 1985. *Hispanics in the United States.* Englewood Cliffs, N.J.: Prentice Hall.

Mouw, Ted, and Yu Xie. 1999. Bilingualism and the academic achievement of first- and second-generation Asian Americans: Accommodation with or without assimilation? *American Sociological Review* 64 (April), pp. 232–252.

Nagel, Joane. 1986. "The political construction of ethnicity." In *Competitive ethnic relations,* edited by Susan Olzak and Joane Nagel. Orlando, Fla.: Academic Press.

Nahirny, Vladimir C., and Joshua A. Fishman. 1996 [1965]. "American immigrant groups: Ethnic identification and the problem of generations." In *The-*

ories of ethnicity: A classical reader, edited by Werner Sollors. New York: New York University Press.

Navarrette, Rubén Jr. 1994. At the birth of a new—and younger—Latino activism. *Los Angeles Times,* 13 November.

Navarro, Mireya. 1996. Bilingual parents dismayed by English's pull on children. *The New York Times,* 31 August, p. A-1.

Nelson, Candace, and Marta Tienda. 1985. The structuring of Hispanic ethnicity: historical and contemporary perspectives. *Ethnic and Racial Studies* 8 (January), pp. 49–74.

Nijman, Jan. 2000. The paradigmatic city. *Annals of the Association of American Geographers* 90, pp. 135–145.

Olsen, Laurie. 1997. *Made in America: Immigrant students in our public schools.* New York: New Press.

Olson, David H., Hamilton I. McCubbin, Howard Barnes, Andrea Larsen, Marla Muxen, and Marc Wilson. 1983. *Families: What makes them work.* Beverly Hills, Calif.: Sage.

Olson, James M., Neal J. Reese, and Mark P. Zanna. 1996. "Expectancies." In *Social psychology: Handbook of basic principles,* edited by E. Tory Higgins and Arie W. Kruglanski. New York: Guilford Press.

Oropesa, R. S., and Nancy S. Landale. 1997. In search of the new second generation: Alternative strategies for identifying second generation children and understanding their acquisition of English. *Sociological Perspectives* 40 (Fall), pp. 429–455.

Owens, Timothy J. 1994. Two dimensions of self-esteem: Reciprocal effects of positive self-worth and self-deprecation on adolescent problems. *American Sociological Review* 59 (June), pp. 391–407.

Passel, Jeffrey S., and Barry Edmonston. 1992. Immigration and race: Recent trends in immigration to the United States. Research paper PRIP-VI-22. Washington, D.C.: Program for Research on Immigration Policy, The Urban Institute.

Peal, Elizabeth, and Wallace E. Lambert. 1962. *The Relation of bilingualism to intelligence.* Washington, D.C.: American Psychological Association.

Pedraza, Silvia, and Rubén G. Rumbaut, eds. 1996. *Origins and destinies: Immigration, race, and ethnicity in America.* Belmont, Calif.: Wadsworth.

Penfield, Wilder. 1965. Conditioning the uncommitted cortex for language learning. *Brain: A Journal of Neurology* 88 (November), pp. 787–798.

Pérez, Lisandro. 1996. "The households of children of immigrants in South Florida: An exploratory study of extended family arrangements." In *The new second generation,* edited by Alejandro Portes. New York: Russell Sage Foundation.

Pérez Firmat, Gustavo. 1994. *Life on the hyphen: The Cuban-American way.* Austin: University of Texas Press.

———. 1995. *Next year in Cuba: A Cubano's coming of age in America.* New York: Anchor Books.

Perlmann, Joel, and Roger Waldinger. 1997. Second generation decline? Children of immigrants, past and present—A reconsideration. *International Migration Review* 31 (Winter), pp. 893–922.

Petersen, Trond. 1985. A comment on presenting results from logit and probit models. *American Sociological Review* 50 (February), pp. 130–131.

Phinney, Jean S. 1990. Ethnic identity in adolescents and adults: Review of research. *Psychological Bulletin* 108 (November), pp. 499–514.

Piore, Michael J. 1979. *Birds of passage: Migrant labor and industrial societies.* Cambridge, Mass.: Cambridge University Press.

Pitts, Leonard Jr. 1999. José is just as American as baseball, apple pie and John. *The Houston Chronicle,* 15 January.

Portes, Alejandro. 1984. "The rise of ethnicity: Determinants of ethnic perceptions among Cuban exiles in Miami." *American Sociological Review* 49 (June), pp. 383–397.

———. 1987. The social origins of the Cuban enclave of Miami. *Sociological Perspectives* 30 (October), pp. 340–372.

———. 1995. "Children of immigrants: Segmented assimilation and its determinants." In *The economic sociology of immigration: Essays on networks, ethnicity, and entrepreneurship,* edited by Alejandro Portes. New York: Russell Sage Foundation.

———, ed. 1996. *The new second generation.* New York: Russell Sage Foundation.

———. 1998. Social capital: Its origins and applications in modern sociology. *Annual Review of Sociology* 24, pp. 1–24.

Portes, Alejandro, and Robert L. Bach. 1985. *Latin journey: Cuban and Mexican immigrants in the United States.* Berkeley: University of California Press.

Portes, Alejandro, and Juan M. Clark. 1987. Mariel refugees: Six years later. *Migration World* 15, no. 5, pp. 14–18.

Portes, Alejandro, and Lingxin Hao. 1998. *E pluribus unum:* Bilingualism and loss of language in the second generation. *Sociology of Education* 71 (October), pp. 269–294.

Portes, Alejandro, and Leif Jensen. 1989. The enclave and the entrants: Patterns of ethnic enterprise in Miami before and after Mariel. *American Sociological Review* 54 (June), pp. 929–949.

Portes, Alejandro, and Dag MacLeod. 1996. Educational progress of children of immigrants: The roles of class, ethnicity, and a school context. *Sociology of Education* 69 (October), pp. 255–275.

———. 1996. What shall I call myself? Hispanic identity formation in the second generation. *Ethnic and Racial Studies* 19 (July), no. 523–547.

———. 1999. Educating the second-generation: Determinants of academic achievement among children of immigrants in the United States. *Journal of Ethnic and Migration Studies* 25 (July), pp. 373–396.

Portes, Alejandro, Juan M. Clark, and Robert D. Manning. 1985. After Mariel: A survey of the resettlement experiences of Cuban refugees in Miami. *Cuban Studies* 15 (Summer), pp. 35–59.

Portes, Alejandro, Samuel A. MacLeod, and Robert N. Parker. 1978. Immigrant aspirations. *Sociology of Education* 51 (October), pp. 241–260.

Portes, Alejandro, and Rubén G. Rumbaut. 1996. *Immigrant America: A portrait.* 2d ed. Berkeley: University of California Press.

Portes, Alejandro, and Richard Schauffler. 1996. "Language and the second generation: Bilingualism yesterday and today." In *The new second generation,* edited by Alejandro Portes. New York: Russell Sage Foundation.

Portes, Alejandro, and Julia Sensenbrenner. 1993. Embeddedness and immigration: Notes on the social determinants of economic action. *American Journal of Sociology* 98 (May), pp. 1320–1350.

Portes, Alejandro, and Alex Stepick. 1985. Unwelcome immigrants: The labor market experiences of 1980 (Mariel) Cuban and Haitian refugees in South Florida. *American Sociological Review* 50 (August), pp. 493–514.

———. 1993. *City on the edge: The transformation of Miami.* Berkeley: University of California Press.

Portes, Alejandro, and Min Zhou. 1993. The new second generation: Segmented assimilation and its variants. *Annals of the American Academy of Political and Social Sciences* 530 (November), pp. 74–96.

———. 1996. Self-employment and the earnings of immigrants. *American Sociological Review* 61 (April), pp. 219–230.

Prince, Robert. 1985. *The legacy of the Holocaust: Psychohistorical themes in the second generation.* Ann Arbor, Mich.: UMI Research Press.

Pyle, Amy, and Simon Romero. 1994. Prop 187 fuels a new campus activism. *Los Angeles Times,* 25 October, p. B-1.

Raijman, Rebecca. 1996. Pathways to self-employment and entrepreneurship on an immigrant community in Chicago. Ph.D. diss., University of Chicago.

Raijman, Rebecca, and Marta Tienda. 1999. "Immigrants' socio-economic progress post-1965: Forging mobility or survival?" In *The Handbook of International Migration,* edited by C. Hirschman, P. Kasinitz, and J. DeWind. New York: Russell Sage.

Rieff, David. 1987. *Going to Miami: Exiles, tourists and refugees in the new America.* Boston: Little, Brown.

Riley, Richard W. 1998. Statement by Secretary of Education Richard W. Riley on California Proposition 227. Washington, D.C.: U.S. Department of Education, 27 April.

Roberts, Bryan. 1995. "Socially expected durations and the economic adjustment of immigrants." In *The economic sociology of immigration,* edited by Alejandro Portes. New York: Russell Sage Foundation.

Rodríguez, Richard. 1982. *Hunger of memory: The education of Richard Rodríguez.* Boston: David R. Godine.

———. 1993. *Days of obligation: An argument with my Mexican father.* New York: Penguin.

Romo, Frank P., and Michael Schwartz. 1995. The structural embeddedness of business decisions: The migration of manufacturing plants in New York State, 1960 to 1985. *American Sociological Review* 60 (December), pp. 874–907.

Rosenberg, Morris. 1965. *Society and the adolescent self-image.* Princeton, N.J.: Princeton University Press.

———. 1979. *Conceiving the self.* New York: Basic Books.

Rosenberg, Morris, Carmi Schooler, and Carrie Schoenbach. 1989. Self-esteem and adolescent problems: Modeling reciprocal effects. *American Sociological Review* 54 (December), pp. 1004–1018.

Rosenberg, Morris, Carmi Schooler, Carrie Schoenbach, and Florence Rosenberg. 1995. Global self-esteem and specific self-esteem: Different concepts, different outcomes. *American Sociological Review* 60 (February), pp. 141–156.

Rosenblum, Gerald. 1973. *Immigrant workers: Their impact on American labor radicalism.* New York: Basic Books.

Roth, Henry. 1992 [1934]. *Call it sleep.* New York: Farrar, Straus & Giroux.

Rother, Larry. 1998. Island life not idyllic for youths from U.S. *The New York Times,* 20 February.

Rumbaut, Rubén D., and Rubén G. Rumbaut. 1976. The family in exile: Cuban expatriates in the United States. *American Journal of Psychiatry* 133 (April), pp. 395–399.

Rumbaut, Rubén G. 1985. "Mental health and the refugee experience: A comparative study of southeast Asian refugees." In *Southeast Asian mental health: Treatment, prevention, services, training and research,* edited by Tom C. Owan. Rockville, Md.: National Institute of Mental Health.

———. 1989. "Portraits, patterns, and predictors of the refugee adaptation process: Results and reflections from the IHARP panel study." In *Refugees as immigrants: Cambodians, Laotians, and Vietnamese in America,* edited by David W. Haines. Totowa, N.J.: Rowman and Littlefield.

———. 1989. The structure of refuge: Southeast Asian refugees in the United States, 1975–1985. *International Review of Comparative Public Policy* 1 (1), pp. 95–129.

———. 1990. *Immigrant children in California public schools: A summary of current knowledge.* CDS report No. 11. Baltimore: Center for Research on Effective Schooling for Disadvantaged Students, Johns Hopkins University.

———. 1991. "The agony of exile: A study of the migration and adaptation of Indochinese refugee adults and children." In *Refugee children: Theory, research and practice,* edited by Frederick L. Ahearn Jr. and Jean Athey. Baltimore: Johns Hopkins University Press.

———. 1991. "Migration, adaptation, and mental health: The experience of Southeast Asian refugees in the United States." In *Refugee policy: Canada and the United States,* edited by Howard Adelman. Toronto: York Lanes Press.

———. 1992. "The Americans: Latin American and Caribbean peoples in the United States." In *Americas: New interpretive essays,* edited by Alfred Stepan. New York: Oxford University Press.

———. 1994. The crucible within: Ethnic identity, self-esteem, and segmented assimilation among children of immigrants. *International Migration Review* 28, no. 4 (Winter), pp. 748–794.

———. 1994. Origins and destinies: Immigration to the United States since World War II. *Sociological Forum* 9, no. 4 (December), pp. 583–621.

———. 1995. "The new Californians: Comparative research findings on the educational progress of immigrant children." In *California's immigrant chil-*

dren: Theory, research and implications for educational policy, edited by Rubén G. Rumbaut and Wayne A. Cornelius. La Jolla, Calif.: Center for U.S.-Mexican Studies, University of California, San Diego.

———. 1996. "A legacy of war: Refugees from Vietnam, Laos, and Cambodia." In Origins and destinies: Immigration, race, and ethnicity in America, edited by Silvia Pedraza and Rubén G. Rumbaut. Belmont, Calif.: Wadsworth.

———. 1997. "Assimilation and its discontents: Between rhetoric and reality." International Migration Review 31, no. 4 (Winter), pp. 923–960.

———. 1997. "Ties that bind: Immigration and immigrant families in the United States." In Immigration and the family: Research and policy on U.S. immigrants, edited by Alan Booth, Ann C. Crouter, and Nancy S. Landale. Mahwah, N.J.: Lawrence Erlbaum Associates.

———. 1998. Coming of age in immigrant America. Research Perspectives on Migration 1, no. 6, pp. 1–14.

———. 1998. Transformations: The post-immigrant generation in an age of diversity. Paper presented at the annual meeting of the Eastern Sociological Society, Philadelphia, March.

———. 1999. "Assimilation and its discontents: Ironies and paradoxes." In The handbook of international migration: The American experience, edited by Charles Hirschman, Josh DeWind, and Philip Kasinitz. New York: Russell Sage Foundation.

———. 1999. "Passages to adulthood: The adaptation of children of immigrants in southern California." In Children of immigrants: Health, adjustment, and public assistance, edited by Donald J. Hernández. Washington, D.C.: National Academy of Science Press.

———. 2000. "Profiles in resilience: Educational achievement and ambition among children of immigrants in southern California." In Resilience across contexts: Family, work, culture, and community, edited by Ronald Taylor. Mahwah, N.J.: Lawrence Erlbaum Associates.

Rumbaut, Rubén G., and Kenji Ima. 1988. The adaptation of southeast Asian refugee youth: A comparative study. Washington, D.C.: U.S. Office of Refugee Resettlement.

Samora, Julián. 1971. Los mojados: The wetback story. Notre Dame, Ind.: Notre Dame University Press.

Sassen, Saskia. 1988. The mobility of labor and capital: A study in international investment and labor flow. Cambridge, U.K., and New York: Cambridge University Press.

———. 1991. The global city: New York, London, Tokyo. Princeton, N.J.: Princeton University Press.

Sassen, Saskia. 1983. The new labor demand: Conditions for the absorption of immigrant workers in the U.S.: Summary. New York: UNESCO.

Schoepfle, Gregory K., and Jorge F. Pérez-López. 1990. Employment implications of export assembly operations in Mexico and the Caribbean Basin. Washington, D.C.: Commission for the Study of International Migration and Cooperative Economic Development.

Sewell, William Hamilton, and Robert Mason Hauser. 1975. Education, occupation, and earnings: Achievement in the early career. New York: Academic Press.

Sewell, William H., Archibald D. Haller, and Alejandro Portes. 1969. The educational and early occupational attainment process. *American Sociological Review* 34 (February), pp. 82–92.

Sharp, Deborah. 1993. English: Kids' language of choice. *USA Today,* 7 July, p. A-1.

Simmons, Roberta G., Richard Burgeson, Steven Carlton-Ford, and Dale A. Blythe. 1987. The impact of cumulative change in early adolescence. *Child Development* 58 (October), pp. 1120–1234.

Simon, Rita J. 1993. Old minorities, new immigrants: Aspirations, hopes and fears. *Annals of the American Academy of Political and Social Science* 530 (November), pp. 61–73.

Smith, Madorah Elizabeth. 1939. *Some light on the problem of bilingualism as found from a study of the progress in mastery of English among preschool children of non-American ancestry in Hawaii.* Provincetown, Mass.: The Journal Press.

Smith, Michael P., and Luis E. Guarnizo, eds. 1998. *Transnationalism from Below.* New Brunswick, N.J.: Transactions.

Smith-Hefner, Nancy Joan. 1999. *Khmer American: Identity and moral education in a diasporic community.* Berkeley: University of California Press.

Sontag, Deborah. 1993. A fervent "no" to assimilation in new America. *The New York Times,* 29 June.

Stepick, Alex. 1992. "The refugees nobody wants: Haitians in Miami." In *Miami now! Immigration, ethnicity, and social change,* edited by Guillermo Grenier and Alex Stepick. Gainsville: University Press of Florida.

———. 1998. *Pride against prejudice: Haitians in the United States.* Boston: Allyn and Bacon.

Suárez-Orozco, Marcelo. 1987. "Towards a psychosocial understanding of Hispanic adaptation to American schooling." In *Success or failure? Learning the languages of minority students,* edited by Henry T. Trueba. New York: Newbury House Publishers.

Suárez-Orozco, Marcelo M., and Carola Suárez-Orozco. 1995. "The cultural patterning of achievement motivation: A comparative study of Mexican, Mexican Immigrant, and non-Latino white American youth in schools." In *California's immigrant children: Theory, research, and implications for educational policy,* edited by Rubén G. Rumbaut and Wayne A. Cornelius. San Diego: Center for U.S.-Mexican Studies, University of California.

Sullivan, Mercer. 1989. *Getting paid: Youth crime and work in the inner city.* Ithaca, N.Y.: Cornell University Press.

Szapocznik, José, Mercedes A. Scopetta, William Kurtines, and María D. Aranalde. 1978. Theory and measurement of acculturation. *Revista Inter-Americana de Psicología* 12, no. 2, pp. 112–130.

Tan, Amy. 1989. *The Joy Luck Club.* New York: Putnam.

Tajfel, Henri. 1981. *Human groups and social categories.* London: Cambridge University Press, 1981.

Thomas, Brinley. 1973. *Migration and economic growth: A study of Great Britain and the Atlantic economy.* Cambridge, U.K.: Cambridge University Press.

Thomas, William I., and Dorothy Swaine Thomas. 1928. *The child in America.* New York: Knopf.

Thomas, William I., and Florian Znaniecki. 1958 [1918–1920]. *The Polish peasant in Europe and America.* New York: Dover.

Tienda, Marta, and Haya Stier. 1996. "The wages of race: Color and employment opportunity in Chicago's inner city." In *Origins and destinies: Immigration, race, and ethnicity in America,* edited by Silvia Pedraza and Rubén G. Rumbaut. Belmont, Calif.: Wadsworth.

Tilly, Charles. 1996. "Citizenship, identity, and social history." In *Citizenship, identity, and social history,* edited by Charles Tilly. New York: Cambridge University Press.

Trillin, Abigail. 1998. Policy by anecdote. *The New York Times,* 19 May.

Tumulty, Karen. 1989. When Irish eyes are hiding. *Los Angeles Times,* January 29, p. A-1.

Turner, R. Jay, Blair Wheaton, and Donald J. Lloyd. 1995. The epidemiology of social stress. *American Sociological Review* 60 (February), pp. 104–125.

Unz, Ron. 1999. California and the end of white America. *Commentary* 108 (November), pp. 17–28.

Updegrave, Walter. 1999. Assessing your wealth. *Money* 28 (July), pp. 63–73.

U.S. Census Bureau. 1998. *U.S. employment data: 1950–1997.* Washington, D.C.: U.S. Bureau of Labor Statistics.

———. 1999. *Profile of the foreign-born population in the United States: 1997.* Current population reports, special studies P23–195. Washington, D.C.: U.S. Department of Commerce.

Veerasarn, Oi. 1999. The faces of Asian America. *Common Quest* 4, no. 1, pp. 46–55.

Vega, William A., Thomas Patterson, James Sallis, Philip Nader, Catherine Atkins, and Ian Abramson. 1986. Cohesion and adaptability in Mexican-American and Anglo families. *Journal of Marriage and the Family* 48 (November), pp. 857–867.

Vega, William A., and Rubén G. Rumbaut. 1991. Ethnic minorities and mental health. *Annual Review of Sociology* 17, pp. 351–383.

Veltman, Calvin J. 1983. *Language shift in the United States.* New York: Mouton.

Viadero, Debra. 2000. Generation gap. *Education Week,* June 7, pp. 6–7.

Vigil, James Diego. 1988. *Barrio gangs: Street life and identity in southern California.* Austin: University of Texas Press.

Viglucci, Andrés, and Marilyn Marks. 1993. Family and community ties help immigrant students excel. *Miami Herald,* 26 December.

Wacquant, Loïc J., and William J. Wilson. 1989. The cost of racial and class exclusion in the inner city. *Annals of the American Academy of Political and Social Science* 501, pp. 8–26.

Waldinger, Roger, and Mehdi Bozorgmehr. 1996. "The making of a multicultural metropolis." In *Ethnic Los Angeles,* edited by Roger Waldinger and Mehdi Bozorgmehr. New York: Russell Sage Foundation.

Waldinger, Roger, and Joel Perlmann. 1998. Second generations: Past, present, future. *Journal of Ethnic and Migration Studies* 24 (January), pp. 5–24.

Warner, W. Lloyd, and Leo Srole. 1945. *The social systems of American ethnic groups.* New Haven, Conn.: Yale University Press.

Waters, Mary C. 1990. *Ethnic options: Choosing identities in America.* Berkeley: University of California Press.

———. 1994. West Indian immigrants, African Americans, and whites in the Workplace: Different perspectives on American race relations. Paper presented at the annual meeting of the American Sociological Association, Los Angeles.

———. 1996. "Ethnic and racial identities of second generation black immigrants in New York City." In *The new second generation,* edited by Alejandro Portes. New York: Russell Sage Foundation.

———. 1997. "Immigrant families at risk: Factors that undermine chances for success." In *Immigration and the family: Research and policy on U.S. immigrants,* edited by Alan Booth, Ann C. Crouter, and Nancy S. Landale. Mahwah, N.J.: Lawrence Erlbaum.

Whyte, William F. 1955 [1943]. *Street corner society: The social structure of an Italian slum.* 2d ed. Boulder, Colo.: Westview Press.

Wilson, Franklin D. 1999. "Ethnic concentrations and labor market opportunities." In *Immigration and opportunity: Race, ethnicity, and employment in the United States,* edited by Frank D. Bean and Stephanie Bell-Rose. New York: Russell Sage Foundation.

Wilson, Kenneth, and W. Allen Martin. 1982. Ethnic enclaves: A comparison of the Cuban and black economies in Miami. *American Journal of Sociology* 88 (July), pp. 135–160.

Wilson, William J. 1987. *The truly disadvantaged: The inner city, the underclass, and public policy.* Chicago: University of Chicago Press.

Wolf, Diane L. 1997. Family secrets: Transnational struggles among children of Filipino immigrants. *Sociological Perspectives* 40 (Fall), pp. 455–482.

Woo, Elaine. 1997. School success of immigrants' children tracked. *Los Angeles Times,* 16 June, p. A-1.

———. 1998. Home life plays a crucial role in students' success or failure. *Los Angeles Times,* 18 May, p. A-1.

Wright, Lawrence. 1994. One drop of blood. *The New Yorker,* 25 July, pp. 46–55.

Yabiku, Scott T., William G. Axinn, and Arland Thorton. 1999. Family integration and children's self-esteem. *American Journal of Sociology* 104 (March), pp. 1494–1524.

Zaldivar, R. A. 1997. Cubanos en el último lugar de sondeo: imagen negativa en la prensa parece originar opinión. *El Nuevo Herald,* 16 June.

Zhou, Min. 1992. *Chinatown: The socioeconomic potential of an urban enclave.* Philadelphia: Temple University Press.

———. 1997. Growing up American: The challenge confronting immigrant children and children of immigrants." *Annual Review of Sociology* 23, pp. 63–95.

Zhou, Min, and Carl L. Bankston III. 1998. *Growing up American: The adaptation of Vietnamese adolescents in the United States.* New York: Russell Sage Foundation.

———. 1996. "Social capital and the adaptation of the second generation: The case of Vietnamese youth in New Orleans." In *The new second generation,* edited by Alejandro Portes. New York: Russell Sage Foundation.

Zimmerman, B. A., A. Bandura, and M. Martínez-Pons. 1992. Self-motivation for academic attainment: The role of self-efficacy beliefs and personal goal-setting. *American Educational Research Journal* 29 (Fall), pp. 663–676.

Zolberg, Aristide. 1997. "Modes of incorporation: Toward a comparative framework." In *Citizenship and education,* edited by Veit Bader. New York: St. Martin's Press.

Zolberg, Aristide, Astri Shurke, and Sergio Aguayo. 1986. International factors in the formation of refugee movements. *International Migration Review* 20 (Summer), pp. 151–169.

INDEX

academic achievement. *See* education;
educational achievement
acculturation: adaptation and, 68f; ambition and, 106, 107, 226, 228t; educational achievement and, 235; ethnic
self-identity determinants, 181, 182t,
187; ethnic self-identity development,
149–50, 153, 190, 191; ethnic self-
identity patterns, 160, 166–67,
168–70t; family status and, 85; psychological well-being and, 222t; racial
self-identity determinants, 181, 184t,
188; role reversal and, 49–54; time
and, 281–84. *See also* consonant
acculturation; dissonant acculturation;
language acculturation/adaptation; residency; selective acculturation
achievement: community and pride, 108,
110; general trends, 72–73; nationality
and, 73–76, 77; parental economic,
76, 78–85. *See also* citizenship; education; educational achievement; occupational status; socioeconomic status
active encouragement, 46, 47
adaptation, 70–72, 90; ambition and,
107; Children of Immigrants Longitudinal Study, 22, 25, 31, 42; early,
72–85; immigrant incorporation and,
46–49, 50t; nationality and family

composition, 85–90; second-
generation, 55–62
additive effects, 76, 78–82
African Americans: identity, 151,
152–53; Los Angeles riots and, 148
African immigrants and descendants: ethnic self-identities, 163t; language
acculturation, 129t; nativity patterns,
164t; racial discrimination and, 55;
racial self-identity, 179t
age: additive effects and, 78, 79t, 80;
ambition and, 226, 228t, 230; bilingualism and, 116, 139t, 142t; Children of Immigrants Longitudinal
Study, 28t, 30t; educational achievement, early, 240t, 242; educational
achievement, late adolescent, 248t;
family status and, 86, 87t, 88; immigrant incorporation and, 50t; psychological well-being and, 222t; racial
self-identity determinants, 184t; school
attrition and, 256t; U.S. Census, 34
Alba, Richard, 149
Alvarez, Julia, 230
ambition, 103–7, 225–30; acculturation
and, 282; education and, 219, 365n.
10; ethnic identity and, 171, 191; fluent bilingualism and, 364–65n. 9;
Mexican immigrants and descendants,

ambition (*continued*)
276, 280; reactive ethnicity and, 285; school attrition and, 252, 255, 258; selective acculturation and, 275

American identity, 154; development of, 150; ethnic identity and, 154–55, 157, 182–83t, 190; family status and language, 166, 167, 168–70t; immigrant parents and, 171, 172t; national-origin identity and, 161, 162–63t; nativity patterns and, 165–66; region, schools, and discrimination, 173, 174–75t, 176; stability and salience, 157–58. *See also* hyphenated American identity

Americanization: ambition and, 106; ethnic identity and, 189–90; European immigrants and descendants, 360n. 36; language acculturation and, 125f; permissiveness and, 98–99, 101t

ancestor worship, 260

Anglos. *See* European immigrants and descendants; white identity

animists, 260

apathetic reaction, 152

Argentinean immigrants and descendants, 128t

Armenian immigrants and descendants, 148

Asian identity, 154; Americanization and, 190; ethnic self-identity and, 160–61, 163t; national origin and, 177, 178–79t; racial self-identity and, 180f, 181, 188; school attrition and, 259f; shifts in, 155. *See also* ethnic identity; panethnic identity; *specific nationalities*

Asian immigrants and descendants, 21, 22; achievement, 74, 74t; additive effects and, 78, 80, 81; ambition, 103, 104t, 105; bilingualism, 137, 139t, 141, 142t; Children of Immigrants Longitudinal Study, 27t, 29t, 32t, 40–41t, 38; community and pride, 109t, 110; discrimination, 55; educational achievement, 235, 236t, 237, 243, 362–63n. 19; educational expectations, 216, 217t, 219; ethnic self-identities, 160–61, 163t; family cohesion, conflict, and change, 198f, 200, 201; family status, 86, 87t, 88, 89; government assistance for, 73; homework, 362n. 15; language acculturation, 123t, 124, 126, 127, 129t; nativity patterns, 164t, 164; parent-child interactions, 194; permissiveness and, 99, 100–101t, 102; psychological well-being, 207, 208t, 224; racial self-

identity, 177, 179t; reception of, 281, 364n. 6; role reversal, 52; school attrition, 253, 254f, 259f; school engagement and effort, 212t, 213–14, 215, 357n. 41; U.S. Census, 37. *See also specific nationalities*

aspirations, 193, 215; ambition and, 106f, 226, 227, 228–29t, 230; Children of Immigrants Longitudinal Study, 30t; community and pride, 111; educational achievement and, 250; educational expectations and, 215–16, 217–18t, 219; family status and, 86; gender and, 64; language acculturation and, 131, 132f; Mexican immigrants and descendants, 278, 280; permissiveness and, 102; school engagement and effort, 212t

assimilation: forceful, 271, 272, 273, 276, 277; identificational, 150. *See also* Americanization; downward assimilation; ideologies; segmented assimilation

Bay of Pigs, 262

Belize, 61

bias, Children of Immigrants Longitudinal Study, 25

bilingual education: cognitive development and, 117; language acculturation and, 128–34; language instruction and, 146

bilingualism, 114; ambition and, 227, 228t; determinants of, 134–43; discrimination and, 363n. 20; educational achievement, early, 238, 239, 240t, 242, 243; educational achievement, late adolescent, 248t, 250; educational expectations and, 218t; ethnic self-identity patterns and, 169t; family cohesion, conflict, and change, 199t, 201; language acculturation and, 121–22, 123t, 126, 127; language instruction and, 145–46; Mexican immigrants and descendants, 278, 280; past and present, 115–18; psychological well-being and, 209t, 221, 222t; psychosocial adaptation and, 364–65n. 9; racial identity and, 180; school attrition and, 256t; school engagement and effort, 214; schools and, 357n. 41; selective acculturation and, 274–76; subtractive, 135. *See also* California Proposition 227

birthplace. *See* nationality/national origin

black identity, 154; ethnic, 152–53; immigrant, 153; national origin and, 177,

178–79t; racial self-identity and, 153, 180f, 181, 184–85t, 188, 189; region, schools, and discrimination, 173; school attrition and, 258, 259f; shifts in, 156f. *See also* ethnic identity; panethnic identity; *specific nationalities*

black immigrants. *See specific nationalities*

Bracero labor contract program, 271–72

Brazilian immigrants and descendants, Children of Immigrants Longitudinal Study, 23

Brigham, Carl, 115

Buddhism, 260

California, 34, 35t, 37; educational achievement, 238, 240t, 248t; educational aspirations and expectations, 228t; ethnic identity, 173, 182–83t, 186, 189–90; Mexican immigrants and descendants, 277, 279; psychological well-being, 222t, 224; racial self-identity determinants, 184–85t, 188; school attrition, 256t. *See also specific cities and immigrant nationalities*

California Proposition 187: ethnic identity and, 147–48, 152, 160; ideology and, 270, 271; reactive ethnicity and, 148, 160, 284–85; unconstitutionality of, 357–58n. 4

California Proposition 227: forced-march acculturation and, 130–31; ideology and, 269–70, 271, 273–74; language instruction and, 144, 366n. 3

Cambodian immigrants and descendants, 21; achievement, 74t; additive effects and, 79t, 80, 82; ambition, 103, 104t, 105, 229t; Children of Immigrants Longitudinal Study, 23, 27t, 29t, 31, 32t, 40–41t, 38; community and pride, 108, 109t, 110; educational achievement, early, 235, 236t, 237, 241t, 243, 244; educational achievement, late adolescent, 245f, 246f, 249t, 250; educational achievement paradox, 258, 260–61; educational expectations, 217t; ethnic identity, 154, 163t; family cohesion, conflict, and change, 198f, 200, 201; family status, 86f, 87t, 88; immigrant incorporation, 50t; Keng, Sophy (fictitious name), 12–14, 19; language acculturation, 123t, 127, 129t; language instruction, 144, 145; nativity patterns, 164t, 164; parent-child interactions, 194–95; permissiveness and, 97, 99, 100–101t; psycho-

logical well-being, 207, 208t, 223t; racial self-identity, 179t; school attrition, 254f, 257t; school engagement and effort, 212t; school environment, 203; student occupational status, 265, 267

Canadian immigrants and descendants: achievement, 73–74; Children of Immigrants Longitudinal Study, 27t, 38; educational expectations, 216, 217t; ethnic identity and, 161, 163t; family cohesion, conflict, and change, 198f, 201; language acculturation, 125, 129t; nativity patterns, 164t, 165; psychological well-being, 207, 208t, 210; discrimination and, 55; racial identity and, 177, 179t, 180; school engagement and effort, 212t, 214

capitalism, corporate, 271, 272

careers. *See* occupational status

Caribbean immigrants and descendants, 21, 22; Children of Immigrants Longitudinal Study, 38; family cohesion, conflict, and change, 201; family status, 86, 88, 90. *See also* West Indian immigrants and descendants; *specific nationalities*

Castro, Fidel, 149, 262

Catholicism (Roman), 260

Caucasians. *See* European immigrants and descendants; white identity

census. *See* U.S. Census

Center for Epidemiological Studies-Depression (CES-D) short-form scale, 133, 207, 221, 224

Central American immigrants and descendants. *See specific nationalities*

Chicago, 20t

Chicano identity, 153, 154, 155, 160. *See also* ethnic identity; panethnic identity; *specific nationalities*

Child, Irvin, 152, 193

children. *See* immigrant second generation

Children of Immigrants Longitudinal Study (CILS), 22–33; follow-up questionnaire, 25, 28–29t, 287–306; parental questionnaire, 307–38; results, 37–43

Chilean immigrants and descendants, 128t

Chinese immigrants and descendants, 21; achievement, 74t; ambition, 103, 104t, 105, 229t; Children of Immigrants Longitudinal Study, 23, 27t, 40–41t; community and pride, 109t, 110; educational achievement, early, 235, 236t,

Chinese immigrants and descendants (*continued*)
241t, 242, 244; educational achievement, late adolescent, 244, 245f, 246f, 249t, 250, 251; educational expectations, 216, 217t, 362–63n. 19; ethnic self-identities, 160–61, 163t; family cohesion, conflict, and change, 198f, 201; family status, 86f; immigrant incorporation, 50t; language acculturation, 123t, 129t; permissiveness and, 100–101t, 102; psychological well-being, 208t, 223t; school attrition, 253, 257t; school engagement and effort, 212t; selective acculturation, 275; speech patterns, 115; student occupational status, 265t

cholos, 153

Christianity, 260

citizenship: achievement and, 74t, 75, 75f; adaptation and, 73; Children of Immigrants Longitudinal Study, 26t, 28t, 30t, 31, 33t; ethnic self-identity determinants, 182t, 186, 188–89; racial self-identity determinants, 186, 188–89

Clinton, William Jefferson, 262

cliques, 361n. 7

cognitive development, 115, 117

college education. *See* education

Colombian immigrants and descendants: achievement, 74t; additive effects and, 79t; ambition and, 104t, 229t; Children of Immigrants Longitudinal Study, 23, 24, 27t, 29t, 32t, 40–41t; community and pride, 109t; educational achievement, 241t, 249t; educational expectations, 217t; ethnic self-identities, 160–61, 162t; family cohesion, conflict, and change, 198f; family status, 86f, 87t; immigrant incorporation, 50t; language acculturation, 123t; nativity patterns, 164t; permissiveness and, 97, 100–101t; psychological well-being, 208t, 223t; Restrepo, Rodolfo (fictitious name), 70, 72; school attrition, 254f, 257t; school engagement and effort, 212t, 214; school environment, 206; student occupational status, 265t

colonialism, 271, 272

community. *See* immigrant community; neighborhoods

Confucian ethic, 260

Consciousness Explained (Dennett), 225

consonant acculturation, 367n. 10; definition of, 54; educational expectations and, 219; family cohesion, conflict, and

change, 199; language instruction and, 145; outcomes, 53t, 66t

consonant resistance, 53t

consumerism, 65, 102, 106

corporate capitalism, 271, 272

corporate downsizing, 57

Costa Rican immigrants and descendants, 126, 128t

countercultures, 59–62, 66t. *See also* crime; drugs; gangs; permissiveness; violence

crime: countercultures and, 60; family cohesion, conflict, and change, 198; Mariel Cubans and, 365n. 19

Cuban immigrants and descendants, 21; acculturation, 281; achievement, 74, 74t; additive effects and, 79t, 80; ambition, 103, 104t, 106, 227, 229t; bilingualism, 137; Children of Immigrants Longitudinal Study, 23, 24, 27t, 29t, 31, 32t, 39, 40–41t; community and pride, 109t, 110; crime and, 365n. 19; de los Angeles, María (fictitious name), 2–3, 18; discrimination, 365n. 21; educational achievement, early, 235, 236t, 237, 241t, 242–43, 244; educational achievement, late adolescent, 245f, 246f, 249t, 250; educational achievement paradox, 261–67; educational expectations, 216, 217t; ethnic identity, 154, 160, 161, 162t, 190–91; family cohesion, conflict, and change, 198f, 200; family status, 86f, 87t; government assistance for, 73; immigrant incorporation, 50t; interaction effects and, 83, 84; language acculturation, 123t, 124, 127, 128t; language instruction, 145; Marín family (fictitious name), 91–93, 94; Montejo, Efrén (fictitious name), 7–8, 18; nativity patterns, 164t, 165; permissiveness and, 100–101t; psychological well-being, 207, 208t, 210, 223t; racial self-identity, 177, 178t, 180; refugees, 149; Santana, Yvette (fictitious name), 2–3, 18, 106; school attrition, 253, 254f, 257t, 258; school engagement and effort, 212t, 214; school environment and, 203; selective acculturation, 275; U.S. arrival date, 365–66n. 22, 366n. 23; unpopularity of, 358n. 8

culture. *See* acculturation; countercultures

Current Population Survey (CPS), 351n. 12

Davis, Gray, 357–58n. 4

deindustrialization, 56–59

Dennett, Daniel C., 225
depression: gender and, 362n. 12; language acculturation and, 132f, 133; self-esteem and, 207–10, 211f, 220–25
discipline: ambition and, 104t, 105; Asian educational achievement and, 260; countercultures and, 60; educational expectations and, 218; permissiveness and, 98; school engagement and effort, 212, 215; school environment and, 203
discrimination: acculturation and, 66t; adaptation and, 55–56; ambition and, 228t; Children of Immigrants Longitudinal Study, 40–41t, 38–39; countercultures and, 59, 60; ethnic identity and, 152–53, 159–60, 171, 173–76, 181, 183t, 186, 187, 189; Haitian immigrants and descendants, 354n. 4; interaction effects and, 83; language acculturation and, 124; Mariel Cubans, 365n. 21; Mexican immigrants and descendants, 280; nativism and, 272; psychological well-being and, 221, 222t, 225; racial identity and, 181, 185t, 186, 187–88, 189; self-esteem and, 363n. 20; West Indian immigrants and descendants, 354n. 4. See also race
dissonant acculturation, 52, 53t, 54, 268, 283f; ambition and, 106, 107, 227, 230; bilingualism and, 140; community and pride, 108; educational achievement, early, 238, 239, 243; educational achievement, late adolescent, 246, 250; educational expectations and, 219; family cohesion, conflict, and change, 85, 193, 199, 201; forceful assimilation and, 273; immigrant community and, 65, 66t; language acculturation and, 126, 127, 130, 134; language instruction and, 144, 145–46; Mexican immigrants and descendants, 276, 279; permissiveness and, 98, 99, 102; psychological well-being and, 210, 225; school attrition and, 258; school engagement and effort, 214
Doctorow, E. L., 156
Dominican immigrants and descendants, 21; Children of Immigrants Longitudinal Study, 23, 27t; Cruz, Betty (fictitious name), 98; educational expectations, 216, 217t; ethnic identity, 151, 160–61, 162t; family cohesion, conflict, and change, 198f, 201; Hernández, family (fictitious name), 4–6, 19, 61; immigrant incorporation, 50t; language acculturation, 128t; Mendoza, Josè, 151; nativity patterns, 164t; permissiveness and, 98, 99; psychological well-being, 208t; school engagement and effort, 212t, 214
Dominican Republic, 61. See also Dominican immigrants and descendants
downsizing, 57
downward assimilation, 65, 66t; acculturation and, 283; adaptation and, 59–62; ambition and, 106f; ethnic identity and, 151; language instruction and, 144; Mexican immigrants and descendants, 279, 280; permissiveness and, 99, 102; reactive ethnicity and, 285
dropouts. See school attrition
drugs: as adaptation challenge, 59, 62; family status and, 85; immigrant parent optimism and, 96t; school environment and, 203, 204–7

earnings. See income; socioeconomic status
East Indian immigrants and descendants, 73
East Los Angeles, 285
economic achievement, parental, 76, 78–82. See also achievement
economy. See global economy; labor market
Ecuadorian immigrants and descendants, language acculturation, 128t
education: achievement and, 73, 74, 75, 75f; adaptation and, 68f, 73; additive effects and, 76, 78, 79, 80, 81, 82f; ambition and, 103, 104t, 365n. 10; Children of Immigrants Longitudinal Study, 26t; community and pride, 108; countercultures and, 60, 61; ethnic identity and, 166–67, 168t, 169t; family status and, 86, 87t, 88; gender and, 64; immigrant communities and, 65; immigrant incorporation and, 46, 48, 49, 50t; immigrant parent optimism and, 95, 96t; interaction effects and, 83t, 84; labor market and, 58–59; Mexican immigrants and descendants, 278–79, 280; permissiveness and, 98, 99, 100–101t, 102; racial identity and, 180, 181; reactive ethnicity and, 285; school engagement and effort, 211–15; U.S. Census, 34, 35t. See also bilingualism; language; language acculturation/adaptation; schools

educational achievement, 233–34, 267–68; acculturation and, 282–83; Cuban Americans, 261–67; early, 234–44; fluent bilingualism and, 364–65n. 9; forceful assimilation and, 273; immigrant parents and, 357n. 46; late adolescent, 244–58, 259f; Mexican immigrants and descendants, 279; motivation for, 351n. 16; selective acculturation and, 274, 275–76; Southeast Asians, 258, 260–61

educational aspirations. See aspirations

educational expectations, 215–19, 220f; acculturation and, 281, 282; adaptation and, 68f; ambition and, 103–7, 226, 227, 228–29t, 230; Asian immigrants and descendants, 260, 362–63n. 19; Children of Immigrants Longitudinal Study, 40–41t, 38, 39; countercultures and, 61; educational achievement, 242, 247–48, 251; fluent bilingualism and, 364–65n. 9; forceful assimilation and, 273; Mexican immigrants and descendants, 278; psychological well-being and, 224; school attrition and, 255, 256t; school engagement and effort, 212, 215; selective acculturation and, 274

educational policy, language acculturation and, 130–31. See also California Proposition 227; government policy; ideologies; politics

embarrassment, 193; ambition and, 228t; family cohesion, conflict, and change, 198–99t, 200, 201; psychological well-being and, 221, 222t, 225

employment: bilingualism and, 274; immigrant communities and, 366; U.S. Census, 36t. See also global economy; labor market; occupational status; socioeconomic status; unemployment

English for the Children initiative. See California Proposition 227

English Knowledge Index, 119f, 120, 127, 356n. 24

English-language dominance: educational expectations and, 218t; ethnic identity and, 169t; family cohesion, conflict, and change, 199t, 201; language acculturation and, 123t, 131, 132f, 133f; predictors of, 136–37t; psychological well-being and, 209t; racial self-identity determinants, 184t. See also limited bilingualism; monolingualism

entrepreneurship: acculturation and, 282, 283f; achievement and, 75–76; ambition and, 103; Cuban educational achievement and, 262, 266, 267; immigrant communities and, 64

Escalante, Jaime, 285

ethnic communities. See immigrant communities

ethnic identity, xvii, 147–49, 189–91; adaptation and, 68f; determinants of, 181–89; discrimination and, 55–56; educational achievement, 246; family status, composition, and language, 166–71; language acculturation and, 130; Latin American immigrants and descendants, 359–60n. 29; Mexican immigrants and descendants, 278; nationality and family, 161, 164–66, 275, 359n. 26, 360n. 33; parental self-identity and, 171, 172t; past research, 152–54; patterns of, 154–61, 162–63t; race and, 55–56, 176–81; region, schools, and discrimination, 171, 173–76; segmented assimilation and, 45; self-development of, 149–52; U.S. Census, 35t; U.S. Office of Management and Budget, 358–59n. 15. See also reactive ethnicity

European immigrants and descendants, 18; achievement, 73–74, 74t; ambition, 104t; Americanization of, 99, 360n. 36; Children of Immigrants Longitudinal Study, 27t; community and pride, 109t, 110f; discrimination and, 55; educational expectations, 217t; ethnic identity and, 149–50, 161, 163t, 189–90; family cohesion, conflict, and change, 198f, 201; labor markets and, 56, 57; language acculturation, 123t, 129t; nativity patterns, 164t, 165; permissiveness and, 100–101t, 102; psychological well-being, 207, 208t, 210; racial self-identity and, 177, 179t, 180; role reversal, 52; school engagement and effort, 212t, 214; social acceptance of, 47, 48; speech patterns, 115

exclusion, 46

expectations. See educational expectations

extended family. See family status/composition; immigrant communities

familism, 198–99t, 201, 202

family change, 197–202, 210

family cohesion, 197–202; educational expectations and, 218t, 219; psychological well-being and, 209t, 210, 211f; school engagement and effort, 213t, 214–15 family conflict (parent-child), 197–202; ambition and, 227, 228t; educational achievement and, 238, 239, 240t, 248t, 250; educational expectations and, 218t, 219; psychological well-being and, 209t, 210, 211f, 222t, 225; school attrition and, 256t

family status/composition, 166–71; acculturation and, 49–54, 283f; adaptation and, 68f, 73; ambition and, 228t; bilingualism and, 116, 135–36, 138, 140; Children of Immigrants Longitudinal Study, 27t, 28t, 30t, 31, 32t, 40–41t, 38, 39; educational achievement, early, 235, 237, 238, 239, 240t, 242, 243; educational achievement, late adolescent, 248, 249; ethnic identity and, 159–60, 161, 164–71, 180–81, 182t, 189; immigrant incorporation and, 49, 50t; nationality and, 85–90, 161, 164–66; permissiveness and, 99; psychological well-being and, 222t, 225; racial identity and, 180–81, 184t, 188, 189; role reversal, 49–54; school attrition and, 252, 255, 256t, 258; segmented assimilation and, 66t; social capital and, 64–65; U.S. Census, 35t, 36t. See also immigrant parent outlooks; immigrant parents

Filipino immigrants and descendants, 21; achievement, 74, 74t; additive effects and, 79t; ambition, 103, 104t, 229t; Aparicio family (fictitious name), 111–12; Children of Immigrants Longitudinal Study, 23, 24, 27t, 29t, 31, 32t, 39, 40–41t; community and pride, 109t, 110; educational achievement, early, 235, 236t, 241t, 244; educational achievement, late adolescent, 245f, 249t; educational achievement paradox, 260–61; educational expectations, 217t, 362–63n. 19; ethnic identity, 154, 157, 160, 161, 163t; family cohesion, conflict, and change, 198f; family status, 86, 87t, 89; immigrant incorporation, 50t; language and, 73, 123t, 125, 129t; Montoya family (fictitious name), 11–12, 19; nativity patterns, 164t, 164; permissiveness and, 100–101t, 102; psychological well-being, 208t, 223t, 224; racial self-identity, 179t, 188–89; school attrition, 254f, 257t; school engagement and effort, 212t; speech patterns, 115; student occupational status, 265t

first generation. See immigrant parents

Florida, 34, 35t, 37; Cuban educational achievement, 261–67; educational achievement, 238, 249; ethnic identity, 173, 174–75t; racial identity, 188. See also specific cities and immigrant nationalities

fluent bilingualism, 116, 117; ambition and, 227, 228t, 230; definition of, 356n. 25; educational achievement, 238, 240t, 242, 243, 248t, 250; educational expectations and, 218t, 219; ethnic self-identity patterns and, 169t; family cohesion, conflict, and change, 199t, 201; language acculturation and, 122, 126, 127, 131, 133–34; Mexican immigrants and descendants, 278; occupational opportunities and, 117–18; predictors of, 135–43; psychological well-being and, 209t, 221, 222t, 224, 225; psychosocial adaptation and, 364–65n. 9; racial self-identity determinants, 184t; school attrition and, 256t; school engagement and effort, 214–15; school systems and, 135; selective acculturation and, 274, 275

Folmar, Kate, 276

Fong-Torres, Ben, 192–93

forced-march language acculturation, 128–34

forceful assimilation, 271, 272, 273, 276, 277

foreign-language dominance: educational expectations and, 218t; family cohesion, conflict, and change, 199t, 201; language acculturation and, 123t, 131, 132f, 133f; psychological well-being and, 209t

Foreign Language Knowledge Index, 120, 127, 356n. 24

Fort Lauderdale. See Children of Immigrants Longitudinal Study; Florida; Miami

French Canadians, 116

friends. See peers

gangs: as adaptation challenge, 59, 62; ambition and, 105; ethnic self-identity and, 153; family status and, 85; school environment and, 203, 204–5t. See also permissiveness

garment industry, 57

gender: achievement and, 76, 77t; adaptation and, 68f; additive effects and, 78, 79, 81, 82f; ambition and, 226, 227, 228t, 230; bilingualism and, 116, 136t, 139t, 140, 141, 142t; Children of Immigrants Longitudinal Study, 26t,

gender (*continued*)
28t, 30t, 32t; discrimination and, 363n. 20; educational achievement and, 240t, 242, 248t, 251; educational expectations and, 216, 217t, 219; ethnic identity and, 151, 159–60, 168t; interaction effects and, 83t; monolingualism and, 136t; psychological well-being and, 208t, 210, 222t, 225, 362n. 12; racial identity and, 184t; school attrition and, 256t, 258, 259f; school engagement and effort, 212t, 215; social capital and, 64–65

German immigrants and descendants, 18, 116

ghettos. *See* countercultures

global economy: ideology and, 273; language skills and, 117–18, 274

Gordon, Milton, 150

government assistance, 193; adaptation and, 73; educational achievement, early, 242; family status and, 88; interaction effects and, 83; psychological well-being and, 224

government policy: additive effects and, 78; immigrant incorporation and, 46, 47. *See also* California Proposition 187; California Proposition 227; ideologies; politics

grades: acculturation and, 281, 282; ambition and, 104t, 105, 226, 228t; Asian educational achievement and, 260, 261; bilingualism and, 117, 138, 139t, 142t; Children of Immigrants Longitudinal Study, 26t, 30t; Cuban educational achievement and, 261, 264f, 266; discrimination and, 363n. 20; educational achievement, early, 234–35, 236t, 237, 239, 240–41t, 242; educational achievement, late adolescent, 245f, 246, 247, 248–49, 250–51; fluent bilingualism and, 364–65n. 9; Mexican immigrants and descendants, 278; psychological well-being and, 221, 223t, 224; school attrition and, 252, 253, 255, 257t, 258; school engagement and effort, 212–13, 214f, 215; senior high school, 245–51

grandparents. *See* immigrant communities

Guatemalan immigrants and descendants: Children of Immigrants Longitudinal Study, 23; de la Puente, Iris (fictional name), 252; language acculturation, 128t

Haitian immigrants and descendants: achievement, 73, 74t; additive effects and, 78, 79t, 80, 81; ambition, 103, 104t, 105, 229t; Children of Immigrants Longitudinal Study, 23, 24, 27t, 29t, 31, 32t, 38, 39, 40–41t; community and pride, 109t; countercultures and, 61; discrimination, 354n. 4; educational achievement, early, 235, 236t, 241t, 242; educational achievement, late adolescent, 245, 246f, 249t; educational expectations and, 217t; ethnic identity, 151, 157, 161, 162t; family cohesion, conflict, and change, 198f, 201; family status, 86f, 87t, 88; immigrant incorporation, 50t; language acculturation, 123t, 126, 128t; Maillol, Aristide (fictitious name), 4, 18, 103, 105; nativity patterns, 164t, 165; permissiveness and, 100–101t; psychological well-being, 208t, 223t; racial barriers, 48; racial self-identity, 177, 178t, 181; school attrition and, 253, 254f, 257t, 258; school engagement and effort, 212t, 213–14; student occupational status, 265t. *See also* Caribbean immigrants and descendants; West Indian immigrants and descendants

Hansen, Marcus Lee, 193

Hawaii, 115

health insurance, 36t

high school. *See* education; schools

Hispanic identity, 150, 154, 359–60n. 29; Americanization and, 190; ethnic self-identity and, 160; Mexican immigrants and descendants, 279; national origin and, 165, 177, 178–79t; racial self-identity, 180, 181, 188, 189; region, schools, and discrimination, 173; school attrition and, 258, 259f; shifts in, 156. *See also* ethnic identity; panethnic identity; *specific nationalities*

Hmong immigrants and descendants: additive effects and, 80; ambition, 103; Cha, Boua (fictitious name), 15–16, 19; Children of Immigrants Longitudinal Study, 27t, 29t, 31, 32t, 38, 40–41t; educational achievement, 260–61; educational expectations, 216, 217t; ethnic self-identities, 160, 163t; family cohesion, conflict, and change, 198f, 200, 201; language acculturation, 123t, 127, 129t; nativity patterns, 164t; psychological well-being, 207, 208t; school engagement and effort, 211, 212t, 214; Thao, Lia, 211, 214; Yang family (fictitious name), 93, 94,

102, 105. *See also* Laotian immigrants and descendants
home ownership, 27t
homework: ambition and, 104t, 105; Asian immigrants and descendants, 362n. 15; educational expectations and, 220f; Latin American immigrants and descendants, 362n. 15; school engagement and effort, 212–13, 214
Honduran immigrants and descendants, 128t
Hong Kong. *See* Chinese immigrants and descendants
household type. *See* family status/composition
Houston, 20t, 280
How the García Girls Lost Their Accent (Alvarez), 230
human capital: acculturation and, 54, 282, 283f; additive effects and, 76, 78–82; Asian immigrants and descendants, 258, 261, 364n. 6; educational achievement and, 235, 244, 250, 267–68; family status and, 89–90; immigrant incorporation and, 46–47, 48, 49, 50t; immigrant parents and, 62, 66t, 68f, 69; immigrant reception and, 280–81; interaction effects and, 82–85; Mexican immigrants and descendants, 277–78; role reversal and, 54; socioeconomic status and, 73–76, 77t. *See also* bilingualism; education; family status; language; socioeconomic status
Hwang, Caroline, 191, 193
hyperghetto, 59–60
hyphenated American identity, 154–55, 174–75t; ethnic identity and, 154–55, 157, 182–83t; family status and language, 167, 168–70t; national origin and, 162–63t, 166; parental self-identities and, 172t; stability and salience, 157–58

identificational assimilation, 150
identity. *See* ethnic identity; racial identity
ideologies: acculturation and, 281–84; California Proposition 227, 269–70; mainstream, 270–74; Mexican immigrants and descendants and, 276–80; reactive ethnicity and, 284–86; selective acculturation and, 274–76
Illinois, 34, 35t
immigrant communities: acculturation and, 53t, 54, 282, 283f; educational achievement and, 243, 260; immigrant

incorporation and, 46, 48; immigrant parent optimism and, 95; interaction effects and, 83; language acculturation and, 124; Mexican immigrants and descendants, 278, 280; nativism and, 272; permissiveness and, 99, 102; pride and, 107–11; role reversal and, 53t, 54; selective acculturation and, 275; social capital and, 64–69
immigrant identity. *See* ethnic identity; racial identity
immigrant parent outlooks, 111–12; ambition, 103–7; community and pride, 107–11; Marín, Aura Lila (fictitious name), 91–93, 94, 103, 145; optimism, 94–96; permissiveness, 97–102; Yang, Pao (fictitious name), 93, 94, 145
immigrant parents: acculturation, 49–54, 281, 282, 283; bilingualism, 135–43; California Proposition 227 and, 366n. 3; Children of Immigrants Longitudinal Study, 26–27t, 28–29t, 30t, 40–41t, 38, 39; discrimination, 354n. 4; economic achievement, 75, 78–82; educational achievement, 235, 357n. 46; educational expectations, 362–63n. 19; ethnic self-identity determinants, 181, 182–83t, 186, 189; ethnic self-identity patterns, 160, 161, 164, 165–66, 168–70t, 171, 172t; family cohesion, conflict, and change, 197–202; forced-march language acculturation, 130, 133f, 134; forceful assimilation, 273; incorporation modes and consequences, 46–49; language acculturation, 121, 122–28, 129t, 357n. 39; language instruction and, 144–45, 146; Mexican immigrants and descendants, 280; monolingualism and, 136t; racial identity, 177, 180, 181, 184t, 186, 188, 189; role reversal and, 49–54; self-identities, 171, 172t; U.S. Census, 34. *See also* achievement; adaptation; bilingualism; embarrassment; ethnic identity; family change; family cohesion; family conflict; family status; ideologies; language; language acculturation/adaptation; racial identity; segmented assimilation; social capital; socioeconomic status; *specific nationalities*
immigrant second generation: census results, 33–37; definition of, 23, 24; educational expectations, 215–19, 220f; family cohesion, conflict, and

immigrant second generation (*continued*)
change, 197–202; psychological well-
being, 207–10, 211f; psychosocial outcome determinants, 220–30; school
engagement and effort, 211–15; school
environments and peer groups, 203–7;
size and concentration of, 19–22. *See
also* achievement; adaptation; bilingualism; Children of Immigrants Longitudinal Study; ethnic identity; ideologies; language; language
acculturation/adaptation; racial identity; segmented assimilation; U.S. Census; *specific nationalities*
immigrant social capital, 62–69
immigrant stories. *See* Miami immigrant
stories; San Diego immigrant stories
immigration, history of, 17–18
imports, 56–57
income: achievement and, 73–74, 75,
75f, 77t; adaptation and, 73; additive
effects and, 76, 78–82; immigrant
incorporation and, 50t; interaction
effects and, 82–85; labor market and,
57, 58; Mexican immigrants and
descendants, 277–78; social capital
and, 62; U.S. Census, 36t. *See also*
achievement; socioeconomic status
Indian immigrants and descendants,
129t, 216
Indochinese immigrants and descendants,
21. *See also specific nationalities*
industrial labor. *See* labor markets
information technology, 57–58
in-group reaction, 152
inner cities. *See* countercultures
instruction quality. *See* teaching quality
intelligence, bilingualism and, 115, 116
interaction effects, 76, 82–85
international economy. *See* global economy
intransigent nativism. *See* nativism
Irish immigrants and descendants, 48, 55
Italian immigrants and descendants, 18,
55, 102, 152

Jamaican immigrants and descendants:
achievement, 74t; ambition, 104t;
Children of Immigrants Longitudinal
Study, 23, 27t, 32t, 38, 39, 40–41t;
community and pride, 109t; educational achievement, 244; educational
expectations, 217t; ethnic identity,
154, 162t; family cohesion, conflict,
and change, 198f; immigrant incorporation, 50t; language acculturation,
73, 122, 123t, 124, 128t; nativity pat-

terns, 164t; permissiveness and,
100–101t; psychological well-being,
208t; racial self-identity, 177, 178t,
181; school engagement and effort,
212t. *See also* Caribbean immigrants
and descendants; West Indian immigrants and descendants
Japan, 56
Japanese immigrants and descendants,
22; Children of Immigrants Longitudinal Study, 23; educational expectations, 216; language acculturation,
129t; speech patterns, 115
Jewish immigrants and descendants, 18
jobs. *See* global economy; labor market;
occupational status; socioeconomic
status; unemployment

Khmer immigrants and descendants. *See*
Cambodian immigrants and descendants; refugees
Korean immigrants and descendants, 21;
ambition, 229t; Children of Immigrants Longitudinal Study, 23; educational achievement, early, 235, 236t,
241t, 242, 244; educational achievement, late adolescent, 245f, 246f,
249t, 250, 251; educational expectations, 216, 362–63n. 19; ethnic identity, 151, 191; family status, 86f;
immigrant incorporation, 50t; language acculturation, 129t; Los Angeles
riots and, 148–49, 358n. 7; school
attrition, 253, 257t; selective acculturation, 275; speech patterns, 115; student occupational status, 265t

labor market: acculturation and, 66t;
adaptation and, 56–59; ideologies and,
271–72, 273; inner city decline and,
353n. 34; language skills and, 117–18;
Mexican immigrants and descendants,
271–72, 276, 277, 280
La Esperanza Improvement Association,
42, 43
language, 113–15; acculturation and, 282;
adaptation and, 68f, 73; additive effects
and, 78, 79, 80, 81, 82f; ambition and,
227, 228t, 230; Children of Immigrants
Longitudinal Study, 27t, 30t, 31,
40–41t, 38, 39; educational achievement and, 235, 237, 238, 239, 246,
248t; educational expectations and,
218t, 219; ethnic identity and, 150,
151, 153, 156–57, 159–60, 166–71;
family cohesion, conflict, and change,
199, 201; forceful assimilation and,

273; gender and, 64; immigrant parents and, 357n. 39; interaction effects and, 83t; nationality and achievement, 74, 75, 77t; psychological well-being and, 209t; racial discrimination and, 55; reactive ethnicity and, 284; role reversal and, 52, 53t, 54; school engagement and effort, 214–15; U.S. Census, 34, 35t, 36t; U.S. English movement 355n. 4. *See also* bilingualism; California Proposition 227; language acculturation/adaptation
language acculturation/adaptation, 113, 115, 230, 240t, 243; ethnic self-identity determinants, 182t, 186; ethnic self-identity patterns, 169t, 171; family cohesion, conflict, and change, 197; forced-march, 128–34; general trends, 118–22; language instruction and, 143–46; Mexican immigrants and descendants, 280; national origin and, 122–28, 129t, 138; psychological well-being and, 210, 221, 222t, 224; racial self-identity determinants, 184t, 186, 187–88; school attrition and, 256t. *See also* California Proposition 227
language instruction: California Proposition 227, 144, 366n. 3; language acculturation and, 143–46
Laotian immigrants and descendants, 21; achievement, 74t; additive effects and, 78, 79t, 80, 81, 82; ambition, 103, 104t, 229t; Children of Immigrants Longitudinal Study, 27t, 29t, 31, 32t, 39, 40–41t; community and pride, 108, 109t, 110; educational achievement, early, 235, 236t, 237, 241t, 243, 244; educational achievement, late adolescent, 245f, 246f, 249t, 250; educational achievement paradox, 258, 260–61; educational expectations, 216, 217t; ethnic self-identities, 160, 161, 162t, 163t; family cohesion, conflict, and change, 198f; family status, 86t, 87t, 88; immigrant incorporation, 50t; language acculturation, 123t, 127, 129t; nativity patterns, 164t, 165; parent-child interactions, 194, 195; permissiveness and, 99, 100–101t; psychological well-being, 207, 208t, 223t; racial self-identity, 179t; school attrition, 254f, 257t; school engagement and effort, 212t; school environment and, 203; student occupational status, 265, 267. *See also* Hmong immigrants and descendants

Latin American immigrants and descendants, 21, 22; achievement, 74t; Alvarez family (fictitious name), 126; ambition, 104t; bilingualism, 118, 135–43; Children of Immigrants Longitudinal Study, 27t, 29t, 31, 32t, 40–41t; community and pride, 109t, 110; discrimination, 55; educational achievement, 236t; educational expectations, 217t; ethnic identity, 162t, 359–60n. 29; family cohesion, conflict, and change, 198f, 200–201; family status, 86t, 87t, 89–90; homework, 362n. 15; language acculturation, 120, 123t, 125, 126, 127, 128t; nativity patterns, 164t; permissiveness and, 100–101t; psychological well-being, 207, 208t, 223t; racial self-identity, 177, 178t; role reversal, 52; school attrition, 254f; school engagement and effort, 212t, 213–14, 357n. 41. *See also specific nationalities*
Latino identity, 154, 359–60n. 29; ethnic self-identity and, 160; national origin and, 177, 178–79t; racial self-identity and, 181, 188; shifts in, 156. *See also* ethnic identity; panethnic identity; *specific nationalities*
Liberty City, 60
limited bilingualism, 114, 116, 117; ambition and, 227, 228t; costs of, 135; educational achievement, 238, 239, 240t, 243, 248t, 250; ethnic identity and, 169t; family cohesion, conflict, and change, 199t, 201; forceful assimilation and, 273; language acculturation and, 130, 131, 132f, 133, 143; language instruction and, 145–46; psychological well-being and, 209t, 221, 222t; racial self-identity determinants, 184t; school attrition and, 256t. *See also* English-language dominance
linguistic assimilation. *See* language acculturation/adaptation
Los Angeles, 20t, 21; bilingualism, 274; California Proposition 187 protest, 147–48; Mexican immigrants and descendants, 280; riots of 1993, 148, 270, 358n. 7
Los Angeles Times, 362n. 15
lunch program, subsidized, 242

Mahayana Buddhism, 260
marginality, 151, 152, 191, 285–86
marginal reaction, 152
Mariel Cubans, 149; crime and, 365n. 19; discrimination, 365n. 21;

Mariel Cubans (*continued*)
  educational achievement, 258,
  260–67; selective acculturation, 275;
  unpopularity of, 358n. 8; U.S. arrival
  date, 365–66n. 22, 366n. 23
marital status: Children of Immigrants
  Longitudinal Study, 32t; ethnic identity and, 149, 161; family cohesion,
  conflict, and change, 197; immigrant
  communities and, 64–65; U.S. Census,
  35t. See also family status
Martelli, Scott, 276
math test scores, Children of Immigrants
  Longitudinal Study, 30t
McClelland, David, 351n. 16
media, language acculturation and, 127
Merton, Robert K., 360n. 36
mestizo immigrants. See specific nationalities
Mexican immigrants and descendants,
  21–22; achievement, 74, 74t; additive
  effects and, 78, 79t, 80; ambition,
  103, 104t, 105, 227, 229t, 230;
  Bernal, Stephanie, 147, 152; Bracero
  labor contract program, 271–72; California Proposition 187 and, 147–48;
  Cardozo family (fictitious name),
  8–9, 18; Children of Immigrants Longitudinal Study, 23, 24, 27t, 29t, 31,
  32t, 38, 39, 40–41t; community and
  pride, 109t, 110, 111; countercultures
  and, 59, 60; educational achievement,
  early, 235, 236t, 241t, 242; educational achievement, late adolescent,
  245f, 246f, 249t, 250; educational
  expectations, 216, 217t; ethnic identity, 153, 157, 160, 162t; family
  cohesion, conflict, and change, 198f,
  201; family status, 85, 86f, 87t;
  Higareda, Jorge, 148; ideology and,
  276–80; immigrant incorporation,
  50t; interaction effects and, 82–83,
  84; language acculturation, 123t,
  124, 125, 127, 128t; Muñoz family
  (fictitious name), 14–15, 18; nativity
  patterns, 164t, 164; parent-child
  interactions, 194, 195–96; permissiveness and, 100–101t, 102; psychological well-being, 207, 208t, 223t;
  racial self-identity, 177, 178t, 181,
  188, 189; reactive ethnicity, 284; Santos, Roberto (fictitious name), 111,
  145; school attrition, 253, 254f, 257t,
  258; school engagement and effort,
  212t, 214; student occupational status, 265t; U.S. Census, 37; Velasco,
  Vicky, 148. See also California

Proposition 187; California Proposition 227
Miami, 20t, 21; bilingualism, 118, 134,
  137, 274; Colombian immigrants and
  descendants in, 70, 72; countercultures, 60, 61; Cuban educational
  achievement and, 261–67; educational
  achievement, 235; educational expectations, 216; language acculturation,
  124, 127; language instruction, 143,
  145; Nicaraguan immigrant communities in, 65, 66–67, 69; school attrition,
  255, 258, 259f; school environment
  and peer groups, 203, 206. See also
  Children of Immigrants Longitudinal
  Study; U.S. Census; specific immigrant
  nationalities
Miami Herald, The, 149
Miami immigrant stories, 2–8, 18–19;
  ambition, 226; educational achievement, 244, 245; Marín, Aura Lila (fictitious name), 91–93, 94; permissiveness, 97
Middle Eastern immigrants and descendants: achievement, 73–74; Children
  of Immigrants Longitudinal Study, 27t;
  ethnic self-identities, 163t; language
  acculturation, 129t; nativity patterns,
  164t; racial self-identity, 179t
migrant labor, 271–72, 277, 280. See
  also labor market
mismatch theory, 353n. 34
monolingualism, 114, 116, 117; family
  cohesion, conflict, and change, 201;
  language acculturation and, 126, 130,
  133, 143; language instruction and,
  146; predictors of, 136–37t; racial
  identity and, 180, 187–88; schools
  and, 135, 357n. 41; selective acculturation and, 274. See also English-
  language dominance; nativism
Mormonism, 260
mulatto immigrants. See specific nationalities
multiculturalism, attacks on, 116
multiracial identity. See panethnic identity
multivariate analyses variables: bilingualism, 341–42; educational attainment,
  346–47; ethnic and racial self-
  identification, 342–44; self-esteem,
  depression, and educational aspirations and expectations, 344–46

names, Americanization of, 189–90
nationality/national origin, xvii, 19–21;
  additive effects and, 78, 79t, 80–81,
  82f; ambition and, 103, 104t, 105,

226, 229t; achievement and, 73–76, 77t; bilingualism and, 136t, 137t, 138, 139t, 140, 142t; Children of Immigrants Longitudinal Study, 27t, 29t, 31, 42; community and pride, 108, 109t, 110, 111; Cuban educational achievement and, 265t; discrimination and, 363n. 20; educational achievement, early, 235, 236t, 238, 241t, 242, 243; educational achievement, late adolescent, 245f, 246f, 248, 249t, 250, 251; educational expectations and, 216, 217t; ethnic identity and, 160–66, 167f, 181, 182t, 186, 187, 189, 359n. 26, 360n. 33; family cohesion, conflict, and change, 197, 198t; family status and, 85–90; immigrant parent optimism and, 95; interaction effects and, 82–85; language acculturation and, 113–14, 122–28, 129t; monolingualism and, 136t, 137t; permissiveness and, 99, 100–101t, 102; psychological well-being and, 208t, 221, 222t; racial identity and, 177, 178–79t, 180f, 181, 184t, 186, 188–89; school attrition and, 253, 254f; school engagement and effort, 212t, 214; school environment and, 204t, 206. See also California Proposition 187; ethnic identity; specific nationalities
national-origin identity, 154, 174–75t; ethnic identity shifts, 154–55; ethnic self-identity and, 160–61, 162–63t, 186–87; family status and language, 167, 168–70t; nativity and, 164t, 165, 177, 178–79t; parental self-identities and, 171, 172t; racial self-identity and, 180f, 184–85t, 188–89; shifts in, 157; stability and salience, 157–58
nativism, 114; bilingualism and, 118; California Proposition 187, 271–72; Mexican immigrants and descendants, 280; reactive ethnicity and, 284–85; selective acculturation and, 274–75, 276. See also California Proposition 187; ideologies; monolingualism
nativity. See nationality/national origin
Nebraska, 116
neighborhoods: countercultures in, 59; immigrant parent optimism and, 95, 96t; permissiveness and, 98. See also immigrant communities
net worth. See socioeconomic status
New Deal, 56
"New Faces of Orange County's Future, The" (Folmar and Martelli), 276

New Haven, 117, 152
New Orleans: community and pride, 108; language instruction, 144; Vietnamese immigrant communities in, 65, 67, 69
New York (state), 34, 35t
New York City, 20t, 21; bilingualism, 117–18, 274; countercultures in, 65; permissiveness and, 98
newspapers, 127, 149, 362n. 15, 365n. 19
Nicaraguan immigrants and descendants: acculturation, 49–51; achievement, 74t; additive effects and, 79t, 80; ambition, 104t, 227, 229t; Argüelles family (fictitious name), 49–51; Children of Immigrants Longitudinal Study, 23, 24, 27t, 29t, 31, 32t, 40–41t; community and pride, 109t, 110–11; educational achievement, 235, 236t, 241t, 249t; educational expectations, 217t; ethnic identity, 154, 157, 160, 162t; family cohesion, conflict, and change, 198f; family status, 86f, 87t; Fernández-Rey family (fictitious name), 3–4, 18, 106; immigrant incorporation, 50t; interaction effects and, 83, 84; language acculturation, 123t, 127, 128t; Miami immigrant community, 65–67; nativity patterns, 164t, 165; permissiveness and, 97, 100–101t; psychological well-being, 208t, 223t; racial self-identity, 177, 178t; reception of, 281; role reversal, 49–51; school attrition, 254f, 257t, 258; school engagement and effort, 212t; student occupational status, 265t

occupational aspirations. See aspirations
occupational opportunities: acculturation and, 282–83; additive effects and, 76, 78; ambition and, 106f; Cuban educational achievement and, 266–67; educational achievement and, 267; immigrant parent optimism and, 95, 96t; language skills and, 117–18; school engagement and effort, 212; selective acculturation and, 274
occupational skills: Cuban educational achievement and, 262; immigrant incorporation and, 46, 47, 48, 49
occupational status: acculturation and, 282, 283f; achievement and, 73, 74, 75, 75f, 77t; adaptation and, 73; additive effects and, 78, 79t, 80; ambition and, 103; bilingualism and, 138;

occupational status (*continued*)
Children of Immigrants Longitudinal
Study, 30t; Cuban educational achievement and, 263, 264, 265, 266, 267,
275; discrimination and, 56; family
status and, 88; immigrant communities
and, 366; immigrant incorporation
and, 48; interaction effects and, 83,
84; labor markets and, 56–59; U.S.
Census, 36t
Olmos, Edward James, 285
optimism, 94–96; acculturation and, 281;
ambition and, 107; educational
achievement and, 268; Mexican immigrants and descendants, 279
Orange County, 20t, 21, 148

Pacific Islanders. *See* Asian identity;
Asian immigrants and descendants
Pakistani immigrants and descendants,
129t
Panamanian immigrants and descendants, 128t
panethnic identity, 150, 154; Americanization and, 190; ethnic identity and,
154–55, 182–83t, 186; family status
and language, 167, 168–70t;
national origin and, 160, 162–63t,
166, 177, 178–79t; parental self-
identities and, 171, 172t; racial self-
identity and, 180f, 181, 184–85t, 188,
189; region, schools, and discrimination, 173, 174–75t, 176; shifts in,
156f, 157; stability and salience, 157,
158. *See also* Asian identity; black
identity; Chicano identity; ethnic identity; Hispanic identity; Latino identity;
specific nationalities
parent-child conflict. *See* family conflict
parents. *See* immigrant parent outlooks;
immigrant parents
passive acceptance, 46, 47
peers: ambition, 106; bilingualism, 136t,
139t, 140, 142t, 143; educational
achievement, 239, 240t, 242, 248t,
250, 260; ethnic identity, 169t, 176,
182t, 187; language acculturation,
121, 123t, 133f, 134; monolingualism,
136t; permissiveness and, 98, 99,
100–101t, 102; racial self-identity
determinants, 184t, 188; reactive ethnicity, 285; school attrition, 256t;
school engagement and effort, 213t;
school environments and, 203–7
People's Republic of China. *See* Chinese
immigrants and descendants
permissiveness, 97–102

Peruvian immigrants and descendants,
language acculturation, 128t
phenotype, ethnic self-identity and, 151
Philippines, U.S. colonialist occupation
of, 272. *See also* Filipino immigrants
and descendants
phonemes, 135
plain American. *See* American identity
policy. *See* California Proposition 187;
California Proposition 227; educational policy; government policy; ideologies; politics
Polish immigrants and descendants, 18,
55, 102
politics: bilingualism and, 114, 116;
mainstream ideologies, 270–74; reactive ethnicity and, 284–85; refugee
educational achievement and, 258,
260–67; U.S. Office of Management
and Budget, 358–59n. 15. *See also*
California Proposition 187; California
Proposition 227; educational policy;
government policy; ideologies
Portuguese immigrants and descendants,
115
postgraduate education. *See* education
poverty: ambition and, 106, 107; bilingualism and, 116; community and
pride, 108, 111; immigrant incorporation and, 50t; Mexican immigrants
and descendants, 277–78, 280;
nativism and, 272
pregnancy. *See* teenage pregnancy
pride, 107–11, 113; 124
professionals. *See* occupational status
Proposition 187. *See* California Proposition 187
Proposition 227. *See* California Proposition 227
psychological well-being, 207–10, 211f,
219, 220–25. *See also* depression; self-
esteem
psychosocial adaptation, 68f; determinants of, 220–30; educational achievement and, 247–48, 250; educational
expectations and, 219; ethnic identity
and, 171; family cohesion, conflict,
and change, 198–99; fluent bilingualism and, 364–65n. 9; gender and, 64;
language acculturation and, 131, 132f,
134; language instruction and, 146;
school attrition and, 252, 256t
Puerto Ricans, 59, 60, 117

race: acculturation and, 66t; adaptation
and, 55–56; Asian educational
achievement and, 260; Children of

Immigrants Longitudinal Study, 39; countercultures and, 59; ethnic identity and, 159–60, 176; immigrant incorporation and, 47–48; marginality and, 191; U.S. Census, 35t. *See also* discrimination

racial discrimination. *See* discrimination

racial identity: adaptation and, 68f; determinants of, 181–89; ethnic identity and, 177–81. *See also* black identity; ethnic identity; panethnic identity

racism, 188. *See also* discrimination

radio, language acculturation and, 127

reactive ethnicity: aftermath of, 284–86; discrimination and, 171; dissonant acculturation and, 283f; ethnic identity and, 148–49, 186, 358n. 6

reactive nativism, 274–75

reading test scores, Children of Immigrants Longitudinal Study, 30t

rebels, 152

refugees: achievement, 74; additive effects and, 78, 80, 81; ambition, 103, 105, 227; community and pride, 108, 110; educational achievement, 235, 242–43, 258, 260–67; educational background, 364n. 6; family cohesion, conflict, and change, 201; family status, 88; government assistance for, 73; immigrant incorporation, 47; interaction effects and, 83, 84; language acculturation, 124, 125; parent-child interactions, 194, 195; permissiveness and, 99, 102; psychological well-being, 207, 224; reception of, 281; U.S. interventions and, 272. *See also specific nationalities*

region: ambition and, 228t; educational achievement, 238, 240t, 248t; ethnic identity and, 171, 173–76; psychological well-being and, 222t; school attrition and, 256t. *See also specific states and cities*

religion, 260

remedial language training, 130

resettlement assistance. *See* government assistance

residency, 281–84; achievement and, 75, 77t; additive effects and, 78, 79t; ambition and, 228t; bilingualism and, 136t, 139t, 140, 141, 142t; Children of Immigrants Longitudinal Study, 26t, 28t; Cuban educational achievement and, 261; educational achievement, 235, 236t, 237, 239, 240t, 243, 250; ethnic identity and, 167, 168t, 176, 186; family cohesion, conflict, and

change, 202; family status and, 88; interaction effects and, 83–84; language acculturation and, 125f; Mexican immigrants and descendants, 278; monolingualism and, 137t; psychological well-being and, 221, 222t; racial self-identity determinants, 186; school attrition and, 255, 256t; school engagement and effort, 214f, 215

Rice Room, The: Growing up Chinese-American (Fong-Torres), 192

Riley, Richard W., 144, 146

role models, 95, 102, 203

role reversal, 193; acculturation and, 49–54; community and pride, 111; language instruction and, 145f; permissiveness and, 99

Roman Catholicism, 260

Roosevelt, Theodore, 113, 114, 116

Rosenberg's Self-Esteem Scale, 133, 207, 221, 224, 248

salience, ethnic identity and, 157–60

Salvadoran immigrants and descendants, 23, 42–43, 128t

San Diego, 20t, 21; bilingualism, 117; California Proposition 187 and, 148; community and pride, 108; educational achievement, 237, 249; ethnic identity, 173, 174–75t; Mexican immigrants and descendants, 280; psychological well-being, 224; school attrition, 252, 255, 258, 259f; school engagement and effort, 211; school environment and peer groups, 203; school suspensions, 361n. 9; Vietnamese immigrants and descendants, 71, 72. *See also* Children of Immigrants Longitudinal Study; U.S. Census; *specific immigrant nationalities*

San Diego immigrant stories, 8–16, 18–19; educational achievement, 245; parent-child interactions, 194–97, 230–31; permissiveness, 97; Yang, Pao (fictitious name), 93, 94

Save Our State proposition. *See* California Proposition 187

Schkolnick, Meyer R., 360n. 36

school achievement. *See* educational achievement

school attendance, 40–41t

school attrition (dropouts), acculturation and, 281, 282; aspirations and, 106f; countercultures and, 59; Cuban educational achievement and, 263–64, 266, 267, 275; educational achievement and, 251–58, 259f; family cohesion,

school attrition (*continued*)
conflict, and change, 198; Mexican immigrants and descendants, 279; peers, 205t, 206f, 213t

school performance. *See* educational achievement

schools: acculturation and, 282; additive effects and, 78; ambition and, 227; bilingualism and, 117, 135–43; California Proposition 187 and, 147–48; cliques in, 361n. 7; countercultures and, 59, 60, 61–62; Cuban educational achievement and, 261, 267; educational achievement, early, 235, 237, 238, 241t, 242–43; educational achievement, late adolescent, 247t, 249t, 250; engagement and effort, 211–15; ethnic self-identity correlates, 171, 173–76; ethnic self-identity determinants, 183t, 187; ethnic self-identity patterns, 156, 157, 160, 161, 162t, 164t, 173, 174t; family cohesion, conflict, and change, 198f; forceful assimilation and, 273; grades in, 245–51; immigrant parent optimism and, 95, 96t; language acculturation and, 123t, 124, 127, 130–31; language instruction, 145–46; monolingualism and, 137t; peers and, 203–7; permissiveness and, 98, 100t; racial self-identity determinants, 185t; selective acculturation and, 275; suspensions, 361n. 9

school safety, 203, 204–5t, 206f, 211f

schoolwork. *See* homework

second generation. *See* immigrant second generation

segmented assimilation, 44–46, 69; acculturation and role reversal, 49–54; adaptation challenges, 55–62; educational achievement and, 268; incorporation modes and consequences, 46–49, 65, 66t, 68f; Mexican immigrants and descendants, 276; social capital, 62–69

selective acculturation, 53t, 54, 64, 65, 66t, 282, 283f; bilingualism and, 143, 274–76; educational achievement and, 238, 239, 242, 243, 246, 250; educational expectations and, 219; ethnic identity and, 167, 170–71; family cohesion, conflict, and change, 199, 201; language instruction, 145; psychological well-being and, 210, 221, 225; reactive ethnicity and, 285; school engagement and effort, 214, 215

self, development of, 149–52

self-employment: achievement and, 75–76, 74t, 75f, 77t; additive effects and, 78, 79t; U.S. Census, 36t. *See also* occupational status

self-esteem, 193; adaptation and, 68f; ambition and, 106f, 227; Asian educational achievement and, 258; depression and, 207–10, 211f, 220–25; discrimination and, 363n. 20; educational achievement and, 247, 248, 250, 251; educational expectations and, 218, 219, 220f, 362–63n. 19; ethnic identity and, 171, 191; family status and, 86; fluent bilingualism and, 364–65n. 9; forceful assimilation and, 273; gender and, 64, 362n. 12; language acculturation and, 130, 131–33; reactive ethnicity and, 285; school attrition and, 252, 256t; selective acculturation and, 274, 275

self-identity. *See* ethnic identity; racial identity

senior high school. *See* education; schools

service employment, 57. *See also* occupational status

sex. *See* gender

Smith, Madorah, 115

social capital: community and pride, 108, 111; definition of, 353n. 47; educational achievement and, 267–68; immigrant community, 64–69; parental status, family structure, and gender, 62, 64; permissiveness and, 99; reactive ethnicity and, 285

social networks. *See* immigrant communities

socioeconomic status, 282, 283f; acculturation and, 281; adaptation and, 68f, 69, 73; ambition and, 106, 226, 228t, 230; Asian educational achievement and, 260; bilingualism and, 116, 117, 138, 139t, 140, 142t; Children of Immigrants Longitudinal Study, 30t; community and pride, 108, 109t, 110, 111; countercultures and, 61; Cuban educational achievement and, 263; determinants of, 76, 78–82; educational achievement and, 238, 239, 240t, 241t, 242, 244, 249, 267; educational expectations and, 216, 217t, 219; ethnic identity and, 149–50, 160–61, 181, 182t; family cohesion, conflict, and change, 197, 199t, 201; immigrant incorporation and, 47, 48, 49, 50t; labor market and, 57, 58; language acculturation and, 122, 124; Mexican immigrants and descendants,

277–78; nationality and, 73–76, 77t; permissiveness and, 99, 102; psychological well-being and, 208t, 221, 222t; racial self-identity determinants, 181, 184t; school attrition and, 256t, 257t; school environment and, 203, 204t, 206; social capital and, 62, 64; U.S. Census, 35t

solidarity: ambition and, 105; community and pride, 108, 110; countercultures and, 60; Korean immigrants and descendants, 358n. 7; language and, 113; Mexican immigrants and descendants, 278; reactive ethnicity and, 148–49, 284, 285

South American immigrants and descendants. See specific nationalities

southeast Asians. See Asian immigrants and descendants; specific nationalities

speech patterns, bilingualism and, 115

Srole, Leo, 45

stability, ethnic identity and, 157–60

Stand and Deliver (film), 285

standardized tests: ambition and, 365n. 10; Asian educational achievement and, 260; bilingualism and, 117; Cuban educational achievement and, 263, 264f; educational achievement, 234–35, 236t, 237, 242, 243, 246, 247t; language acculturation and, 131, 132f; Mexican immigrants and descendants, 278–79

Street Corner Society (Whyte), 359n. 21

stressful life events, 197–98; family cohesion, conflict, and change, 197–98; psychological well-being and, 209t, 210, 224

subcultures. See countercultures

subsidized lunch program, 242

subtractive bilingualism, 135

suspension, from school, 361n. 9

Taiwanese immigrants and descendants. See Chinese immigrants and descendants

teaching quality, 203, 204–5t, 206f; California Proposition 227 and, 269; educational achievement, early, 238, 240–41t; psychological well-being and, 210, 211f; reactive ethnicity and, 285

technology, labor markets and, 56, 57–58

teenage pregnancy, countercultures and, 60

television, language acculturation and, 127

tests. See standardized tests

Texas, 34, 35t, 189–90

Theravada Buddhism, 260

Trinidadian immigrants and descendants: ethnic self-identities, 162t; language acculturation, 128t; nativity patterns, 164t; Patterson family (fictitious name), 6–7, 19. See also Caribbean immigrants and descendants; West Indian immigrants and descendants

unemployment, U.S. Census, 36t

unhyphenated American. See American identity

U.S. Census, 19–22, 33–37, 176, 351n. 12

U.S. English movement 355n. 4. See also monolingualism; nativism

U.S. immigrant population. See immigrant parents; immigrant second generation; specific immigrant nationalities

U.S. Office of Management and Budget (OMB), 358–59n. 15

Unz, Ronald, 269–70, 271, 273–74

Venezuelan immigrants and descendants, 23, 128t

Vietnamese immigrants and descendants, 21; achievement, 74t; additive effects and, 78, 79t; ambition, 103, 104t, 105, 227, 229t; Children of Immigrants Longitudinal Study, 23, 24, 27t, 29t, 31, 32t, 39, 40–41t; community and pride, 107–8, 109t, 110f, 111; educational achievement, early, 233–34, 235, 236t, 241t, 242, 243; educational achievement, late adolescent, 245, 249t, 250; educational achievement paradox, 258, 260–61; educational expectations, 216, 217t; ethnic identity, 154, 160, 163t; family cohesion, conflict, and change, 198f; family status, 86f, 87t, 88; immigrant incorporation, 50t; interaction effects and, 83, 84; language acculturation, 123t, 125, 127, 129t; language instruction, 144; Le, Van (fictitious name), 233–34, 235; nativity patterns, 164t, 165; New Orleans immigrant community, 65, 67, 69; Nguyen family (fictitious name), 9–11, 19, 71, 72, 107–8; parent-child interactions, 194, 196–97, 230–31; permissiveness and, 97, 99, 100–101t, 102; psychological well-being, 207, 208t, 223t; racial self-identity, 179t; school attrition, 254f, 257t; school engagement and effort, 212t; school

Vietnamese immigrants and descendants (*continued*)
environment and, 203; selective acculturation, 275–76; student occupational status, 265t
violence: immigrant parent optimism and, 95, 96t; school fights, 203, 204–5t, 206f
Vuong, Joseph, 144

Warner, Lloyd, 45
Washington, D. C., 20t
Waters, Mary, 61, 153
wealth. *See* socioeconomic status
well-being. *See* psychological well-being
West Indian immigrants and descendants: achievement, 74, 74t; additive effects and, 79t; ambition, 103, 104t; Children of Immigrants Longitudinal Study, 23, 27t, 29t, 31, 32t, 38, 39, 40–41t; community and pride, 109t; countercultures and, 61; discrimination, 55, 354n. 4; educational achievement, 236t, 241t, 249t; educational expectations, 217t; ethnic identity, 153, 160–61, 162t; family cohesion, conflict, and change, 198f; family status, 86, 87t, 88; language acculturation, 73, 123t, 124, 125, 128t; nativity patterns, 164t; permissiveness and, 100–101t, 102; psychological well-being, 207, 208t, 223t, 229t; racial self-identity, 177, 178t, 181, 187–88; school attrition, 254f, 257t, 258; school engagement and effort, 212t, 213–14; student occupational status, 265t. *See also* Caribbean immigrants and descendants; *specific nationalities*
white identity, 154; national origin and, 177, 178–79t; racial self-identity and, 180, 181, 188, 189; school attrition and, 258, 259f. *See also* European immigrants and descendants
Whyte, William F., 359n. 21
Wilson, Pete, 357–58n. 4
work. *See* occupational status
work experience: additive effects and, 78, 80; interaction effects and, 84
work habits, 60
World War I, 59, 115
World War II, 56, 152

Youth Adaptation and Growth Questionnaire (II). *See* Children of Immigrants Longitudinal Study (CILS), follow-up questionnaire
youth gangs. *See* gangs

Compositor: Impressions Book and Journal Services, Inc.
Text: Sabon
Display: Syntax
Printer and Binder: Edwards Brothers, Inc.